Political corruption in Ireland, 1922–2010

MANCHESTER
1824

Manchester University Press

Political corruption in Ireland, 1922–2010

A crooked harp?

ELAINE A. BYRNE

Manchester University Press

Manchester and New York

distributed in the United States exclusively
by PALGRAVE MACMILLAN

The right of Elaine A. Byrne to be identified as the author of this work has been asserted by her in accordance with the Copyright, Designs and Patents Act 1988.

Published by Manchester University Press
Oxford Road, Manchester M13 9NR, UK
and Room 400, 175 Fifth Avenue, New York, NY 10010, USA
www.manchesteruniversitypress.co.uk

Distributed in the United States exclusively by
Palgrave Macmillan, 175 Fifth Avenue, New York,
NY 10010, USA

Distributed in Canada exclusively by
UBC Press, University of British Columbia, 2029 West Mall,
Vancouver, BC, Canada V6T 1Z2

British Library Cataloguing-in-Publication Data
A catalogue record for this book is available from the British Library

Library of Congress Cataloging-in-Publication Data applied for

ISBN 978 0 7190 8687 8   hardback

ISBN 978 0 7190 8688 5   paperback

First published 2012, reprinted in paperback 2012 (twice)

The publisher has no responsibility for the persistence or accuracy of URLs for any external or third-party internet websites referred to in this book, and does not guarantee that any content on such websites is, or will remain, accurate or appropriate.

Typeset in 10.5 on 12.5 Minion Pro
by Servis Filmsetting Ltd, Stockport, Cheshire
Printed in Great Britain
by Bell & Bain Ltd, Glasgow

Dedication
Patrick (Paddy) McHugh 1977–2010
For saying it like it was. Veritas.

Contents

List of Figures and Tables

Figures

Tables

Preface and acknowledgements

This book would not have been possible but for the counsel of Michael Marsh, Kevin Whelan, Sean McGraw, Maurice Manning and Stuart Gilman who encouraged the book from the outset and kept it alive when it sought to yield. Thank you.

I am enormously grateful to Michael Gallagher, David McCullagh, Eoin O'Dell, Raj Chari, Peter Murtagh, Ronan Fanning, Felix Larkin, Patrick Holden and Myles Duggan for their comments on various draft chapters and for allowing me to trespass on their goodwill.

I am especially indebted to my colleagues, past and present, at the United Nations Office on Drugs and Crime, the University of Limerick and Trinity College Dublin who obliged this project by providing perspective and encouraging scholarship. Thank you in particular to my students who challenged my views and made me think differently about assumptions taken for granted.

The *Irish Times* provided me with the remarkable opportunity to test the thesis of this book to a wider audience and I am very thankful to them for the trust that was placed in those columns. Above all, my editor and friend, Peter Murtagh, gave me the confidence to believe that the written word does make a difference. I am particularly grateful for the fortitude shown by several Irish journalists who ploughed a lonely furrow over many years to expose the underlying malignant behaviour that corrupted Irish public life. The consequence of their courage, and that of the whistleblowers, provided the cornerstones of this book and my appreciation and admiration for their work is referenced throughout the text.

This book is a much-modified version of a PhD thesis, *The Moral and Legal Development of Corruption: Nineteenth and Twentieth Century Political Corruption in Ireland*, submitted to the University of Limerick in 2006. The support and commitment of Maura Adshead and Tom Lodge at this initial stage of the journey is deeply appreciated, as is the ever-encouragement of Gary Murphy, Eunan O'Halpin, Jac Hayden, Pat Leahy and Anita Kelly.

The staff of the National Library and National Archives, where much of this work was completed, offered not only the conditions conducive to cerebral study but also a sense of humour that sustained it. Grateful acknowledgment is made to Thomas Kinsella for permission to reproduce his beautiful poem, 'Nightwalker', and to Brian Warfield of the Wolfe Tones for permission to reproduce the 'Helicopter Song'.

The patience of Msgr. Luke Hunt, Helen Young, Scarlett Griffin, Dearbhail and many other friendships that nourished this book and who kept this project in line. To those who began the journey in Kilquiggan and in Tullow Community School – Anne-Marie, Niamh, Loraine, Catherine, Peter, Marie and Joylen. Thanks especially to the Zalzbergs in Jerusalem, the McKees in Omagh, the Munnellys in Mayo, the Glasers in Vienna and the Morris family in Ottawa. My Gaelic football teammates in Coolkenno, Carnew, Monaleen and Ballyboden St Enda's provided indispensable distraction. As always, Jack and his blue horse kept faith. Thanks to Ross Curran for compiling the index.

To my parents for always encouraging me to do what I wanted to do, even if it did not always make sense. To my sisters, Aine, Roisin, Eadaoin and Shauna and my brothers Johnny and Eoin for their love and support. To Tony, Amie and Niall, welcome!

A final note of thanks is to Michael Lowry who tolerated the eighteen-year-old who spent her Leaving Certificate summer sitting beside him at the McCracken Tribunal in Dublin Castle in 1997. He corrupted her with an abiding sense of curiosity.

This book should have been finished years ago but when I went exploring the archives I got lost and distracted by stories of corruption that are absent in Irish historical texts. In the end I wrote enough material for three books (and at the time of writing the Flood / Mahon Tribunal was still to report). By the time this much-abridged version came to light, Ireland had rendered her economic sovereignty to the European Commission, the European Central Bank, and the International Monetary Fund. The book was no longer a quaint history of corruption incidents since the foundation of the state. The narrative now had a beginning, middle and end.

Henry Grattan is one of my heroes. This anti-corruption crusader and campaigner of constitutional and political rights retired from the Irish House of Commons in 1797 in protest that his proposed political reforms were being ignored. In his 24 page *Letter to the citizens of Dublin*, Grattan explained his dramatic decision. In order to 'save the country', he wrote, it was 'absolutely necessary to reform the state'. That was the precisely the course of action taken when Ireland obtained political independence in 1922. The consequences of deep-seated injustice provoked Irish public life to demand and imagine political sovereignty. A similar challenge, albeit an economic one, confronts Ireland almost one hundred years later. The lesson from a narrative stretching from 1922 to 2010, is that there are always new beginnings. A sense of renewal even.

Foreword

For the degree of corruption to which the kings had sunk was such that, if it had continued for two or three successive reigns, and had extended from the head to the members of the body so that these were also corrupt, it would have been impossible ever to have reformed the state. (Machiavelli, *The Discourses*, Chapter XVII).

From the classical writings of Plato, corruption has been seen as the most dangerous cancer of republican government. Ironically, in much of the last century it was rarely addressed in the academic literature. In fact, often when corruption was focused upon it was seen as a necessary 'lubricant' for development in poor nations. This attitude changed in the late twentieth century as a result of multiple corruption scandals, most notably the Watergate scandal in the United States. But for some inexplicable reason most of the subsequent research focused on developing countries and what was most often characterised as endemic corruption. Corruption became the focus of the multi-lateral community as undermining governance and destroying democracy in these fledgling nations.

As much as this perspective held some validity, curiously corruption was seen as a disease of the poor, coloured nations of the world. The EU, Australia, the USA and Canada viewed corruption scandals as isolated events having little impact on the vitality and legitimacy of their governments.

In this important work, Dr. Elaine Byrne challenges the presumption that developed countries are somehow immune to the corrosive impact of corruption. By using an in-depth analysis of the 'new' Irish question, she points out the weakness of government efforts. A legislative hearing, some senior politician brought up on charges, a special commission are seen as palliative. Yet the truth underneath this thin patina is far more disturbing. Corruption affects Old Europe as much as it does New Europe. Ireland is not an isolated case; it is simply symptomatic of the rest of the EU. The tendency to ignore problems at home simply unveils the hypocrisy of the 1st world telling the third world to do something about corruption. Sadly, this often leads to a corruption spiral for both sides of this equation.

Her theoretical framework follows the excellent thread begun by Dennis Thompson,[1] seeing corruption not as a 'thing' but rather as an organic concept that changes with community and political circumstances. Many politicians get caught up in doing things that were 'right' some fifty years ago without understanding that the ethical ground has shifted beneath them.

Dr. Byrne's in-depth analysis of corruption in Ireland and its impact on the government and the public brings home the fact that no country is exempt from corruption. It has a far deeper impact on the social fabric of society and impacts how the average citizen not only view government but view each other. The detail of corruption's pernicious influence on Irish politics and its people is at once both disturbing and enlightening.

It is important to put this into a global context. In late 2005, the United Nations Convention against Corruption came into force. More than 140 countries have ratified the Convention and as of November 2011, Ireland has finally joined that list. There were probably good reasons for such a delay. But, I would argue, after reading this forceful book, there were probably bad reasons as well. Ratification now requires Ireland to address corruption head-on. There is no longer anything to lose.

Ireland justifiably relishes its image of the Gaelic miracle and wants to regain it. But even if this economic prosperity returns, can it be sustained? Arguably, one of the lynch pins to sustainability is addressing corruption. Dr. Byrne's research compellingly details the corruption problem, why it exists and how it can be dealt with. The question is will anything be done.

> Let not princes complain of the faults committed by the people subject to their authority, for they result entirely from their own negligence and bad example. (Machiavelli, *The Discourses*, Chapter XXIX)

Dr. Stuart C. Gilman,
Former Head, United Nations Global Programme against Corruption,
Washington, DC

Note

1 Dennis F. Thompson, 'Mediated corruption: the case of the Keating five', *American Political Science Review*, 87:2 (1993).

1

Introduction

Ireland's national emblem, the harp, has since medieval times, resonated as an official symbol for Irish nationhood. Today, this immediately recognisable icon is found in the seals of the President, Taoiseach, naval flags, on courthouses and Irish embassies. It appears on the back of Irish coins, on postage stamps and pints of Guinness. This distinctive Irish musical instrument has an additional significance within political folklore. It has become symbolic of the adage that in order to get anything done in Ireland, it is necessary to pull strings. The implication, therefore, is that concepts of meritocracy and legitimate entitlement are superseded by notions of special advantage through unorthodox and clandestine influence.

This is a study of the history of corruption in Ireland which, by inference, reveals a hidden chronicle of Irish politics. This book will outline specific corruption incidents since the foundation of the state to determine if this proverb of a corrupted harp has some resonance or if the eloquence and exaggeration of the Irish storytelling tradition is in evidence. The purpose therefore, is to document if a decline in standards occurred since the inauguration of Irish independence in 1922 to the loss of economic sovereignty in 2010. Although the Irish public mind is perhaps convinced that corruption is a prevailing feature of political life, there has been almost no empirical investigation into the veracity of this assumption.

The main assumption underpinning this book is that contemporary corruption, and the political culture which sustains it, can best be understood by charting how the phenomenon has incrementally changed over a significant period of time, in this case over ninety years. In doing so, it seeks to reintroduce a philosophical and moral emphasis to the definition of corruption by focusing on its legal and moral keystones. The definition of corruption is an evolving one. As the nature of the state changed, so too did the type of corruption. This longitudinal inquiry provides an in-depth historical insight into the predominant trends of corruption at different stages of Ireland's political development. A central thematic focus therefore is the relationship between different notions of loyalty and its influence on public trust. Loyalty to the political individual, the political party and the state are evaluated. It is examined whether aspects of Irish political culture incentivised and condoned certain conduct. The extent to which interpretations of the national interest, economic crises and the thirty year conflict in Northern Ireland prevented and distracted due attention are also surveyed.

This is explored through a case study methodological approach which examines representative cases of corruption within an empirical perspective. Such extensive description and contextual analysis facilitates an awareness of why corruption occurred as it did within its real-life context.[1] The selection of cases is central to this approach because it defines the limits for generalising the findings.[2] To that end, the selected cases were chosen because they are representative of key Irish political events since the foundation of the state and illustrate different forms of conventional political practice which best represent the characteristics and patterns of Irish corruption. The suitability of this methodology is illustrated by case studies on corruption in Africa and focused country studies in Italy and Japan.[3]

Incidents which have attracted significant public attention are not necessarily included, or may only be referenced in passing, because the parameters of the book do not allow for a more thorough analysis, and in many cases, are deserving of a manuscript in their own right. It is not intended to provide an exhaustive inventory of every corruption incident. As the purpose of this study is to catalogue changing behaviour, such an exercise would quickly become futile because it inevitably repeats itself. Instead, it is more constructive to identify the key turning points which demonstrate different types of corruption and why behaviour changes.

The originality of the in-depth archival evidence is complemented by the extraordinary process of self-scrutiny engaged in Ireland by political and other institutions since the 1990s. The research is primarily qualitative and interdisciplinary, and derived from political, historical, sociological, anthropological and economic data. The vast majority of the corruption cases surveyed is not identified within any aspect of the literature. Primary source material consists of previously unpublished and un-accessed material from the collections of the National Archives, National Library, National Manuscripts, UCD Archives, Linen Hall Library and the Enhanced British Parliamentary Papers on Ireland. These include internal government correspondence on proposed legislation and reports, private and published correspondence, manuscripts, pamphlets, speeches and letters. Primary source material also comprises formal and informal interviews with leading political figures, members of the judiciary, senior public servants and other experts. As such, this study provides the groundwork or foundation for studies of corruption in Ireland.

Corruption has played no small part in determining the course of Irish history. The United Irishman and father of Irish Republicanism, Theobald Wolfe Tone, recognised its corrosive influence as early as the eighteenth century. In his very first political pamphlet in 1790, Wolfe Tone wrote of the 'choice of open or concealed corruption'.[4] The consequence of the blatant bribery by agents of the British King which procured the Act of Union, 1801, was the robbery of native Irish legislative independence until 1922. The quid pro quo of the £10,000 political donation by the diamond entrepreneur, Cecil Rhodes, to the Irish Parliamentary Party leader Charles Stewart Parnell in 1888, ultimately found expression in the settlement of the Irish question in 1920 with the retention of Irish MPs at the Northern Ireland Parliament.

The selected case studies are sourced from pivotal points in Irish history and reflect not only the changing nature of ethical behaviour but also the often-unacknowledged impact of these corruption scandals on political events. Chapter 2 examines how the deliberate policy of Augustine Birrell, Chief Secretary to Ireland from 1907–16, to 'green' Dublin Castle through patronage contributed to the downfall of the Irish party and had a profound bearing on the development of post-independent Ireland. This set the context for the austere conditions of probity which were a defining feature of Irish politics and the civil service in the 1920s. This is explored through an examination of the £4 9s 6d restaurant bill and the character of legislation implemented in this period.

Chapter 3 reveals how the policy of economic protectionalism in the 1930s and 1940s provided the opportunity to exercise discretionary decisions to political allies in the issuing of licences, shares, leases and export quotas. The Tribunal trilogy from 1943 to 1947 contributed to the government collapse in 1944 and the removal of Fianna Fáil from power for the first time in sixteen years in 1948. The seeds of Taoiseach Seán Lemass' *New Departure* economic policy of the 1950s, which opened up the Irish economy, were in part sown from his experience before the Tribunals as Minister for Industry and Commerce in the 1940s.

Chapter 4 makes the assessment that discretionary political decisions, made under the cloak of economic protectionalism, were replaced by the authorisation of planning permission in the 1950s, 1960s and 1970s. The shortcomings of planning legislation in the 1960s and the response of the 1973–77 National Coalition government to alleged corruption, determined the framework for political culture in the subsequent thirty years.

Chapter 5 scrutinises allegations of political favouritism towards the beef industry and within the privatisation process of state sponsored bodies in the 1980s and 1990s. The consequent 1991–94 Beef Tribunal ultimately precipitated the collapse of the 1992 and 1994 coalition governments. This remarkable period was distinct from previous scandals because it marked the possibility of state capture within political decision-making.

Chapter 6 demonstrates how previous practices within the planning system, the privatisation process and the relationship between politics and business remained largely unchanged. The Tribunal trilogy which began in 1997 and which is expected to conclude in 2011, outlines how the definition of corruption evolved from a narrow interpretation of legal statutes to a greater awareness of the ethical dimensions of improper political behaviour. A consequence of this growing public appreciation of the wider understanding of political ethics, was the untimely retirement of popular Taoisigh, Charles J. Haughey and Bertie Ahern.

In previous chapters, the unorthodox link between political donations and business or personal interests became the principal cause of scandal over time. Chapter 7 details how Fianna Fáil's financial reliance on the beef industry in the 1980s was replaced by property and construction interests in the 1990s and 2000s. This chapter explores the degree to which this dependence impacted on policy decisions which exacerbated the depth of Ireland's economic collapse in 2008 and necessitated the subsequent intervention by the International Monetary Fund and the European Central Bank in 2010.

The final chapter assesses how the definition of corruption evolved in Ireland from 1922 to 2010. Apart from discretionary political decision making, which is analysed at length in the case studies, this chapter presents three variables – Irish party system, Irish political culture and Irish media – which impacted on the character of corruption exercised in Ireland.

Towards a new definition

The central thesis of this book is to challenge the conventional definition of corruption which is widely understood to be the 'abuse of public office for private gain'. Corruption however is as much implicit as it is explicit. John Noonan's definitive study on bribery emphasises that bribery can only be understood from a historical context and definitions depend upon culture.[5] In other words, public and political response to scandal can readily be held hostage to an outdated understanding of ethical transgressions. The case studies will demonstrate how this is the case.

The concept of corruption has continually wrestled between an awareness of what is legally and what is morally regarded as corrupt. A legal understanding narrowly interprets the concept of corruption as obligations defined by legal statutes where the law is clearly broken. A moral concept place a greater emphasis on behaviour defined not just by legal codes, but to expectations of behaviour characterised by a broader moral compass. The word corrupt is derived from the Latin verb *rumpere* which means, 'to break'. This implies that something is broken.

History has at different times placed greater weight on moral codes of

conduct over legal codes of conduct and vice versa. This was the case in classical antiquity where corruption was defined in generalist terms as inequality
and the loss of civic virtue, rather than as any individual political action. The
'Pledge of the Athenian City State' in ancient Greece reflected this sense of a
broad duty to a public trust.

'The Pledge of the Athenian City State'
We will never bring disgrace to this our city
by any act of dishonesty or cowardice,
nor ever desert our suffering comrades in the ranks;
We will ever strive for the ideals and sacred things
of the city, both alone and with many;

We will revere and obey the city's laws
and do our best to incite to a like respect and reverence
those who are prone to annul or set them at naught;
We will unceasingly seek to quicken the sense of public duty;

That thus, in all these ways, we will transmit this city
not only not less, but greater, better and more beautiful
than it was transmitted to us.[6]

For Plato, corruption was the systemic collapse of the moral vitality of an
entire society and the inability to pursue justice for the common good.[7] In
the same way, the sixteenth-century Republican political thinker, Niccoló
Machiavelli, regarded political corruption as the destruction of *virtu*, which
he defined as civic loyalty.[8] Corruption could only be prevented through creating and sustaining citizenship which facilitated loyalty to the state rather
than to any individual vested interest. From this perspective, the polity is
organically integrated. The individual represents the organs of the polity and
the collective comprises the body of the polity. The interdependent nature
is such that when individual self-interested behaviour occurs, corruption is
systematic, because it is the corruption of the body politic. The self-interested
private citizen is subordinate to the public-minded citizen which may explain
why the ancient Greek word for private citizen is *idiota*, which is the origin of
the contemporary word, idiot.

Irish religious teaching placed similar moral emphasis on corruption. In
1111, the Synod of the sons of Óengus, a meeting of Ireland's bishops, priests
and ecclesiastics, took place at Fiad mic Oengusso in Co. Westmeath, to
make 'certain regulations concerning public morals'.[9] Suffice to say, the age
when Ireland had Synods, or national governing councils, to determine the
boundaries of public morality are no longer in existence. The unconscious
solidarity of simpler societies that Plato espoused is not a practical application for contemporary society. The nineteenth-century French sociologist,
Emile Durkheim, believed that there was no going back to a society where the

individual was subordinated to a collective conscience.[10] The dense division of labour that greeted modernity encouraged interdependence between people which precluded such communal moral harmony, if such a thing ever actually existed. This made absolute self-regulation no longer appropriate, like that envisaged by Plato and the Irish Synods.

As the nature of the state changed, so too did the shift in emphasis from the moral to the legal concept of corruption. The eighteenth and nineteenth centuries bore witness to a fundamental redefinition of the very meaning of the state. The growth in government functions compelled greater intervention by the state in the affairs of its citizens which in turn necessitated a further reliance on legal statutes to determine and regulate conduct.

Indeed the early struggles for democratic government were marked by widespread corruption which was then regarded as a necessary means to check the absolute power of the monarchy. Both Charles Louis de Montesquieu and Jeremy Bentham, the French and British philosophers of the Enlightenment, advocated the buying and selling of political offices because it raised money for the public treasury and offered an alternative route for economic and social advancement. The twin pillars of democracy - the principles of majoritarianism and the separation of powers - were conceived from eighteenth-century corrupt practices. The first Prime Minister of Great Britain, Sir Robert Walpole (1721–42), pioneered what we know today as the majority principle. This was where the ruling party of the House of Commons gained its position on the basis of majority support. Royal patronage and nepotism were used to provide appointments and favours to political allies in cooperation with the then leader of the Opposition, Lord Henry St John Viscount Bolingbroke. This transfer of monarchical control to a parliamentary system was the prologue to the modern concept of the state. The introduction of bureaucracy was a symbolic end of aristocratic and monarchical privilege and advantage. The state, and by implication public office, was no longer regarded as the private property of the King. Distinctions between public and private became more prominent as the practice of politics was transformed.

This was also the case in Ireland as the character of Irish politics dramatically altered. Irish constituencies, no longer the private property of the landlord, became the public property of its citizens from the mid nineteenth and twentieth century. The concept of the State shifted from the living embodiment of an inheritance to an impersonal legal entity. The use of public office as a private property was no longer acceptable or tolerated. Rule thus developed from a private activity to a public duty.

It was in this context that Lord John Acton, a former MP for the County Carlow constituency, wrote to Bishop Mandell Creighton in 1887 with the often repeated phrase: 'I cannot accept, your canon that we are to judge Pope and King unlike other men, with a favourable presumption that they do no wrong. If there is any presumption, it is the other way holders of power . . . Power tends to corrupt, and absolute power corrupts absolutely'.[11] Acton challenged the assumption that traditional authority figures, such as the Pope and the King, can do no wrong. He believed that a person's sense of morality diminished as an individual's power increased.

Traditionally, intellectual argument on ethics in Ireland has qualified as assuming that corrupt conduct is wrong, albeit qualified with cultural considerations. Although corruption is a commonly used word, it is most often misused, misunderstood and misdirected. The power of its meaning and impact has become weakened by overuse which has rendered it as a hackneyed, clichéd, and stereotyped expression. Public debate has often been reduced to blandly labelling an unethical act as corrupt. This is meaningless. The analogy of cancer is useful in this context insofar as cancer cannot be cured unless it is known what type of cancer it is. Any understanding of corruption must be accompanied by an appreciation of the different types so that a long-term strategy for its prevention can be achieved.

The critical challenge then is to diagnose and explain the distinctions within corruption. By being able to define what something is, it is possible to learn how to prevent it. This can be realised by distinguishing between moral and legal corruption; clientelism and brokerage; and the rumours and reality of corruption. In doing so, a new definitional approach to corruption will be provided.

Any attempt to define corruption has been deeply problematic because, by its nature, it is secretive and does not lend itself to overt analysis earned from empirical evidence. Human beings, by their very nature, are flawed creatures. This fragility within our value system does not cease to exist with the passing of time nor when countries become more modern. Instead, our limitations grow to become more nuanced and intricate as our lives become more complicated. The ethical dimension of wrongdoing also hinders objective analyses because any such scrutiny is suggestive of a judgmental and self-righteous undertone. This is especially the case when any historical analysis of corruption is attempted. The well-known opening line of L. P. Hartley's 1953 novel, *The Go-Between*: 'The past is a foreign country, they do things differently there' is a frequently cited charge when any retrospective examination of behaviour is undertaken. This justifiably recognises that the political culture and context of the period under scrutiny deters a value neutral contemporaneous appraisal.

What is corrupt today may be the kernel of tomorrow's norms and vice-versa. What is unethical in one culture may be socially acceptable in another. Political culture, defined as the inherited set of beliefs, attitudes, opinions and norms held by a population, ultimately decides what types of political conduct is considered acceptable. As the set of values within which a system operates, political culture may place particular significance on informal rules of behaviour which elevate the importance of gratitude, respect, loyalty and secrecy. Thus, any failure to reciprocate and not offer due deference are regarded as acts of disrespect and disloyalty which in turn are severely frowned upon by wider society.

Yet caveats regarding political culture, historical conditions and traditional customs can often become champions for justifying unprincipled actions and enable ethical ambiguity or a muddying of the moral waters. In Ireland, as elsewhere, consensual attitudes towards political indiscretion can become so entrenched within a political system that it is regarded as perfectly normal. This ' culturally relativistic' argument suggests that a society tolerates corruption because it is part of the culture.

The Hartley doctrine is used to suggest that the corruption of the past is incapable of ever being subject to enquiry. This argument follows that lines should be drawn underneath such episodes and the body public would best be served by moving forward without the indulgence of looking back. A society can only learn from its mistakes when it acknowledges that mistakes have been made. This unwillingness to unconditionally learn from the mistakes that have been made, ultimately filters down into wider public life. If it is no one's fault, then of course, no one can be held accountable and for that reason nothing needs to change. In this scenario there is no obligation to learn from the past because the mindset of the past remains that of the present. Such intellectual paralysis can be circumvented by studying how corruption evolved and developed as it did, in order to understand the rationale for why it occurred. A descriptive case study analysis focuses on the context of an incident which allows the reader to evaluate how such behaviour occurred without imposing any obligation to make the judgement why.

The extensive volume of literature reflects the consensus that any classification is contested and divided between the public office,[12] market[13] and public interest[14] centred approaches, definitions based upon law[15] and philosophical interpretations[16] and various anthropological descriptions.[17] Recent theoretical approaches have tended to view corruption from an economic and rational outlook where economic transaction is the central unit of analysis.[18] This emphasis on rational choice based theorems and economic modelling neglects ethical dimensions of corruption.

These Byzantine philosophical and economic considerations, which have dominated academic discourse on different theoretical approaches, have been lost on a public more concerned about the practical repercussions of corruption. The focus on the difficulties in defining corruption can obscure the fact that a general definition actually exists.

A basic definition accepts that corruption occurs where there is a violation of laws or norms. Joseph S. Nye's 1967 explanation still holds water today:

'Corruption is behaviour which deviates from the normal duties of a public role because of private-regarding (personal, close family, private clique) pecuniary or status gains; or violates rules against the exercise of certain types of private regarding influence'.[19] Nye's approach however assumes a clear grasp of the terminology: benefit, abuse, public and private. His understanding of private gain does not include situations where the purpose of the misuse of public office is to benefit the official's religion, political party, ethnic group or other affiliation.

A legal definition treats corruption as fixed, stemming from legal statutes where the law is clearly broken. This requires that all laws are precisely stated, leaving no doubts about their meaning and no discretion to the public officials.[20] This approach assumes that although certain activities are legal, it may lie outside norms of society. It does not take into account that the law itself may originate in corrupt practices or that the legitimacy of that law may be contested. A corrupt act can be camouflaged by lawful justification. For instance, 'If an official's act is prohibited by laws established by the government, it is corrupt; if it is not prohibited, it is not corrupt even if it is abusive or unethical'.[21]

Legislating for behaviour focuses on the legality of an action but not the morality of that same action. Dependence on legal interpretations of corruption cannot 'divide shades of grey, but instead may separate the darkest black from the brightest white'.[22] When a legal definition is exclusively applied to define personal conduct, legislation replaces obligations to personal ethical responsibility. Contemporary political life in Ireland, for instance, has consequently borne intimate witness to the defence that 'I have broken no law; therefore I have done no wrong'. In this scenario, in the absence of an acknowledgement of personal ethical responsibility, the law will always play catch up.

Towards a new definition: clientelism and brokerage

The academic focus in Ireland on the distinctions between clientelism and brokerage is demonstrative of a legalistic understanding of corruption. It is argued, in the Irish case, that it is more accurate to describe the constituency work of politicians as brokerage, as distinct from clientelism. Ireland's political culture, small size of society and administrative structures are cited as reasons why brokerage is predominant within Irish politics. The inability of citizens to negotiate the myriad structures of the state bureaucracy in order to access their rightful entitlements necessitates the legitimate intervention of a broker. In that academically celebrated phrase, politicians are said to be merely 'busy harassing civil servants on behalf of constituents'.[23] The capacity failure of the Irish bureaucracy has warranted 'inflexibility, rigid adherence to the rules and perhaps impatience with people who do not fully understand these rules'.[24]

'In many ways politicians brokerage activities are similar to the activities of a range of professional mediators (such as priests, advice centre personnel and trade union officials); the difference derives from their special access to the state bureaucracy and their specific motives in carrying out brokerage functions'. A broker deals in access to those who control resources rather than directly in the resources themselves.[25] The difficulty with this interpretation, that Irish politics is characterised not by clientelism but brokerage and that brokerage is a necessary evil given the traditional character of Irish politics, is that it is limited. It ignores the broader definition of clientelism and the long-term corollaries of brokerage.

Moreover, the narrow definition of clientelism is said to encompass the direct exchange of public goods and state resources to reward, support and bestow privilege to individuals for their political support.[26] The political actor acts as the patron and facilitates direct access to the state for their clients, the voters, who more often than not are friends, associates and family members. In return, the client is obliged to reciprocate through a demonstration of their loyalty by voting and engaging in political activity as directed by the patron. The client has to engage in this practice because without a patron, the client is politically isolated and without access to basic economic and social benefits in the gift of the state, such as government jobs and contracts, land rights, public services, public housing, special welfare benefits or public sector jobs. A patron-client exchange relationship is characterised by an imbalanced vertical pattern of reverence where 'persons of higher social status (patrons) are linked to those of lower social status (clients) in personal ties of reciprocity that can vary in content and purpose across time'.[27]

These key characteristics of clientelism are said to be 'simply not present in (contemporary) Irish electoral politics' because these direct benefits 'are simply not in the gift of TDs'.[28] This is because politicians are 'dependent on the votes of anonymous constituents with whom they could have no direct links'.[29] This interpretation of clientelism and the implicit tolerance of brokerage analyses Irish political culture within a context that accepts that because the formal system was inadequate, informal intervention by brokers were justifiable. This means to an end approach is reminiscent of modernisation theory, predominant within academic literature in the 1960s and 1970s. Behaviour which embraced informal influence was regarded as functional and as 'a welcome lubricant', necessary to grease the wheels of administrative incompetence in order to deliver a system of social and personal welfare that the official system could not.[30] It was the rational outcome of an inefficient rigid bureaucracy which suffocated flexibility and business exigency. Market considerations and self-interested behaviour took pre-eminence over moral concerns and was considered as a normal part of the political process within the traditions of contemporary political culture.

This approach also overlooks the enduring and undermining 'moral connotations and value judgments with regard to democracy by stressing the beneficial effect'.[31] The presumption about the absence of impropriety is systematic of a refusal to countenance it. This premise may account for why academic literature in Ireland has neglected to empirically research or theorise on grand corruption. It has been instead content to preoccupy itself with petty corruption, the presumed outcome of the brokerage and clientelistic intricacies of the Irish political system. The belief that brokerage humanises 'the state in the eyes of people who would otherwise see it as remote', counters the cynicism that attaches to politicians generally, and fails to appreciate that brokerage self-perpetrates the perception of impropriety.[32]

A broader definition of clientelism accepts that a client or voter is not obliged to reciprocate in order to benefit from the direct exchange of public goods and state resources by a patron. The element of dependency, conditionality or contract in this exchange relationship is not explicit. However, the clientelism is implicit when the politician claims credit for having provided a clearly defined constituency with important benefits. It is not required that the politician discriminate between voters within his electoral district based on their voting preferences. It is sufficient that he discriminates against voters across constituencies by exacting disproportionate benefit on a particular constituency for political advantage.[33] When public officeholders focus on serving a particular client group linked to them by geographic ties, this shapes the public landscape and ultimately creates the conditions that are ripe for corruption.[34] Such conditions include blurring of the line between the public and private interest. The legitimacy of the state may be contested when the rule of law is used to advance private interests rather than protecting the public interest and where national leaders express weak commitment to combating corruption. The terminology of clientelism will be used in this study and unless specifically defined, will be taken to infer its wider interpretation.

Clientelism and brokerage do not stand for competing concepts and are not mutually exclusive but are mutually complementing terms. They can be subsumed as a specific form and concrete manifestation of a corrupt act. 'When a patron occupies a public position or extracts favours from those in public positions, patronage and corruption overlap'.[35] Ultimately, each of these concepts concerns the relationship of power between those that hold public power and how this is utilised for private or public benefit. In this way, the conditions for corruption are established because clientelism and brokerage ultimately distort the relationship of power between public and private interests.

As contemporary political and cultural practices transform themselves, so too, does the conventional twentieth-century definition of corruption, the abuse of public office for private gain. The state has become more involved in people's lives since the 1960s and consequently, modern governance has become more intricate as the demarcations between public and private have become more blurred. In turn, corruption as a multifaceted, systemic and global phenomenon continues to be redefined.

In this way, the United Nations Convention against Corruption (UNCAC) deliberately does not provide for a generic, one-dimensional definition of corruption. This allows for the broadest possible interpretation and captures a typology of situations. The UNCAC came into force in 2005 and contains innovative measures on international cooperation, asset-recovery and the prevention and criminalisation of corruption. By August 2010, 140 countries had ratified the UNCAC, solidifying it as the basis for agreement on international anti-corruption action. As difficult as it is to present a universally satisfying list of corruption types, the UNCAC provides such a framework in Articles 15–28, within Chapter III of its Treaty.

The list of corruption offenses include, but are not limited to, bribery, embezzlement, trading in influence, abuse of function, illicit enrichment, money laundering, concealment, obstruction of justice, participation and attempt and knowledge. In defining and criminalising these offences, it becomes de-facto a definition. 'Corruption is a fluid concept, signifying different things to different people. More importantly, it is an evolving concept . . . in view of the multifaceted nature of the phenomenon and the consequent difficulty of constructing a legal definition, the Convention adopted a descriptive approach, covering various forms of corruption that exist now'.[36] This approach by the UN, and its recognition of the evolving nature of corruption, underlines the central hypothesis of this book. Corruption is constantly changing and the case-studies presented illustrate this journey from one type of corruption to another.

Towards a new definition: mediated corruption

To that end, 'mediated corruption' is a more appropriate definition to account for the difficulties inherent within Nye's explanation, such as the challenges of perception and the tensions between legal and moral approaches. Mediated corruption is defined as:

> (1) the gain that the politician receives is political, not personal and is not illegitimate in itself, as in conventional corruption; (2) how the public official provides the benefit is improper, not necessarily the benefit itself, or the fact that the particular citizen receives the benefit; (3) the connection between the gain and the benefit is improper because it damages the democratic process, not because the public official provides the benefit with a corrupt motive.[37]

This approach redefines the traditional assumption of private gain as a financial benefit and takes into consideration other types of gains, such as power, prestige, authority and symbolic capital through illicit means. It challenges the traditional means of defining reciprocity. It also places emphasis on the recipient of the illegitimate gain. The individual who abuses public office for private gain does not necessarily always directly benefit. Instead, the misuse of public office may indirectly benefit the public officials' family, friends, political associates, political party, constituency or other affiliation associated with the public official. The gain is political, often indirect, and valuable within its own context. Corruption therefore is the use of public office for private gain without any direct link to a precise favour but in anticipation of future benefits. It may encompass undue influence in the formulation of policy and legislation by vested interests at the expense of the public interest but which benefit political actors through popular and political support.

Policy may be tailored to benefit specific geographic, demographic or socio-economic interest groups.[38] As Michael Johnston advocates: 'If an official sponsors legislation, or uses her discretion to make administrative decisions, popular with a segment of the public, do the popularity and political support that may result constitute a "private benefit?"'[39] The benefit the political actor may accrue is popular or political support which influences the outcome of an election or secure promotion within the ranks of the political party or government structures. Or, the benefit that the politician gets is the preservation of existing political support because of a decision not to be forthright during the process of implementing an unpopular policy or legislation. Moreover, favourable decisions may be introduced just before an election and difficult choices are postponed until after an election. The case studies will demonstrate how such behaviour was regarded as part and parcel of Irish politics and which remained unchallenged until the 2000s.

The Metherall / Greiner circumstances are a case in point. Anthony (Tony) Metherall resigned as a minister within the Australian Parliament and as a member of the Liberal National Party in January 1992 because of tax offences. Although he remained in the parliament as an independent, he continued to vote with the minority government of the Prime Minister, Nick Greiner. In April of that year, Metherall resigned from the parliament itself. On the very same day, Greiner appointed him to a lucrative position within the New South Wales public service. The Australian Independent Commission Against Corruption (ICAC) subsequently initiated an investigation. The Prime Minister was found to have contravened the anti-corruption legislation that he himself had sponsored through parliament.

The ICAC made the finding that Metherall's appointment was improper because it damaged the democratic process, as it implied that Metherall was rewarded for his political support to the minority government despite his resignation. Greiner did not knowingly engage in wrongful conduct and made no private or personal gain from Metherall's appointment. Nonetheless, he had created a public service job which had not existed heretofore and did not use proper public service appointment procedures. Greiner was instead deemed to have made a political gain because he solved a politically embarrassing problem. The elimination of Metherall from parliament created the political vacuum for a Liberal party member to become elected in his place and thus increased support for the Liberal government. Greiner subsequently made a clear case for his actions insofar as it was a normal part of the political process within the traditions of the New South Wales political culture.[40]

Greiner's statement to the ICAC was indicative of the struggle in how to define this very wide interpretation of corruption: 'What the Opposition and media have opened up there is the very nature of politics itself – that is, the conflict between the demands of politics and the demands of public office . . . the standards that are implied in this censure of me today are entirely new standards . . . I am not sure . . . that those standards are going to produce a workable system of democracy in our State'.[41] Meredith Burgmann, President of the Australian Legislative Council, referred indirectly to Greiner's specific situation: 'Basically, if you are taking on public office to some extent you end up with less rights than a normal member of the public, and you've just got to cop it, even if it means that your spouse gets less rights as well'.[42] This raises the legitimate question, what is the 'naturally sound condition of politics?' Greiner's demise was his assumption that such a thing existed.

The resignation of the Ceann Comhairle in October 2009, the first Speaker of the Irish parliament to do so in the history of the state, brought to the fore the questions about moral and legal responsibilities. John O'Donoghue resigned following intense public scrutiny regarding his political expenses which included five-star hotels, chauffeur-driven cars on stand-by, Michelin-starred restaurants and official trips with his wife that coincided with prestigious race meetings at Longchamp, Chantilly and Sandown.[43] In his resignation speech the Fianna Fáil TD stated that all 'travel, accommodation and related costs . . . were made in accordance with established Department of Finance guidelines and practices . . . I never transgressed any procedure, guideline or regulation'. O'Donoghue in effect provided a legal justification for his behaviour without any recognition of a moral responsibility for his actions. Like Metherall, O'Donoghue himself noted this variance: 'I find somewhat discomforting is the concept of a new parallel system of accountability'.[44]

The mediated approach recognises that the preservation of public trust is not just a question of discerning legal rights from wrongs, but upholding the very spirit of the law. As Robert Louis Stevenson wrote, 'to tell the truth, rightly understood, is not just to state the true facts, but to convey a true impression'.[45] Although political action may be within the letter of the law, it does not always account for the spirit of the law. An awareness of mediated corruption reintroduces notions of moral responsibility which have been lost on an over dependence on legal definitions of corruption.

It also acknowledges that servants of the public trust have an extraordinary set of responsibilities which are accompanied by public expectations. Any suggestion of impropriety becomes corrosive to the public trust. There is an imperative that political leadership comprehend how the volatility of perception becomes defined by the public which, in due course, acts as a tide-water mark, to which laws and regulations ultimately rise. George Berkeley, the eighteenth century Irish philosopher, coined the Latin phrase, *esse is percipi*, to be is to be perceived. Perception is inevitable. Actual and perceived corruption is often regarded as one and the same. In this way, the definition of corruption has itself become corrupted because of the failure to articulate an unambiguous definition uncoloured by the imprints of political culture. The role perception plays challenges any attempt to present a unified definition. Those in public office underestimate the corrosive power of perception which is sometimes enough to undermine the public's confidence in the moral authority of their political leadership. Public expectations of political leaders necessitate that Caesar's wife must be above suspicion, or be able to dispel it, if it arises. This is unfair, but this is the reality of modern political life. A correlation between trust and corruption recognises that 'trusting societies have less corruption. People who have faith in others are more likely to endorse strong standards of moral and legal behaviour'.[46]

The Metherall and O'Donoghue cases demonstrate that 'corruption is profoundly influenced not simply by how corruption is defined but, more deeply, by how we are to understand the character of politics'.[47] This is determined to a large degree by the role of perception. Mediated corruption takes into account the integrity of the political process. This definition is more susceptible to perception than conventional definitions of corruption. Perception is determined by how political culture is perceived by the body public. Cultural change, rather than legal change, may therefore be necessary to prevent corrupt behaviour.

Chapters 5 and 6 develop the mediated definition of corruption by focusing on case-studies which underline specific instances of this behaviour. These chapters go further and suggest that mediated corruption lends itself to legal corruption which is defined as the undue, as distinct from illegal, influence by vested interests over regulation and policy-making where elites have access to insider information that they utilise for their private benefit.

The history of Irish corruption from the foundation of the state is one where a narrow definition predominated. A growing appreciation of the limitations of this approach became more acutely evident in 2010 when political decisions regarding economic policies came under immense public scrutiny.

The unprecedented involvement by the International Monetary Fund, the European Union and the European Central Bank has challenged Irish citizens to examine their tolerance of behaviour as defined within the mediated and legal definitions of corruption.

Notes

1 R. K. Yin, *Case Study Research, Design and Method*, 3rd edn. (Sage Publications, 2002).
2 K. M. Eisenhardt, 'Building theories from case study research', *Academy of Management Review*, 14:4 (1989), pp. 532–50.
3 K. R. Hope and B. C. Chikulo (eds), *Corruption and Development in Africa: Lessons from Country Case Studies* (Palgrave, 1999); D. Gambetta, *The Sicilian Mafia: The Business of Private Protection* (Harvard University Press, 1993); P. B. E. Hill, *The Japanese Mafia Yakuza, Law, and the State* (Oxford University Press, 2003).
4 T. W. Moody, R. B. McDowell and C. J. Woods, 'A review of the conduct of administration during the seventh session of Parliament, By an independent Irish Whig, ie Tone, 6 April 1790', *The Writings of Theobald Wolfe Tone 1763–98: Volume 1: Tone's Career in Ireland to 17 June 1795* (Oxford University Press, 1998), p. 38.
5 J. T. Noonan, *Bribes* (Macmillan, 1984).
6 C. W. Lewis and Stuart Gilman, *The Ethics Challenge in Public Service: A Problem-Solving Guide*, 2nd edn (Jossey-Bass, 2005), p. 54.
7 Plato, *The Republic*, trans. H. D. P. Lee (Penguin, 1987). 421d–422b, 547a–553e.
8 N. Machiavelli, *Discourses*, trans. L. J. Walker (Yale University Press, 1950), Book 1, Ch. 2–7, pp. 211–30.
9 R. A. Stewart Macalister (ed.), and M. Murphy, *Lebo Gabála Erin: The Book of the Taking of Ireland, Part 6* (2008), www.ucc.ie/celt/LGQS.pdf.
10 E. Durkheim, *De la division du travail social: étude sur l'organisation des societies superiors*, trans. G. Simpson (Macmillan, 1933).
11 Lord Acton, 'Letter to Bishop Mandell, 3 April 1887', in L. Creighton, *The Life and Letters of Mandell Creighton* (Longmans, 1904).
12 D. H. Bayley, 'The effects of corruption in a developing nation', *Western Political Quarterly*, 19:4 (1966), pp. 719–32.
13 Theobald, *Corruption, Development, and Underdevelopment* (Macmillan, 1990).
14 C. J. Friedrich, 'Political pathology', *Political Quarterly*, 37 (January-March 1966), pp. 70–85.
15 N. H. Leff, 'Economic development through bureaucratic corruption', *American Behavioural Scientist*, 7:3 (November 1964), p. 423; V. Tanzi, *Policies, Institutions and the Dark side of Economics* (Edward Elgar, 2000), p. 94.
16 P. J. Dobel, 'The corruption of a state', *American Political Science Review*, 72:3 (September 1978), pp. 958–73.
17 J. C. Andvig, Odd-Helge Fjeldstad, I. Amundsen, K. Tone Sissener, and Tina Soreide, *Corruption: A Review of Contemporary Research* (Christian Michelsen Institute, NUPI Report NO 268 NOK 175, 2002).

18 A. Dixit, 'On the modes of economic governance', *Presidential Address Regional Meeting of Econometric Society* (2001), pp. 449–81.
19 J. S. Nye, 'Corruption and political development: a cost-benefit analysis', *American Political Science Review*, 61:2 (June, 1967), pp. 417–27.
20 Tanzi, *Policies, Institutions and the Dark Side of Economics*, p. 94.
21 J. A. Gardiner, 'Defining Corruption', *Corruption and Reform*, 7. (1993), p. 115.
22 D. H. Lowenstein, 'Legal efforts to define political bribery', in Heidenheimer *et al.*, *Political Corruption*, p. 30.
23 B. Chubb, 'Going about persecuting civil servants: the role of the Irish parliamentary representative', *Political Studies*, 11:3 (1963), pp. 272–86.
24 M. Gallagher and Lee Komito, 'The constituency role of Dáil deputies', in J. Coakley and M. Gallagher (eds), *Politics in the Republic of Ireland*, 5th edn (Rutledge, 2009), p. 250.
25 *Ibid.*, pp. 237, 243.
26 S. N. Eisenstadt and L. Roniger, *Patrons, Clients and Friends: Interpersonal Relations and the Structure of Trust in Society* (Cambridge University Press, 1984), pp. 48–9; S. Piattoni (ed.), *Clientelism, Interests, and Democratic Representation* (Cambridge University Press, 2001); H. Kitschelt and S. I. Wilkinson (eds), *Patrons Clients, and Policies: Patterns of Democratic Accountability and Political Competition* (Cambridge University Press, 2007).
27 P. D. Hutchcroft, 'The politics of privilege: rents and corruption in Asia', in A. J. Heidenheimer and M. Johnston (eds), *Political Corruption: A Handbook* (Transaction 2002), p. 495.
28 Gallagher and Komito, 'The constituency role of Dáil deputies', p. 242.
29 L. Komito, 'Irish clientelism: a reappraisal', *Economic and Social Review*, 15:3 (1984), p. 181.
30 S. P. Huntington, *Political Order in Changing Societies* (Yale University Press, 1968), pp. 59–72; A. K. Cohen, 'The study of social disorganization and deviant behaviour', in R. K. Merton, L. B. Broom and L. S. Cottrell, Jr. (eds), *Sociology Today*, (Basic Books, 1959), p. 71–81.
31 D. della Porta and Y. Mény (eds), *Democracy and Corruption in Europe: Social Change in Western Europe* (Pinter, 1997), p. 2.
32 Gallagher and Komito, 'The constituency role of Dáil deputies', p. 256.
33 I. H. Indridason, 'Coalitions and clientelism: explaining cross-national variation in patterns of coalition formation' (Department of Political Science, University of Iceland, 26 July 2006), www.notendur.hi.is/ihi/CoalitionsClientelism.pdf.
34 A. Shah, 'Tailoring the fight against corruption to country circumstances', in A. Shah (ed.), *Performance Accountability and Combating Corruption* (World Bank, 2007), p. 242.
35 J. Waterbury, 'Endemic and planned corruption in a monarchical regime', *World Politics*, 25:4 (July 1973), p. 555.
36 United Nations Office on Drugs and Crime, *Fact sheet 2, Convention Against Corruption: Q&A (2003)*, www.un.org/webcast/merida/pdfs/03-89373_factsheet2.pdf.
37 D. F. Thompson, 'Mediated corruption: the case of the Keating five', *American Political Science Review*, 87:2 (1993), p. 369.

38 S. Rose-Ackerman, 'Democracy and "grand" corruption', *International Social Science Journal*, 158:3 (1996), pp. 365–80.

39 M. Johnston, 'The search for definitions: the vitality of politics and the issue of corruption', *International Social Science Journal*, 48:149 (1996), pp. 3, 25.

40 M. Philip, 'Defining political corruption', *Political Studies*, 45:3 (1997), p. 438.

41 Commissioner Ian Temby, 'Report on Investigation into the Metherall Resignation and Appointment', (Sydney: ICAC, June 1992), quoted in: Philip, 'Defining political corruption', p. 437.

42 M. Burgmann, 'Constructing legislative codes of conduct lecture in the department of the senate', *Occasional Lecture Series at Parliament House Australia* (23 July 1999).

43 E. Byrne, 'Irish politics big on perks, but what of values?', *Irish Times* (6 October 2009).

44 'Statement by John O'Donoghue', *Irish Times* (13 October 2009).

45 R. L. Stevenson, 'Truth of intercourse', *Cornhill Magazine* (May 1879).

46 E. M. Uslaner, 'Trust and corruption', in J. G. Lambsdorff, M. Taube and M. Schramm (eds), *The New Institutional Economics of Corruption*, p. 76.

47 Philip, 'Defining political corruption', p. 437.

2

Why so little corruption? 1900s–1920s

Introduction

In the nineteenth century, limited Irish independence was thwarted on several occasions by corruption through the patronage of Irish political representatives. The barefaced purchase of Irish legislative independence through the direct bribery of Irish MPs at the Irish House of Commons before the passage of the Act of Union, 1801 embodied what the English journalist and radical reformer, William Cobbett described as 'old corruption'.[1] This also proved to be the case with the politically motivated patronage of members of Daniel O'Connell's Repeal party of the 1840s and members of the Independent Irish Party in the 1850s.[2]

A myth developed in the Irish sub-consciousness that the fall of Charles Stewart Parnell, and thus that of Home Rule, occurred because anti-Parnellite Irish Parliamentary Party members accepted promises of patronage by Gladstone, the Prime Minister of the United Kingdom, as a reward for opposing Parnell's leadership. Concessions were granted to Nationalists as a conciliatory strategy of diverting attention from the demand for Home Rule by implementing a policy known as 'Killing Home Rule by Kindness'. The 1890–91 anti-Parnellite split in the Irish Party between John Dillon (Dillonites) and Timothy Healy (Healyites) centred, among other issues, on patronage. Healy, a vociferous opponent of Parnell, listed Irish Party MPs who 'make use of their position to secure jobs for their relations' in his *Nation* newspaper.[3]

A sustained Sinn Féin propaganda campaign from 1906 successfully depicted their Irish Party political opponents as corrupt because of their acceptance of Dublin Castle patronage. These memories of the consequences of patronage had an acute effect on the policy choices of the Free State government. Memories of the long-term implications of a disreputable political system were the underlying motivation of the governments and civil servants of the early 1920s to prevent the perception of history repeating itself.

Administrative legacies of British rule: conditions for Irish probity

The appointment of Augustine Birrell as Chief Secretary to Ireland from 1907 to 1916, had two profound effects on the character of post-independence government. His actions solidified the perception that the Irish Party were besmirched by patronage from the British Crown, thereby generating an anti-corruption zeal among the Sinn Féin representatives who founded the state. Yet, paradoxically these same policy decisions by Birrell ensured the success-ful transition to Irish independence, even though he had already left Dublin Castle five years before the 1921 Anglo-Irish Agreement.

Birrell created a new dimension to Dublin Castle policy and resolved many pertinent questions surrounding the transfer of power. Birrell believed that Home Rule was inevitable and saw patronage as an opportunity to create a native Irish governing class reflective of the religious and political character of the country. Birrell's tenure marked 'the greening of Dublin Castle'.[4] This had a direct bearing on the development of the modern Irish state. In 1892, forty-five of the top forty-eight administrative positions were controlled by Protestant and Unionist officials. By 1914, these positions were divided between twenty Catholics and twenty-eight Protestants.[5] This transforma-tion was also reflected in the judiciary. Birrell appointed clearly identifiable Irish Party members to the middle echelon of the civil service, the county court system and local government. His appointees included former report-ers and editors of Nationalist newspapers, including the *Freeman's Journal* and the *Evening Telegraph* and members of the 'Standing Committee of the United Irish League' which were perceived as political allies of the Irish Party. Controversially, Max Sullivan Green, the son in law of the leader of the Irish Party, John Redmond, was appointed to the prestigious position of private secretary to the Lord Lieutenant.[6]

This courted considerable debate among both the Unionist and Nationalist communities. Unionists coined the term, Birrellism, to describe such patron-age. Arthur Griffith, founder of Sinn Féin and editor of the *United Irishman*, William Martin Murphy, owner of the Irish Catholic newspaper, *National Press*, D. P. Moran, editor of the *Leader* newspaper and Pádraig Pearse, editor of the Gaelic League newspaper, *An Claidheamh Soluis*, articulated concerns about patronage, place hunting, and maladministration.[7] Indeed, 'Arthur Griffith believed it would be a more difficult task to end favouritism and family influence in appointments under local bodies in Ireland that to drive the British away from the country'.[8] In the Sinn Féin 1906 political manifesto, Griffith advocated a nationalised Irish civil service where patronage would be exercised in the interest of the nation and not in the interest of the individual.

In the 1906 Irish Party minute book, members of the party pledged, as a sign of their independence, 'not to champion the cause of any one individual or become involved in any appointment process'.[9] As early as 1908, Redmond was defending the Irish Party's record on patronage. In a meeting with the Liberal party in Manchester, he told those present that he was proud to say that in his twenty-five years of public life 'no single member of his Party has ever violated that pledge or has accepted any honour, office, or employment for himself or his friends'.[10] The accusation of accepting 'the Saxon shilling' proved difficult to shake off.[11] Sinn Féin successfully used the issue of patronage as a propaganda tool. This was evident during Éamon de Valera's electoral breakthrough at the 1917 East Clare by-election. The Sinn Féin election literature portrayed the by-election as a simple choice between that of a 'Placehunter v Patriot'. Patrick Lynch, Irish Parliamentary Party candidate, was satirised as supportive of 'Dublin Castle jobbery'.

> A vote for Lynch is a vote for a place hunter.
> A vote for Lynch is a vote for the corrupt English Government.
> A vote for De Valera is a vote for Ireland.

The Shan Van Vocht, a widely distributed Sinn Féin poem to East Clare electors, noted

> And their God is Saxon pay,
> for four hundred pounds a year,
> (And deny it over here),
> Lies must choke their traitor breath. . .
> Won the course of Judas gain[12]

The Irish Party of Parnell which had held the seat of the British Empire to political ransom following the seminal 1885 election, was decimated within thirty years. The unprecedented 1918 election left them with just six seats and the great party of Parnell, John Redmond and John Dillon was dead. Redmond's support for the Irish Volunteers in the First World War and his party's failure to fully appreciate the significance of the 1916 Easter Rising, are two reasons often cited why the electorate lost trust in the establishment party.[13] Historians have underestimated the influence of Sinn Féin's sustained propaganda campaign. The depiction of a corrupt Irish Party which accepted Dublin Castle patronage to the civil service, the county court system and local government proved impossible to shake off.

Yet, it was because of Birrell, that many of the preconditions necessary for democracy had been achieved on the eve of Irish independence. During Birrell's stewardship, an average of five pieces of legislation for Ireland per year reached the statute book and he has been described as 'the most productive chief secretary from 1801–1922'.[14] Between 1895 and 1905 the Irish Supreme Court of Judicature was reorganised, the Department of Agriculture and Technical Instruction and the Estates Commission were established, and significant local government and Grand Jury Reform were introduced. The introduction of Land Purchase legislation was responsible for an unprecedented transfer of land. The Land Commission averaged about fifty purchases per working day from 1904 to 1914.[15] This process of state sponsored land purchases was revolutionary. The political struggle between tenants and landlords, which had dominated nineteenth century Irish politics, was essentially over as a growing peasant proprietorship warranted the departure of the Irish landlord class.

Administrative reform was also in place in advance of independence – down to the most mundane detail. In the case of the Post Office, six parliamentary committees of inquiry into wages and conditions of service had already occurred between the 1890 Raikes Committee and the 1922 Douglas Committee. The 1919 application procedures for the uniform of an auxiliary postman went so far as to detail the exact hours of service per month before waterproof capes, leggings, belts and aprons could be provided.[16] The continuity of Irish administration from Birrell's reforms to post-independence is rooted in these reforms.

Birrell was responsible for the Irish Universities Act, 1908 which was of prodigious consequence to that first independent government. The Act formally recognised the Catholic university established in the 1850s by John Henry Newman. The National University of Ireland was thus established and given the right to confer degrees. Until this time, Catholics had limited opportunity to access third level education. A dispensation, or explicit permission, was required from the Archbishop of Dublin in order to attend Trinity College Dublin. Names associated with the National University College as students, academics or both during this period included: Hugh Kennedy, Éamon de Valera, Eoin MacNeill, John A. Costello, Kevin O'Higgins, Patrick Hogan, Patrick McGilligan, Richard Mulcahy, John M. O'Sullivan, Michael Hayes and Kevin O'Sheil. It was here that the majority of the highly able and public spirited young men of the civil service, the army, the police, the magistrates, and experts, who served on the government commissions of inquiry, were educated.

An emerging Catholic governing class was relatively well educated with national literacy levels approaching ninety per cent. Land reform had largely been achieved, thus essentially forestalling challenges to the economic foundations of the state. A comparatively homogenous state, Ireland benefited from long experience of democratisation, imperfect as it was. The principle of the ballot box and the legitimate mobilisation of public opinion had dominated political activity throughout the nineteenth century. Together, these instances were what the historian, Bill Kissane, has described as 'consequences, in one way or another, of British policy, and were more tangible evidence of a positive imperial legacy'.[17]

The administrative legacies of British rule set in train the conditions for probity. The young ministers of the early 1920s governments adopted these principles wholesale, introduced further ethical reforms and disregarded established practices of patronage. Coupled with pre-independence reform, the new state initiated substantial post-independence reform. These reforms served to largely eliminate patronage and outright corruption within the civil service and local government. Determinations of kinship and community solidarity were for the most part ignored. The reformism was due to a genuine hatred by the new political elite of old Irish Tammany Hall politics. It was also due to the courage in defying popular traditions and local vested interests and challenging corrupt local authorities.

Context: ministers and the £4 9s 6d Civil War restaurant bill

The political failures since the Act of Union to the fall of the Irish Party, due to the complicit role of corruption and patronage, served as an ethical benchmark for the Sinn Féin movement. In the public mind, the loss of legislative independence and the subsequent struggle for greater political freedoms had time and again been undermined by self-interest. These mistakes of the past were implicitly understood by the young generation of politicians that entered office in 1918. A critical juncture had been breached.

The threat by British Prime Minister, Lloyd George, of 'immediate and terrible war' compelled the Irish plenipotentiaries to sign the Anglo-Irish Treaty on 6 December 1921. Éamon de Valera, Head of Government and President of the Irish Republic 1918–22, resigned, citing dissatisfaction with its terms. The Treaty proved divisive on three grounds. It demanded that Irish parliamentarians take an oath of allegiance to the British monarch; it gave Britain control over Irish ports and most controversially, conferred the six counties in the north-east of the country the right to decide their own fate. This ultimately meant partition of the island.

The Irish Parliament, Dáil Éireann, ratified the Treaty with sixty-four votes in favour and fifty-seven against in January 1922, signalling an imminent split between the Pro-Treaty and Anti-Treaty factions of the Sinn Féin party. The first provisional Government was subsequently elected and sat from January-September 1922. This period was distinguished by widespread guerrilla fighting and a gradual descent into Civil War. Public order remained fragile. Pro-Treaty Sinn Féin won the Irish general election of June 1922. Civil War, also referred to as *Cogadh na gCarad* or the *War of Brothers*, formally broke out from June 1922 until May 1923 between those who supported and opposed the Treaty.[18] The human sacrifice of the Civil War is reckoned at between 4,000 and 5,000 deaths.[19]

The Provisional government, and the Free State government which replaced it in December 1922, was composed of men primarily in their thirties with no political experience.[20] Captain William Archer Redmond and Major Bryan Cooper, both Independents, were the only two members of the Dáil that had significant previous parliamentary experience in the House of Commons at Westminster. W. T. Cosgrave, was regarded as the elder statement in cabinet, at only forty-two years, when he became the first President of the Executive Council of the Free State government in 1922. Thrust immediately into the responsibilities of office, the young ministers had no practical experience of parliamentary life and for the most part, no exposure to local government representation.

At the outbreak of hostilities at the end of June 1922, ministers, deputies and officials were forced to live under military guard in the newly acquired government buildings, formerly the headquarters of the Irish Department of Agriculture, in Upper Merrion Street. Some two years later, Ernest Blythe, then the Minister for Finance, wrote to each individual seeking reimbursement for their subsistence which had been met out of public funds:

> I am directed by the Minister of Finance to refer to the circumstances during the months of June and July 1922 when owing to dangerous conditions in the city it was necessary for Ministers, Deputies, Officials and other persons occupied on duties at Government Buildings, to remain there for some days, having their meals supplied from a neighbouring restaurant (Messrs. Mills on Merrion Row). The cost of these meals was met out of Public Funds, and the C+AG on examining the accounts thereof, has questioned the propriety of such a charge. The Minister agrees that the expenditure is not such as should be met from Public Funds and has directed that steps be taken for the recovery thereof from the persons concerned. The cost of meals supplied to you in the above mentioned period is found to be £4 9s 6d, and in the circumstances I am to ask that you will be so good as to forward a cheque for this amount drawn in favour of the Secretary, Ministry of Finance. Mise le meas, JJ McElligott Ministry of Finance.[21]

This letter was in the archives of Hugh Kennedy, Legal Adviser to the Free State government, with a letter confirming the acknowledgement of receipt and the intention of payment. These were remarkable times made extraordinary by the accomplishments of the young and inexperienced men who presided over the birth of a state. The death of Arthur Griffith, President of the Republic, of natural causes on 10 August 1922 and the assassination of General Michael Collins, Chair of the first Provisional government and Minister for Finance, in his native Cork at Béal na mBláth ten days later on 22 August 1922, deprived the Treatyites of their strongest leaders.

The enormity of their achievements can be understood by understanding the conditions which the new government had to establish an independent

Ireland. Kevin O'Higgins, Minister for Justice, told the Dáil in September 1922: 'this thing that was trying so hard to be an Irish nation would go down in chaos, anarchy, and futility'.[22] Patrick Hogan, Minister for Agriculture wrote to O'Higgins in January 1923 warning that 'two months more like the last two months will see the end of us and the Free State'.[23] The vulnerability of these early years was best summarised by O'Higgins' address to the Irish Society at Oxford University:

> To form a just appreciation of developments in Ireland in 1922, it is neces-
> sary to remember that the country had come through a revolution and to
> remember what a weird composite of idealism, neurosis, megalomania and
> criminality is apt to be thrown to the surface in even the best regulated revo-
> lution. It was a situation precipitated by men who had not cleared the blood
> from their eyes... there was no state and no organised forces. The Provisional
> Government was simply eight young men in the City Hall standing amidst
> the ruins of one administration, with the foundations of another not yet laid,
> with wild men screaming through the keyhole. No police force was function-
> ing through the country, no system of justice was operating, the wheels of
> administration hung idle, battered out of recognition by the clash of rival
> jurisdictions.[24]

The basic political structures of the Pro-Treaty government party were still being built when nine Pro-Treaty TDs resigned following the 1924 Army Mutiny which challenged the supremacy of civil authority. In all, five sets of national elections occurred between 1922 and 1927. These elections (1922 (two), 1923, and 1927 (two) and a series of by-elections known as the 'mini general election') happened in an exceptionally volatile period and immedi-ately after the introduction of universal adult suffrage to Ireland in 1922. Such electoral endeavours must be considered in the context of inter-war Europe. The practice of political stability was the exception in a period when European democracies routinely collapsed.[25]

Yet, the governments, of the early 1920s established, legitimised and consolidated many of the institutions of government, which remain with us today, in the midst of a bitter and divisive Civil War. These achievements – 'constitutional, political, administrative and diplomatic – made possible the constitutional, economic, and foreign policy adventures of the next decade'.[26] Against this background, the principle of probity was obsessively upheld, notwithstanding a period of intense political instability coupled with eco-nomic uncertainly. The concept of the state as a moral entity and the exercise of public power as 'a compelling sense of duty', as Blythe later described it.[27] Early Dáil debates denoted corruption as an evil political depravity which undermined democracy and called for those who violated their citizenship duties to be deprived of citizenship.[28]

Unsung heroes: a civil service obsession with probity

The concern about impropriety was one also shared by the civil service. Their formative influence in forming the machinery of the state's administration was astonishing. The Irish administrative system, pre-independence, was characterised by cumbersome complexity and was said to have 'as many boards as would make her coffin'. The resulting perception, as logged in the diary of Dublin Castle official Andrew Philip Magill, was one where 'in the eyes of the populace' the Castle was 'both extravagant and corrupt'.[29] A team of British senior civil servants led by Sir Warren Fisher, Permanent Under-Secretary of the Treasury and Head of the British civil service, carried out a special investigation into Dublin Castle in 1920. Fisher succinctly concluded: 'The Castle Administration does not administer'.[30]

The British Treasury believed that 'the efficient administration not merely of the Minister of Finance but of the civil service generally in the Free State is of very great importance'.[31] Handpicked, high-ranking civil servants were temporarily transferred from London with a mandate to introduce sweeping reorganisation changes to Dublin Castle and to prepare for the smooth transfer of power. The subsequent Whitley report culminated in the restructuring of the Irish Treasury from 1919 to 1921. The Provisional government were the beneficiary of a financial administration exposed to the most internationally advanced Treasury reforms of its time, which had been implemented by the most able civil servants of an entire Empire.

These included A. P. Waterfield, J. B. Gilbert, T. K. Bewley, J. N. Ryan and C. J. Flynn. Cornelius James (Corny) Gregg was 'Secretary for Establishment Matters', directly responsible to the Minister for Finance, from March 1922 until October 1924. Cosgrave created this position especially for the Kilkenny man whom he regarded as a personal friend and of special importance to his government in those early years. Gregg was on loan from the British Treasury and his extended transfer was agreed at the highest levels with approval from the Permanent Secretary to the Colonial Office and the Permanent Secretary to the Treasury. Though Gregg was anxious to return to London, Cosgrave persuaded him to remain. Cosgrave had personal contacts with Gregg's wife's family. The Crottys were prominent supporters of the Pro-Treaty government, now regrouped into the Cumann na nGaedhael party.[32] Gregg was responsible for the establishment and organisation of the Department of Finance and the civil service.

Ronan Fanning, in his historical text, *The Irish Department of Finance* noted 'how few men made so many big decisions'.[33] J. J. McElligott, influential Assistant Secretary at the Department of Finance 1923–27 and promoted as Secretary 1927–53, noted that the beneficial effect of Ministerial inexperience and distraction by the Civil War was that it enabled senior civil servants to construct the administrative fabric of the Free State without political interference.[34]

Finance officials had wide-ranging freedom of action in decision-making throughout 1922 and 1923. It was in this period that the Revenue Commissioners, the Civil Service Commission, the Comptroller and Auditor General were instituted, as were proposals for the reorganisation of government. This two year phase of exceptional decision-making from 1922 until 1923 ensured the primacy of the Department of Finance, the formulation of probity standards and the formation of basic democratic institutions. This was the only time in the history of the state, that the positions of head of government and finance were simultaneously held by the same individual. Michael Collins, Minister for Finance 1919–22, and W. T. Cosgrave, Minister for Finance 1922–23, trusted and depended on their finance officials. In fact, until 1924, officials from the Department of Finance were occasionally present at Executive Council meetings when matters relating to finance were being discussed. Apart from the Government Secretariat, no other government department has had this privilege. Leon Ó Broin, Department of Finance administrative officer in the 1920s, observed how reliant Collins was on his civil servants:

> (Collins) . . . accepted the minutes he (Joseph Brennan, Secretary of the Department of Finance 1923–27) prepared for them and signed his draft letters. He (Brennan) appears to have had a free hand in setting up an Irish Exchequer on the British model, in devising how the Exchequer account in the Bank of Ireland would operate and be controlled, in introducing the British system of Parliamentary control over public finances via annual estimates, vote on account, and appropriation accounts, and in solidly establishing the role of the Comptroller and Auditor General.[35]

Collins' meticulous concerns for financial probity and the introduction of proper accounting and auditing procedures were evident as early as August 1919 when he appointed Donal O'Connor & Company of Westmoreland Street as auditor of the Loan Accounts. These fully audited half-yearly statements were presented, notwithstanding the ongoing Anglo-Irish War and the Civil War. On the day of the largest military action in Dublin, the burning of the Custom House, Collins made a complaint to Diarmuid Ó hEigeartaigh in the Department of the Secretariat that he had yet to receive the estimates due for the half year July / December 1921 from many of the Dáil Departments.[36] In June 1920 Collins appointed George McGrath as Accountant General to his Finance Ministry. Collins believed in the scrutiny, examination and audit of public accounts to ensure their 'accuracy, authority and conformity'. Collins told the Dáil:

> The value of this would be uniformity and constant check. The report. . . would show exactly the financial position of all Departments, the outgoings and receipts, the amount being spent, and the return if any; by a general coordination all books and accounts expenses would be saved and, by paying a first class man, all expenditure will be regularised and placed upon a business basis.[37]

The pre-eminence of the Department of Finance, intentionally modelled on its British counterpart, was now established. No minister or government department could initiate any policy, or draft any Bill, involving the expenditure of public funds without the consent of Finance. Finance also had statutory responsibility for the regulation of civil service recruitment, staffing levels, promotions, salaries and expenses. Insistence upon accountability through transparent procedures, wide discretionary powers and considerable independence characterised this new department. This dominance was reinforced through Kennedy's amendment to the Ministries and Secretaries Act, 1924. 'Apportionment of funds between Ministers: If and whenever any question or doubt shall arise. . . every such question or doubt shall be determined by the Minister for Finance whose decision shall be final and conclusive'.[38]

Gregg was the key drafter of this Act which remains the basic statute governing the central administration of the state. The Act consolidated the cumbersome and inefficient collection of forty-seven departments, commissions and boards into eleven new departments. The functions of these new departments were centralised and directly under the control of the Minister. The historian Eunan O'Halpin has described it as 'the single most important piece of public service legislation passed in independent Ireland'.[39]

The Ministries and Secretaries Act also clarified the role of the Attorney General's office. Amendments were made to ensure the independence of the office. The principle of a full-time paid Attorney General, uncompromised by potential conflicts of interest because of private practice commitments was initiated.[40] Kennedy believed that:

> the basis and the whole character of proceedings to be ordered will be the strict letter of the law which will be fairly administered and which will be the safeguard and the bulwark of every citizen of the State, ensuring to everyone his rights and in return demanding his duty. . . but it is right that I should point out that this Bill (Ministers and Secretaries) is next perhaps in importance, from the point of view of the State, to the Constitution.

Memories of Birrell's blatant practice of patronage motivated the new Ministers to introduce the principle of meritocracy within local government and civil service appointments. Kennedy advocated a distinct break from the past. In his personal letter to his mother in 1923 he outlines his deep-seated rationale for such a policy:

My Dearest Mother, With reference to the office of State Solicitor in the County of Clare, I must say I have been greatly distressed by the amount of personal pressure brought to bear with reference to filling the vacancy, by the Sinn Féin party. One of the outstanding principles of the Sinn Féin movement was the eradication of the horrible system of jobbery, which was corrupting public life and public administration in this country. It had become one of the worst features of the late Irish Party. People do not seem to me to have quite realised that it is not the Irish Party which has carried the country to freedom. If it had been, canvassing for jobs might have been one of the features of public life. I am determined, for my part, not to permit it in connection with any office with which I have any say. It is bad enough in the case of any appointment to have that kind of thing going on, but in the case of a professional appointment such as a solicitor to act on behalf of the state in public business, I can only say that in my opinion it is extremely reprehensible. The government is gradually setting up machinery which will I hope, save people like me from continual persecution by the friends of those who are seeking offices of profit. Affectionately, H.[41]

The removal of patronage from the political system served a number of purposes. From a practical standpoint, the government were relieved of the burden of being beleaguered by requests for patronage. The private papers of Desmond FitzGerald, Minister for External Affairs and Hugh Kennedy, Attorney General reveal their irritation at the 'innumerable applications for posts'.[42]

The appointment of candidates based on open examination and promotion on merit for certain civil service positions had been enshrined in British statutes following the recommendations of the 1855 Northcote-Trevelyan report. This link between professionalism and honesty was a by-product of a moral code inherited from Victorian values. Gregg's Memorandum to Government petitioned for a Civil Service Commission to ensure the continuation of established procedures introduced by the British Civil Service Commission before independence.

The Blythe Committee, so called after Ernest Blythe, Minister for Local Government and chair of the committee, was subsequently appointed in January 1923 to present such proposals. Eamon Duggan, Gregg, Gordon Campbell, Secretary of the Department of Industry and Henry Friel, Secretary of the Department of Home Affairs, were the other members of this industrious committee. Within five months it had reported and the Civil Service Regulation Act 1923 was pioneered. Under the supervision of the Department of Finance, the first Civil Service Commission was created and comprised of three commissioners. Michael Hayes, Ceann Comhairle (chairman) of the Dáil, chaired and was assisted by J. O'Neill, Secretary of the Department of Education and Gregg, Secretary of the Department of Finance. From the outset, the Commissioners were resolute and in no uncertain terms issued notice of their independence to each government minister:

It has been brought to the notice of the Civil Service Commissioners that attempts
have been made to use influence in favour of candidates for examination or for
interview by Selection Boards set up by the Commission. The Commission
desire to give public notice that any attempt to influence any Commissioner, or
any member of a Selection Board which has been set up by the Commission in
favour of any candidate for any public appointment will automatically disqualify
the candidate for the position which he is seeking.[43]

The vivacity by which one of the most influential pieces of legislative reform
was prosecuted in these turbulent Civil War years of the young state was
striking. The enduring impact of this meritocracy policy led to a professionalised and competent civil service, defined by rule based behaviour, and
detached from local and national political considerations. The assumption of
impartial recruitment, rather than patronage, into the state bureaucracy was
a concept before its time in many parts of Europe in the 1920s. Apolitical and
impersonal competitive examination became the norm by which candidates
were recruited into the administrative organs of the Free State. John Regan's
historical account of the early 1920s, *The Irish Counter-Revolution*, is not particularly marked by his enthusiastic recognition of the achievements of the
early Provisional and Free State governments. In that light, it is worth observ-
ing that Regan regarded the Civil Service Commission as 'arguably the most
important long-term achievement of the post-revolutionary settlement'.[44]

The Provisional and Free State governments inherited a local government
system which was a by-word word for corruption in its appointments.[45]
Gerald William Balfour, Chief Secretary for Ireland, instigated the 1898 Local
Government Act as part of the 'Kill Home Rule By Kindness' policy. This Act
abolished the landlord dominated Grand Jury system and introduced county,
urban and rural district councils largely controlled by Nationalist interests.
The multiplicity of local government structures encouraged administrative
confusion and inefficiency. The power to make local appointments to dispensary doctor positions, clerkships and local government officer posts had now
simply transferred from landlords to Nationalists. The rules governing tenure,
status and pay for these highly coveted positions were essentially dependent
on the strength of political connections.

Local government was regarded as the access point for power rather than
Dublin Castle, which was deemed foreign and Unionist. In advance of Irish
independence, local government had become a firmer concept in the Irish
mind rather than national government. Irish people had long identified with
representative local democracy instead of the Unionist controlled national
democracy. This was to have a profound long-term effect on the structure of
the democratic political process in the newly independent state.

The Local Government Act 1925 reorganised the entire system of local government. The new broom swept relentlessly clean. The 214 Rural District Councils, a bastion for public appointment abuses under the 1898 Act, were abolished. The Local Authorities (Officers and Employees) Act, 1926 introduced the Local Appointments Commission (LAC) along similar lines to the Civil Service Commission. Though a corresponding body to the Civil Service Commission existed earlier than independence, this was not the case for the Local Appointments Commission and represented a complete departure from Dublin Castle practice. This autonomous statutory body was responsible for the independent appointment of senior and professional positions in local government and public sector through competitive examination. Appointments were no longer politically or religiously motivated; however, councillors could still appoint lesser grades. A national, standardised set of qualification criteria and remuneration for local officials was devised and enforced, thereby bypassing local networks.

These reforms were welcomed by Ministers for Local Government and Public Health, Seamus de Burca and Richard Mulcahy. In 1926, de Burca claimed that the LAC represented 'the ideal cherished by the founders of the Sinn Féin movement. . . the establishment of a national service which should be arrived on the principle of merit'. Mulcahy was relieved of the burden of patronage requests. He wrote in 1927 that 'outside persons, including Ministers, have as little influence or right to influence appointments to the Civil Service, where candidates are appointed as a result of definite examination'.[46] The 1929–30 report of the Ministry of Local Government and Public Health on Local Appointments concluded that with 'the expansion of the functions of local authorities, it became more and more evident that the appointment of local officials should no longer be exposed to the evils of patronage, of family, local and political influences'.[47]

There was an expectation by government supporters that Unionists and Protestants would be removed from their positions in their favour. Public appointments were a contentious issue following independence. To some minds, it reinforced the concept of a Dublin based elite imposing appointments at local level and encouraged existing centre-periphery tensions. Resistance to merit based nominees in Kerry and Mayo led to the dissolution of these Councils. Not everyone was suitably impressed. Despite Fianna Fáil TD Frank Aiken's nostalgia for the 'old days', the principle stood.

> It used to be that one could only get a job if one had some friends in an influential position in the County Council. But this conspiracy was pretty open. Everyone in the county knew that certain people got jobs because they were related to so-and-so on the County Council. Then people had an opportunity of weighing up that man and of voting against him when he next came along for re-election. To-day the conspiracies are not quite so open.[48]

As Minister for Local Government, Cosgrave had to overcome a number of direct challenges to his authority. In 1923 he dissolved the county councils of Kerry and Leitrim and other minor bodies. In 1924 he also dissolved Roscommon Town Commissioners, New Ross Urban District Council, the Cork and Dublin Corporations and Offaly County Council. Cosgrave believed these bodies to be negligent or incompetent in its administration and appointed Commissioners for periods extending to three years, after which time the local body was to be re-elected. These Commissioners proved to be an effective determinate against the notorious corruption which had infected these authorities. The Commissioners overruled vested interests and instead set a new standard of civic responsibility and achievement.

The principles of an efficient and fair administration were pioneered and substantially reformed in advance of independence. This negated attempts to circumvent a rigid, ineffective bureaucracy perceived to be unjust and corrupt for the benefit of the old order. The civil service provided continuity and stability in equal measure. There was no struggle for control of the administrative machinery. The Unionist and Protestant communities had accepted a realignment of power structures, content that the 'new' Irish civil service had absorbed the positive values of its predecessor. The civil service were as loyal to new political masters as they had been under British rule.

Conclusion

The historical character of Irish politics had a deep influence upon future malpractice. In newly established states with recently won freedom, the natural inclination is to preserve power by distributing patronage among political supporters. The Free State government did the very opposite and created structures, such as the Local Appointments Commission, to prevent the abuse of authority in this way. Though it may also be argued that such crude mechanisms of consolidating political support within the institutions of the state was unnecessary because the transition from British rule to Irish independence did not challenge the position of the existing economic or social elites. The assumption of impartial recruitment and the principle of meritocracy, rather than patronage, into Ireland's bureaucracy was a concept before its time for much of Europe. This is often taken for granted, yet accounts for why Ireland has not experienced overwhelming systemic corruption within its administration structures and civil service, as occurred in other post-colonial and newly independent countries.

A consequence of the sacrifices and struggles for independence was a deep sense of state. Political culture placed extraordinary degrees of trust in its institutions. It was in this context that the remarkable decision was made to restructure the Garda Síochána as an unarmed police force in 1922. In the words of first Commissioner, Michael Staines, TD 'The Garda Síochána will succeed not by force of arms or numbers, but on their moral authority as servants of the people'.[49] Despite the shadow of Civil War and the historical precedent of an armed Royal Irish Constabulary, the Free State government had astonishing confidence in the Irish people's reverence for moral authority.

This unconditional respect for the rule of law, and the pride in the 1922 Free State Constitution, generated a collective moral bond. The letter from the Minister for Finance to government ministers seeking the reimbursement of the paltry sum of £4 9s 6d for their subsistence during the dangerous days of the Civil War, is one example of how political culture earnestly upheld ethical standards. Although Ireland was now partitioned, this revolutionary generation not only restored legislative independence lost through the Act of Union, 1801, but secured wider sovereignty for post-independence Ireland. They achieved this because they sacrificed their self-interest for the public good and assumed that the lessons of Irish history were enough for this principle to endure after them.

Notes

1   H. Harling, 'Rethinking "old corruption"', *Past and Present*, 141:1 (May 1995) pp. 127–58.
2   T. Hoppen, *Elections, Politics, and Society in Ireland, 1832–1885* (Oxford, 1984).
3   T. W. Healy, *Why Ireland Is Not Free* (Dublin, 1898), p. 99; *The Nation* (19 September 1896); *The Nation* (26 September 1896); *The Nation* (3 October 1896).
4   L. McBride, *The Greening of Dublin Castle: The Transformation of Bureaucratic and Judicial Personnel in Ireland, 1892–1922* (University of America Press, 1991), p. 190.
5   R. B. McDowell, *The Irish Administration, 1808–1914* (Routledge & Kesal Paul, 1964), pp. 46–51.
6   McBride, *The Greening of Dublin Castle*, p. 145.
7   'The Muses 'tribute to Parnell', *United Irishman* (5 October 1895); 'D. P. Moran Editorial', *Leader* (4 April 1908); 'Editorial', *Irish Independent* (27 September 1909).
8   J. J. Lee, *Ireland 1912–1985, Politics and Society* (Cambridge University Press, 1989). Quotes from *Connacht Telegraph*, p. 162.
9   National Manuscripts, Dublin, Ms 12081, Irish Parliamentary Party Minute Book, 14 February 1906.
10 *Freeman's Journal* (13 November 1908).
11 Saxon Shilling' is an alliterative term meaning money given by the British government as an inducement for Irish recruits to join the British army. The term is understood to denote traitorship.
12 National Library, Dublin, LOP 414; LOP 417, East Clare election literature: 'Placehunter v patriot', 1917. The letter 'v' does not exist in the Irish language but election agents phonetically spelt 'bh' as 'v'. Éamon was invariably spelt as Edward and Edmond.

13 D. Meleady, *Redmond the Parnellite* (Cork University Press, 2008).

14 L. O Broin, *The Chief Secretary: Augustine Birrell in Ireland* (Chatto & Windus, 1969), p. 41.

15 McBride, *The Greening of Dublin Castle*, pp. 120–1.

16 National Library, 2A 2571, William Norton, Civil Service Reference Book, 1929.

17 B. Kissane, *Explaining Irish Democracy* (University College Dublin Press, 2002), p. 223.

18 T. P. O'Neill and F. A. Pakenham, Earl of Longford, *Éamon de Valera* (Arrow Books, 1974), p. 195.

19 R. Fanning, *Independent Ireland* (Educational Company of Ireland, 1998), p. 39.

20 Collins was President of the first Provisional government from January to August 1922; Cosgrave was President of the second Provisional government from September to December 1922 and the first Executive Council from December 1922 to September 1923 and the second Executive Council from September 1923 to June 1927.

21 University College Dublin Archives, P4/737 7, Hugh Kennedy Papers (March 1924).

22 Kevin O'Higgins, Dáil Éireann, *Precedence for Ministerial Business.* 1 (27 September 1922).

23 M. Hopkinson, 'Civil War and aftermath, 1922–4', in J. R. Hill (ed.), *A New History of Ireland VII: Ireland 1921–1984* (Oxford University Press, 2003), p. 49.

24 T. de Vere White, *Kevin O'Higgins* (Methuen, 1948). pp. 83–4, 'Three years hard labour: an address to the Irish Society at Oxford University in 1924'.

25 L. Karvonen, *Fragmentation and Consensus: Political Organisation and the Interwar Crisis in Europe* (Columbia University Press, 1993); D. Berg-Schlosser, and J. Mitchell (eds), *Conditions of Democracy in Europe 1919–1939* (Macmillan, 2000), p. 464.

26 E. O'Halpin, 'Politics and the State 1923–32', in Hill (ed.), *A New History of Ireland VII: Ireland 1921–1984*, p. 125.

27 M. McInerney, 'Ernest Blythe: A Political Profile IV', *Irish Times* (4 January 1975).

28 Darrell Figgis and Professor William Magennis, Dáil Éireann, *The Prevention of Corrupt Practices at Elections. 1* (20 October 1922).

29 C. W. Magill (ed.), *From Dublin to Stormont Castle: The Memoirs of Andrew Philip Magill, 1913–1925* (Cork University Press, 2003), p. 128.

30 Report of Sir Warren Fisher to the Chancellor of the Exchequer. 12 May 1920. Quoted in C. Townshend, *The British Campaign in Ireland 1919–1921* (Oxford University Press, 1975), p. 75.

31 R. Fanning, *The Irish Department of Finance 1922–58* (Institute of Public Administration, 1978), pp. 77–8. 739/18 Materson-Smith to Warren Fisher (1 August 1923).

32 Liam Cosgrave, interview (March 2008).

33 Fanning, *The Irish Department of Finance 1922–58*, p. 98.

34 *Ibid.*

35 L. O Broin, *No Man's Man: A Biographical Memoir of Joseph Brennan* (Institute of Public Administration, 1982), pp. 106–7.

36 Fanning, *The Irish Department of Finance 1922–58*, p. 28.

37 *Ibid.*, p. 26.

38 University College Dublin Archives, Hugh Kennedy Papers.

39 O'Halpin, 'Politics and the State 1923–32', p. 111.

40 University College Dublin Archives, Dublin, P4/529. Hugh Kennedy Papers: 'Tomás MacEoin'.

41 University College Dublin Archives, P4/13. Hugh Kennedy Papers (24 September 1923).

42 Desmond FitzGerald, *Memoirs of Desmond FitzGerald, 1913–1916* (Liberties Press, 2006), p. 12; University College Dublin Archives, P4/617, Hugh Kennedy Papers: '1923 MS drafts of circular letters'.

43 University College Dublin Archives, P4/742, Hugh Kennedy Papers: Department of Finance Circular letter 29/24 to Ministers from Civil Service Commissioners. 'Use of influence on behalf of candidates for public appointments', 1 May 1924.

44 J. M. Regan, *The Irish Counter-Revolution: 1921–1936 Treatyite Politics and Settlement in Independent Ireland* (Gill and Macmillan, 1999), p. 216. University College Dublin Archives, Dublin, P7a/95. Richard Mulcahy Papers, 1927.

45 Lee, *Ireland 1912–1985*, p. 161.

46 University College Dublin Archives, P7b/23, 24, 25, Richard Mulcahy Papers, 1927.

47 Report of the Ministry of Local Government and Public Health 1929–30, See: N. Mansergh, *The Irish Free State: Its Government and Politics* (Allen and Unwin, 1934), p. 14.

48 Frank Aiken, Dáil Éireann, *Orders of the Day: Local Government Bill, 1931. 39* (17 June 1931).

49 Michael Staines last instructions as Garda Commissioner, given to Gardai being sent out to the country. (9 September 1922).

3

Setting standards: 1930s–1940s

Introduction

In 1932, the newly formed Fianna Fáil party entered government for the first time. Éamon de Valera's party came to dominate Irish politics, emerging as the largest party at every general election until 2011. Fianna Fáil's protectionist platform centred on a policy of economic self-sufficiency and was a significant shift from W. T. Cosgrave's Cumann na nGaedheal policy of economic liberalism. Translated as 'soldiers of destiny' in English, Fianna Fáil promised to protect Irish industry through the imposition of tariffs.

The scandals of the 1930s and 1940s were as a direct consequence of protectionalism because it enabled discretionary decision-making. The establishment of the Control of Manufacturing Acts 1932–34, initiated under Patrick McGilligan and enacted under Seán Lemass, provided the Minister for Industry and Commerce with varying degrees of latitude in the issuing of licences, shares, leases and export quotas. The minister's department presided over an extraordinarily regulated environment. In 1931, the year before its introduction, the list of tariffs on Irish goods covered 68 articles. The *Economist* magazine calculated that by 1938, the number of articles subject to state restriction or control had risen to 1,947.[1] The Irish economy was heavily protected, largely subsidised and principally controlled by the state. The 1932–38 'Economic War' with Great Britain, where coal and cattle tariffs were used as retaliatory devices, reinforced this self-sufficiency policy. World War Two served to intensify Ireland's economic isolation, which in turn placed greater value on tariffs controlled by the department.

T. K. Whitaker, senior civil servant at the Department of Finance 1938–69, described Lemass as 'the chief protagonist of protection'.[2] In later life Lemass described himself as a 'pragmatic protectionist' and defended his early advocacy of the self-sufficiency doctrine: 'Had you any example from another small country that had achieved this blend of industrialisation and agriculture? . . . We were working entirely on our own without any guidance of any kind.'[3]

The 1935 Wicklow Gold inquiry and the 1943–47 Tribunal trilogy – Great

Southern Railways, Ward and Locke – occurred, in part, because of the personal antagonism between McGilligan and Lemass. The emergence of scandal was as much personality driven, as it was ethically motivated. This chapter details the nuances of the various inquiries to illustrate how corruption changed because of new economic circumstances and how the influence of a political rivalry was fundamental in bringing these concerns to public attention.

The Wicklow Gold inquiry 1935

Patrick McGilligan (1889–1979), a leading figure of Cumann na nGaedheal, the precursor of Fine Gael, was Minister for Industry and Commerce 1924–32 and Minister for External Affairs 1927–32. He was instrumental in establishing Irish influence at the Court of International Justice, the League of Nations and the Commonwealth and oversaw the speedy expansion of the new Irish diplomatic service. These initiatives may have proved detrimental to him in the long-term as they 'may conceivably have reduced his effectiveness in the more electorally significant Department of Industry and Commerce, and certainly offered his formidable shadow, Seán Lemass, an opportunity to accuse him of neglect'.[4]

When Seán Lemass (1899–1971) replaced McGilligan as Minister for Industry and Commerce, McGilligan shadowed Lemass' portfolio and proved a formidable opponent until his return to government in 1948–51 as Minister for Finance. In every way, both men represented the two distinct political forces of Irish public life. Lemass, a proud Dubliner, was a member of the Irish Volunteers and an active participant in the 1916 Easter Rising, the War of Independence and the Civil War. Free State soldiers murdered his brother Noel in 1923, the same year that McGilligan was first elected to the Dáil as a Free State TD.[5] McGilligan's political career began as secretary to Kevin O'Higgins, Minister for Justice, in the first Dáil, a deeply hated figure within the Lemass Anti-Treaty tradition for authorising the execution of Republican prisoners during the Civil War. As a founding member of Fianna Fáil in 1926, Lemass famously described Fianna Fáil as a 'slightly constitutional party'.[6]

McGilligan on the other hand was a Northern Catholic from Coleraine in Derry.[7] His father was a businessman opposed to Parnell, and sat in the House of Commons from 1892 to 1995 as the South Fermanagh MP. In direct contrast, Lemass' grandfather, John Lemass, was a Northern Catholic from Armagh, elected to Dublin City Council in 1885 as a Parnellite Irish Party member. Lemass' 'earliest political experience' was memories of his father, John Timothy Lemass, as an active member of the Irish Party.[8]

The politics of McGilligan and Lemass were as different to one another as their educational experiences. A student of the prestigious Clongowes Wood College and University College Dublin, McGilligan later became a prolific Senior Counsel and a Professor of Constitutional, International and Criminal Law at UCD. Lemass' education was more modest, his schooling limited to Westland Row Christian Brothers School, in the heart of Dublin city, when his participation in the 1916 Easter Rising spelt the end of his formal education.

Lemass and McGilligan politically marked one another for almost two decades which in time came to personify a clash of characters of two men deeply at odds with each other. McGilligan, a vociferous and informed debater was not to be challenged without prudence. Renowned for his sharp wit and, at times, uncompromising tenacity, McGilligan 'withheld longer than most the hand of friendship from those who had refused to accept the treaty and whose actions had added to the difficulties of state-building'. His tongue could be vitriolic and he did not suffer fools gladly, which matched Lemass' 'resolute and unswerving' and 'independent-minded and most impatient' character.[9] McGilligan's trenchant religious views were at one with his robust character. These spirited personality traits regularly collided with those of Lemass' who also processed strength of character in equal measure but without McGilligan's staunch Catholicism.

Perhaps more than any other government sector, the Department of Industry and Commerce determined the economic policy of the state. The Mines and Minerals Act 1931 gave the Minister for Industry and Commerce the authority to issue a lease for the mining of state owned minerals. By 1935, Lemass had granted eighteen leases from the fifty applications received.[10] This included a prospecting lease with exclusive mining rights in 982 acres of three townlands near Woodenbridge, Co. Wicklow to Senator Michael Comyn and Robert (Bob) Briscoe TD, both Fianna Fáil, in 1934. The lease was initially limited to a two year period, but contained a proviso for an extension of a further ninety-seven years.

Comyn and Briscoe also had a further application for an additional six townlands in Wicklow, totalling some 2,000 acres. The lease was issued for an initial two years with rent payable to the department at five pounds annually with a royalty of 1/25 part of the value of the minerals obtained by both men. Comyn and Briscoe were the only applicants for the Wicklow lease, the availability of which was not advertised.[11]

In 1935, Comyn and Briscoe made an agreement to sub-lease their lease to M. E. Heiser,[12] managing director of a London syndicate. McGilligan believed that it was 'an extra big scandal that the contract document was drawn up on Seanad Éireann notepaper to give an official stamp, as it were, to the whole matter'.[13] Comyn and Briscoe had invested just £200 into the mining project, vis-à-vis mining tools and wages. Under the terms of Heiser's contract, they were now to receive 48,000 five shilling fully paid up shares (£12,000) and a royalty of 2¼ per cent on all minerals found.[14] The syndicate agreed to form a company; Consolidated Goldfields of Ireland, Ltd. The syndicate led Comyn and Briscoe to believe that they had £80,000 in capital to invest in their mining venture.

This proved not to be the case. Instead, the syndicate intended to raise the money by selling shares on the stock market. This was a very controversial subject in Ireland at the time. Mining speculation was rife internationally in the late 1920s. Indeed, the 1929 Wall Street crash was in part caused by Latin American mining companies raising enormous sums of money on dubious prospects in America. The London syndicate was similarly attempting to raise money on the stock market based on a mining prospect which had poor expectations with potential investors none the wiser. The syndicate did not disclose their full intentions to the Fianna Fáil representatives. Lemass' consent was necessary for the sub-lease to be lawful. Confusion arose as to whether Comyn and Briscoe made an application for a sub-lease following McGilligan's accusations. Lemass had said in an earlier Dáil debate that an application had been made and was to be considered but later retracted this statement. 'It was incorrectly stated on Saturday that an application had been made. No application, in fact, has been made'.[15]

The role of the department in issuing licences, leases, export quotas and so forth was new and rapidly expanding. The system of licence allocation was hotly disputed in the 1930s on the most mundane of items, including sheepskins for export. In 1934, the Fine Gael TD, James Dillon 'objected to giving licensing powers to the Minister because the administration of the licensing powers the Minister already has is corrupt. I want to repeat that. The administration of these licensing powers is corrupt and grossly corrupt'.[16]

McGilligan was suspicious that those benefiting from licence decisions made by the department were Fianna Fáil supporters and sought a broad inquiry into the 'the granting of licences in relation to cattle, flour, and thread'.[17] The Fine Gael shadow spokesperson on Industry and Commerce was angry that potentially valuable state mining rights were sold at token value for the perceived private gain of his bitter Fianna Fáil political rivals. To add insult to injury, he was incensed that the state's gold mines were being exploited by an English syndicate to fraudulently take money from Irish investors. He believed that Fianna Fáil, wittingly or otherwise, was a party to this. In particular, he contended that the lease was issued under conditions of secrecy. This was a bone of contention for Lemass. The Mines and Minerals Act 1931 was enacted when McGilligan was Minister and McGilligan himself had insisted that secrecy was essential as far as prospecting leases were concerned.[18]

Matters came to a head when McGilligan formally alleged in the Dáil in June 1935 that Lemass had improperly allocated the lease to his Fianna Fáil associates.[19] Lemass moved a Dáil motion to establish a Select Committee on the Demise of Certain State Mining Rights in June 1935,[20] comprising of Dáil deputies, to investigate McGilligan's allegations.[21] Curiously, the Select Committee was nominated by a Committee of Selection which included both the person who made the allegation and the accused, McGilligan and Briscoe. William Norton TD, leader of the Labour party, chaired the cross-party inquiry.[22]

John Leydon, Secretary of the Department of Industry and Commerce, rebuffed the suggestion that Lemass had exercised any 'radiated influence'. The inquiry, which included McGilligan's Fine Gael colleagues, Desmond FitzGerald and John A. Costello, rejected the allegations. The inquiry did however point to the dangers of selling state mining rights to companies which were 'company-promoting and share-pushing. . . undesirable specula-tion'.[23] It sought more rigid state control over leases being used for the flota-tion of companies. Significantly, it also had reservations regarding the receipt of government contracts by Oireachtas members and recommended that in future, mining leases allocated to members should lie in public on the table of both Houses. McGilligan believed that the terms of reference of the inquiry did not correspond with the charges made. He had specifically sought an examination of Comyn and Briscoe's private financial resources and an inves-tigation into the procedures which determined how these and other mining rights were allocated.

Lemass testified before the inquiry that 'members of the Oireachtas should be treated exactly as anyone else, and that there was nothing improper in their benefiting by privileges available to all citizens'.[24] Cross-examination of R. C. Ferguson, Assistant Secretary of the Department of Industry and Commerce, by John A. Costello, member of the inquiry, supported Lemass' view:

> *Costello* – When it came to your notice that the applicants were members of the
>   Oireachtas and that they were both members of the Government Party, did
>   it strike you as in any way a matter in which you should have consulted the
>   Minister on, or that it required more consideration than in the case of an
>   ordinary member of the public. You make no differentiation between them
>   and ordinary members of the public?
> *Ferguson* – No.
> *Costello* – It did not strike you as being improper in any way?
> *Ferguson* – No.[25]

Ferguson protested that Costello's cross-examination was unfair. He stressed that 'in the ordinary course of his duty in connection with the lease, he treated a member of the Dáil the same as a member of the public'.[26] Comyn and Briscoe were elected public figures whose private business interests benefited from a ministerial decision. The very concept of conflict of interest and the

notion that those in a position of trust had competing professional or personal interests were uncharted waters. There were no formal or informal
benchmarks on how to manage such situations when they arose. Codes of
ethics, procedures of disclosure and practices of recusal or abstention were
not part of the political culture at this time. Public life did not distinguish
between private and public interest but instead warranted commitment to the
interests of the state itself.

In response to the Comyn and Briscoe incident, the Taoiseach Éamon de
Valera told the Dáil that 'corruption, of course, properly means using one's
political office, one's public office, for personal gain. It was not personal gain
the Minister (Lemass) was accused of, but partisanship and giving gain to his
friends'.[27] At this time personal interest was defined purely as a financial gain
and not as special advantage to a political associate, business colleague, friend
or family member.

McGilligan's accusations were always conspicuously on cue with pertinent
political events. The Wicklow Gold accusations emerged two days before
the County Dublin by-election and four days before the Galway by-election.
The timing of the allegations, on a Friday afternoon, gave the government no
opportunity to respond prior to the by-elections.

The *Irish Press* was understated in their assertion that the Wicklow
Gold mining lease incident 'is expected to produce an animated debate'.[28]
There was no space to discuss the niceties of political ethics and the tenor
of parliamentary discussion was antagonistic. Lemass was incredulous at
the suggestion that the Wicklow Gold inquiry should be 'considered apart
from Party rivalries and without any partisan spirit. I never heard such
nonsense in all my life'.[29] MacEntee described McGilligan as 'a woman
with a serpent's tongue'.[30] The first Fianna Fáil government was now three
years in office. The exceptionally intense, protracted and bitter Dáil debates
surrounding the corruption inquiry certainly illustrated the strength of bitterness between Lemass and McGilligan. Lemass described McGilligan's
rather longwinded technical motion on the circumstance of the allocation
of the Wicklow mining lease, as 'the most disgusting motion that has ever
appeared on the Order Paper in the House'. Exasperated, he went further
and decried:

> I do not know how to deal with Deputy McGilligan. One could deal with
> him as an impish schoolboy, sitting in a pool of mud, squirting slime at his
> more respectable companions, or possibly as an unfortunate person whose
> mind has become so warped by hatred and rancour that he is incapable of
> seeing anything except the rottenness and corruption – of seeing everything
> but decency; or probably he might be more correctly regarded as an unfortu-
> nate investigator all of whose mares' nests have turned out to be booby traps
> for himself.[31]

The *Irish Times* pulled no punches either regarding conduct in the Dáil:

> Responsible deputies comport themselves like ill mannered schoolboys, and occupants of the front benches, who ought to know better. . . how far the Free State's standards have fallen. . . to think of our country when they hear a Minister declare that an opponent 'would make a dog sick' and a Deputy describe the same Minister as 'a snarling dog'.[32]

The Wicklow Gold inquiry tested the very integrity of the new Irish state, only thirteen years old. For decades to come, Dáil references to 'Wicklow Gold' became synonymous with corruption. The first parliamentary inquiry into corruption was born. Significantly, it pioneered debate on concepts of conflict of interest and definitions of public and private.

The Great Southern Railways Tribunal 1943

As Minister for Industry and Commerce, Lemass also had responsibility for rail reform. Years of extensive under-funding in the rail network had almost caused it to collapse. In November 1943, he sought to introduce a Transport Bill which would reform the rail network. This proved to be no ordinary Bill though – the government collapsed, a snap election followed, the first corruption tribunal in the history of the State was initiated and a civil servant was compulsorily retired.

The evening before Lemass was due to present his Bill to the Dáil, John James Cole TD, Cavan Independent, alleged that Lemass was involved in dubious transactions on the stock exchange between August and November 1943: 'The Stock Exchange valuation of the total Great Southern Railway Stocks has increased by over £2,500,000 sterling since that date, as a result of inspired speculation'.[33] McGilligan attributed this speculation to improper disclosure of insider information to friends of government ministers.

Lemass and A. P. (Percy) Reynolds, Chair of Great Southern Railways (GSR), they maintained, had intentionally depreciated the stock value by giving the company false prospects. The controversy may have had been motivated by the Opposition's hostility to the Emergency Powers Act 1942 which empowered the government to appoint a chair of the GSR. Reynolds, a long time friend with Lemass having served with him in the General Post Office during the 1916 Rising, was appointed with an annual salary of £2,500.[34] Colonel George O'Callaghan Westropp, President of the GSR Shareholders Protection Association, mobilised shareholder opinion against the proposed Railways Bill of 1943, fearing that that the government was introducing a policy of nationalising private enterprise.

Lemass was determined to meet the allegations head on. The day after they were made, he sponsored a Dáil motion for a Tribunal of Inquiry. The

Tribunal was appointed on 1 December 1943 and issued its fifty-two page report ten months later on 18 September 1944. The Tribunal cost £1,295 and examined 107 witnesses. It was chaired by Mr. Justice Andrew Kingsbury Overend of the High Court and assisted by Mr. Justice Cahir Davitt and Mr. Justice Barra Ó Briain of the Circuit Court and sat at the Four Courts.

The Opposition pointed to public statements made by the Minister and the GSR chair between March and October 1943 as evidence of the allegations. Lemass and Reynolds had agreed upon a seven year restructuring plan for GSR through a private exchange of memorandums in February 1943. The two public transport companies, the practically bankrupt GSR and the traditionally prosperous and well-managed Dublin United Transport Company, would amalgamate under a new statutory transport organisation, Córas Iompair Éireann (CIÉ). Ten million pounds in capital would initially be provided with any additional capital required guaranteed by the government.

Despite this, in his annual report to shareholders in March, only a month later, and in a circular to the shareholders in October, Reynolds was downbeat and suggested that the stock was not very valuable.[35] The Tribunal found this speech was 'gloomy and had a very depressing effect on the market. Some holders proceeded to get rid of their stocks and this occasioned some activity and a sharp fall in prices'. The Tribunal also determined that Lemass' 'non-committal. . . and not regarded as encouraging' March and May 1943 speeches on GSR prospects saw prices fall to such an extent that 'the stock exchange considered suspending all dealings in the company stocks until the position became clearer'. Moreover, Lemass told the *Irish Times* that May, 'The present financial position of the company is very serious. The anticipated revenue of the company in the present year would not meet its working expenses'.[36] Lemass told the Tribunal that he made these statements based on information contained in the GSR's register which the Tribunal subsequently found to be incomplete.

The fluctuation of GSR shares was nothing new. For example, the price for guaranteed preference stocks in 1944 was lower than in 1937.[37] The fortunes of the company were volatile because of unpredictable supplies of coal and petrol due to war shortages. At any rate, the War would have made shareholders nervous about future prospects. Share appreciation occurred in part due to an increase in passenger and goods traffic and the successful reorganisation under new management. Lemass argued that as far back as 1939, a Transport Tribunal into the GSR had sought capital reorganisation and that this had been approved by the government.

McGilligan held that Lemass and Reynolds had intentionally spooked the shareholders, a tenth of whom had sold their shares. McGilligan made the case that shareholders were 'jockeyed' out of their holdings and ought to be compensated.[38] The Tribunal agreed with Opposition claims that between

August and November 1943, a 'definite inflationary boom period' in GSR shares occurred.[39] Lemass, the stock-exchange brokers and the Tribunal had very different interpretations of this 'boom'. Lemass alleged that the fluctuations were 'infinitesimal' and 'insignificant'.[40] The brokers testified that Lemass' response bore little or no relation to the actualities of the situation and were 'completely illusory' and instead described the boom as 'absolutely abnormal', 'absolutely hectic' and 'inexplicable'.[41] The Tribunal agreed that an 'abnormal amount of dealing' had occurred but believed that the extent and nature of this was exaggerated.

The GSR Tribunal was in session when the Transport Bill was presented for a second time to the Dáil on 9 May 1944. The Opposition stirred up popular emotion claiming that the Bill was favourable towards speculators. For many, the concept of shares and stock markets was alien and fears were easily fanned. The memory of the 1929 Wall Street crash was still very much alive. Almost a dozen years out of government, Fine Gael was happy at the opportunity to harvest political advantage from the government's discomfort. The Tribunal was a David and Goliath opportunity and Fine Gael portrayed themselves as firmly in the corner of the small investor.

The government were unsuccessful in its attempts to distinguish the Transport Bill from the ongoing Tribunal process. An Opposition Dáil motion to defer the Bill until the publication of the GSR Tribunal report was passed by only one vote. Ironically, it was not only the Transport Bill that undid the government but a train as well. Cole voted with the Opposition and became known as the 'sixty-fourth vote'. The Beltubert man arrived in Leinster House only twenty minutes before the division bells rang, having rushed to the Dáil as soon as his Cavan train reached Dublin.

The government, only one year in office, lost the vote and in response, the Taoiseach asked the President's permission to dissolve the Dáil and subsequently announced a snap election for June 1944. This was the first time that Article 28 of the 1937 Constitution was invoked. The Taoiseach believed that if the 'working of public business and trying to get the nations work done, were not to be accepted, it meant that they had responsibility without power'.[42] During the eighteen day election campaign, Lemass claimed victory from the jaws of defeat and insisted that the downfall of the Bill 'was no accident, it was carefully planned'.[43] His rationale was that the government had to be cruel to be kind. In dismissing the minority government they would thus create a majority government, as had happened in the 1933 and 1938 elections. This actually turned out to be the case. Lemass, also Minister for Supplies (1939–45), rationed sixteen gallons of petrol for each candidate. Ireland and Sweden were the only European states to hold wartime elections.[44] The front page of the *Irish Press* announcing the election was shared with the headline 'Sebastopol is captured by Russian Army: Allied offensive in

West'.[45] The Tribunal overshadowed campaigning and the Taoiseach, Éamon de Valera, attacked McGilligan for making 'very great use during the election' of the allegations.

The Tribunal concluded that although the summer of 1943 was dominated by 'rumours and "tips" alleged to emanate from persons in procession of inside information concerning the details of the plans for re-organisation of the Company were exceedingly prevalent. . . none of the rumours. . . contained a single accurate reference to the confidential and secret matters'.[46] McGilligan's allegations were not however entirely baseless. The concluding paragraph of the report stated that there was 'no improper disclosure of such information except in one case. . . which we consider unimportant and to which no dealings can be attributed'.

Reynolds acknowledged to the Tribunal that he had personally contacted and given advance information about government plans to heavily invest and nationalise the railways to Dr. John Charles McQuaid, Archbishop of Dublin, the Representative Body of the Church of Ireland and the Bank of Ireland (BOI).[47] He justified this exchange of information on the basis that these three trustees held large qualities of railways shares and that it would be 'discourteous to allow them to have the first intimation of the reorganisation proposals through the Press'. The Tribunal were of the opinion that Reynolds' 'judgement was at fault' and tactfully reprimanded his actions: 'We find it difficult to conceive that any of these trustees would not strongly deprecate the receipt of such advance information. . . We are of the opinion that all stockholders, large and small. . . should have received precisely equal treatment with rigid imparity'. That was as far as the Tribunal were prepared to go: 'It is hardly necessary to say that the evidence showed no dealing which could be possibly attributed to this disclosure'.[48]

An examination of the Archdiocese of Dublin's accounts, suggests that McQuaid invested more heavily in GSR railway shares around the time Reynolds gave him the advance information. McQuaid managed a large portfolio of investments on behalf of the Archdiocese, much of which was dominated by railway interests since before the War. The 1941–45 Archdiocese account book show regular dividends from Dublin Corporation, War Stocks, Bank of Ireland, the National Loan, Land Bonds and Canadian and Argentinean railways. Substantial investments were also held in Irish railway companies, including Dublin United Transport, Great Western Railways, Great Northern Railways and the Great Southern Railways. McQuaid was an astute investor and obtained advice from (Hubert) Briscoe and (Desmond) Butler government stock brokers.

In 1941 and 1942, the Dublin Archdiocese held £2,562 in ordinary and preferential shares in GSR yielding a total return of £136 15s 0d for the two years. The Archdiocese of Dublin had a good war. It substantially increased its GSR shareholding in early 1943 to £19,472. On behalf of its seven trustees, this investment yielded a dividend of £243 8s 0d in January and a total of £731 4s 0d in 1943. The end of year dividends for the Dublin Archdiocese increased from £13,939 in 1942 to £22,891 in 1945, a not insignificant sum in the context of a war.[49]

Although Reynolds gave the Tribunal access to his financial accounts for examination, it is not clear if the Tribunal scrutinised the accounts of McQuaid and the other two entities or if it just assumed that men of such stature were above reproach. William Davin TD, Labour, never did get an answer to his parliamentary question regarding what 'percentage of ordinary, preference and guaranteed preference shares were held by these three representatives?'.[50] What is clear, is that McQuaid did increase the Archdiocese's shareholding in GSR in 1943, the period under Tribunal investigation.

This was also the case regarding William Claude Odlum, Chair of BOI. Odlum confirmed to the Tribunal that he and his brother bought £1,132 in shares in July 1943 which were worth £2,050 in 1944. J. P. Goodbody, a GSR director who had purchased £500 in shares, was censured for 'improper use of such information'.[51] A high ranking civil servant in the Transport and Marine branch of Lemass' Department of Industry and Commerce was compulsorily retired. John O'Brien, a principal officer, had bought shares in GSR. The Tribunal report noted many 'coincidences', including the fact that the same O'Brien, the brokerage firm and large purchasers of shares 'were all members of Milltown golf club'.[52] Lemass told the Dáil: 'I do not believe that he [O'Brien] took the action he did with any intention of doing anything wrong. But the action he did take led to the possibility of a leakage of information'.[53] Several other civil servants and employees of GSR who bought shares were also interviewed by the Tribunal but were not censured.

Lemass took the allegations of corruption very seriously and swiftly responded. He established a Tribunal immediately and those found guilty were censured or punished. The extent of insider share dealing was not established nor was the identity of all those involved. Without this information it is difficult to assess how lenient the punishment of censure was, though media coverage was favourable to the Tribunal findings. The *Irish Times* noted:

> It would be impossible to exaggerate the importance to the Irish state of popular confidence in the unblemished integrity of the nation's public life. Ministers, public servants, and officials of all kinds must be without fear and without reproach; and we are happy to say that, after more than twenty years of native Government, public standards in this country remain remarkably bright.[54]

Nonetheless, Lemass was angry at newspaper reporting on the Tribunal and expressed his 'contempt of the tactics of the *Irish Times* in the manner in which it presented the report to the public. Nobody reading the headlines in that paper, or the sub leader or sub-editors observations on it, could possibly understand the significance of the Tribunal's decision.'[55] The *Irish Times* were at a complete loss. 'On the morning of the [Tribunal] Report's publication, our "sub-leader" was entitled "Dear Fruit"; on Thursday it dealt with the subject of the harmless, necessary bee.' The paper queried if it had something to do with the Shakespearean quote 'Where the bee suck, there suck I.' In all, it was an odd end to an extraordinary episode. Lemass and McGilligan's bitter and personal duel, first evident by the Wicklow Gold affair, was unrelenting.

> *McGilligan* – I wonder why the Minister is so bad-tempered at the word 'speculators'.
> *Lemass* – I am so bad-tempered because of the disgusting manners displayed by the Opposition.
> *McGilligan* – There are disgusting matters which we want to have disclosed.[56]

Lemass' tetchiness throughout this period can be attributed to the politicisation of the corruption allegations which he became the focus of. He especially found the rumours of his alleged transgressions hurtful.[57] He 'took a strict view of personal integrity' and family and close civil servants commented on 'his insistent propriety in refusing gifts and favours. . . in fact neither then nor later was there anything in his lifestyle or possessions to give any credible support to the round of rumours and innuendos'.[58] Biographies of Lemass have justifiably focused on his transitional, progressive leadership between the first generation of politicians to the professional era of politics. Research on Lemass has tended to focus on his accomplishments as Tánaiste and Taoiseach when his contribution to public life was the most obvious and not on the episodes referred to in this chapter.

The Transport Act 1944 merged the GSR and the Dublin United Transport Company to form CIÉ as a private company. A. P. Reynolds, GSR chair, was appointed chair of the first CIÉ board. Lemass' brother, Frank Lemass, was appointed as CIÉ's first Assistant General Manager in 1945 and served as CIÉ General Manager from 1947 to 1970. Lemass' sister-in-law, Moll Lemass, noted the difficulties Frank's transfer from the Dublin United Tramway Company to CIÉ caused, 'when Frank moved to CIÉ, a special job title had to be created for him to avoid any semblance of a potential conflict of interest with his older brother'.[59]

The Ward Tribunal 1946

Dr. Francis Constantine (Con) Ward (1891–1966), represented Fianna Fáil in the Monaghan constituency from 1927 to 1948 and was Parliamentary Secretary to the Minister for Local Government and Public Health from 1932 to 1946. The Taoiseach announced in 1946 that a new Department for Health would be created and it was widely anticipated that Ward would become Ireland's first Minister for Health. Ward was not well liked among the Irish medical profession and was regarded as antagonistic though reform minded. A 1945 departmental report sought to introduce major proposals for 'sweeping administrative reorganisation and phased introduction of a free comprehensive service, funded largely from general taxation, employing the bulk of general practitioners as state district medical officers, with private medicine a peripheral activity'.[60] Ward's legislative ambition, articulated through his 1945 Health Bill, did not curry him any favour with the medical profession and his proposals were essentially a 'legislative time bomb'.[61]

In the late 1930s, Lemass' Department of Industry and Commerce allocated Ward and two associates a licence and several loans to establish a pig factory known as the Monaghan Curing Company.[62] In advance of his anticipated promotion as Minister for Health, Ward was compelled to resign his managing directorship of the pig factory. This would have left him with a serious financial shortfall. Dr. Patrick MacCarvill wrote to the Taoiseach in May 1946 outlining his personal concerns about Ward's pending appointment.[63] MacCarvill, a former Sinn Féin and Fianna Fáil TD for Monaghan from 1922 to 1927, was a constituency rival of Ward. When MacCarvill did not contest the 1927 election, Ward was elected as the Monaghan TD for Fianna Fáil.

MacCarvill was also a former leader of the Irish Medical Organisation (IMO), an organisation vehemently opposed to Ward's health reforms. MacCarvill alleged that Ward had dismissed his brother, John, as manager of the pig factory and installed Ward's son instead. 'My brother Johnny' therein became a derisive phrase in political folklore. MacCarvill asserted that the factory had cheated the taxman and that Ward had pocketed £12,000 from the factory's accounts. Moreover, he contended that Ward was still receiving a salary as a Monaghan Dispensary District medical officer even though a temporary medical officer was doing his work. He also alleged that Ward had taken several hundred pounds from the Monaghan Public Utility Building Society to erect a Fianna Fáil hall on land rented by Ward.[64] MacCarvill gave the Taoiseach a copy of the company accounts, balance sheets and correspondence as evidence. A brother of the previous owner of the pig factory had also written to the Taoiseach a month earlier. Ward was blamed for steamrolling the original owners from the factory by threatening 'transportation and gaol' and 'done his Hitler act of bullying everybody to get out'.[65]

In essence, this amounted to a personal dispute between two prominent members of the medical profession and members of Monaghan Fianna Fáil whose families had connecting business interests. MacCarvill's letters caught everyone, particularly the Taoiseach, by surprise. De Valera told the Dáil that he was in an 'impossible position'. Without any pre-warning, he read MacCarvill's rather lengthy letters into the Dáil record. This was an unusual course of action for a Taoiseach to take. His motivation to do so may have been due to the controversial circumstances regarding the evidence given by Robert Briscoe TD, Fianna Fáil, in a Special Criminal Court case some weeks earlier.[66] Ward's political opponents were unsure of how to react. Echoing the sentiments of Lemass' testimony to the 1935 Wicklow Gold inquiry, James Dillon TD, Independent Fine Gael and future leader of Fine Gael and also from Ward's Monaghan constituency, accepted the distinction between public and private activities of a politician:

> What has Dáil Éireann got to do with the private activities of Dr. Ward or the management of his business?... Dr. Ward stands at the head of a splendid family. Whatever expedition may be required in business, the rights of that family are far more important, far superior and far more enduring; and the honour and integrity of the head of that family has been put in issue.[67]

De Valera was perhaps anxious to address MacCarvill's allegations immediately and not allow them to fester, as was the case with Briscoe. He manoeuvred the Dáil into accepting his proposal for a tribunal because he made the charges public. The Taoiseach was happy to delegate the matter to the judiciary: 'I do not think anybody here or in the country is likely to suggest that these three judges, who are independent of us, are going to make any report other than in accordance with the facts as they find them, that there will be a genuine and fair investigation that will be fair to Dr. Ward and to the public and to everybody concerned.'[68] Ward then also insisted on a tribunal because he believed it would be quicker than a potentially lengthy court procedure.[69] Senator William Quirke, Fianna Fáil, proposed a motion in the Seanad for a tribunal.[70] Oliver J. Flanagan TD, Independent Monetary Reform party and later Fine Gael, responded by instantaneously moving the writ for the Cork city by-election.

The Tribunal was chaired by Mr. Justice John O'Byrne, Supreme Court and assisted by Mr. Justice Kevin Haugh, High Court and Mr. Justice J. Shannon, Circuit Court. O'Byrne and Haugh would later serve in the 1947 Locke Tribunal of inquiry. The Tribunal opened on 25 June 1946 and sat for just nine days. Ward was exonerated of the grosser charges against him. The Tribunal did make the finding that income tax evasion had occurred and that there were undisclosed sales.[71] Ward resigned immediately and was the first politician in the history of the state to do so for alleged personal impropriety. He did so on the grounds that the issues raised 'might embarrass the Government were I to continue to discharge official duties'.[72] Dr. Jim Ryan instead became Ireland's first Minister for Health. He served for just one year and was succeeded by Dr. Noel Browne in the 1948 Inter-Party government. Ward later made restitution to the Revenue Commissioners.[73]

The Tribunal attracted unprecedented media attention and transfixed the public imagination. McGilligan alleged that the Department of Agriculture were complicit in the supply of inferior and tainted bacon to the army because Ward's pig factory had no other means of 'getting rid of it'. McGilligan repeated previous concerns about the criteria of the Department of Industry and Commerce in allocating licences. McGilligan pointed to the 'public wonderment that has been caused by learning this, that a man [Ward] who never was in the curing business at all, a man who was trained as a professional man and a doctor, could become a bacon curer, that he could get a loan of £8,000 from the Government and repay it in record time'.[74] The Taoiseach adopted a hands-off approach. On receipt of the Tribunal findings he simply read the *Tribunal of Inquiry Report into the charges made against Dr. Conn Ward by Dr. Patrick MacCarvill* into the Dáil record shortly before the Dáil's summer recess. He did not defend Ward nor make any comment on the Tribunal findings.

Prompted by Ward's resignation, the Briscoe incident and recent convictions for Seanad bribery, the Taoiseach sought to legislate for political standards in the context of a Privileges Act.[75] A resolution for a Joint Oireachtas Committee passed the Dáil and Seanad in 1947 which was to consider advice and report on: (1) the powers and privileges of the Oireachtas (2) the limitations and obligations on members concerning their external activities and conduct, and (3) the procedures, method for investigation and penalties in connection with alleged breaches of members' conduct or privilege.[76]

Support for his initiative was not forthcoming. Major Vivion de Valera TD, the Taoiseach's son, said 'it is very difficult to say where one is to draw the line between representations which are tinged, shall I say, by a personal interest and representations which are not'.[77] Flanagan was robustly defensive of such practice. 'I am one Deputy in this House who would strenuously resent and strongly oppose any action which might be taken by the Government to restrict the rights of Deputies as far as representations to Departments are concerned.'[78] The consensus emerged that the existing criminal legislation, the principles of the Ten Commandments and 'the ordinary principles of decency and good conduct' were enough.[79] General Richard (Dick) Mulcahy TD, Fine Gael, stated that 'you cannot legislate to make people more moral or more honest'.[80]

De Valera agreed and conceded that 'ultimately, of course, the conduct of members will be determined by their own sense of what is fit and right and proper'.[81] He did not secure cross-party support for the committee and these early attempts to legislate for political conduct failed. The Opposition was mistrustful of his motives as the government had a majority on the committee which was to present a majority report. Alfie Byrne TD, Independent, summed up the public weariness with corruption allegations: 'Instead of coming in here and talking seriously about the. . . blizzard, scarcity of fuel, scarcity of potatoes, scarcity of food. . . The House assembles here to-day and proceeds calmly to discuss a motion that nobody outside ourselves cares two straws about. The people can go hungry and naked and cold.'[82]

The Locke Tribunal 1947

Oliver J. Flanagan made a series of allegations in the Dáil in October 1947 regarding the sale of Locke's Whiskey Distillery at Kilbeggan in Co. Westmeath.[83] Founded in 1757, and believed to be the oldest distillery in the world, the distillery was being sold as a going concern by sisters, Mrs. Hope-Johnston and Mrs. Eccles. The distillery management had unsuccessfully attempted to buy it and were unhappy with the prospect of the sale. The secretary of the distillery, Joseph Cooney senior, wrote to Flanagan with his concerns in October 1947. Cooney's correspondence formed the basis for Flanagan's accusations:

> Negotiations are still proceeding for the sale. . . The bait for the Vendors is that they would carry on the Industry and extend it; and for the Government that they would pay in dollars or Swiss Francs [*sic*]. In pursuit of this deal they are assisted by Senator Quirke. . . all are actively engaged in trying to bring off the deal and to get concessions from the Government to allow the removal of whiskey from the country. Minister Lemass' Department – if not actually himself – is already committed to some sort of undertaking of this nature.[84]

A 'notoriously great shortage of whiskey in England'[85] following World War Two made Locke's whiskey stocks exceptionally valuable. Indeed the phrase 'locked' in terms of over consumption of alcohol may originate from this period. A foreign syndicate, *Trans-World Trust of Lausanne,* agreed to buy the distillery in mid-1947. Flanagan alleged that in the course of this sale, the syndicate procured dollars from the Department of Industry and Commerce though the sale of tweed; that the Taoiseach's son, Éamon de Valera, an eminent surgeon, improperly accepted a Swiss gold watch from a member of the syndicate; that the government were complicit with the syndicate in selling black market whiskey in England and that the Department of Justice was lax in allowing members of the syndicate remain in Ireland.

In essence, Flanagan accused Éamon de Valera, his son also Éamon, Seán Lemass and Gerry Boland, Minister for Justice, of political favouritism and abuse of position. De Valera appointed a tribunal of inquiry almost immediately in November 1947.[86] The judges selected to chair the inquiry, which sat at the Four Courts, were well-versed in tribunal procedure. Mr. Justice John O'Byrne of the Supreme Court presided and had previously sat at the 1946 Ward Tribunal together with Mr. Justice Kevin Haugh of the High Court. Mr. Justice Cahir Davitt was a veteran of the 1943 GSR Tribunal.

The inquiry sat for only eighteen days and heard the evidence of forty-nine witnesses.

In order to appreciate why the Tribunal spiralled into a life of its own, it is necessary to understand the versatile character of Flanagan (1920–87). The twenty-seven-year-old Mountmellick apprentice carpenter was the son of a stonemason who built bridges for GSR and represented Laois-Offaly from 1943 to 1987. A strong vote getter and acute constituency operator, Flanagan's political outlook was defined by traditional parish pump parochialism. Folklore persists about his canvassing methods. The sign on the front of his bicycle read: 'Here Comes Oliver J' with a matching: 'There Goes Flanagan' on the back. The contemporary popular folk musician, Christy Moore, would later sing of, 'Oliver J. Flanagan goes swimming in the Holy Sea' in *Lisdoonvarna*. The Tribunal became enormously personalised, due in no small part to Flanagan's capricious personality. It was also a politicised venture due to the nature of legal representation at the Tribunal of the various witnesses.

Senator Gerard Sweetman, Fine Gael, was Flanagan's legal representation before the Tribunal. Thomas F. O'Higgins and his brother Michael O'Higgins, sons of Dr. Thomas F. O'Higgins TD, Fine Gael, who testified in support of Flanagan before the Tribunal, also legally represented Flanagan. Thomas F. and Michael O'Higgins were both elected as Fine Gael TDs in the 1948 election. Thomas shared the same constituency as Flanagan, as his father. In all, six former, sitting and future Fine Gael TDs were legal representatives at the Tribunal. These included John A. Costello, acting for Joseph Cooney senior, Patrick McGilligan, for Joseph Cooney junior and Cecil Lavery, former Fine Gael TD, and later Attorney General and Supreme Court Judge, for Senator William Quirke.

The syndicate engaged the services of Senator Quirke's auctioneering firm, Stokes and Quirke, based at 33 Kildare Street, to negotiate the sale of the distillery. The Department of Industry and Commerce was five doors down at 23 Kildare Street. Quirke (1896–1955), a Tipperary born farmer, was a prominent member of Fianna Fáil and was a family friend of President Seán T O'Kelly. He was leader of the Seanad from 1938 to 1948, and again from 1951 to 1954.

Before the final sale was agreed, Quirke and Cooney (distillery secretary) met with civil servants from the Department of Industry and Commerce to request an increase in the distillery's export quota. The quota was doubled the next day from 4,000 to 8,000 gallons of whiskey. Quirke testified to the Tribunal that:

> Government policy was to accept whatever could be exported to hard-currency countries and I think the Department would be very pleased to do whatever

they could do, within reason. . . He [Department of Industry and Commerce civil servant] then said 'in what way do you want the blessing of the Department or the goodwill of the Department' and I said 'Well, a good way to express the goodwill of the Department would be to increase the Export quota. . .' I told [the syndicate] 'you will be amazed to hear the quota is doubled and whatever the place was worth yesterday when they bought it, it is worth more today'.[87]

Payment by foreign currency in such a large amount in an economic depression made the sale very valuable. 'Sterling had ceased to be freely convertible into American dollars. The advisability of developing export trade to hard currency countries thereupon became a matter of added importance. . . that it was intended to develop an export trade in whiskey with Switzerland: that such exports would be paid for in Swiss francs: and the purchase price of the distillery, £305,000, would be brought to this country in America dollars.'[88]

Quirke told the Tribunal that it was not unusual for him to meet with the department's civil servants: 'The normal thing for me to do (which I probably did that day) was to ring up the Minister's Private Secretary and ask him "who is dealing with distilleries, whiskey and that kind of thing."'[89] In his evidence to the Tribunal, Dr. Thomas F. O'Higgins, Fine Gael TD noted that his experience was in stark contrast:

My Lord, I have twelve years' experience of trying to get facilities, permits, and concessions of one kind or another for various types of people. . . It took me, my lord; I think two months to get a permit to export a woollen dressing gown. . . I certainly was struck with the extraordinary speed with which this permit was given. . . it is my opinion that no other firm of Auctioneers in Ireland would have got the same facilities with the same speed.[90]

Flanagan believed that the quota was increased improperly because of Quirke's political affiliation. The Tribunal rejected Flanagan's conflict of interest charge. The Tribunal determined:

as a matter of Ministerial policy that, upon application, the quota might be increased on the basis of the presentations which had been made to the officers of the Department by Senator Quirke and Mr. Cooney. The circumstances that a Departmental conference, at which such a decision would be given took place on the afternoon of the same day on which Senator Quirke and Mr. Cooney visited the Department was obviously quite accidental.[91]

It was fortuitous for Quirke and Cooney that they were the only people aware of this ministerial policy. They were the only applicants that applied for what was a remarkably large increase on an exceptionally valuable quota. The quota was only increased when a request was made to change it. The syndicate had agreed to pay Quirke a 2 per cent commission, or £6,000, on the sale. Quirke told the Tribunal that subsequent to the quota increase he increased the bid on the distillery from £250,000 to £300,500.

The syndicate asked Quirke to be one of the three Irish directors, along with Tom Morris and Joseph Cooney senior, with a 51 per cent controlling stake in the distillery.[92] The Deputy Secretary of the Department of Industry and Commerce informed the solicitor for Locke's Distillery that 'the Minister wished to make it clear that he would deprecate the sale to undesirable purchasers – any company or persons outside the state'.[93] Lemass testified to the Tribunal that his fears that the distillery would be acquired by foreign 'undesirable people were dispelled' when 'men of standing in the community', such as Quirke, were 'connected with its purchase'.[94] The sale of Irish whiskey abroad was a means of attaining access to foreign currency and the government did not wish to concede Irish control. Quirke's role in the sale of the distillery was now promoted from that as an auctioneer to a controlling stake in the company. Quirke later denied this was the case.[95]

Quirke was not aware that the syndicate planned to sell 60,000 gallons of whiskey from the distillery on the English black market for £11 a gallon. The syndicate would thus earn £660,000 after purchasing the distillery for £305,000, a considerable sum in the context of a post-war depression. Quirke was adamant that when the syndicate failed to pay the deposit for the distillery he became suspicious of the syndicate, and immediately relayed his concerns to the Minister for Justice, Gerry Boland and the Guards.[96] James Dillon TD, Independent and future leader of Fine Gael, said in the Dáil that Quirke had only done so when he felt that Hubert Kurt Saschsell, a key member of the syndicate, was going to cut in on his commission.[97] The historian Maurice Manning believes that Dillon was not 'convinced that the full truth had been brought to light'.[98]

Of the ten allegations examined, the Tribunal rejected nine, including that against Quirke. The only allegation established was against Seamus Sweeney, the syndicate's solicitor who was married to the niece of President Seán T. O'Kelly. Sweeney was found to have improperly introduced the syndicate to the President at a reception at the President's residence thereby giving them 'a fictitious standing and social importance'.[99]

Two specific issues hampered the Tribunal's investigation. Those who made the allegations failed to substantiate them. Cooney, the original source of the allegations and whistleblower to Flanagan, backtracked on his earlier statements. He later said that the controversy was a 'storm in a tea cup. . . I cannot see where any member of the Government is to blame. Cannot be advanced by any rational being that they were guilty of the things that happened. Rumours are wafted on every breeze, but when they come down to concrete facts, it is quite another matter'.[100] Moreover, the Tribunal had difficulty in determining how to define a personal interest. This was particularly evident from their protracted cross-examination of Flanagan.[101] The

Taoiseach had a similar difficulty and neglected the basis of the charge against Quirke, where his private life influenced his very actions as a public representative. The Taoiseach told the Dáil:

> Senator Quirke happens to be also a businessman. Is it to be suggested that he should not, because he is a member of the Seanad, engage in any business? Are we to have wholetime politicians, only, in this Parliament?... Businessmen, then, who are members of this House or of the other House, in so far as their private actions are concerned, are subject only to the ordinary law, and also subject, of course, to popular judgment on their conduct.[102]

The Tribunal raised more questions than it answered. It failed to hear evidence from key members of the syndicate including Ms. Dunnico, the Austrian Hubert Kurt Saschsell, the Swiss businessman Georges Einidiguer and his British interpreter, Alexander Maximoe, acting under the alias of Horace Henry Smith. Maximoe was later presumed drowned on the mail boat to Holyhead, which was in fact an elaborate escape from Garda custody. The Tribunal found that the application by Flanagan's counsel to hear their evidence outside the country was 'frivolously made'.[103] A complaint was made to the Bar Counsel which stated that Flanagan's counsel had 'acted with professional propriety in making their application for a Commission'.[104] Though in hindsight this appears to have been an extraordinary decision which ensured that one part of the story was not to be told.[105]

The Tribunal was very definite in its conclusion regarding Flanagan: 'We found it necessary to exercise extreme caution in dealing with the evidence of Deputy Flanagan. We found him very uncandid and much disposed to answer questions unthinkingly and as if he were directing his replies elsewhere than to the Tribunal.'[106] The Tribunal described one of his accusations as 'a degree of recklessness amounting to complete irresponsibility'. This was unfair to the Laois-Offaly TD.[107]

The Locke Tribunal became an examination of Flanagan's credibility. In the context of crippling weather conditions and the severe fuel and food scarcities of that year, Flanagan's lengthy stint in the witness box dominated newspaper headlines from mid-November. Much of his cross-examination centred on whether he took notes or used his mental memory, why he had crossed out words in his notebook and not underlined them, the specific times he meet with specific individuals, how long he met with them and who they had met before him.

> *Conolly* (Counsel for Sweeney) – Didn't you, on October 22, call Mr. Sweeney a chancer? (Syndicate's solicitor and married to the niece of President Seán T. O'Kelly)
>
> *Flanagan* – I did, meaning, according to the Oxford Dictionary, a risky man, one that chances his arm, an adventurer.

Conolly – Does it necessarily involve some insinuation of dishonesty or sharp practice?

Flanagan – I am going on the greatest authority possible, and that is the Oxford Large Dictionary.

Mr. Justice Haugh – Did you look at the Oxford Dictionary before making that remark?

Flanagan – No, I did not; but I always refer to it when I come to big words.

Mr. Justice Davitt – You didn't find 'chancer' in the Oxford Dictionary?

Flanagan – I did, and I have it here.

Conolly – Did you consult the dictionary before referring to Mr. Sweeney?

Flanagan – Not in referring to Mr. Sweeney: but I have called other people 'chancers.' I consulted the dictionary about the term 'chancer' five years ago, and I don't usually forget things. . .

Conolly – You again insulted him openly in the Dáil by calling him a racketeer?

Flanagan – Yes.

Conolly – That is an offensive term necessarily involving dishonesty?

Flanagan – I do not know what it involves.

Connolly – Did you consult the Oxford Dictionary before you used the term?

Flanagan – No because I put the whole group down as racketeers, including Mr. Sweeney.[108]

The undertone that emerged was that allegations of corruption were in themselves anti-Irish. The Roscrea Fianna Fáil branch passed a resolution calling on the government to enact legislation to remove the TDs responsible for the Locke inquiry from the Dáil.[109] In a thinly veiled attack on Flanagan, de Valera quoted from the seventeenth-century text of the Irish historian, Geoffrey Keating, and said that the allegations reminded him of:

> the primpealláin, a beetle, which from the moment in the summer time when it began to use its wings and fly about, went about, not attracted by any flower in the field or any flower in the garden, no matter how beautiful they were, whether they were roses or lilies. The primpealláin went about looking for some cow dung or horse dung in which they might roll themselves.[110]

Flanagan made his Locke allegations a week before the Tipperary, Waterford and Dublin County October 1947 by-elections. A Department of Taoiseach memo noted the 'significant and interesting fact that these allegations of corruption against the Government are timed, to a remarkable extent, to coincide with pending by-elections'.[111] Clann na Poblachta's breakthrough occurred with the election of Seán MacBride, the party's leader, in the Dublin County by-election where he narrowly defeated the Fianna Fáil general secretary, Tommy Mullins. De Valera's official biographer, Lord Longford, made no reference to the three Tribunals and suggested that the by-election victories were due to the severe October 1947 'unpopular supplementary budget'.[112]

The perception of corruption, however, was certainly a dominant theme in

Irish public life in the mid 1940s. Clann na Poblachta was established in July 1946 in Barry's Hotel Dublin, just weeks after Briscoe's evidence in a controversial Special Criminal court case and the publication of the Ward Tribunal report. MacBride spoke impassionedly on alleged impropriety in public life at Clann na Poblachta by-election rallies in October 1947. In his maiden speech to the Dáil, he called for a 'new political morality'[113] and said that the government 'could have inquiries week after week, but they would not deal with the suspicion that existed in the public mind so long as they allowed the granting or withholding of licences to be made behind closed doors, either by Ministers or their appointees'.[114] Noel Browne, Clann na Poblachta Minister, later held that an anti-corruption campaign had been a 'major plank' in the party's platform.[115]

Liam Cosgrave, Government Chief Whip, Fine Gael Parliamentary Secretary to the Taoiseach and to the Minister for Industry and Commerce in the 1948–51 inter-party government, believed that the knock-on effect of Fianna Fáil losing two and narrowly winning one of these by-elections proved that de Valera was not electorally invincible.[116] These losses prompted the Taoiseach to announce in November 1947, before the Locke Tribunal was established, that 'the Dáil is to be dissolved as soon as practicable and a general election held early next year'.[117] The timing of these events and the rise of the party were not coincidental. Clann na Poblachta won a respectable 13.2 per cent in their inaugural election of 1948, the highest percentage attained by a new political party at its first electoral test.

The Tribunal report was published three days before Christmas, the same week de Valera called the general election. Flanagan promptly telegrammed the Taoiseach: 'People not surprised at report of Locke Tribunal inquiry. Proud of manner in which I discharged my public duty and would gladly do likewise again. Right will win over might eventually. People are best judges.'[118] Fianna Fáil lost office in February 1948, for the first time in sixteen years and less than two months after publication of the Locke Tribunal report. Economic factors certainly contributed to the government's defeat, particularly prolonged war rationing, the bad winter and bitter industrial disputes. Lemass, outgoing Tánaiste, believed that the government was defeated because its association 'with all the restrictions and hardships, the wage limitations imposed by the war – everything that was unpleasant during the war was associated with Fianna Fáil. . . The defeat of the British government which had won the war was an indication of the mood of the time'.[119]

Yet historians have underestimated the significance of the Tribunal and how it took on a life of its own and gave unprecedented oxygen to anti-Fianna Fáil sentiment in the run up to the election. Flanagan became a mini-celebrity. On receipt of the findings of the Locke Tribunal, the headline of the de Valera controlled *Irish Press* stated: 'Locke Inquiry Finds Charges 'False and Reckless' Deputy Flanagan's Evidence "Untrue"'. The front page of the *Irish Press* was dominated by large profile pictures of the 'TDs who figured in the Inquiry'. Though, no doubt, Mulcahy, Dillon, O'Higgins, McGilligan and Flanagan would have been more than happy with such publicity in the weeks leading up to the pending election. This was particularly the case in a paper that traditionally gave prominent coverage to Fianna Fáil branch meetings at the expense of Opposition Dáil statements. For the first time in months, the main headline of the *Irish Press* related to something other than post-war issues. The Locke Tribunal was a release valve from the mundane seriousness of international affairs, an indication of which was the *Irish Press*'s subheading the day of the publication of the report: 'Truman asks Marshall Aid to Save Peace'.[120]

Whether deserved or earned, an undercurrent of scepticism, suspicion and distrust towards Fianna Fáil gathered momentum. The various corruption incidents positively swung the balance in the Opposition's favour and this swing was amplified through the mechanisms of the single transferable vote.[121] Flanagan successfully portrayed himself in his rural constituency as a casualty of Dublin based justice and his first preferences increased by an incredible 5,000 votes. Flanagan telegrammed the Taoiseach: 'Laois/Offaly's answer to Locke Tribunal leaves no doubt as to belief in existence of corruption. Eagerly awaiting assembly Dáil Éireann to reopen this and other similar public scandals.'[122] A view de Valera disagreed with.

> *de Valera* – Is the Minister going to suggest that the question at the election was the question of the Locke Tribunal?
> *McGilligan* – Yes. I say this: that if Deputy Flanagan had been believed by the people of Leix-Offaly to be the sort of perjurer he was made out to be in the Report he could not have got elected.[123]

McGilligan's first accusations against Lemass were in the context of the 1935 Wicklow Gold inquiry. Now, some twelve years later, McGilligan finally had the opportunity to cross-examine his greatest political adversary in the witness box. The *Irishman's Diary* noted that it gave 'McGilligan the chance of a lifetime.'[124] McGilligan's cross-examination of Lemass was perhaps recognition by the both men of the failure of an isolationist economic policy. The seeds of Lemass' New Departure economic policy of the 1950s, which opened up the Irish economy, were perhaps sown from his Tribunal experience in the 1940s.

> *McGilligan* – Under Emergency Powers, you will recognise that you are allowed considerable interference with private property. . . you are given power to interfere with distilleries export quotas. Is that not considerable interference?
> *Lemass* – I am given power to regulate exports, and I am responsible to the Dáil. I cannot take an arbitrary decision.[125]

Although it only sat for a mere eighteen days, the Locke Tribunal entered political mythology. Flanagan was constantly jibbed by political opponents as a 'perjurer'. Some years later, in January 1952, Flanagan's response in the Dáil to such heckling resulted in the notorious Dáil Restaurant incident.[126] Flanagan was in conversation with James Dillon TD 'when a member of the Fianna Fáil Party, Deputy (Stephen) Flynn, came behind him, caught hold of him, turned him round, used a very offensive and obnoxious expression and struck him violently in the mouth.'[127] Flynn took exception to the 'gross personal nature by innuendo' remarks Flanagan had made about him in the context of the Adoption of Children Bill.[128] Flynn believed that 'there was no adequate remedy, under existing Standing Orders, available to him.'[129] Following a complaint by John A. Costello TD, a Committee on Procedure and Privileges was established to investigate the matter and subsequent to their report, the Ceann Comhairle publicly reprimanded Flynn.[130]

Conclusion

Oireachtas debates in the 1940s demonstrate an uncertainty about recourse to the tribunal method of inquiry. Senator Professor Michael Hayes, Fine Gael, former Ceann Comhairle of the Dáil from 1922 to 1932, was apprehensive about the ability of judiciary to conduct a tribunal: 'Judges as an investigating Tribunal. The whole notion of asking a judge to investigate a charge by himself is like asking a doctor to make a suit of clothes, as it is something completely outside his ordinary functions.'[131] De Valera did not regard tribunals 'as satisfactory, but if we examine the alternatives we will find that they would not be satisfactory either. . . At the present time our hands are manacled'.[132] With everything considered, the Taoiseach believed that a tribunal was the most time efficient way of carrying out an inquiry: 'When the ribunal will have made its report, the position will be fairly clear. The report might be of such a kind as to relieve us of any responsibility, from the executive side, of pursuing any particular matter.' Senator Thomas Foran, Independent, was adamant that the tribunal's job was very simple:

> It does not require a lot of eloquent and very able lawyers; the charges are set out there definitely. The prosecutor will have to produce his evidence to prove them. That is a simple job and he knows all about it. The defendant will have his opportunity of refuting the evidence brought before the Tribunal. That is a simple procedure. The report of the Tribunal will be available for the whole community. . . All I want to do is to appeal to the House to cut the cackle and get on with the work.[133]

This revolutionary generation of de Valera, Lemass and Costello exhibited a deep sense of state and their initial response to charges of corruption was to immediately restore confidence in the political system. They believed that integrity did not need to be legislatively defined. They did not believe that those in authority could be culpable of moral transgression and demonstrated reluctance to intervene in the absence of concrete evidence of corruption. Their assumptions were dependent on a stagnant notion on how these ethical concepts were defined. In the years to come, the spirit of these intentions would be forfeited for political expediency and immense abuses of public trust would occur.

Trends established themselves in the course of these incidents. Corruption allegations tended to emerge from the same political representatives who affected the maximum political impact by timing their public abhorrence before by-elections and the government's Transport Bill. A sense of deference to authority was evident as those who made allegations generally withdrew or failed to substantiate them. This was in part facilitated perhaps by a historically entrenched apprehension of publicly informing on someone. Attitudes towards 'informers' have traditionally been hostile and perceived as having traitorous qualities. The treachery of informers was a regular theme in the eighteenth-century speeches of condemned Fenians in the docks of English courts for instance.[134] Liam O'Flaherty, celebrated Irish author, portrayed this mind-set in his 1925 book, *The Informer*. It tells the story of Gypo, former policeman and informer, who takes blood money for betraying his friend. 'Everybody remembered with horror that there was a suspicion abroad, a suspicion that an informer had betrayed Francis Joseph McPhillip. Informer! A horror to be understood fully only by an Irish mind.'[135] Informing was regarded as a weakness of integrity and character. A Dáil exchange between the Taoiseach, Éamon de Valera, and Eamonn Coogan TD, Fine Gael, perfectly illustrates these difficulties.

> *Coogan* – I have information which might perpetrate another crisis in this House.
> *de Valera* – If that is so the Deputy should give it to me.
> *Coogan* – If, again, I can get immunity for some of the people who may speak. If the Taoiseach presses me perhaps I can interview certain individuals.
> *de Valera* – I do not press the matter. It is your simple duty.
> *Coogan* – I do not want to become a common informer.[136]

Any assumptions that Irish public life was free from corruption in the 1940s is not borne out. The Tribunals confirmed that when the opportunity arose, transgressions occurred. Political favouritism, improper disclosure of confidential information, use of position to ascertain favourable access to key decision-makers and the circumvention of normal bureaucratic procedures existed. Of special concern were conflicts of interest between the public and private lives of the politicians, where business concerns collided with political responsibilities. This was a period when the distinctions between different types of unethical imprudence were not definite in the public mind. These uncertainties about the boundaries of political behaviour were highlighted in a Dáil debate some years earlier:

> *Eamonn O'Neill* – I would like to draw a distinction between political corruption and political favouritism.
> *Seán Lemass* – I know of no such distinction.[137]

Within a month of coming to office in 1948, the new Taoiseach, John A. Costello, announced that every member of the government 'will comply with the principle that he should not engage in any activities whatever that would interfere, or be incompatible, with the full and proper discharge by him of the duties of his office'. Costello sought to address the conflict of interest difficulties that had wounded the previous government and that had been raised regarding the predominance 'legal deputies' with Fine Gael. He acknowledged however that 'It would not be practicable, however, to lay down [these rules] in a rigid form' and that 'the first guide must be the Minister's or Parliamentary Secretary's own judgment [*sic*]'.[138]

The immediacy of Costello's stance was a reflection of the rumbling questions about de Valera's personal business concerns. When Patrick Cogan TD, Clann na Talmhúain (Farmers Party) asked de Valera in December 1947 about the existence of any conflict of interest rules, de Valera responded: 'To lay down precise rules as to the private activities [by ministers]. . . is obviously a matter of considerable difficulty.'[139] Yet, as controlling director of the *Irish Press* group since its establishment in 1931, de Valera held an extraordinary position of power within both the media and Irish political life. The *Irish Press* was Ireland's second largest chain of national newspapers, which existed to promote Fianna Fáil's view of the world, and was comprised of the influential *Evening Press, Irish Press*, and *Sunday Press*. According to the company's articles of association, the functions of the controlling director merited the 'sole and absolute control of the public and political policy of the company and of the editorial management thereof'. He also had the responsibility to 'appoint and at his discretion, remove or suspend all editors, sub-editors, reporters, writers, contributors of news and information and all such other persons as may be employed in or connected with the editorial department'.

De Valera defended this apparent conflict of interest by stating that he was not financially remunerated as controlling director and that the day-to-day business of the newspaper was delegated to board members. Dr. Noel Browne TD was not convinced: 'He is remunerated by having his speeches reported at great length; his photograph appears on page one, page three or page five – everything he does from the time he gets up in the morning till the time he goes to bed at night.'[140] Browne proved to be doggedly persistent. In a January 1959 Dáil motion, the Dublin South-East TD charged de Valera of rendering 'a serious disservice to the principle of integrity in parliamentary Government and derogated from the dignity and respect due to his rank and office as Taoiseach'.[141]

Browne outlined how de Valera had turned the *Irish Press* into a family concern by using his power as controlling director to bring family members onto the board of directors. De Valera's 1919 American fundraising tour raised substantial finances from Irish-Americans for the 'Republican Loan' which would be repaid in full as soon as an independent Ireland gained international recognition. This was diverted to the de Valera family through the *Irish Press* in an underhand share transaction that Browne described as a 'grossly deflated undervaluation.' By 1959, the de Valera family 'were the effective majority shareholders in the Irish Press and controlled well over half the shares of a company then worth £918,000'.[142] In effect, de Valera used his public office for the enrichment of his family by means of financing the establishment of the *Irish Press*.

Debates on conflicts of interest were not new, but the attention they received was. Questions on whether the private life of a politician influenced their actions as a public representative were raised in a sustained way. This was a new departure. However, no measures were introduced on foot of the Ward Tribunal to address conflicts of interest where politicians were associated or engaged in private business and using their position to make representations to government departments. Nor were measures introduced to prevent undue influence regarding quotas, permits or licences where politicians had a financial interest.

Ireland would not witness such an intensity of corruption allegations for another fifty years. This was perhaps due to the extraordinary personalisation of corruption allegations and the fallout from the Tribunals. McGilligan commented in the Dáil that the Tribunal judges had been wrong in their findings in respect of Flanagan.[143] Mr. Justice Cahir Davitt, who had presided over the Tribunal, 'bitterly resented' these remarks and wrote to the Taoiseach, John A. Costello: 'The effect of this unpleasant business upon my mind is to leave me with an acute personal distaste for any further extra-judicial assignments.'[144] The unpleasantness of the Locke Tribunal endured for many years to come with a marked reluctance to resort to the tribunal method as a means of investigating allegations of corruption. James Dillon, Minister for Agriculture, failed, for example, to secure support among his colleagues to establish a Tribunal of Inquiry in 1949 to investigate his allegations against Martin Corry TD, Fianna Fáil, regarding the acquisition of lime from Tuam sugar beet factory.

Ray Burke, disgraced Fianna Fáil Minister found corrupt by the 1997–2011

Flood / Mahon Tribunal of Inquiry into Certain Planning Matters and Payments, was born in 1943. This was the same year that the first Tribunal in the history of the state, the GSR Tribunal, was initiated. Frank Dunlop, chief whistleblower to the Flood / Mahon Tribunal, was born in October 1947, on the same day as Flanagan was meeting his Tribunal whistleblower. We would have to wait this long for things to come full circle.

Notes

1 T. K. Whitaker, *Interests* (Institute of Public Administration. 1983), p. 7.
2 *Ibid.*
3 M. Mills, 'Interviews', *Irish Press* (24 January 1969).
4 Lee, *Ireland 1912–1985*, p. 156.
5 McGilligan interchangeably represented the constituencies of the National University of Ireland and Dublin North-West, later Dublin North-Central from 1923 to 1965.
6 Initially elected in the 1924 Dublin South by-election for Sinn Féin, Lemass represented Fianna Fáil thereafter until his retirement in 1969. Served as Minister for Industry and Commerce (1932–48 and 1951–54); Minister for Supplies (1939–45); Tánaiste (1945–48 and 1951–54); and Taoiseach 1959–66.
7 D. Harkness, 'Patrick McGilligan: man of commonwealth', *Journal of Imperial and Commonwealth History*, 5 (1979) pp. 117–35.
8 M. Mills, 'Interviews', *Irish Press* (20 January 1969).
9 D. Harkness, 'Patrick McGilligan' and R. Fanning 'Seán Lemass', in J. McGuire and J. Quinn (eds), *Dictionary of Irish Biography: From the Earliest Times to the Year 2002* 4 (Royal Irish Academy, Cambridge University Press, 2009), www.dib. cambridge.org.
10 Seán Lemass, Dáil Éireann, *Committee on Finance Vote 57: Industry and Commerce (Resumed). 57.* (19 June 1935).
11 *Ibid.*
12 McGilligan's predecessor as Minister for Industry and Commerce, Joseph McGrath, had previously been "associated" with gold mining projects which included Heiser in 1930. McGrath founded the Irish Hospitals Trust or sweepstakes in 1930 which was later found to have serious questions regarding the distribution of its profits. RTÉ One, 'Irish Sweepstakes', *Hidden History*, (1 December 2003). McGrath donated £500 to Fianna Fáil in 1931. (Gerry) 'Boland's initial efforts to return the money were overturned by the Fianna Fáil National Executive on the insistence of Lemass.' R. Dunphy, *The Making of Fianna Fáil Power in Ireland* (Clarendon Press, 1995), p. 80.
13 McGilligan, 19 June 1935, Dáil Éireann.
14 General Richard Mulcahy, Dáil Éireann, *Questions. Oral Answers. Wicklow Mining Lease. 57.* (25 June 1935).
15 Lemass, Dáil Éireann, *Committee on Finance Vote 57.*
16 James Dillon, Dáil Éireann, *Sheepskin (Control of Export) Bill, 1934: Committee Stage. 51.* (22 March 1934).

17 McGilligan, Dáil Éireann, *Committee on Finance Vote 57*.

18 Patrick McGilligan, Dáil Éireann, *Twenty-Seventh Report of the Committee of Selection: Mines and Minerals Bill, 1931 – Committee. 40.* (19 November 1931).

19 Patrick McGilligan, Dáil Éireann, *Finance Bill, 1935: Second Stage (Resumed). 57* (14 June 1935).

20 National Library, Dublin, OPIE PP / 36/4, Interim and Final Report Select Committee on the Demise of Certain State Mining Rights, Dáil Éireann Reports of Committees 1932–35. May 1936.

21 Seán Lemass, Dáil Éireann, *Wicklow Mining Lease: Appointment of Select Committee. 57.* (25 June 1935).

22 Norton was the longest serving leader, from 1932 to 1960, in the history of the Labour party. He would later serve as Tánaiste in the first (1948–51) and second (1954–57) Inter-Party governments.

23 National Library, Dublin, Interim and Final Report Select Committee on the Demise of Certain State Mining Rights, p. 52.

24 Seán Lemass, Dáil Éireann, *Wicklow Mining Lease*.

25 *Irish Times* (24 July 1935).

26 *Ibid.*

27 Éamon de Valera, Dáil Éireann, *Financial Resolutions Report (Resumed) Proposed Sale of Distillery: Motion for Select Committee (Resumed). 108.* (30 October 1947).

28 *Irish Press* (25 June 1935).

29 Seán Lemass, Dáil Éireann, *Wicklow Mining Lease*.

30 Seán MacEntee, Dáil Éireann, *Public Business: Finance Bill, 1935: Second Stage (Resumed). 57.* (18 June 1935).

31 Lemass, Dáil Éireann, *Committee on Finance Vote 57*.

32 'Towards Sanity', *Irish Times* (29 June 1935).

33 John Cole, Dáil Éireann, *Questions. Reorganisation of Great Southern Railways Company. 91.* (17 November 1943). See: Dunphy, *The Making of Fianna Fáil Power in Ireland*

34 'Mr. A. P. Reynolds, An Appreciation', *Irish Times* (29 March 1983).

35 General Richard Mulcahy, Dáil Éireann, *Transport (No. 2) Bill. Committee (Resumed: Amendment No. 18). 94.* (21 September 1944).

36 *Irish Times* (27 May 1943).

37 General Richard Mulcahy, Dáil Éireann, *Transport (No. 2) Bill. Committee (Resumed: Amendment No. 18). 94.* (21 September 1944).

38 *Ibid,* McGilligan.

39 *Report of the Tribunal of Inquiry into Dealings in Great Southern Railway Stocks between the 1st day of January and the 18th day of November 1943* (Dublin Stationery Office, 1944).

40 Seán Lemass, Dáil Éireann, *Questions. Reorganisation of Great Southern Railways Company. 91.* (17 November 1943).

41 *Report of the Tribunal of Inquiry into Dealings in Great Southern Railway Stocks,* p 12.

42 *Irish Press* (11 May 1944).

43 *Irish Times* (13 May 1944).

44 C. O'Leary, *Irish Elections 1918–1977: Parties, Voters and Proportional Representation* (Dublin, 1979), p. 35.

45 *Irish Press* (10 May 1944).

46 *Report of the Tribunal of Inquiry into Dealings in Great Southern Railway Stocks* pp. 25; 44.

47 de Valera, Dáil Éireann, *Financial Resolutions Report*.

48 *Report of the Tribunal of Inquiry into Dealings in Great Southern Railway Stocks*, pp. 26–7.

49 Archbishop John Charles McQuaid archives, Dublin: Bishops House. Finance 1111 A. Book 4. 1939–46.

50 *Report of the Tribunal of Inquiry into Dealings in Great Southern Railway Stocks*, *p. 35*; William Davin, Dáil Éireann, *Transport (No. 2) Bill. Committee (Resumed: Amendment No. 18) 94.* (21 September 1944).

51 *Great Southern Railway Stocks Tribunal*, p. 52.

52 *Ibid*, p. 43.

53 Seán Lemass, Dáil Éireann, *Transport (No. 2) Bill, 1944: Committee (Resumed). 94.* (28 September 1944).

54 *Irish Times* (21 September 1944).

55 *Irish Times* (22 September 1944).

56 Patrick McGilligan, Dáil Éireann, *Transport Bill, 1944: Second Stage (Resumed). 93.* (9 May 1944).

57 J. Horgan, *Seán Lemass: The Enigmatic Patriot* (Gill and Macmillan, 1997). p. 131.

58 B. Farrell, *Seán Lemass* (Gill and Macmillan, 1991), pp. 71–2.

59 Horgan, *Seán Lemass*, p. 100.

60 L. W. White, 'Francis Constantine Ward', in McGuire and Quinn (eds), *Dictionary of Irish Biography*, www.dib.cambridge.org.

61 T. P. Coogan, *De Valera: Long Fellow, Long Shadow* (Hutchinson, 1993), p. 647.

62 Patrick McGilligan, Dáil Éireann, *Report of (Ward) Tribunal: Adjournment Debate. 102.* (11 July 1946).

63 Éamon de Valera, Seanad Éireann, *Allegations against Parliamentary Secetary: Motion for Tribunal 31* (5 June) 1946.

64 *Ibid*.

65 National Archives, Dublin, S 13866/A, Taoiseach: Locke's Distillery Kilbeggan, Purchase by Aliens 1947, 'Allegations against Dr. F. Ward', 6 May 1946.

66 E. Byrne, 'Ethics in Public Office Act 1995: public, political & legislative responses' (Degree dissertation, University of Limerick, 2001). Briscoe received financial accommodation which amounted to ten sums of £50 from a Dublin watch company in return for representations on the companies' behalf to the Department of Finance regarding an allocation of Swiss francs to import watches from Switzerland. Briscoe later repaid the money.

67 James Dillon, Dáil Éireann, *Motion for Tribunal. 101.* (10 June 1946).

68 de Valera, Seanad Éireann, *Allegations Against Parliamentary Secretary: Motion for Tribunal. 31.* (5 June 1946).

69 National Archives, S 13866/A, 'Letter from Ward to Taoiseach', 4 June 1946.

70　William Quirke, Seanad Éireann, *Allegations Against Parliamentary Secretary*. de Valera moved the same motion in the Dáil earlier that day.

71　A. Maltby and B. McKenna, *Irish Official Publications: A Guide to Republic of Ireland Papers, with a Breviate of Reports 1922–1972* (Pergamon Press, 1981), p. 45.

72　Dr. F.C. Ward, 10 July 1946.

73　National Archives, Dublin, S13866/B, Taoiseach: Memorandum to Taoiseach, 19 January 1948.

74　Patrick McGilligan, Dáil Éireann, *Report of (Ward) Tribunal: Adjournment Debate. 102.* (11 July 1946).

75　James Derwin, a low ranking Department of Education civil servant was convicted for bribing councillors to vote for particular candidates in the 1943 Seanad election. He was released on a good behaviour bond for three years His stepbrother, John A. Corr, formerly United Ireland Party/Fine Gael and Independent Councillor, Chairperson of Dublin County Council was sentenced to three months imprisonment for the same offence in 1945. Byrne, 'Nineteenth and Twentieth Century Political Corruption in Ireland'.

76　de Valera, Dáil Éireann, *Powers and Privileges of the Oireachtas: Motion. 104.* (11 March 1947).

77　Major Vivion de Valera, *Dáil Éireann, Private Deputies' Business: Motion for a Select Committee: Question of Members' Conduct. 101.* (15 May 1946).

78　Flanagan, *ibid*.

79　Eamonn Coogan, Dáil Éireann, *Powers and Privileges of the Oireachtas: Motion. 104.* (11 March 1947).

80　General Richard Mulcahy, *ibid*.

81　de Valera, *ibid*.

82　Alfie Byrne, *ibid*.

83　Flanagan, Dáil Éireann. (22, 29, 30 October 1947).

84　National Manuscripts, Dublin, Ms 949-52, Ref1238-1 Locke Tribunal Report: 'Letter from Cooney to Flanagan', 19 October 1947.

85　Cross-examination of Joseph Cooney senior, secretary of Locke's Distillery by John A. Costello.

86　Éamon de Valera, Dáil Éireann, *Proposed Sale of Distillery: Motion for Tribunal 108.* (5 November 1947).

87　Locke Tribunal Report: Ref5717-2.

88　*Ibid,* Ms 949-52, Ref1238- 1.

89　*Ibid,* Ref5717.

90　*Ibid,* O'Higgins cross-examination, Ref5482 5485-2.

91　*Ibid,* pp. 12–5. 1.

92　*Ibid,* Ref5717. 2.

93　*Irish Press* (20 November 1947).

94　*Irish Press* (9 December 1947).

95　*Irish Press* (3 December 1947).

96　*Lock Tribunal Report,* Ref6350-2.

97 James Dillon, Dáil Éireann, *Motion for Select Committee. Proposed Sale of Distillery. 108.* (29 October 1947).

98 Evident from Dillon's memoirs and detailed in: M. Manning, *James Dillon: A Biography* (Wolfhound Press, 1999), p. 215.

99 *Locke Tribunal Report,* 1. pp. 12–15.

100 *Locke Tribunal Report* Ref1731: Letters to Mr. Patrick Brady (wine and spirit business) from Cooney, 3, 9 November 1947; Letter to Mr. Kelleher (wine and spirit business) from Cooney, 17 October 1947.

101 *Locke Tribunal Report,* 2.

102 Éamon de Valera, Dáil Éireann, *Financial Resolutions Report (Resumed) Proposed Sale of Distillery: Motion for Select Committee (Resumed). 108.* (30 October 1947).

103 *Locke Tribunal Report,* para 45.

104 National Archives, Dublin, AGO/2002/15/166, Justice: Complaint by Sweetman and O'Higgins addressed to Bar Counsel, 'Bar Counsel letter', 30 December 1947.

105 Manning, *James Dillon,* p. 213.

106 *Locke Tribunal Report,* 1. p. 11.

107 A. Bielenberg, *Locke's Distillery: A History* (Lilliput, 1993), p. 88.

108 *Irish Press* (27 November 1947).

109 *Irish Press* (22 December 1947).

110 de Valera, Éamon, Dáil Éireann, *Financial Resolutions Report.*

111 National Archives, Dublin, S 13866/A, Taoiseach: Locke's Distillery Kilbeggan, Purchase by Aliens 1947, 'An Taoiseach Memo', 29 October 1947.

112 De Valera to Lynch, 27 November 1922 in O'Neill and Pakenham, *Éamon de Valera,* p. 430.

113 'Seán MacBride', *Irish Times* (8 July 1946).

114 *Irish Press* (6 November 1947).

115 Seán MacBride and Caitriona Lawlor, *That Day's Struggle: A Memoir 1904–1951* (Curragh Press, 2005), pp. 140–1.

116 Liam Cosgrave, interview, (March 2008).

117 *Irish Press* (1 November 1947).

118 National Archives, Dublin, S 14153/B, Taoiseach: Locke's Distillery Kilbeggan, Purchase by Aliens 1947, 'Telegraph Flanagan to de Valera', 6 February 1948.

119 M. Mills, 'Interviews', *Irish Press* (27 January 1969).

120 *Irish Press* (20 December 1947).

121 'Lemass: a profile', *Nusight* (December 1969). For a full account: David McCullagh, *A Makeshift Majority: First Inter-party Government 1948–51* (Institute of Public Administration, 1998).

122 National Archives, Dublin, S 14153/B, Taoiseach: Locke's Distillery Kilbeggan, Purchase by Aliens 1947, 'Telegraph Flanagan to de Valera', 6 February 1948. telegraph note dated 9 February.

123 Patrick McGilligan, Dáil Debates, *Committee on Finance: Vote 5, Office of the Minister for Finance. 116.* (21 June 1947).

124 *Irish Times* (12 December 1947).

125 *Irish Times* (9 December 1947).

126 Report of the Committees of Dáil Éireann 1950–53, *Report of the Committee*

on *Procedure and Privileges on the Assault Committed by a Member on another Member in the Oireachtas Restaurant on 31 January 1952* (February 1952).

127 John A. Costello, Dáil Éireann, *Private Deputies' Business- Dáil Restaurant Incident. 129.* (31 January 1952).

128 Oliver J. Flanagan, Dáil Éireann, *Order of Business Social Welfare Bill.* 532. (31 January 1952).

129 *Report of the Committee on Procedure and Privileges on the Assault Committed by a Member on another Member in the Oireachtas Restaurant on 31 January 1952.*

130 Ceann Comhairle, Dáil Éireann, *Report of Committee on Procedure and Privileges, Deputy Reprimanded. 129.* (5 March 1952).

131 Michael Hayes, Seanad Éireann, *Allegations Against Parliamentary Secretary.*

132 de Valera, *ibid.*

133 Thomas Foran Seanad Éireann, *Allegations Against Parliamentary Secretary.*

134 Stephen Joseph Meany, Speeches from the Dock, (Project Gutenberg eBook, Part I, June 1867). www.gutenberg.org.

135 L. O'Flaherty, *The Informer* (Jonathan Cape, 1925), p. 66.

136 Eamonn Coogan, Dáil Éireann, *Report of (Ward) Tribunal: Adjournment Debate. 102.* (11 July 1946).

137 Seán Lemass, Dáil Éireann, *Sheepskin (Control of Export) Bill, 1934: Committee Stage. 51.* (22 March 1934).

138 *Irish Times* (9 March 1948).

139 Éamon De Valera, Dáil Éireann, *Questions, Oral Answers: Parliamentary Secretaries and Business. 109.* (11 December 1947).

140 Noel Browne, Dáil Éireann, *Private Members' Business: Office of Taoiseach, Motion. 171.* (12 December 1958).

141 Noel Browne, Dáil Éireann, *Private Members' Business: Office of the Taoiseach, Motion. 172.* (14 January 1959).

142 RTÉ One, 'Family fortune: De Valera's *Irish Press*', *Hidden History* (November 2004); M. O'Brien, *De Valera, Fianna Fáil and the Irish Press* (Irish Academic Press, 2001). p. 111.

143 *Irish Times* (21 June 1949).

144 National Archives, Dublin, S 15153/C, Taoiseach.

4

At a crossroads? 1950s–1970s

Introduction

Ireland's quiet demographic revolution had profound implications for the direction of Irish politics. Demographic shifts to urban areas and population increases in the 1960s and 1970s led to demands for increased housing. Consequently, the shortage of serviced land necessitated the rezoning of large tracts of agricultural land.[1] This was exacerbated because the growth and expansion of Dublin took place in a predominantly rural area.

The 1961 census also recorded Ireland's lowest population figures since records began, with just under three million. Yet the census also revealed that Ireland's urban population had increased by almost 20 per cent since the foundation of the state. For the first time since independence, more people were living in urban rather than rural Ireland (see figure 4.1). Such growth was remarkable given the stagnant nature of overall population growth. The period 1971 to 1981 actually documented 3.4 per cent immigration into the state, figures only to be replicated in the late 1990s and early 2000s.

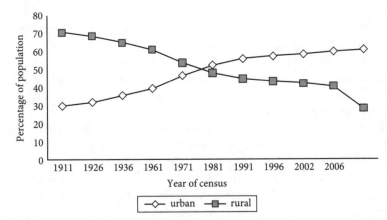

4.1 The percentage of population living in rural and urban areas, 1911–2002

The 1960s were a turning point for Ireland. Demographic transformation, economic adjustment and political modernisation combined to challenge preconceived traditional ways of approaching public life. A more confident and outward looking Ireland was coming of age. As Fergal Tobin put it, 'the blinds were let up, the windows were thrown open, the doors were unlocked; and good, bad or indifferent, the modern world came in among us at last'.[2] The consequence of this change was an unprecedented demand for planning permission and ancillary services. This created a similar incentive for discretionary decision-making by those in power as had occurred in Irish politics in the 1930s and 1940s. The shortcomings of planning legislation in the 1960s and the response of the 1973–77 National Coalition government to alleged corruption, determined the framework for political culture for the subsequent thirty years.

The 1963 Planning Act and the 1974 Kenny Report

The 1963 Planning Act created eighty-seven planning authorities with responsibility for the preparation of development plans for Irish cities and towns. The failure of the Town and Regional Planning 1934 and 1939 Acts, a rapidly growing population and a new political mindset towards long-term economic planning, provided the underlying rationale for the ninety-two lengthy sections of the 1963 Act. Members of the public who wished to build now had to obtain planning permission from their local authority. Planning permission was dependent on the availability of serviced land, such as sewage, water and drainage amenities. Where access to such services was non-existent, the local authority had the power to zone un-serviced agricultural land for residential and commercial purposes.

The 'section four' motion within the City and County Management (Amendment) Act 1955 authorised local government representatives to override the decision of a county or city manager or planning officials on such matters where application for planning permission was denied. In short, the capacity to zone agricultural land incentivised property speculation. The potential for enormous financial profits created an added inducement for corrupt transactions between developers and local officials and representatives.

The rise in population and the economic boom inflated the cost of building land. This thereby restricted the supply of land for public use, such as schools, hospitals and other public amenities. Public disquiet grew when it emerged that large financial windfalls could be made because of the provisions under the Act. It also became obvious that the Act facilitated dubious tax anomalies. Seven years after its introduction, the Minister for Local Government, Bobby Molloy, commissioned a committee in 1970 to inquire into these matters. Mr.

Justice John Kenny of the High Court, who had particular expertise on Irish jurisprudence, was appointed chair. The committee first met at the Custom House in January 1971.

The *Report of the Committee on Price of Building Land*, which became known as the Kenny report, was published in 1974. The Majority report was signed by Kenny and committee members Martin O'Donoghue, economist at the Department of the Taoiseach and two civil servants from the Revenue Commissioners and the Valuation Office. The two officials from the Department of Local Government rejected the report on constitutional grounds.

This report was the first broadly based assessment of problems connected with building land and highlighted the vast profits in rezoning and the sophistication of tax avoidance measures. The Kenny report outlined an October 1964 land transaction where 60 acres at Castleknock, County Dublin, was sold for £67,000. Just six months later, the purchaser sold this land to a finance company for £160,000, at a profit of 140 per cent. Planning permission to develop the lands was granted to the finance company in September 1968.[3] The ultimate value of the redeveloped land is unknown, but in line with similar land transactions at the time, it can be assumed that the return on this four-year investment was considerable, subsequent to planning permission being granted. A 1980 report by the government funded environmental research institute, An Foras Forbartha, echoed the Kenny report's findings. From the 417 land transactions examined between 1974 and 1978, they concluded that agricultural land prices increased by 150 per cent while private housing land increased by 500 per cent.[4]

The Kenny report, initially accepted in principle by the government, proposed that development / industrial land should be compulsorily purchased by local authorities at a small margin above its existing agricultural value, or in other words, at less than its potential market value. At the outset there was public enthusiasm for the Kenny proposals. *Business and Finance* magazine congratulated the 'admirably detailed and lucidly presented review of an extraordinarily complex problem which has defeated the ingenuity of successive governments'.[5]

The Kenny report exposed the anomalies of transferring benefits from land deals between companies under the same beneficial ownership. Such a company would inevitably be placed into voluntary liquidation to ensure, what An Foras Forbartha described as, one of the 'many elaborate devices' which were used to ensure 'that the real purchase price of land is not recorded'.[6] The true number of land transactions in the 1960s and 1970s is unknown because these tax avoidance incentives, particularly on capital gains tax, encouraged non-disclosure of land sales. As *Hibernia* magazine enquired in 1974:

The first question is to ask why such lucrative loopholes in the tax laws have been allowed to survive for so long . . . the second point concerns the penalties attached to tax dodging on a large scale . . . the really big tax dodgers are encouraged in this country by the certain knowledge that, if all comes to all, the revenue authorities will settle on a compromise.[7]

It was not until 1979 that all property, particularly that which transferred between parent and subsidiary, and land sold to an independent purchaser, was legally obliged to be recorded as a land transaction. A clause within the Act warranted that where outline planning permission had been granted, subsequent full planning permission refusal would entail a liability for compensation by the property owner against the local authority at the full development value of the land. Journalist Frank McDonald blames this legal proviso for the granting of controversial planning permission to Green Property Company on the corner of Hume Street and St. Stephen's Green in March 1970. Architectural students from University College Dublin squatted at No. 45 St Stephens Green for six months in an attempt to prevent the destruction of these Georgian buildings. John Garvin, city commissioner, did not rescind the Hume Street planning decision made by Kevin Boland, Minister for Local Government. McDonald notes that this was, 'mainly because it would open the door to a massive claim for compensation by the Green Property Company. The same fear was uppermost in Boland's mind and, more than anything else, this explains why he acted as he did'.[8] In a similar manner, the Oireachtas Select Joint Committee on Building Land, established in 1985 to further examine the Kenny report, remarked, 'The magnitude of certain claims for compensation by landowners has coerced some authorities into granting permissions against their better judgement, or into some sort of compromise arrangements with developers.' These concerns were not acted on. The 1985 Committee on Building Land innocently concluded that it was 'not possible to show the number of cases in which such pressures has been exerted. However, an indication of the size of the problem is the small amount of money actually paid out in compensation. Up to March 1981, for example, Dublin Corporation paid only £135,000 in compensation to landowners, since the introduction of the 1963 Act'.[9]

In 1989, Grange Developments Ltd, a property development company owned by developers, Thomas Brennan and Joe McGowan, were awarded £1.9 million in compensation following the decision by Dublin County Council to refuse planning permission at Montgorry near Swords. Dublin County manager, George Redmond, signed off on the cheque. This was at the time the largest compensation award in the history of the state. Journalist Paul Cullen concluded that 'for the builders, it was a "win-win" situation: a refusal to grant planning permission could prove as profitable as a positive outcome'.[10] It was only after this 1989 payout that the loophole in the 1963 Act was closed.

Builders, developers and speculators protested against thé Kenny proposals. The Kenny report's timing was unfortunate as the property market was struggling to emerge from a downturn in the industry. Newspaper banner headlines shouted 'Disaster looms for builders'. The *Irish Press* noted that house buildings in the first three months of 1974 had dropped 43 per cent below the same period the previous year.[11] Immediately following the Kenny report's publication, the government established the 'Building and Construction Industry' cabinet subcommittee 'to recommend the steps to be taken to increase output and employment in industry with due regard to the financial and economic implications'.[12] *Business and Finance* magazine suggested that the government pushed through its capital taxation package at the expense of not implementing the Kenny proposals. 'Wealth tax and capital gains tax are bad enough, but for builders. . . things could be much worse . . . inflation has produced other more pressing problems. Kenny, like old soldiers, may now slowly fade away.'[13]

Political support quickly waned. Councillor Dermot O'Rourke, failed Dublin South-Central candidate in the 1969 and 1973 elections, chair of the key Dublin corporation housing committee and former Vice-Chair of the Labour party, set the tone for the defeat of the proposals. O'Rourke believed the Kenny report 'would inflict undue hardship on the owners of land on the periphery of the cities and towns of Ireland . . . the role of speculators in pushing up land prices had been over estimated . . . worried about the basic constitutionality of the Kenny report'.[14]

The Kenny report had however pre-empted charges of the unconstitutionality of the proposals. It recommended 'that the President, when asked to sign the Bill, should refer it to the Supreme Court under Article 26 of the Constitution for a decision whether it is repugnant to the Constitution'.[15] M. Ó Flathartaigh, Secretary to the President's Office, wrote to the Department of the Taoiseach, taking umbrage at this 'exceptional' recommendation. 'I do not recall that any enquiry body, or member of the Judiciary in any capacity, has hitherto subscribed to a recommendation of this kind.'[16] The Legal Adviser to the Minister for the Environment told the Committee on Building Land that the Kenny report 'would have little chance of surviving a Constitutional challenge in the Courts based on the argument that it would amount to an unjust attack on landowners property rights'.[17] He believed that the primacy of Articles 40 and 43 of the Constitution which provide distinct and separate protection to the property rights of citizens would win out. This argument gained legislative precedent with the 1982 *Blake v Attorney General* Supreme Court case.[18] Despite the proficient expertise of Mr. Justice Kenny, 'one of the foremost constitutional lawyers in Ireland', Frank McDonald believed that 'the oft-repeated excuse for doing nothing about the commit-tee's majority report was that it might be unconstitutional – an issue never tested in the courts'.[19] *The Committee on Building Land Report* concluded that there were 'alternative ways of dealing with land problems which would be effective, more wide ranging than Kenny,' though these 'alternative' methods were never identified. In all, the committee displayed remarkable short- sight-edness: 'Windfall gain and larger profits are both residual and result from general market conditions unless it can be shown that landowners and/or builders have some monopoly type influence on supply. The committee has no evidence that such is the case'.[20]

The 1968 High Court bribery case and 1975 Tully Tribunal

Apart from the tax loopholes and financial windfalls on rezoning decisions, the provisions of the 1963 Planning Act granted the Minister for Local Government, or his Parliamentary Secretary, absolute discretion on planning appeal decisions. Inevitably, these wide discretionary powers gave rise to accusations of political favouritism in return for private gain. The 1968 High Court bribery case and the 1975 Tully Tribunal of Inquiry underlined the potential consequences of any such abuses of discretion.

Kelly v Dundrum Enterprises opened at the High Court on 7 March 1968. The plaintiff, Mr. Kelly, sued the property development company, Dundrum Enterprises, in a civil action for £2,500. Dundrum Enterprises alleged that Kelly had intimated that due to his close relationship with the then Minister for Local Government, Neil Blaney, he could secure planning permission for the build-ing company. To all intents and purposes, Kelly sued Dundrum Enterprises for not paying what essentially amounted to a bribe. Kelly was a teacher and from a well known Fianna Fáil family in the same Donegal constituency as Blaney. His brother had unsuccessfully run for the party in the Seanad elections.

Kelly had demanded a financial 'consideration' for his services, amount-ing to six cheque instalments of £500, £3,000 in total. Dundrum Enterprises however, paid just one instalment and stopped the cheques as soon as plan-ning permission was granted. The building company were perhaps aware of the immense legal difficulties Kelly may have had if he sought to enforce a contractual agreement tainted with illegality (a bribe). Ultimately, Dundrum Enterprises settled with Kelly out of court for £1,500, a thousand pounds less than Kelly had sued for. The pleadings were not published and no admission of impropriety was made by either side. In essence, the court case amounted to a set of circumstances where financial 'consideration' for political assist-ance rendered was not paid. Some thirty years later, the various Tribunals of Inquiry would turn this ethos on its head and investigate matters where money was paid for political returns.

The Fine Gael Chief Whip, Gerry L'Estrange TD, extensively quoted from these confidential High Court documents into the Dáil record under privilege a week after the court case concluded. 'Here was an admission of corruption,' L'Estrange contended, 'when both the defendant and plaintiff came to the court and saw that the court was littered with journalists and photographers, neither could afford to fight it and wash their dirty linen in open court'.[21] L'Estrange alleged that Fianna Fáil supporters had financially benefited from planning appeal decisions made by Blaney at the Department of Local Government.

Jack Lynch's Fianna Fáil government considered establishing a Tribunal of Inquiry but were advised by the Attorney General, Colm Condon, that witnesses could not be compelled to give evidence incriminating themselves. Blaney's successor at the Department, Kevin Boland, requested the Gardaí to investigate the claims made in the course of the court case. This proved to be beyond the legislative capability of the authorities. All the individuals concerned refused (and could not be compelled) to make statements to the investigating detective superintendent. The month long investigation found that the court documents contained no suggestion that Dundrum Enterprises had alleged that improper influence was used though they did demonstrate that Kelly had held himself out as 'being able [to] potentially' use such influence. Kelly stated that he had merely assisted in the planning appeal and had sought appropriate compensation. The case rested on the subjective interpretation and distinction between *assistance* and *influence* in obtaining planning permission. This tacit linguistic differentiation is significant because it highlights the recurring difficulty of alleging corrupt activity in the absence of *explicit* evidence but in the knowledge of *implicit* evidence. Unfortunately, files from the Department of Local Government, Attorney General, the Garda Investigation and the High Court are unattainable. It would have been interesting to learn how assistance and influence were defined and determined.

Following L'Estrange's Dáil contribution, the Minister for Transport and Power, Erskine Childers, wrote to the Taoiseach, Jack Lynch, outlining his disquiet about the discretionary powers invested in the Minister for Local Government:

> This greatly disturbs me. While accepting the absolute incorruptibility of the Minister . . . there is a very great necessity not only to be incorrupt but to appear to be so. I am trying to think of any other case where a Minister makes personal decisions on matters involving such huge amounts of money. I doubt there is . . . I cannot help feeling that in our own interest we should examine some new method of making these decisions as soon as possible.

In response, Lynch suggested to Boland that he 'might consider the formulation of proposals to change the present (planning appeals) procedures'.

Boland was not enthusiastic: 'The matter is quite a difficult one'.[22] The 1968 annual congress of the Association of Municipal Authorities unanimously called for the transfer of planning appeals from the Minister to an appeals board.[23] Notwithstanding these calls for legislative action, the legislation remained unchanged.

Not unlike earlier corruption controversies, the accompanying political theatre distracted from the allegations and served only to further political antagonism. An assertion of corruption was a by-word for intensely sharp verbal exchanges on the moral reputation of both the individual and political party. Those on the receiving end interpreted such charges as an attempt at character assassination and were especially robust in their response.

Kevin Boland, nephew of Harry Boland, shot by Free State forces during the Civil War, played a leading role in the ensuing drama. Boland was a larger than life figure in Fianna Fáil. The *Hibernia* magazine profile of the Minister suggested that he would make 'an interesting psycho-analytic study and his must be one of the most tortuous personalities in the cabinet'. A teetotaller and non-smoker, *Hibernia*'s anonymous political correspondent contended that Boland was 'incapable of controlling sudden fits of blind rage' and shared with Neil Blaney 'the image of the party fixer, the Tammany politician'.[24] The 1968 electoral referendum was quickly identified as Boland's referendum and the Minister became a particular target for Fine Gael. Boland was known to have a hot temper which Fine Gael delighted in stroking. The *Irish Press* headline – 'angry exchanges in Dáil debate' fantastically underestimated Boland's tone in response to L'Estrange's Dáil disclosure of the High Court documents.[25]

> *Boland* – It is being investigated by the proper authorities. If Deputy L'Estrange has the information – if he has not, he is a liar – let him go to the proper authorities, to the Garda, with it . . . He is a dirty, cowardly cur, a dirty swine.
>
> *L'Estrange* – I am exposing corruption . . . I am proud – and I am neither a cur, nor a liar nor a swine.
>
> *Boland* – And a coward, a yellow coward . . .
>
> *An Ceann Comhairle*: I would ask the Minister to withdraw the word 'liar'. . .
>
> *Boland* – Do not meet me outside if you are wise . . .
>
> *L'Estrange* – Dare you lay one hand on me. If the dead hand of Fianna Fáil has fallen on this country, you're live or dead hand will not fall upon me.
>
> *Boland* – I know. You are a good runner.
>
> *L'Estrange* – Thanks be to God, I never had anything to run from.
>
> *Boland* – You will . . .[26]

The High Court case and the media attention it attracted were advantageous to Fine Gael, now eleven years in opposition. L'Estrange's timing for dramatic accusations of Fianna Fáil corruption, on the eve of crucial by-elections, proved to be as scrupulous as Oliver J. Flanagan in the 1940s. L'Estrange and

Flanagan had in fact much in common. Both vociferously highlighted concerns of corruption as young TD's in their first Dáil term. The day after his allegations, the *Irish Independent* ran with two headlines: 'Fianna Fáil accused of corruption' and 'Wicklow Uncertain'.[27] Polls opened at the Wicklow by-election that same day, which did not allow Patrick (Paudge) Brennan, Wicklow Fianna Fáil TD and incidentally, Parliamentary Secretary for Local Government, the opportunity to counteract these damaging newspaper headlines.

The Fine Gael candidate, Godfrey Timmins, was elected on the fifth count without reaching the quota. This was the sixth by-election in eighteen months and the first that Fianna Fáil had lost. Jack Lynch's seemingly unshakable popularity as Taoiseach was tested for the first time. Timmins's narrow election victory, a mere 546 votes ahead of the Fianna Fáil candidate, gave momentum to the campaign against the pending electoral referendum which sought to substitute the proportional representation electoral system at Dáil elections and introduce the 'straight vote' system in single-member constituencies. The Opposition believed that this would provide a permanent Fianna Fáil government. Subsequently, and for only the second time in the state's history, the government lost the referendum.

Successive Ministers for Local Government were confronted by two competing housing policy objectives. The severe shortage of housing, the appalling conditions of existing housing and the squatting phenomenon were dominant political issues. The unorthodox campaigning methods of the Dublin Housing Action Committee, including the Mountjoy hunger strike by founding member Denis Donehey, received considerable media attention. *Hibernia* magazine noted that although delegates to the 1970 Fianna Fáil Ard Fheis were besieged by 'longhaired housing action protesters,' representatives from the 1,800 Fianna Fáil Cumann 'pledged themselves to the defence of property and Fianna Fáil'.[28]

On the other hand, civic groups which sought to protect Dublin's Georgian historic structures were suspicious of the closed nature of decision-making within the planning appeals process. The Minister was not obliged to justify why he had changed decisions, no matter how controversial. It quickly became evident that his decision-making process was guided by a priority to facilitate housing and business needs rather than petitions for preservation. Kevin Boland, Minister for Local Government, was acutely frustrated with such petitions, as evident from his inflammatory 1970 Dáil contribution where he disparaged 'the consortium of belted earls and their ladies, and left-wing intellectuals'.[29] Moreover, his correspondence to the Taoiseach in 1969 during the Fitzwilliam square, Stephen's Green / Hume Street and the Central Bank development controversy was indicative of such short-sighted irritation:

I like the appearance of Georgian Dublin myself – although I seldom find time to contemplate the entity of Hume Street and Ely Place. I also dislike the unsightly collection of caravans along the Naas Road and at other places in County Dublin . . . If I have to choose between preserving the entity of Hume Street and Ely Place for these who have time to enjoy its beauty *and* providing the houses that will eventually eliminate the eyesores on the Naas Road, I will choose the latter and accept the vilification . . . And with capital scarcity this is fundamentally the choice.[30]

Petitions from business interests to government requesting intervention to expedite the planning process were common in the 1970s. When Dublin Corporation rejected planning permission for a proposed development at O'Connell Street Upper in 1971, the chartered architects and planning consultants wrote to the Taoiseach and the Minister for Local Government warning that 'our Clients . . . are now seriously considering withdrawing from further building investment in Dublin unless a speedy and satisfactory decision can be given'.[31] In the context of an economic recession, direct measures which checked the high unemployment and emigration rates were publicly well received. In response to a 1972 United Nations questionnaire on the 'relationships and decision-making processes in the planning and building of houses' the Department of Local Government advised that local planning authorities should adhere to a policy of doing:

> all they can to facilitate desirable developments, including housing developments, and not to frustrate these developments by the unduly rigid application of controls . . . to cooperate with and help prospective developers to the maximum possible extent; to press ahead with those parts of their sanitary services programmes required to open up more land for development in built up areas; to continue to acquire land develop land for housing . . . and, where feasible, not to hinder minor housing development by individuals or small builders.[32]

The variety of coercion relating to planning decisions was wide-ranging. Michael (Mickey) Mullen, general secretary of the Irish Transport and General Workers Union (ITGWU), was one such actor. The ITGWU's unreserved backing of a Labour / Fine Gael Coalition in 1973 was crucial to ending internal Labour deadlock on the coalition question, especially given the union's earlier strong stance against coalition. Mullen's ITGWU was the largest financial backer to Labour in the 1973 general election, donating a considerable £23,000.[33] In all, ten members of the ITGWU were elected as Labour TDs. Financially and politically a powerful figure in the Labour party, Mullen, formerly a Labour councillor and Dublin North-Central TD, was subsequently appointed to the 1973–77 Seanad. Mullen also had a close relationship with Charles J. Haughey and was later the sole witness of the famous 1982 'Gregory Deal' between the inner-city independent socialist TD, Tony Gregory, and Haughey, the then Taoiseach.

On eleven occasions in 1972, Mullen wrote to the Taoiseach, Jack Lynch and Fianna Fáil Ministers for Local Government, Labour and Industry and Commerce – Robert Molloy, Joseph Brennan and Patrick J. Lalor – seeking rezoning at Turnapin Little, near Santry in North County Dublin. The Dublin city planners rejected planning permission on three grounds because of the land's hazardous proximity to the Dublin airport runway. Turnapin Little, owned by a failed Labour Dáil candidate, also had a complete absence of drainage facilities while its proximity to the proposed Northern Cross Route motorway would necessitate the bisecting of the site. Mullen adopted three separate approaches to cajole the Fianna Fáil government. At first he applied economic pressure, then utilised the voting capacity of the Union's membership and finally, intimated negative publicity and legal action against the government.

> We have been advised by one such industrialist . . . that if a site on the said lands is not made available to him on or before the 31st inst., that he will abandon his intention of establishing an industry in Ireland. This will mean the loss of approximately 200 jobs which we can ill afford.
>
> We fail to understand the irresponsible and callous approach adopted by your Department in this matter. Once again, may we remind you that, as the largest trade union in the country representing 150,000 workers, we expect our representations to you to be treated more seriously.
>
> Because of your attitude . . . It will be necessary for us to be completely open and above board and explain the position exactly to them [industrialists] . . . If any publicity results which could adversely affect us at home or abroad we wish to make it clear that the said responsibility could properly be placed at your door . . . Should Mr. Geraghty [landowner who sought lands rezoned] have recourse to the courts we would be prepared to assist him in any way we can.[34]

James Tully, Labour party, replaced Molloy as Minister for Local Government in the Fine Gael / Labour Coalition government 1973–77. Tully rezoned the land and granted planning permission. This was the subject of much comment at the time. Although, planning experts estimated that it would cost £250,000 to move the proposed motorway, Tully did so anyway because, as he advised the Dáil, 'it would cost less eventually because of the type of land that would be acquired'.[35] In June 1974, Tully told the *Sunday Independent* journalists Joe McAnthony and Paul Murphy that his decision to rezone Turnapin Little was 'incidental to that site'.[36] The *Sunday Independent* estimated that Tully's rezoning decision increased the value of the lands by one and a half million pounds. The auctioneer for the land, Senator John Boland, Fine Gael, subsequently set an asking price of two million pounds. The rezoning at Turnapin Little had ramifications for the value of land at Rolon Caravans, owned by the same family, which lay in the path of the motorway. This was later sold at an undisclosed price. In response to the McAnthony and Murphy article, Tully circulated a statement at the June 1974 cabinet meeting which simply read,

'The Minister wishes it to be clearly understood that the decision was made on objective professional advice'.[37]

Tully (1915–92), the 'gutsy anti-intellectual', was the archetypal 'grass roots politician par excellence'.[38] His celebrated remark 'To hell with the rich' in an RTÉ interview earned the Meath TD a popular reputation. *Hibernia* credited the Labour deputy leader with introducing 'Madison avenue personality tactics to the Irish Labour party'.[39] As Minister for Local Government, Tully famously introduced what became to be known as the 'Tullymander'. This scheme of redrawing the country's constituency boundaries in order to maximise the return in seats for the National Coalition in the subsequent election, spectacularly backfired when Fianna Fáil recorded its biggest ever majority. Frank McDonald, pulled no punches in his description of Tully.

> The worst minister for local government in the history of the state . . . Almost every county in Ireland is littered with the consequences of his decisions . . . his four years in office marked the very nadir of planning in Ireland. He appeared willing to grant permission for almost any development, no matter how appalling in itself and no matter what dreadful precedent it would create . . . the fallout from what became known as 'Tully permission' – the inexplicable decisions made by the Minister who called himself a socialist.[40]

Together with Brendan Crinion TD, Fianna Fáil, Tully's predecessor at the department, Robert (Bobby) Molloy, alleged that Tully had an improper business connection with building contractor, Robert (Bobby) Farrelly (also known as James Farrell). Molloy and Crinion asserted under Dáil privilege in December 1974, June and July 1975 that Tully personally issued signed cheques every Thursday into Farrelly's account which was used to pay Farrelly's staff. Tully, Crinion and Farrelly were all from Meath.[41]

Jack Lynch, angry at Molloy's solo-run on the Tully incident and his failure to substantiate the allegations, described Molloy's actions as 'most grave'.[42] Molloy, a former Mayor of Galway, Parliamentary Secretary to the Minister for Education and Minister for Local Government, resigned from the Fianna Fáil frontbench. Nonetheless his resignation letter was couched with the qualification: 'I wish to make it quite clear that I acted in good faith in making these allegations'.

The Dáil Committee on Procedure and Privileges investigated the Molloy and Crinion allegations but made inconclusive findings. Both men refused to make a statement to the committee because of doubts whether the committee proceedings were privileged. The committee, chaired by Sean Treacy TD and with a Fine Gael / Labour government majority, did not recommend a Garda inquiry because 'the allegations were not properly the subject for such an inquiry'.[43]

To much surprise, the Taoiseach, Liam Cosgrave, established a Tribunal of Inquiry on 3 July 1975 to investigate the matter because 'The nature of the allegations directly affects the Minister for Local Government in the perform-ance of his duties as Minister and the matter cannot be left unresolved'.[44] The *Irish Press* headline announced 'Tully Case for Judge' the following day. The other front page headline was the rather far-sighted: 'EEC to investigate Irish beef stocks: £10m irregularities?' Some fifteen years later, Julien de Kassell's story would also be given Tribunal treatment with the establishment of the 1991–94 Tribunal of Inquiry into the Beef Industry, chaired by Mr. Justice Liam Hamilton.

Subsequent to Cosgrave's announcement and immediately prior to a Seanad motion to ratify establishment of the Tribunal, Molloy and Crinion publicly apologised to the Minister for Local Government. Tully was not in the Dáil to receive the Molloy and Crinion act of contrition. Molloy withdrew his allegations because the three people from whom he had obtained the information refused to disclose their identity and give evidence on the matter. A week later, Tully launched Farrelly's housing development in Kells with the words 'Good luck, Bobby, and to hell with the begrudgers'. Farrelly was quite happy with the adverse publicity that the forthcoming Tribunal had brought. He told the *Irish Times* journalist, Jack Fagan, 'I'm building 12 houses at the moment and nine of them are already sold. I haven't time to build a show-house. They are selling as fast as they go up'. The weeklong ceremonies in Oldcastle, ten miles from Kells, to mark the elevation of local saint, Blessed Oliver Plunkett, were interrupted by the vice rector of the Irish college in Rome, Right Rev. Monsignor John Hanly, to congratulate Tully on the good news of Molloy's withdrawal of the allegations.[45]

Although Cosgrave had the option to discontinue Tribunal proceedings in light of the apology, he persevered. This may have been due to a common bond both Cosgrave and Tully shared having both joined the army at the outset of the "Emergency". Tully rose to the rank of corporal which accounted for his moniker 'the little corporal from Laytown'. The Tully Tribunal of Inquiry was the first Tribunal established to investigate political corruption since the 1947 Locke Tribunal, some three decades earlier. Proceedings opened at Court No. 4 in the Four Courts on Monday, 21 July 1975. Mr. Justice Seamus Henchy, Supreme Court, chaired and was assisted by Mr. Justice Weldon R. C. Parke of the High Court and Mr. Justice John Charles Conroy, President of Circuit Court. After only two hours, the Tribunal was adjourned indefinitely and became the shortest tribunal in the history of the state.[46]

The Tribunal heard evidence from Tully, the building contractor and eight Bank officials. Molloy and Crinion were not legally compelled to attend or present evidence to the Tribunal and chose not to. Counsel for both men, Donal Barrington SC, 'submitted that the terms of reference of the tribunal were not authorised under the (1921 Tribunal) Act, in so much as that act was never intended to deal with an inquiry into utterances made in Dáil Éireann or any house of Parliament'.[47] The Tribunal determined that there was no foundation or evidence for any of the allegations.

The Dáil Committee on Procedure and Privileges was again invoked to consider the Tribunal report and found that Molloy and Crinion were in 'grave breach of privilege in making the allegations'.[48] Eight months after the Tribunal, the government passed a Dáil motion which strongly condemned and censured Molloy and Crinion's actions. Lynch described the motion as 'mean, petty, vindictive and totally unnecessary' and instructed his party to vote against the motion and not to engage in Dáil debate on the issue.[49] In response, Cosgrave made perhaps the shortest speech in Leinster House with the three Latin words: 'Res Ipsa Loquitur' which translates as, 'the thing speaks for itself'.

Molloy's allegations were met with hostility by the wider media and all political parties, including his own. Editorials in the *Irish Press*, a Fianna Fáil friendly paper, were tenacious throughout the controversy: 'the principle is that if there is something amiss in public life the public have a right to know, and if something is not amiss public figures have a right to their reputation and public esteem, which should not lightly be impugned'.[50] Focus centred on the abuse of Dáil privilege in making the allegations. The tribunal may only have taken two hours but the affair was drawn out over a year due to the Dáil Committee and motion. The Molloy experience may have prompted reluctance among potential whistleblowers and Parliamentarians to come forward and engage with allegations of political wrongdoing.

Response by the National Coalition to corruption allegations

The Joe McAnthony and Paul Murphy *Sunday Independent* article of June 1974 asked questions not only of Tully but also of Raphael (Ray) Burke, Fianna Fáil TD, and Senator John Boland, Fine Gael. Burke was the son of P. J. Burke, a Fianna Fáil TD for Dublin North, originally from Westport in County Mayo. He became a director of his father's Swords based auctioneers and estate agents business, P. J. Burke (Sales) Limited from 1968. Burke entered public life as a Fianna Fáil councillor in 1967 and served as a member of Dublin County Council until 1978 and then as a TD for Dublin North from 1973 to 1997. He was a key figure in Fianna Fáil and served in nine ministerial offices including Industry, Commerce and Energy, Environment, Energy, Communications, Justice and Foreign Affairs. As Minister for Justice, he initiated the first comprehensive review of the Garda Fraud Squad.

Dublin County Council's planning committee and professional planning staff rejected a rezoning application for 35 acres at Montgorry near Swords in 1971. The Assistant County Manager strongly argued that 'the land was in a noise zone, there were no provisions for sewage and to give permission was contrary to good planning'. Only a week after this rezoning refusal, Independent Cllr Jim Guinan, an auctioneer like Burke and Boland, again proposed the lands for rezoning under a section four motion. Under the provisions of the City and County Management (Amendment) Act, 1955 a council majority can require the City / County manager to carry out a particular action under the provisions of a section four motion. This process was often used to overrule the manager in order to grant planning permission for an application already denied. To avoid such ignominy, the manager would often grant a permission simply to avoid the inevitable section four motions.[51]

This motion was seconded by Burke. The Moutgorry lands were subsequently rezoned and their value increased to the tune of £388,000. McAnthony and Murphy's detailed and well-researched article reproduced a document from the Companies Office in Dublin with the returns for the Dublin Airport Industrial Estates Ltd, (DAIE), a company connected to property developers Tom Brennan and Joseph McGowan and auctioneer Patrick Langan. Under the title 'Professional Fees,' the document read 'Ray Burke planning £15,000'.

The Montgorry land was owned by the DAIE. Following the rezoning of this land, Burke received a £15,000 'fee' from this same company. As an influential member of Dublin County Council, Burke was a key participant in a political decision which radically benefited the DAIE and thus by inference, himself. At the very least, this was a clear case of conflict of interest. When this proposition was put to Burke, he told the *Sunday Independent* that he 'made it clear that he regarded the zoning motion which he seconded and his later contracted payment from the sale of the land as entirely unrelated. He said he had no interest in the site when he urged its new zoning'. The *Sunday Independent* article appeared a week after the June 1974 local elections where Burke topped the poll with 3,296 votes in the Swords electoral area. At the time of the article, Burke was also a recently qualified auctioneer and a newly elected member of the Dáil.

Provisions under the Local Government Act, 1946 curiously rescinded obligations under section 36 (6) of the Application of Enactments Order 1898. That Order had declared that a Local Authority member could not vote or take part in a discussion on any matter before the Council or Council committee in which they or their partner had a direct or indirect pecuniary interest. Indeed the conflict of interest segment of the Housing Act 1966 had yet to be implemented. In all, conflict of interest legislation was far more robust when Ireland was under British rule. Thus, councillors who pushed through rezoning were not legally obliged to declare their occupation as auctioneers. They were not required to disclose their close relationship with those developers who sought to have the land rezoned. Ultimately, this absence of statuary disclosure requirements allowed a *carte blanche* approach by elected representatives. McAnthony forcefully suggested that councillors had pecuniary interest in the rezoning of the land. The *Sunday Independent* article fatalistically concluded that 'None of these representatives acted illegally. Their business activities were entirely within the law'.[52] This was legally correct. The extraordinary activities of councillors were entirely within the law because there was no law.

James Tully, the Minister for Local Government, referred the *Sunday Independent* and subsequent *Hibernia* articles to the Attorney General, Declan Costello, for 'such action as he might consider appropriate'.[53] Three separate Garda inquiries consequently declared that a 'thorough and painstaking investigation had not disclosed evidence to warrant any prosecutions'.[54] The thoroughness of the Garda investigation was later queried in Mr. Justice Feargus M. Flood's *Tribunal of Inquiry into Certain Planning Matters and Payments Second Interim Report* of 2002. In what was called 'The Brennan & McGowan Module', the Tribunal found that Brennan and McGowan's transfer of a house to Burke in 1973 amounted to a corrupt payment. Burke later sold the house for £3 million in the 1990s. The Tribunal found that a 1974 letter from a Bank of Ireland branch assistant manager was 'written for the sole purpose of satisfying the Gardaí as to how he [Burke] had paid for his house'.[55]

The John Poulson corruption affair (1972–74) in Britain had put into focus the need for politicians to disclose their interests. Poulson was convicted of fraud for bribing senior British politicians in return for building contracts. The political scandal compelled the House of Commons to initiate a Register of Members' Interests. Tully stated that similar legislation on the matter was in progress. The administrative council of the Labour party, he said, had 'decided that every Labour candidate should indicate in writing the nature of any interest in property or building companies or dealings in land. The same request will be made of every candidate in the next general election'.[56] Nonetheless, when Cllr Niall Andrews, Fianna Fáil, attempted to pass a motion on Dublin County Council obliging councillors to declare their financial interests in 1974, nobody seconded his proposal. Despite varied political concern, the initial enthusiasm to regulate any potential conflicts of interest was progressively watered down.

The *Irish Press* was concerned that any such legislation would inhibit professional people such as solicitors, accountants or company directors from going forward for election because of client confidentiality obligations. The newspaper was sanguine in its editorial. 'The law, as it stands, is adequate to deal with the question of financial inducements. And perhaps a simple declaration which an elected person could swear to . . . a solemn promise not to use the office for personal gain would be a minimum statuary requirement'.[57] The editorial reflected a benign media consensus that 'fortunately, Irish public life is fairly free of large-scale corruption. This is partly because of the intimacy of our society in which very little goes on that is not found out. It is also due to the small scale of the economy'.[58]

At the 18 October 1974 cabinet meeting, Tully presented a three page Memorandum to the cabinet which sought to amend the planning legislation to 'deal with pecuniary and other interests of councillors'. Tully was initially ambitious in his proposals. He believed that legislation on conflict of interest matters should not only be extended to local representatives, but members of the Oireachtas and officers and employees of local authorities. He accepted that decisions taken under the Planning Act 1963:

> can affect the value of the land directly concerned . . . councillors can influence the manager, or require him to act in a particular way . . . It is clear that a direct conflict of interests could arise . . . Indirect interests could also be involved; for example, a councillor could be acting as architect, engineer, solicitor, auctioneer etc. for a person who has an interest in the land concerned.

However he went on to say that the 'complex' nature of the reforms would ensure that it would be 'likely to be some time before legislation on a comprehensive basis could be prepared'. The Minister would ultimately conclude that 'amendments of the Prevention of Corruption Acts would be quite inappropriate for inclusion in planning legislation'.[59] Nevertheless and somewhat misleadingly, Tully announced the introduction of 'conflict of interest' legislation at his party's annual conference three days later which the *Irish Independent* reported was 'greeted with loud applause and he later received a standing ovation'.[60]

The Attorney General, Declan Costello, also presented a 'Memorandum for the Government on the reform in the law relating to conflict of interest of members of local authorities and of members of the Oireachtas' at the same cabinet meeting. The tone and implicitness of the language used suggest that he was exceptionally frustrated by the conduct of politicians and the absence of legislative reform. His detailed legal opinion condemned the legislation as 'completely inadequate and needs to be amended and reformed'. Costello was forthright in his assessment that the need for legislative reform did not just derive from recent newspaper reports but from the existence of 'widespread public disquiet at the manner in which public affairs are conducted in this country . . . in relation to the activities of public representatives at national level and, in particular, to the activities of office holders'.

Costello was critical of the Local Government Act 1946 which as noted earlier, repealed the 1898 Order obliging local councillors to declare a conflict of interest. He also drew attention to the conflict of interest segment of the 1966 Housing Act which had yet to be applied and the difficulties of proving an offence under the outdated Public Bodies Corrupt Practices Act 1889.

In all, his lengthy submission suggested the immediate establishment of a comprehensive Register of Interests which would be open for public inspection, the prohibition of gifts and hospitality, the criminalisation of using confidential information for private gain and the proscription of verbal communication between Local Authority members and developers and those with a vested interest in the development of land. A motion along similar lines by Independent Senators John Horgan and Mary Robinson was defeated earlier that year.

Costello succeeded in persuading the government to establish an internal committee 'to consider their [Costello's recommendations] detailed implementation and to bring forward detailed proposals to the Government for legislative action'.[61] At the October 1974 cabinet meeting, seven members of the government were delegated to Costello's Committee. Tully was the first appointment. He was joined by Richard (Richie) Ryan, Mark Clinton, Tom Fitzpatrick, Patrick Cooney, Frank Cluskey and Declan Costello, Ministers for Public Service, Agriculture and Fisheries, Lands, Justice, the Parliamentary Secretary to the Minister for Social Welfare and the Attorney General.

A civil servant's handwritten note on the cabinet minutes noted that 'This Committee had not reported before this Govt (*sic*) went out of office in July 1977.' In an interview some thirty years later, Costello confirmed that the committee met at least once and expressed a sense of disillusionment at the experience.[62] Costello's recommendations were not implemented. Analysis of the 1974–76 cabinet minutes illustrates that apart from the establishment of this committee, there were no further formal discussions on corruption prevention and on the day of the Tully Tribunal report, the cabinet instead discussed commissioners of charitable donations and bequests.

Costello was a strong critic of the spoils system of allocating state briefs based on party allegiance.[63] In 1974, as Attorney General, he established the office of the Director of Public Prosecutions (DPP) which eliminated this practice. He drew on recent legislative initiatives in Britain which had responded to similar ethical questions. Costello's 1974 recommendations were striking similar to post 1995 Irish corruption legislation.[64] Would Ireland have experienced three corruption tribunals in the 1990s on such issues if this legislation had been implemented earlier?

The enthusiasm to address these matters was not immediately evident in media comment or among the political parties, suggesting that political culture was not as pre-disposed to ethical legislation as was the case in Britain. Despite demographic, economic and social change, Ireland remained an inward looking state, suspicious of external influence and resistant to self-scrutiny or criticism. The *Irish Press's* dismissive editorial regarding the initial 1974 Burke allegations was illustrative of the hostility brought to bear on suggestions of political misconduct: '"They are in it for what they can get out of it" is a phrase frequently used in relation to members of the local authorities. It is an unfair and an unjust one, simply because there are many, poor and well off, who give voluntary public service without expectation of any reward'.[65] The futility of exposing corruption to an ambivalent public was best summed up by McAnthony: 'It was so naked we published it; it was so naked I thought there was no way he [Ray Burke] would get away with this. I thought we have him, there is no question about this now but the policeman who came to interview me about it said "forget it, he'll never go to jail, nothing's going to come out of this" and that was true.'[66]

The only legislative outcome from this period was the Local Government (Planning and Development) Act, 1976. The Act provided for an 'independent' planning board, An Bord Pleanála, to replace the Minister's sole power of discretion. This legislation was first put forward in 1968 when Kevin Boland, Minister for Local Government, obtained cabinet approval for two provisos which ensured the Minister's proxy control of the board through the power of appointment and included this amendment proposed by Boland which was accepted: 'The deletion of the first sentence . . . and the substitution therefore of the words "the term of office of the chairman shall be fixed by the Government" . . .. "if there is disagreement in any particular case between the chairman and the ordinary members, the chairman shall report to the minister, and the minister shall give the decision."'[67]

The ineffectiveness of the legislation became apparent when, on his last day in office in 1981, Burke, now Minister for Local Government, made three appointments to An Bord Pleanála. These appointments included the main architect for Brennan and McGowan, John P. Keenan, who also designed Burke's home, and Michael Cooke, formerly a quantity surveyor for Brennan and McGowan. Burke ignored all precedent and did not appoint a civil servant from his own department. Coincidentally, again on his last day in Ministerial office in 1982, Burke appointed two Fianna Fáil constituency workers to An Bord Pleanála. The Local Government (Planning and Development) Act, 1983 addressed this shortcoming and restructured An Bord Pleanála. The new Minister for Local Government, Dick Spring, believed this was necessary 'to restore public confidence in the [planning] system'.[68] As a mark of protest, Haughey, leader of the Opposition, led Fianna Fáil out of the Dáil when debate began on the Bill. Burke denounced the 'clear innuendo' of corruption and stated that he stood over 'every appointment I made'.[69] This Board was not without controversy. In 1980 a Garda investigation was conducted into alleged planning irregularities surrounding the Board's decision to grant planning permission to a housing development at Killiney, County Dublin. The investigation centred on a senior member of the board who had made the decision. A file was forwarded to the DPP who ruled no prosecution take place.

Conclusion

Despite the persistence of allegations on planning related matters, the 1960s and 1970s did not share the same intensity of formal corruption investigations as the 1940s. A two hour Tribunal of Inquiry and a failed internal government committee were the only political responses to disquiet on planning decisions. The absence of official inquiry is not to suppose that corruption did not occur, but that the prevailing characteristics within Irish public life dictated that they were *not* reported or taken seriously. Yet, despite the promise of transformation that the outset of the 1960s seemed to suggest, unethical political actions which were later to become the subject of over a decade of tribunal inquiries from the 1990s, became more ubiquitous.

Economic and social modernisation coincided with the entry of a new political generation to the Dáil, unburdened by a living memory of the Civil War. The puritan revolutionary ethic of the first generation of political leaders in independent Ireland was evident in the austerity which characterised their private lives. Richard Mulcahy, controversial commander of the Provisional government military forces during the Civil War and leader of Fine Gael (1944–59) believed in 'hard work, early rising, walking' and had a love of 'plain, simple food'.[70] The subconscious piety of de Valera was deliberately expressed in his 1943 St Patrick's Day speech where he dreamed an Ireland which would value 'material wealth only as a basis of right living, of a people who were satisfied with frugal comfort'.[71]

Dominant first generation political figures were permanently departing the political stage. W. T. Cosgrave died in 1965, Seán Lemass in 1971 and Éamon de Valera in 1975. A wave of career orientated politicians entered the 1960s with the ascent of Brendan Corish in 1960, Liam Cosgrave 1965 and Jack Lynch 1966. Donogh O'Malley, Haughey and Brian Lenihan, 'the three musketeers', came to represent the new pragmatic, business minded approach of Fianna Fáil. First elected in 1954, 1957 and 1961 respectively, the 'men in the mohair suits' came to dominate positions of power from the 1960s. Lenihan would later write that the 'escapades' of the three became 'mythologised beyond the mundane reality of a society that was quite simply modernising'.[72] This changing face of Fianna Fáil was 'to be found in the company of self-made men, speculators, builders and architects'.[73]

The period was accompanied by a new generation of young, urban, educated, middle-class voters who were more concerned with social and economic matters than the Treaty debates of the 1920s. The post-war period witnessed the consolidation of a complacent party system built around socially indistinct electoral alliances. The stagnant electoral market of the 1950s became more competitive and political parties were on a permanent election footing in the late 1960s. In a tight election, Fine Gael's Tom O'Higgins came within an unprecedented 10,700 votes of the perpetual de Valera in the 1966 Presidential election. The 1967 local elections were promptly followed by six tightly contested by-elections and a hot tempered referendum on abandoning the proportional representation electoral system in 1968.

Taca

The professionalisation of politics and a greater number of elections in the 1960s cost money and Fianna Fáil's traditional reliance on national church collections as its main source of revenue was not enough. Fianna Fáil established a political fundraising organisation called Taca, which translates as help or support in Irish. This general election fund-raising committee was established on a permanent basis in 1966 and operated from Room 547 of the Burlington Hotel. The £100 annual subscription fee was considerable for its time. Nonetheless, over 500 business figures, including the self-made men of the 1960s economic boom – builders, speculators and successful architects – became members. In essence, Taca facilitated networking between the politically and economically powerful. The *Nusight* journalist, Michael McInerney, outlined the considerable financial 'strength' of Fianna Fáil in advance of the 1969 election:

> That machine, on National Collection Day brings in about £40,000 in an election year, like the present, it will double that sum, perhaps. In addition there is the Taca organisation which last year brought in an additional £40,000, making a total of £80,000. This election year that Taca sum will jump. In addition the Taoiseach will write to thousands of businesses throughout the country seeking contributions to the election fund. A total of £100,000 for the election might not be an exaggeration. It is a formidable machine, more formidable in its money raising potential than any other party.[74]

Dublin city centre hotels, the Gresham on O'Connell Street, the Russell on St Stephens Green and Groomes on Cavendish Row, hosted regular dinners for this new group which excited media attention and greatly exercised an organisationally complacent opposition. Patrick D. Harte TD announced at a 1968 Fine Gael by-election meeting in Wicklow that Taca was 'a secret junta going around the public houses trying to purchase votes by buying drinks for all and sundry'.[75] Kevin Boland, Joint Honorary Secretary of Fianna Fáil and one of the three Taca treasurers, was more modest about Taca's purpose. This 'top hat organisation' allowed party members 'the opportunity of rubbing shoulders with their betters and of exchanging views with them'. Fianna Fáil had moved from the party of the 'small man' to one 'now financially patronised by the bosses . . . the entrepreneurial class'.[76]

McInerney was not convinced that Fine Gael's umbrage at Fianna Fáil's aggressive fundraising was particularly justified. Fianna Fáil, it seemed, had merely robbed Fine Gael of their traditional sources of financial backing. There is no research to back up these observations by the political correspondent but the belief that Fine Gael were financially better off than their political opponents was a well-founded perception of that time. The new money of the emerging entrepreneurial class had chosen Fianna Fáil rather than the business friendly Fine Gael who, McInerney believed:

> had its substitute for Taca. It can 'screw' money out of businessmen also, but has not the success in its national collection. A great number of Fine Gael TDs and leaders are also businessmen and subscribe handsomely to their party funds at election times. Almost all of the Fine Gael TDs unlike Fianna Fáil, finance their own campaigns. In this sense Fianna Fáil retains control over the selection of candidates: money does not – or did not – buy a place in the panel of candidates.[77]

The Taoiseach, Jack Lynch, rejected any whiff of corruption surrounding the party's fundraising organ. 'I want to say categorically that no member of Taca has benefited in any way from his membership, nor do I believe any member ever expected to so benefit'.[78] Although Taca was wound up in the late 1960s, Frank Dunlop, former government press secretary and political lobbyist, noted that while Taca disappeared, the 'goal of raising money from the business community didn't, the party just found more discreet ways of doing it'.[79] As a consequence of the wealth and capital gains taxes introduced by the 1973–77 National Coalition, Fianna Fáil witnessed a surge of financial support by those directly affected by these new taxes. Boland believes that 'These people were making an investment on which they expected a return, and they intended to call the tune'[80] and attributed part of this tune to the give-away Fianna Fáil 1977 manifesto which abolished local business rates and had catastrophic long-term economic consequences for the country.

Machine politics

Self-interested behaviour and the cult of the political leader grew to be more prominent features of Irish political life. The political machine as a professional organisation was one where 'hints of municipal corruption and graft were winked at, even applauded by the machine clientele as the social banditry of an urban robin hood'.[81] The 1969 Devlin report into the Irish civil service implied that such political activity 'helps perpetuate the misconception that everything can be *fixed*'.[82] A wonderful example of such political activity is this correspondence from the Minister for Justice, Michael Moran (Micheál Ó Moráin) to a Mayo constituent a month before the June 1969 general election on a housing matter:

> After discussion and considering the matter I considered the only thing for you to do is to move in quietly to Mrs . . .'s house. If any neighbours ask any ques-

tions, you should say you are in there at Mrs . . . 's cousin and that you looking after the place for her. Once you are in, we will try and find ways and means of keeping you there and ultimately getting you recognised as the official tenant. . . this is strictly confidential . . . for obvious reasons you should destroy this letter, and tell nobody on what basis you are getting into the house.[83]

Moran, a Castlebar solicitor succeeded by Pádraig Flynn on the Fianna Fáil Mayo ticket in 1977, was a focus of ridicule for *Hibernia* magazine. 'The poor country that has to put up with him as Minister for Justice is in even greater need of pity'.[84] Despite more pressing concerns of national importance, the attention of Taoisigh during this time was invariably drawn to localism queries. Analysis of the Taoiseach files from the 1960s reveal how ministers directly contacted the Taoiseach on individual constituent concerns such as an unsuccessful application for a Local Appointments Committee (LAC) advertised posts, particularly veterinary inspectors and dispensary doctors. The decision regarding such posts was the preserve of this independent body, based on principles of meritocracy and free from political interference. The immediacy of the response and the detailed and thorough investigations into the cases by civil servants, suggests that the Taoiseach's department took such complaints very seriously.[85]

In their separate studies on political activity in Donegal and Cork in the 1970s, Paul Sacks and Max Bax found that politicians commonly installed people in positions of powers in order to create a reciprocal network.[86] Nonetheless, politicians could accomplish very little and instead focused their time convincing constituents that they had delivered something for them, when this was in reality was not the case: 'Patronage is rarely solid and substantial and also entirely imaginary. In the grey area in between, the constituent receives some kind of marginal assistance giving him a tiny advantage or edge, on which he often sets exaggerated store'.[87] Yet the image of the harp and its strings which demands to be 'pulled', persisted in Irish political life. As this 1970 poem from the *Donegal Democrat* depicts, real or imaginary, the perception of patronage persevered:

> Without pull in Holy Ireland,
> Though you saint or scholar be,
> You don't stand a bloody earthly
> With selection Committees[88]

'Pulling strings' was regarded as necessary and positive because it overcame apparent inefficiencies within a rigid administration which unjustifiably delayed the building programme in the context of a housing shortage in what was an erratic building industry susceptible to market forces outside of its control. The legal framework was undeveloped to deal with the economic circumstances of the 1960s and 1970s. Inefficient local administration and red

tape were perceived as delaying planning permission in the context of a housing shortage during the biggest building boom in Irish history. Karl Jones, a
self-proclaimed 'unashamedly pro-property' property correspondent for the
Irish Times interviewed several property developers in 1969. They complained
that the planning and development department of Dublin Corporation 'hide
behind bureaucracy and detail . . . they never give a decision until the last day
of the second month after the application is lodged'.[89] An 'eminent planning
source' told Jones that Dublin Corporation's planning staff were overworked
and understaffed, struggling to administer the estimated sixty planning decisions a day- 'we're heading for a city of upwards of a million people. We planners are on a treadmill, and we're operating with a staff at least 20 per cent
under-strength. Qualified planners are desperately scarce, just when we need
them most'.[90]

The Planning Act, 1963 had in its gift considerable financial opportunities which justified circumventing excessive regulations within the system
through unorthodox political influence. To actors involved in such processes, this was not regarded as overtly corrupt but rather rational, judicious
and astute political practice in response to bureaucratic shortcomings. Such
imprudence operated within a context where legislation and regulations on
political ethics were outdated or absent.

Northern Ireland

Apart from lethargy within the political system, the rapidly escalating conflict
in Northern Ireland overshadowed public debate for most of the 1970s, nar-
rowing space on the political agenda for collective and concerted policy action
in other areas. In response to violent clashes in the Civil Rights marches and
growing fears that the Northern Administration would collapse, Taoiseach
Jack Lynch made a televised address to the nation on 13 August 1969. Five
murders the following day confirmed that what was to become known as 'The
Troubles' had begun in earnest.

Despite, or perhaps partly due to, the introduction of internment to
Northern Ireland in August 1971, 467 people lost their lives in 1972, including thirteen shot dead at Derry by the British army, in what became known as
'Bloody Sunday'. The British Embassy in Dublin was burned just a few days
later. October 1973 witnessed an extraordinary incident at Dublin's Mountjoy
Prison when a hijacked helicopter landed in the prison's exercise yard and
facilitated the escape of three IRA men including Séamus Twomey, Chief of
Staff of the IRA. The episode was indicative of the oscillating unpredictability of the Northern conflict on politics in the South. A song on the incident
by the Irish traditional rebel band, the Wolfe Tones, was number one in the
Irish charts for four weeks, indicating undercurrents of public condonation
towards the famous escape. The first verse of the 'Helicopter Song':

Up like a bird and high over the city
'Three men are missing' I heard the warder cry
'Sure it must have been a bird that flew into the prison
Or one of those new Ministers' said the warder from Mountjoy.

In April 1974, some five years after the conflict began; the sad distinction of the one-thousandth casualty of the Troubles was recorded. The Dublin and Monaghan bombings occurred the following month, May 1974. This attack by the Loyalist paramilitary group, the Ulster Volunteer Force (UVF), left thirty-three dead and almost three hundred injured, in what was the largest number of casualties in any single day since the beginning of the Troubles. The collapse of the Northern Ireland Executive was immediately followed by the reinstatement of Westminster direct rule.

Half of all the 3,722 deaths which occurred due to violent political conflict in the North occurred between 1971 and 1976.[91] Such was the extent of the perception of the threat against the state in 1974 that the Taoiseach, Liam Cosgrave, called for the establishment of a local security force, or citizens groups of vigilantes, in coordination with the Gardaí (Irish national police force) to ward against further Loyalist car bombs as had occurred in Dublin.[92] The 1974 state papers and newspaper headlines were dominated by the IRA kidnapping of Lord and Lady Donoughmore, Billy Fox's murder trial, and the crippling Dublin bus strikes. The North, rather than allegations of corruption in the absence of explicit evidence, was most definitely government priority. It was in this context that initial charges of political impropriety within the planning process were made against Burke.

Moreover, the long term consequence of the 1970 Arms Trial was the nurturing of a political culture counterproductive to ethical inquiry. Loyalty to the individual became ensconced at the expense of loyalty to the party. The emotive nature of the Arms Trial was of a similar disposition to the Locke Tribunal, in that it ensured a marked reluctance to go down this route of investigation again and enabled an avoidance of confrontational inquiry into political ethics.

The then Minister for Finance, Charles J. Haughey, was dismissed from government by Lynch and arrested later that same day in 1970. He was charged with conspiring 'with other persons unknown to import arms and ammunition illegally into the state' between 1 March and 24 April 1970. With Haughey's approval, the Minister for Defence, James (Jim) Gibbons, used public funds for the purchase of weapons for the 'relief of distress in Northern Ireland' or as understood by others, for Nationalist civilians to protect themselves following the outbreak of violence in Northern Ireland. It was alleged that Haughey gave Captain James Kelly, an Irish army officer, £10,000 to buy the following: 200 sub-machine guns, eighty-four light machine guns, fifty general purpose machine guns, fifty rifles, 200 grenades, 200 pistols and 250,000 rounds of ammunition.[93] The subsequent court case, or the Arms Trial, as it became known, began that September which found Haughey not-guilty on all counts of any conspiracy to import arms illegally. Haughey contended that by virtue of the fact that the Minister for Defence had approved the shipment; accordingly it was legal, though he was unaware that this involved a consignment of arms. The dismissal of two Ministers, Haughey and Neil Blaney, the Minister for Agriculture and Fisheries, shocked the Irish public. In May 1970, Kevin Boland, Minister for Local Government, and Paudge Brennan, Parliamentary Secretary, resigned in protest at Lynch's decision. Michael Moran, Minister for Justice, had resigned a few days before the Arms Trial broke.

Gibbons and Haughey gave contradictory evidence at the Arms Trial which openly pitted Minister against Minister.[94] With a deep fissure now running through Fianna Fáil, the dilemma this posed was not addressed within the party in any open way. It served merely to reinforce already adopted loyalties: Gibbons supporters were convinced of the truthfulness of his version of events just as Haughey's were that their man was the victim of a monstrous injustice. At the time, the backing of 'Honest' Jack Lynch swayed many in the party to believe Gibbons while a question-mark was placed over Haughey for the rest of his political career.[95]

The affair divided the party for two decades and placed Fianna Fáil in a permanent leadership crisis. The party were splintered by cabals. At a press conference immediately after the trial, Haughey's comments were regarded as a direct challenge to Lynch's authority as Taoiseach. Lynchite supporters responded by organising a guard of loyalty or 'welcoming party' on the tarmacadam of Dublin airport for Lynch upon his return in October 1970 from a United Nations meeting in New York. Most of the Fianna Fáil parliamentary party attended or as Kevin Boland put it: 'Everyone had to be there unless he or she had a doctor's cert.' More ominously, the period was distinguished by a new means of conducting politics.

Those who disagreed with Lynch, on any matter, were tagged as 'dissidents'. Anyone associated with Haughey was under suspicion by Lynchites. At all levels of the party, from Ministers to party members, the circumstances of the Arms Crisis demanded an out-and-out choice between the different factions within the party. Decision-making was centralised and brooding resentment promoted a culture of secrecy within all aspects of party business. Lynch surrounded himself with loyalists George Colley and Des O'Malley. This inner cabinet all shared the distinction of intensely disliking Haughey. Colley's repugnance may have been rooted in Haughey's inaugural election win of 1957 when Colley's father was ousted in the process.

Lynch focused on copperfastening his authority, a process the *Irish Times* journalist, Dick Walsh, described as the 'Jack Lynch Cultural Revolution' and that Lynch's actions had much more to do with enhancing his own power than with modernising the party.[96] *Hibernia* described the consequences of the Arms Crisis as 'a cancer eating at the vitals of the party spreading distrust and bitterness and reducing participation in party affairs . . . more and more decisions are handed down from front bench and fewer originate at the roots of the party'.[97] Brian Lenihan later recalled that 'one of the saddest things that I witnessed in my political life' was Haughey's prolonged stay in hospital when only he and one other government colleague visited the then Minister for Health. Lenihan noted that 'The bitterness from the Arms Trial ran deep'.[98]

Haughey appealed to the grassroots of Fianna Fáil. Following his removal from office, he consolidated and used every opportunity to test his personal support within the party throughout the early 1970s. Haughey's cult of personality grew in his wilderness years on the backbenches. He put this time to good use, travelling around the country meeting small Fianna Fáil branches in what became known as the 'rubber chicken' circuit, because of an Irish affection for chicken sandwiches, a staple diet of country political gatherings.

Fianna Fáil was ultimately a victim of its own success in their phenomenal 1977 general election victory which recorded a twenty seat majority. A high number of marginal seats created instability and backbench opinion made their voice heard. After the disastrous defeats of the two 1979 by-elections in Lynch's native Cork, the Haughey loyalists circulated a petition calling for Lynch to resign. In common with the clandestine nature of politics at the time, deputies were asked to sign without being allowed to see other names on the list. The 1979 Fianna Fáil leadership campaign between Haughey and Lynch's anointed successor, George Colley, firmly fixated the animosity between the different fractions. Colley, the then Tánaiste and Minister for Finance, placed a high premium on loyalty and his supporters made frantic efforts to persuade deputies to support him by threatening to cut off funds already allocated for local projects. Concerns were raised that the privacy of the ballot was not respected. George Colley's 1979 leadership bid, 'amateurish in the extreme', proved no match for Haughey's professional campaign and 'The Boss' was elected leader of Fianna Fáil.[99]

Just as the Irish Party was riven by the Parnellite and anti-Parnellite fractions, Fianna Fáil came to be divided between the pro and anti-Haugheyites. The cult of political leadership eclipsed other political issues. Kevin Boland, an embittered and vitriolic critic of Fianna Fáil, a party he left not long after the Arms Trial, described Fianna Fáil as 'totally dominated by the doctrine of leadership infallibility, and of unquestioning loyalty'.[100] Haughey assumed a larger than life presence in Irish public life. This commanding impression of Haughey was captured well by the acclaimed poet, Thomas Kinsella, in his poem 'Nightwalker'. Kinsella, a civil servant in the early 1960s, implicitly makes reference to 'Our new young minister':[101]

> It is himself! In silk hat, accoutred
> in stern jodhpurs The sonhusband
> coming in his power, climbing the dark
> to his mansion in the sky, to take his place
> in the influential circle, mounting to glory
> on his big white harse!

An examination of the activities of the Committee of Public Accounts (PAC) in the 1960s reveals the extraordinary reluctance to ask questions within political action in the context of Haughey's assent to power. The PAC is a standing committee of the legislature charged with scrutinising the annual reports of the Comptroller and Auditor General (C&AG). The C&AG examine and audit the expenditure of the executive, drawing attention to any instance of apparent misappropriation. In his detailed study of the PAC, Eunan O'Halpin highlights the disregard and indifference that members of the Oireachtas held the committee. From 1961 to 1980, the PAC spent on average of only eighteen hours a year on its activities. Many of its members did not take the committee seriously and its attendance records were dismal. In the case of one TD, his attendance amounted to just twenty-seven out of 172 meetings and was absent from the PAC for three years running. O'Halpin notes that the PAC transcripts demonstrate 'an obvious lack of preparation for and detailed knowledge of most of the matters under discussion.' Recurring failures about the basic rules of financial procedure are frequently explained away as 'merely technical breaches' while 'a great deal of public money is spent by bodies not accountable to the Dáil'.[102]

In one remarkable case, when Minister for Finance, Haughey borrowed 100 million deutschmarks in 1969 on behalf of the Irish exchequer and left it on deposit in Germany in anticipation of a revaluation of the Deutschmark. This duly happened and the money was converted back to the exchequer. Haughey subsequently introduced legislation in the Appropriation Act, 1969 which provided the Minister for Finance with explicit authority to exercise his 'reasonable judgement' for such transactions. The C&AG believed that Haughey's actions circumvented statutory procedures and expressed concern that such vast sums of money 'was completely under the personal control of the Minister and I think, constitutionally, that is wrong'.[103] The Department of Finance dismissed any suggestion that there was a danger of misappropriation arising from exchequer funded deposits being held abroad in the sole name of the Minister for Finance. O'Halpin notes that the members of the PAC 'seemed bemused by the dispute [between the C&AG and the Department of Finance]: neither in their questions to witnesses nor in the interim report did they get to grips with the issues of constitutionality, propriety and efficiency which arose'.[104]

Haughey's liberties with exchequer funds on the German markets in August 1969, occurred in the same month that public funds 'determined by the Minister for Finance would be made available from the Exchequer to provide aid for victims' in Northern Ireland.[105] After the failure of the Arms Trial to convict, a special PAC inquiry was ordered by Dáil Éireann in 1970 to examine the expenditure of public money known as 'grant-in-aid for Northern Ireland relief' to determine if it had been misappropriated. This inquiry effectively collapsed following a Supreme Court decision though an incomplete report found that some public money had been misappropriated.[106] The Supreme Court unanimous judgment of 24 June 1971, delivered by Chief Justice Cearbhall O Daláigh, had implications for future state inquiries. PAC inquiries were deprived of any effective powers in the event of a witness refusing to attend, to produce documents or to answer questions.

Haughey's testimony to the PAC on 2 March 1971 on the Northern Ireland special funds was reflective of general attitudes towards political responsibility, the closeted decision-making process and the administration of public funds: 'None of us ever envisaged that any such accountability would ever be required . . . nobody asked me questions and it went through without any discussion whatsoever'.[107] Moreover, Irish people suspicious of ethical breaches had nowhere to direct their disquiet. For instance, on a letter sent to the President by a member of the public expressing concern about standards in public life, a civil servant at Áras an Uachtaráin noted: 'there is no other dept to whom this letter should be referred. The letter has been acknowledged. In the circumstances I think that no further action is necessary.'[108]

Notes

1 National Industrial Economics Council, *Report of Physical Planning. Report No. 26* (Dublin Stationery Office, 1969), pp. 16–17.
2 F. Tobin, *The Best of Decades: Ireland in the 1960s* (Gill and Macmillan, 1984), p. 8.
3 Mr. Justice John Kenny, Report (of the) Committee on the Price of Building Land to the Minister for Local Government (Kenny Report), (Dublin Stationery Office, 1973), p. 4. Also: Gerry L'Estrange, Dáil Éireann, *Private Members' Business: Planning Appeals Bill, 1967. 233.* (13 March 1968).
4 R. Jennings, *Land Transactions and Prices in the Dublin Area 1974–1978* (An Foras Forbartha, 1980), pp. 7, 10.

5   G. Finn, 'Kenny report: drawing the lines for a new land war', *Business and Finance* (14 February 1974).

6   An Foras Forbartha, 1980. *Land transactions and Prices in the Dublin Area 1974–1978*, pp. 7, 10.

7   *Hibernia* (1 February 1974). p. 26.

8   F. McDonald, *Destruction of Dublin* (Gill and Macmillan, 1985), p. 95.

9   Oireachtas Select Committee on Building Land, *Report of the Joint Committee on Building Land* (Dublin Stationery Office, 5 June 1985), pp. 76–7.

10 P. Cullen, *With a Little Help from My Friends: Planning corruption in Ireland* (Gill and Macmillan, 2002), p. 22.

11 *Irish Press* (21 June 1974).

12 National Archives, Dublin, S 10553C, Taoiseach: Cabinet Minutes, 2005–06, p. 283.

13 'Taxman Socialism', *Business and Finance* (16 October 1975).

14 'Recommendation of Kenny report on land prices queried', *Irish Times* (8 February 1974).

15 *Kenny Report*, paragraph 110, p. 91.

16 National Archives, Dublin, 2005/3/43, President: Price of Building Land Kenny Report, 31 January 1974.

17 Oireachtas Select Committee on Building Land, *Report of the Joint Committee on Building Land*, p. 148.

18 *Blake v Attorney General* [1982] I.R. 117.

19 F. McDonald, *The Construction of Dublin* (Gandon Editions, 2000), p. 204.

20 Oireachtas Select Committee on Building Land, *Report of the Joint Committee on Building Land*, pp. 74, 76, 126, 146, 148.

21 Gerry L'Estrange, Dáil Éireann, *Private Members' Business: Planning Appeals Bill, 1967. 233.* (13 March 1968). Case Reference: 1967, No. 94-OP. Curiously, although L'Estrange was adamant about this case reference, perusal in the National Archives found this to be an incorrect reference and the file was not found.

22 National Archives, Dublin, 99/1/521, Taoiseach: Planning Appeals, 'Department of the Taoiseach Correspondence', 22, 28 March and 3 April 1968.

23 Dáil Éireann, *Private Members' Business: Planning Appeals Bill, 1967. 233.* (13 March 1968).

24 *Hibernia* (July 1968).

25 *Irish Press* (14 March 1968).

26 Kevin Boland, Gerry L'Estrange, Dáil Éireann, *Planning Appeals Bill, 1967: Second Stage (Resumed). 233.* (13 March 1968).

27 *Irish Independent* (14 March 1968).

28 *Hibernia* (12–25 June 1970).

29 Kevin Boland, Dáil Éireann, *Committee on Finance. Vote 26: Local Government (Resumed). 245.* (11 March 1970). Vote 26: Local Government (Resumed).

30 National Archives, Dublin, 2000/6/650, Taoiseach: Planning Appeals General (Planning Appeals Board), 'Letter to Minister for Local Government, Kevin Boland, to An Taoiseach, Jack Lynch', 21 July 1969.

31 National Archives, Dublin, 2003/16/393, Taoiseach: Planning Appeals General: Planning Appeals Board, 'Letter from Arthur Swift and Partners, to Minister for Local Government, Robert Molloy', 2 September 1971.

32 National Archives, Dublin, 2008/79/724 408/137/2 Pt IX, Foreign Affairs: ECE - Housing Sub Committee - Housing, Building and Planning 1971–75, 'Monograph prepared by the Department of Local Government in response to a questionnaire circulated by the UN Economic Commission for Europe', 23 June 1972.

33 'Michael Mullen: the dissident senator', *Hibernia* (16 May 1975).

34 National Archives, Dublin, 2003/16/393, Taoiseach: Planning Appeals General: Planning Appeals Board, 'Letters by Michael Mullen to Jack Lynch, Robert Molloy, Joseph Brennan and Patrick J. Lalor', 18 October, 29 November and 11 December 1972.

35 James Tully, Dáil Éireann, *Local Government (Roads and Motorways) Bill, 1973: Second Stage. 270. 1974. 270.* (7 February 1974).

36 *Sunday Independent,* June 1974.

37 National Archives, Dublin, 2005/7/488, Taoiseach: County councils etc corruption, 'Statement of G.I.S. at today's meeting', 25 July 1974.

38 D. Boucher, 'Jim Tully: Labour party's enigma', *Hibernia* (23 September 1974).

39 *Hibernia* (28 April 1972).

40 McDonald, *Destruction of Dublin*, pp. 197–8.

41 Robert Molloy, Dáil Éireann, *Questions. Oral Answers - Road Safety. 276.* (12 December 1974); *Local Government (Planning and Development) Bill, 1973: Committee Stage (Resumed). 282.* (25 June 1975); *Personal Explanation by Minister. 283.* (2 July 1975).

42 M. Mills, *Irish Press* (8 July 1974). p. 1.

43 31 July 1975. *Report of the Tribunal appointed by the Taoiseach on the 4th Day of July 1975* (Dublin Stationery Office, p. 6).

44 Liam Cosgrave, Dáil Éireann, *Financial Resolutions. Statement by Taoiseach and Motion re Tribunal of Inquiry. 283.* (3 July 1975).

45 J. Fagan, 'Tully and his alleged "business associate" meet for a celebration', *Irish Times* (12 July 1975), quoting James Tully.

46 Mr. Justice Seamus Henchy, *Report of the Tribunal appointed by the Taoiseach on 4 July 1975 (allegations against Minister for Local Government).* (Prl 4745, July 1975).

47 *Irish Press* (22 July 1975).

48 Dáil Committee on Procedure and Privileges, *Draft report from the Parliamentary Secretary to the Taoiseach.* (4 December 1975); Dáil Éireann, *Deputies' Allegations: Censure Motion. 228.* (25 February 1976).

49 Jack Lynch, Dáil Éireann, *Deputies' Allegations: Censure Motion. 228.* (25 February 1976).

50 'Editorial: judicial inquiry', *Irish Press* (4 July 1975).

51 L. Komito, 'Development plan rezoning: the political pressures', in J. Blackwell and F. Convery (eds), *Promise and Performance: Irish Environmental Policies Analysed* (Resource and Environmental Policy Centre, University College Dublin, 1983). pp. 293–302. www.ucd.ie/lkomito.

52　J. McAnthony and P. Murphy, 'Conflict of interests on county council', *Sunday Independent* (23 June 1974).

53　M. Mills, 'Cabinet to act on land deals', *Irish Press* (26 June 1974). p. 1.

54　Cullen, *With a Little Help from My Friends*, p. 16.

55　Mr. Justice Feargus M. Flood, *Tribunal of Inquiry into Certain Planning Matters and Payments: Second Interim Report* (Dublin Stationery Office, 2002), pp. 13, 15.

56　Michael Mills, 'Cabinet to act on land deals', *Irish Press* (26 June 1974). p. 1.

57　'Editorial: declaration of interests', *Irish Press* (26 June 1974).

58　*Hibernia* (13 September 1974).

59　National Archives, Dublin, 2005/7/223, Taoiseach: Local Government (Planning and Development) Act, 1976, 'Memorandum for Government prepared by the Minister for Local Government', 18 October 1974.

60　*Irish Independent* (21 October 1974).

61　National Archives, Dublin, 2005/7/520, Taoiseach: Members of Oireachtas and Members of Local Authority. Financial and other interests, 'Memorandum for the Government prepared by the Attorney General', June 1974.

62　Former Attorney General, Declan Costello, interview, (February 2006).

63　'Declan Costello: leader in the making?', *Hibernia* (31 October 1975).

64　Local Government Act, 2001, Section 175. Part 15, declarations of interest came into operation in 2003.

65　'Editorial: declaration of interests', *Irish Press* (26 June 1974).

66　McAnthony, interview.

67　Taoiseach, 20 December 1968. Cabinet Minutes. In: *Local Government Planning and Development Act, 1963*.

68　Dick Spring, Dáil Éireann, *Local Government (Planning and Development) Bill, 1983: Second Stage. 344.* (28 June 1983).

69　Ray Burke, Dáil Éireann, *Local Government (Planning and Development) Bill, 1983: Motion. 344.* (30 June 1983).

70　Ristéard Mulcahy, *A Family Memoir* (Aurelian Press, 1999) p. 268.

71　Éamon de Valera, 1943 St Patrick's Day speech in Michael Mays, *Nation States: The Cultures of Irish Nationalism* (Lexington Books: March 2007), p. 99.

72　B. Lenihan, *For the Record* (Blackwater Press, 1991), p. 61.

73　T. Ryle Dwyer, *Haughey's Forty Years of Controversy* (Mercier Press, 2005), p. 22.

74　M. McInerney, 'Election Machinery', *Nusight* (June 1969).

75　'Taca destroys political morale, says L'Estrange', *Irish Times* (5 March 1968).

76　K. Boland, *The Rise and Decline of Fianna Fáil* (Mercier Press, 1982), p. 98.

77　Michael McInerney, Election Machinery, *Nusight* (June 1969).

78　C. Keena, *The Ansbacher Conspiracy* (Gill and Macmillan, 2003); p. 46, quoting Lynch from December 1968.

79　Frank Dunlop, *Yes, Taoiseach.* (Penguin, 2004), p. 19.

80　Boland, *The Rise and Decline of Fianna Fáil*, p. 102.

81　J. C. Scott, 'Corruption, machine politics, and political change', *American Political Science Review*, 63:4 (December 1969), p. 1144.

82 Devlin Report, *Report of Public Services Organisation Review Group 1966–1969* (Dublin Stationery Office, 1969), p. 448.

83 Reproduced in *Hibernia* (5–18 December 1969).

84 'Michael Moran by our political correspondent', *Hibernia* (11–24 April 1969).

85 Byrne, 'Nineteenth and Twentieth Century Political Corruption in Ireland'.

86 Mart Bax, *Harpstrings and Confessions: Machine-Style Politics in the Irish Republic* (Van Gorcum, 1976).

87 P. Sacks, *Donegal Mafia: An Irish Political Machine* (Yale University Press, 1976), p. 93.

88 Willie McAffertys, 'If Buchanan comes true: a terrible indictment in Donegal land of problem and promise, special supplement to Fall 1970', p. 29, quoted in Sacks, *Donegal Mafia,* p. 84.

89 K. Jones, '60 planning decisions a day by corporation: overworked and over-staffed', *Irish Times* (21 March 1969). Also see F. McDonald, *Destruction of Dublin* (Gill and Macmillan, 1985), p. 218.

90 Jones, *Irish Times.*

91 D. McKittrick, S. Kelters, B. Feeney and C. Thornton, *Lost Lives: The Stories of the Men, Women and Children Who Died as a Result of the Northern Ireland Troubles* (Mainstream, 1999). This figure is calculated from 1966–98. John Patrick Scullion, West Belfast was the first to die on 11 June 1966. The list concludes in 2007. Also see Mc Donald, *Destruction of Dublin,* p. 218.

92 'S.F. men consider Cosgrave force', *Irish Times* (2 July 1974).

93 P. Bew, *Ireland: The Politics of Enmity, 1789–2006* (Oxford University Press, 2007), p. 500.

94 Ryle Dwyer, *Haughey's Forty Years of Controversy,* p. 62.

95 J. O'Brien, *The Arms Trial* (Gill and Macmillan, 2000).

96 J. Downey, *Lenihan: His Life and Loyalties* (New Island Books, 1998), pp. 97–8.

97 'A party of yes men?', *Hibernia* (16 July - 5 August 1971).

98 Lenihan, *For the Record,* p. 63.

99 *Ibid.,* p. 131.

100 Boland, *The Rise and Decline of Fianna Fáil,* p. 119.

101 T. Kinsella, *Nightwalker and Other Poems* (Dolmen Press, 1968).

102 E. O'Halpin, 'The Dáil Committee of Public Accounts, 1961–1980', *Administration,* 32:4 (1985), pp. 485–511.

103 Comptroller and Auditor General evidence to the PAC 1971 (Interim Report 1969–70 pp. 7–9.) in Halpin, 'The Dáil Committee of Public Accounts, 1961–1980', pp. 501–2.

104 Halpin, 'The Dáil Committee of Public Accounts, 1961–1980', p. 502.

105 *Irish Times* (26 August 1969); Seanad Éireann, *Private Business: Appropriation Bill, 1969 (Certified Money Bill): Second Stage. 67.* (2 December 1969); in the Matter of the Committee of Public Accounts of Dáil Éireann (Privilege and Procedure) Act, 1970, and in the Matter of the Courts (Supplemental Provisions) Act, 1961, and in the Matter of Pádraic Haughey High Court (1971. No. 58 SS.) p. 242.

106 Dáil Committee of Public Accounts, *Northern Ireland Relief Expenditure*

Final Report (13 July 1972), www.193.178.2.84/test/R/1972/en.toc.com. REPORT_13071972_0.html.

107 *Ibid.*, Haughey testimony to Committee of Public Accounts, (2 March 1971).

108 National Archives, Dublin, 2001/6/12, Taoiseach: Ministers, Parliamentary Secretaries and Ministers of States, 'Letter from member of the public to President', 3 December 1968.

5

Golden circles: 1980s–1990s

Introduction

The Fianna Fáil / Progressive Democrat 1989–92 Coalition was a double-edged sword for Irish public life. For the first time since independence, the 1989 general election arithmetic meant that Dáil Éireann failed in its duty to elect a Taoiseach. A deadlocked Dáil forced Fianna Fáil to abandon its core principle of single party government and enter into coalition with its bitter political enemies, the Progressive Democrats (PDs). Charles J. Haughey's pragmatism complemented his ambitious appetite for power. The PDs now had two senior cabinet positions, including the poisoned chalice at the Department of Industry and Commerce.[1] This decision altered the dynamics of Irish electoral politics permanently.

Fianna Fáil were no longer held hostage by an out-dated and unrealistic principle of single party majority government. However, the shrewd consent by Fianna Fáil to coalition government ensured that despite its declining vote it could hang on to power for much longer than it would otherwise have done.[2] The unintended and long-term consequences of Fianna Fáil's decision to enter into coalition ultimately included the establishment of a Tribunal of Inquiry into allegations of political impropriety in 1991 and the collapse of the 1992 and 1994 coalition governments.

Suspicions of favouritism earned credibility following a series of media revelations concerning the probity of state sponsored bodies and commercial businesses. These included the circumstances surrounding the allocation of a licence to Century Radio; the privatisation of Irish Sugar; the sale of land involving Telecom Éireann; the Beef Tribunal; issues surrounding Celtic Helicopters; the provision of passports to foreign nationals; allegations of bribery within the planning process; the installation of an Electricity Supply Board (ESB) wind generator on Haughey's island home of Inishvickillane; and the sale of land at Carysfort College in Blackrock to a friend of Haughey's. This period was distinct from previous scandals because it marked the possibility of the gravest form of corruption, that of state capture within political decision-making.

Greencore

The privatisation of the state owned enterprise, Irish Sugar / Siúicre Éireann (now Greencore), was hit by scandal in 1991. In September of that year, the *Sunday Independent* alleged that the managing director of Greencore plc, Chris Comerford, was involved in a complex financial scheme from which he benefited personally at the state's expense. Reporter Sam Smyth's article outlined how four executives from Irish Sugar formed a company called Gladebrook in 1989 which bought a 49 per cent minority holding in a company called Sugar Distributors Holdings Limited for IR£3.25 million. The four Irish Sugar executives put up no money of their own to pay for Sugar Distributors and incurred no personal borrowings because they secured a loan from a subsidiary of Sugar Distributors which was authorised by two of the said executives. Irish Sugar owned the remaining 51 per cent majority holding.

The Minister for Industry and Commerce, Des O'Malley, appointed Maurice Curran under the Companies Act 1990 to look into payments by Greencore to Comerford. Curran concluded that Comerford had committed a breach of company law because he failed to disclose his interest in Sugar Distributors, a rival private company.[3] Curran's report led to the appointment of High Court inspectors, Aidan Barry and Ciaran Foley, to investigate further. The inquiry cost IR£1.1 million and lasted six months. Of the twenty-four conclusions contained in the March 1992 report, the Inspectors failed to come to any finding on whether the transactions by the four Irish Sugar executives and the managing director, were improper, unethical, or illegal- the central issue which caused the inquiry in the first instance.

The Fine Gael spokesperson on Finance, Michael Noonan, was circumspect about the merits of the report. 'I know it is a widely held view among the professions in this country that dog does not eat dog. I believe, however, that the taxpayer who paid IR£1.1 million for this report was at least entitled to one bite . . . the inspectors in effect funked the issue.'[4] Nonetheless, the report was highly critical of the managing director. 'Mr. Comerford was given and corruptly accepted monies. The purpose for making the payments was to circumvent public policy and may constitute the taking of bribes in consideration for remaining in his employment at Siúicre Éireann at a time when he was managing director of that company.' The inspectors also declared that Comerford was 'an unfit person to be a director of a company in the state'.[5]

In essence, public servants employed by the state used state money to buy a subsidiary of a semi-state company which they then sold back to the state at an inflated price. Private actors, at the expense of the public, unilaterally negotiated the buying and selling of their minority stake in a subsidiary of Irish Sugar before the actual privatisation, thereby making a sizeable sum in the process. Within eleven months, the Irish Sugar executives had made a financial killing of over IR£7 million. The public duties and private interests of the public servants of a state owned company collided.

Comerford said the report was 'subjective and unfair'.[6] A Garda inquiry into the affair took two years and the Minister for Finance, Bertie Ahern, confirmed that a file would be sent to the DPP. The leader of the Labour party, Dick Spring, expressed the hope that 'the white collar criminals uncovered by this report, together with their ill-gotten gains, are brought to book'.[7] There were no prosecutions. Comerford resigned on a generous IR£70,000 per year pension, though did not receive the agreed one million golden handshake, not because of any government intervention, but due to shareholder unrest.

The Supreme Court overturned the High Court in 2001 and ruled that one of the former Irish Sugar executives was liable for income tax on just IR£250,000 of the IR£1.8 million paid for shares in Gladebrook. Apart from the limited tax revenue on the questionable dividend granted to the Irish Sugar executives at the expense of the state, Comerford and the other Irish Sugar executives were exempt from any punishment for their actions. The Irish exchequer would later foot a €7 million fine imposed by the European Commission due, to a large degree, to decisions taken by the same executives which were found to have seriously breached EU competition rules.[8] As it happens, because Irish Sugar deliberately ignored EU competition laws, their monopoly on the Irish Sugar market meant that Irish Sugar prices were 'among the highest in the Community, to the detriment of both industrial and final consumers in Ireland'.[9] The only consequences were to the public purse and the private pocket of the Irish citizen.

Telecom Éireann

The Greencore affair was only two weeks old when the Telecom Éireann controversy emerged. Both scandals involved substantial financial killings made at the expense of the taxpayer and shared similar suggestions of clandestine golden circles between politics and business. The purchase of the former Johnston Mooney & O'Brien bakery site by the semi-state telephone company, Telecom Éireann, in 1990 unleashed a chain of financial and political events which ultimately led to the motion of no confidence in the leadership of then Taoiseach Charles Haughey.

United Property Holdings Limited (UPH), a property investment company linked to financier Dermot Desmond's NCB stockbrokers, paid a liquidator IR£4 million in 1988 for a 5.5 acre site in Ballsbridge. Previously occupied by the Johnston Mooney & O'Brien bakery, this prime Dublin site was then promptly sold to a property consortium which included an offshore company, Freezone Investments Ltd, registered in the Isle of Man. Less than two years later in early 1990, Telecom Éireann paid IR£9.4 million for this same site on which it planned to build a new headquarters. The price was paid despite a IR£6 million valuation by the State Valuation Office. Remarkably, in this short period of under two years, the site had more than doubled in value from IR£4 million to IR£9.4 million – at a time when commercial property prices generally were falling. Telecom later abandoned its Ballsbridge head-quarters plans and, in 1993, developers Sheelin MacSharry bought the site for IR£5.6 million, some IR£3.8 million less than the price paid by the semi-state body only three years earlier. Today, the Herbert Park Hotel forms part of the infamous site.

In February 1990, the *Irish Independent* alleged that the government appointed chair of Telecom, Dr. Michael Smurfit, had a beneficial financial interest in the sale of the Ballsbridge site. Smurfit's solicitor immediately extracted a front page public apology that Smurfit 'does not have, and never had an interest, directly or indirectly, in the site'. These conflict of interest allegations resurfaced in the *Irish Times* over a year later in September 1991. The newspaper alleged that Smurfit did in fact have a 10 per cent investment in UPH. Haughey's response on the *This Week* RTÉ radio programme was emphatic. Certain people should 'step aside' he said and added that 'without making any implication, the slightest scintilla of suggestion that there is any-thing wrong. . . but if that advice and that suggestion of mine is not taken up, then I'll have to see'. Smurfit subsequently resigned as Telecom chair.

O'Malley commissioned the High Court Inspector, John Glackin, to inquire into the allegations. The Glackin report, published in 1993, fully exon-erated Smurfit: 'Dr. Smurfit gave evidence and has submitted that he had no knowledge of this use of his name and did not consent to it. I accept this evi-dence.'[10] Glackin found that although Smurfit was an investor in UPH, there was no evidence to substantiate the claim that he was aware of the internal affairs of UPH when Telecom purchased the Ballsbridge site. Glackin also concluded that Smurfit was not aware of Desmond's interest in the site when he discussed the Telecom purchase with Desmond.[11]

The report did find that although he gave sworn evidence to the con-trary, Desmond controlled the offshore companies involved in the resale of the Ballsbridge site, including Freezone, and was 'financially interested in them'.[12] (Freezone's refit of Haughey's yacht was investigated by the Moriarty Tribunal, see chapter 6). Glackin also found that proper procedures on valu-ation and cost comparisons were not followed. The findings were, and con-tinue to be, strongly contested by Desmond, including in the High Court. But despite this, Glackin's verdict, as stated in the report, still stands.

Before the Telecom scandal, the phrase 'golden circle' in the *Irish Times* archives denoted sunflowers and airline business travellers clubs. The expres-sion only entered the political lexicon around October 1991, during a motion of confidence in Taoiseach Charles Haughey, the second during that phase of his career.[13] From then on, the term was used with increasing regularity to describe the belief that an elite had access to insider information which was making them very rich. The week before the October 1991 no confidence motion, the political editor of the *Irish Times*, Dick Walsh, wrote: 'many have also been struck of late by the way in which the same names keep cropping up in different surrounds; as if running the state in its different guises was a family affair'.[14] The minutiae of the personal and business relationships within these two scandals of the early 1990s, served to illustrate the layered connections between business and politics at this time. Large tracts of public perception believed that Haughey was the common denominator among the different personalities listed concerning the Greencore and Telecom Éireann scandals.

An MRBI opinion poll conducted for an RTÉ television's *Today Tonight* programme in November 1991 cemented this view. A total of 89 per cent agreed that 'there is a Golden Circle of people in Ireland who are using power to make money for themselves.' Some 81 per cent agreed that the people in this Golden Circle were made up in equal measure of business people and politicians. Some 76 per cent thought the scandals were 'part and parcel' of the Irish economic system rather than one-off events. A total of 83 per cent thought that the Greencore, Telecom and Goodman (see next section) scandals were merely 'the tip of the iceberg', while 84 per cent said business people involved in corrupt dealings and fraud get off more lightly than other criminals.[15] The suspicions of those polled proved to be startlingly accurate.

The Beef Tribunal 1991–94: context

The Beef Tribunal of Inquiry (1991–94) was perhaps the most extraordinary political episode in modern Irish history. For the first time since the 1940s, the reciprocal relationship between politics and vested interests was placed under intense political, public, judicial and media scrutiny. This was a period when questions about political corruption, golden circles and the integrity of public officials were raised in a meaningful way.

The Tribunal examined allegations that the 1987–89 Fianna Fáil government abused its power for the benefit of a private company, Goodman International, the beef business owned and controlled by Larry Goodman. In particular, the Tribunal investigated irregularities within the beef process industry and accusations of special dispensations given by the then Minister for Industry and Commerce, Albert Reynolds, to Goodman International. Although it found Reynolds not guilty of wrongdoing, it did illustrate a pattern of large campaign contributions by the company to Fianna Fáil.

The Tribunal findings failed in the eyes of many observers to articulate conclusions suggested by the evidence, conclusions that would have damaged severely the political credibility of Albert Reynolds. It underlined the systematic character of questionable ethical peccadilloes and the way in which such actions were facilitated and condoned at the uppermost echelons of power for decades. The bitter and deeply personal political fallout and the focus on the cost of conducting the Tribunal obscured the more salient aspects of the inquiry. Much of what emerged during its hearings and its conclusions remain as contested today by some interested parties and vested interests as they were in 1994. Simply put, the post-Beef Tribunal period marked a distinctly different phase to modern Irish politics.

Pat O'Malley, a Dublin West TD for the PDs, was not to know that his April 1989 parliamentary question on the export credit insurance scheme for the beef industry would have the consequences that it did. In his response, the Minister for Industry and Commerce, Ray Burke, outlined how his department had underwritten almost IR£120 million in export credit insurance for Goodman International beef exports to Iraq from 1987 to 1988 which amounted to virtually a third of available credit on Irish exports being put at the disposal of just one company.[16]

Larry Goodman owned and controlled Goodman International, a group of 74 companies including Anglo Irish Beef Processors (AIBP).[17] The beef industry was Ireland's largest indigenous enterprise in the 1980s and 1990s and Goodman was Ireland's biggest beef baron. By the mid 1980s, Goodman had a turnover the equivalent of about 4 per cent of Ireland's gross nation product and was Europe's largest beef exporter.

Born in 1938, the low-profile businessman has been described as 'ruthless, shrewd and highly controlled. In private life he is shy, sensitive and said to be very charitable'. A non-drinker and non-smoker, Goodman followed his father into the cattle business when he left school. Adverse to publicity and impatient with bureaucracy, the Louth native was known to be 'intensely proud of the Goodman name' and 'very concerned that in the meat business, often regarded as a slightly underground business, no impropriety should taint it'.[18] An absence of ostentatious aside, the Castlebellingham beef baron was Ireland's J. R. Ewing, the fictional oil baron from *Dallas*, the American television series popular in the 1980s. Goodman's knack of buying meat factories on their last legs, at a time when Ireland was in deep recession, and transforming them into profitable enterprises, made him in the eyes of many, a figure to be admired. Part of the allure came from the fact that his extraordinary business empire stretched from Ardee, a small town in Co Louth, across the rest of Ireland and into England, Scotland and Jersey.

Much of Goodman's success can be attributed to the creation by the European Economic Community (EEC, as the European Union then was) of a protected and entirely fictitious market for his beef products. The export credit insurance and intervention scheme, under which the Community guarantee to buy produce irrespective of market deterrants, were two separate protectionist mechanisms created by the Community artificially to keep European beef prices high. Export credit insurance sought to reduce the EEC surplus beef mountain by encouraging the European beef industry to export beyond the member states of the Community. Beef sold in alternative markets, such as Iraq, would receive guaranteed minimum EEC prices. In other words, the EEC underwrote all beef exports to ensure EEC high prices, even in those countries where the market price was considerably less. The intervention scheme also sought to tackle the thorny issue of European beef overproduction. When beef prices fell below the EEC price, the EEC intervened to buy large quantities of beef, pay meat factories to de-bone it, carve it into different cuts, freeze it, and store it in vast refrigerated warehouses. The resultant European Beef Mountain, as it and other stores of overproduced agricultural products were likewise known, was managed through a twin track policy of export and storage and operated by the Departments of Industry and Commerce and of Agriculture. The export credit insurance and intervention was funded through European Union subsidies and the Irish exchequer.

The Irish beef industry was quick to take advantage of this artificial market nirvana. In 1973, the year that Ireland joined the EEC, the Department of Agriculture bought 2,383 tonnes of Irish beef into intervention. This increased tenfold to 262,000 tonnes by 1992. In that same period, the EEC paid out over IR£4 billion to buy 2 million tonnes of Irish beef into intervention.[19] Larry Goodman was the major beneficiary of this lucrative scheme.

In July 1989 the Fianna Fáil / PD Coalition entered office, in the circumstances outlined in the chapter introduction. Des O'Malley, leader of the PDs, became Minister for Industry and Commerce. Political fate now intervened and the poacher had become the gamekeeper. O'Malley had been a noted critic of the EEC protectionist measures when in opposition, decrying the 'ministerial intervention' which had facilitated the 'serious abuse' of export credit insurance, thus causing substantial 'fraud on the State and the taxpayer.'[20] Within two months of this dramatic Dáil intervention, O'Malley was the Minister with direct responsibility for the administration of this scheme and announced to the Dáil: 'Incredibly, my view does not change'.[21] His first priority as Minister was to review the operation of export credit insurance. Providence intervened. The Department of Industry and Commerce finalised the explosive 'Fisher Report' days before O'Malley became Minister. It blew the political lid on the export credit insurance scheme by showing that 38 per cent of beef covered for Iraq on behalf of the Goodman group between 1987 and 1988, had been sourced outside the state.[22] Something clearly was afoot if more beef was claimed to be exported from Ireland than was actually in Ireland. O'Malley cancelled the export credit insurance to the company. Goodman immediately responded by initiating a legal action against the state for IR£50 million.[23]

There the matter might have ended but for an ITV television *World in Action* programme two years later in May 1991. Produced by Irish woman Susan O'Keefe, the programme, called *Where's the Beef?*, alleged fraud within the export credit insurance scheme, tax evasion through under-the-counter payments to Goodman staff, complicity by the regulatory authorities and inappropriate political influence by Goodman. The programme featured a forthright contribution by Patrick McGuinness, a former Goodman account-ant who had left the company and immigrated to Canada. McGuinness's assertion that: 'There was also a feeling that we were invincible, that we had the right connections at the right places, that could basically control any investigation that would be put in place' was politically explosive, though later rejected by the tribunal.[24]

The day after the documentary, Haughey stonewalled the Opposition and refused to respond to questions on the grounds that 'This matter has been before this House on a number of occasions. I have answered questions at great length with regard to it.'[25] The Dáil record notes thirty-two separate 'interruptions' in what was a fractious but short debate. The Minister for Agriculture and Food, Michael O'Kennedy, moved a motion the next day reaffirming the Dáil's 'confidence in the regulatory and control procedures for the Irish meat industry'. O'Kennedy noted that five Ministers had answered ninety parliamentary questions since 1989 on the matter.[26]

Ironically, the next item of Dáil business, after O'Kennedy's motion had passed, was a private members Bill sponsored by Brendan Howlin on behalf of the opposition Labour party. Howlin's proposed Ethics in Government and Public Office Bill, which sought to regulate political funding and introduce legislation governing conflicts of interest, did not pass. 'The Government do not accept that there is any pressing need for legislation in this area',[27] Albert Reynolds told the Dáil. Reynolds' relationship with Goodman would subse-quently become a focus of public attention.

A couple of weeks later *Where's the Beef?* aired which caused conster-nation within the Fianna Fáil and PD Coalition. Haughey acquiesced to opposition demands for a Tribunal only after O'Malley issued an ultimatum to Haughey – establish an inquiry into the beef industry or the PDs would leave the minority coalition.[28] A Tribunal of Inquiry into the Beef Processing Industry to investigate the allegations was appointed by the Fianna Fáil / PD government on 31 May 1991 and issued its 904 page report four years later on 29 July 1994. At a cost of approximately IR£320 million, with 475 witnesses and 452 books of transcripts, the Tribunal was the subject of seven different applications for judicial review to the High Court and Supreme Court. Mr. Justice Liam Hamilton, President of the High Court, was the sole member of the Tribunal which sat at the upper yard of Dublin Castle. The Tribunal's book of allegations contained 143 claims that ensured, as noted by Hamilton in the report, the terms of reference 'were unusually broad in their drafting and scope'.[29] This may have accounted for the fact that, notwithstanding its exhaustive detail, the report failed to reach clear conclusions even though evidence of systematic malpractice, fraud and tax evasion by the Goodman companies was uncovered. Moreover, despite evidence of 'reckless if not biased decision-making at ministerial level, the tribunal's eventual report was an unwieldy and opaque document'.[30]

Liam Hamilton was born in Mitchelstown, Co. Cork, in 1923. He became a Senior Counsel in 1968 and acted for Neil Blaney TD, Fianna Fáil, when Blaney was charged, together with Haughey and others, in the District Court with conspiracy to import arms in 1970. Hamilton was the product of a system in which politics still plays a major role in judicial preferment. An unsuccessful local elections candidate for the Labour party in 1967, Hamilton was appointed as the legal adviser for Labour when the party entered government with Fine Gael in 1973. He was appointed to the High Court in 1974, presiding judge of the Special Criminal Court in 1976 and President of the High Court in 1985 on the nomination of the Labour party, which was back in government.

When he died in 2000, his *Irish Times* obituary described his Beef Tribunal report as 'characteristically diffuse, setting out great wads of evidence but drawing few definite conclusions and allocating less blame than many felt appropriate'.[31] The newspaper also noted that the timing of Hamilton's deliberation on the report was 'especially invidious as the judge was reporting on the behaviour of members of his government who would have to decide who should succeed Thomas Finlay as Chief Justice'. Hamilton was nominated as Chief Justice two months later in September 1994. Mr. Justice John MacMenamin, a contemporary, has described his characteristics as a judge as that where, 'He considered the practical and fair result of a case of far greater importance than that a judgment be used as a means of expanding legal principles . . . He had no regard for 'intellectualism' of any description . . . Critics sometimes suggested that his desire to remain popular was a weakness as well as a strength.'[32]

The Beef Tribunal: the five political decisions

The following section outlines the five key political decisions made between 1987–89 by the Minister for Industry and Commerce, Albert Reynolds, the Minister for Finance, Ray MacSharry and the Fianna Fáil government which formed the heart of the Tribunal's investigations. These include: (1) Decision to reintroduce cover; (2) Decision to increase export credit insurance ceilings; (3) Decision to limit cover to AIBP and Hibernia; (4) Decision to amend Section 84 of the Finance Act; and (5) Decision to drop Industrial

Development Authority clause. The framework in which these five decisions were made were two matters relating to tax evasion by Goodman companies and the investigation by the Revenue collecting government agency, Customs and Excise, into the beef industry.

Tax evasion

Patrick McGuinness, the former Goodman accountant and whistleblower who features in the ITV documentary, testified about under-the-counter payments by his former company to its employees. The state's biggest bank, Allied Irish Bank (AIB), routinely cashed bogus cheques for the Goodman meat plants in Cahir, Bagenalstown, Dublin and Dundalk. This suggested that the fraud was more systematic than a series of local failures.

'A deliberate policy in the Goodman Group of companies to evade payments of Income Tax', according to the Beef Tribunal report, cost the Irish exchequer IR£8.6 million.[33] Although the Revenue Commissioners made about ninety inspections at Goodman plants between 1985 and 1990, it failed to uncover these practices.[34] Revenue began an investigation into Goodman International shortly after the Tribunal was established and reached a tax settlement in 1994. Nevertheless, the company were exempt from interest and penalties because of the introduction of the Waiver of Certain Tax Interest and Penalties Act 1993. The Tribunal noted that 'were it not for the provision of this Act, the statutory rate of interest [1.25 per cent per month on underpayments] would have applied'.

Haughey's resignation as Taoiseach in February 1992 conferred Albert Reynolds the honour of becoming premier. Reynolds' tenure as Taoiseach in the acrimonious Fianna Fáil / PD Coalition was short-lived and the November 1992 election heralded a new Fianna Fáil / Labour Coalition which governed until December 1994.

The timing of the 1993 tax amnesty was fortuitous for the Goodman group and also prevented the prosecution of those behind the tax scam. The Memorandum for Government on the tax amnesty noted that the Minister for Finance, Bertie Ahern, the Labour party ministers, the Attorney General, two out of three independent experts and the Revenue Commissioners were against the introduction of the amnesty. Nonetheless, the then Taoiseach, Albert Reynolds, persevered, arguing that the amnesty would bring large amounts of 'hot money' back into the state where it would benefit the economy.[35] The Labour party maintained that Ahern led them to believe he would oppose the proposal at cabinet level, as a result of which they saw no need to raise strong objections in advance, but in the event Ahern failed to do so.[36] In his memoir, *Albert Reynolds: My Autobiography*, published in 2009, Reynolds says that he and Ahern both spoke in favour of it. Ahern on the other hand claims in his memoir, *Bertie Ahern: The Autobiography*, also published in

2009, that he had made an agreement with Labour when he spoke against the proposal at cabinet, Labour failed to back him up.

Fintan O'Toole, the *Irish Times* columnist who observed and criticised the workings of the Beef Tribunal more than any other commentator, noted on its tenth anniversary that: 'The bank [AIB] was at best turning a blind eye to a massive tax fraud, at worst colluding in organised crime . . . Yet, when all of this was revealed, there was no Garda investigation, no Revenue scrutiny, and little media interest. The idea that it might have ethical and legal responsibilities simply didn't arise.'[37] To all intents and purposes, there were no consequences.

Customs investigation

An investigation by the Revenue collecting government agency, Customs and Excise, in 1986–87, found that AIBP employees used bogus stamps and deliberately over-declared the weight of export beef. These fraudulent practices at the Goodman controlled AIBP meat plants in Waterford and Ballymun totalled a massive 137,418 tonnes of over-declared beef. The effect of which 'resulted in substantial payments to AIBP in excess of their proper entitlement under the APS [Aids to Private Storage] Scheme and Export Refund Scheme'.[38] The Department of Agriculture determined that the 'financial consequences of the misdeclaration' amounted to IR£1,084,866.[39]

On 5 March 1987, Goodman met James O'Mahony, Secretary at the Department of Agriculture, to discuss the implications of this investigation and asked O'Mahony for 'an opportunity to meet officials to see whether [reputational] damage to his company abroad could be prevented'.[40] O'Mahony told Goodman in January 1988 that a penalty on his company in the 'possible range of IR£1 million to IR£10 million' would be discussed with the European Commission. As the excess claims made by AIBP under the EEC schemes constituted a fraud, the department were obliged to report the matter to the Commission and seek their opinion on the level of sanction that should be imposed.

By coincidence, after receiving this news, Goodman met Haughey in private the following day at his home.[41] Haughey later told the Dáil that he had no '*official* knowledge' (emphasis added) about the fine. In an attempt to utterly wash his hands of the matter, Haughey made it clear in that same Dáil debate, that it was 'not the duty of the Government to bring these irregularities to the attention of the Commission or the Court of Auditors or anybody else. It is the duty of the official side, the administration of the Department of Agriculture'.[42] Ultimately, the option chosen was the lower one, saving Goodman over IR£8 million.[43] O'Mahony subsequently became a non-executive director of a Goodman controlled public company, Food Industries, following his retirement from public service in January 1988.

The Department of Agriculture referred the Customs report to the Fraud Squad thirteen months after irregularities in Waterford had been discovered. The extraordinary lack of urgency in the investigation meant that the Waterford allegations were actually never examined by the Fraud Squad. The Department of Agriculture never asked why.

At the Tribunal, Goodman and other senior AIBP management denied any knowledge of, or involvement in, the irregularities and attributed responsibility to a subcontractor, Eamon Mackle of Daltina Traders Ltd. Mackle blamed Joe Devlin, a checker employed by him. Devlin, now living outside Ireland, refused to attend the Tribunal. Ray Watson was also an employee of Mackle and was responsible for checking the weights and the preparation of the production sheets in the boning hall. According to Watson, his office 'was occupied by a number of girls . . . responsible for the documentation'. He testified to the Tribunal that although he 'merely suggested the alteration of such weights', the two junior office workers took it upon themselves to make the necessary alteration and produced documents showing 'what they considered to be the expected percentage'. In its report, the Tribunal felt it necessary to publicly name the two junior female office workers. The Tribunal went as far to suggest that 'AIBP can and should be criticised for failing to exercise any reasonable degree of supervision over the activities of their staff'.[44]

The episode revealed how quick and easy it was to attribute blame down along the ranks. A complicated and elaborate scheme, where some 137,418 metric tonnes of beef was fraudulently over-declared in one year alone, at an unknown potential cost of millions to the exchequer, was, it appeared, due to the shortcomings of two junior female office workers who had absolutely nothing to gain from taking such an astonishing initiative.

Ultimately, two other low-ranking Goodman executives were sentenced in a subsequent court case to suspended prison terms for their parts in a conspiracy to defraud the Minister for Agriculture by misappropriating intervention beef. Mr. Justice Michael Moriarty made it clear in his sentencing that they were neither the instigators nor the beneficiaries of the crime. Like the girls in Watson's office, they did not make the slightest personal financial gain from any of the dishonest dealings.

Decision to reintroduce export credit insurance cover
Michael Noonan, Minister for Industry and Commerce (1982–87) withdrew all state granted export credit insurance to Irish companies operating in Iraq in 1986. The department had advised Noonan that Saddam Hussein's Iraq, at war with Iran and with ominous trouble in Kuwait on the horizon, would default and effectively leave the Irish taxpayer liable for outstanding export credit insurance. Apart from the military instability, Iraq was deteriorating financially and payments were already overdue. Noonan told the Tribunal

that 'all our colleagues in Europe were going off-cover and that Iraq was too high a risk'.[45]

Albert Reynolds was appointed as Minister for Industry and Commerce on 11 March 1987 and almost immediately overturned Noonan's decision. On 9 April 1987, Goodman spoke to Reynolds 'about the desirability of and necessity for the provision of export credit insurance'. Four days later, Reynolds directed his department to adopt a 'pragmatic approach' and reinstate Iraqi cover.

Reynolds' decision was staunchly against the explicit advice of civil servants from three separate Departments, including Industry and Commerce, Agriculture and Finance. Senior civil servants were already concerned about an outstanding IR£30 million liability for export credit insurance to Iraq. The Beef Tribunal report catalogued the chorus of objections to Reynolds' decision. This included the bluntly worded memo to Reynolds from the Assistant Secretary at the Department of Industry: 'Because it is obviously wrong in terms of a balance in the total exposure, I would be opposed to seeking extended cover for Iraq.' In a memo to the Minister for Finance, officials at the Department of Finance wrote 'the Exchequer would be at a loss for a considerable sum possible of the order of IR£120m . . . In essence, the Minister for Industry and Commerce's proposals are too much of a gamble with the Exchequers resources'. Department of Finance officials also sent a memo to their Minister, Ray MacSharry, outlining six specific reasons why 'the officials recommend strongly that you oppose the Minister for Industry and commerce's proposals'.[46]

The Insurance Cooperation of Ireland (ICI), the body which administered the export credit scheme, was direct in its opposition to the Reynolds decision. Frank Fee, the ICI company secretary, wrote in a memo: 'We strongly recommend that no further credit be offered to Iraq under the export credit scheme.' In his evidence to the Tribunal, Fee stated: 'our view was that there was a fifty-fifty chance of claims. At that particular time, there was a very tight budgetary situation in Ireland. You had hospitals being closed for two or three million pounds'.[47]

The nature of the discussions at cabinet and the extent of debate on these matters never received proper scrutiny. In the 1992 decision of the *Attorney General v Sole Member of the Tribunal of Inquiry into the Beef Processing Industry*, it held that it was unconstitutional for the Tribunal to inquire into the content and details of discussions at meetings of the government.[48] The Attorney General, acting, as the Supreme Court made clear, with at least the tacit approval of 1992–94 Albert Reynolds government, sought and obtained a ruling that the factors which influenced the government in reaching its decision to reintroduce cover and increase the export credit ceilings (see decision on pp. 116–18) were the beneficiary of absolute confidentiality in all circumstances.

Apart from ignoring the clear-cut advice from the ICI and senior civil servants across three departments, the Reynolds decision was all the more curious because the context was completely at odds with the reality of the situation. The company which was to benefit directly from state support was at the same time the subject of a serious criminal investigation by the state. In September 1987, Mr. Justice Michael Moriarty found a senior AIBP executive, Nobby Quinn, guilty of attempting to defraud the Department of Agriculture and Food having been found in possession of forged South African customs stamps. Quinn was fined IR£8,000 and given a two year suspended jail sentence. He later became chief executive of the Goodman controlled Classic Meats company.

And on what basis had Albert Reynolds made his decision? 'I imput into the decision-making process my experience and my knowledge of international markets', Reynolds told the tribunal. This, Fintan O'Toole believed, amounted to Reynolds using 'his experience of selling dogfood to supermarkets in Europe to measure the risks of losing public money in Iraq'.[49] Reynolds' decision would prove to be an expensive one for the Irish taxpayer. By November 1987, within ten months of becoming Minister, he had allocated IR£69.42 million to AIBP and IR£28.42 million to Hibernia Meats in export insurance cover to Iraq, courtesy of the Irish taxpayer.

Hibernia Meats was established in 1977 by Oliver Murphy who was now its chief executive. The refrain of the country and western star, Merle Haggard, 'The worst is yet to come' was a familiar one in the many dancehalls owned by Reynolds the length and breadth of Ireland in the 1980s. In this tone, AIBP and Hibernia subsequently requested more and more cover.

Decision to increase export credit insurance ceilings

Irish legislation limited export credit to Iraq at IR£70 million. 'You can take it from me that every single opportunity both Mr. Goodman or Mr. Britton [Goodman senior executive], or both, took every opportunity to look for the maximum amount of export credit', Reynolds told the Beef Tribunal. 'They believed they were entitled to it all and that nobody else was entitled to any and they made no bones about it', Reynolds said.

Reynolds made the decision to more than double the export credit ceiling to IR£150 million in September 1987. The opinion expressed by the Department of Finance that 'the arguments against any increase in the present effective ceiling for Iraq as overwhelming'[50] were simply ignored. Reynolds never gave any reason why he chose consistently to disregard official advice. Yet, AIBP and Hibernia believed that this new IR£150 million ceiling was not sufficient for their needs and they requested further cover.

In October 1988, Reynolds informed his department that the cabinet had decided the previous June that under the provisions of the Insurance (Export

Guarantees) Act, 1988, the Iraqi export credit insurance ceiling was to be increased to IR£270 million. More ominously, further increases 'should be at the discretion of the Minister for Industry and Commerce'. The provision of such insurance 'should be managed in the national interest so as to avoid damaging competition between exporters'. The Tribunal noted that the effect of these instructions were such that export credit insurance cover in Iraq would only be granted to existing exporters in the market, i.e. AIBP and Hibernia.[51] Although this staggering decision which granted the Minister astonishing discretionary powers in determining the allocation of a valuable state resource was made in June, Reynolds only informed his officials on 21 October. This was the same day, coincidently, as the department officials were scheduled to meet with AIBP executives, who, as it happened, requested additional cover. The department officials requested Reynolds to seek clarification from the cabinet as the decision had not been recorded in the normal manner. The Irish exchequer was fortunate that clarification was sought.

Reynolds told the Tribunal that he had intended to allocate a further credit of IR£80 million to AIBP, IR£20 million to Hibernia and IR£20 million to smaller non-beef exporters to Iraq. In addition, there would be a 'roll over' of the allocations already made to these companies. If the Reynolds decision had been implemented, AIBP's cover would have increased to IR£139.42 million and Hibernia's to IR£48.52 million. This would have amounted to an IR£187.94 million liability to the Irish exchequer. In November 1988, one month later, Reynolds was appointed to the Department of Finance and Ray Burke became the new Minister for Industry and Commerce. These allocations were not honoured and no further allocations were made.

The Tribunal heard evidence from Haughey, Reynolds and Goodman about the timeline of the decision-making process which granted these increases. In untypical candidness, Hamilton said: 'It is difficult to understand how nobody recollects the circumstances under which notice was given to the Minister for Industry and Commerce that the Goodman group would be making an application for export credit insurance in respect of the largest contract for the export of beef ever negotiated by an exporter within the state.'[52]

Reynolds' decisions to repeatedly increase the export credit insurance ceilings were utterly bewildering because more cattle were listed as being exported from Ireland than there were cattle. In fact, a cabinet colleague of Reynolds, the Minister for Food, Joe Walsh, made public comments at that time, as did the wider farming community, about the ever declining cattle numbers.[53] Reynolds failed to ask basic questions. Hamilton noted in his report that if Reynolds had asked the basic questions about the 'benefits to the Irish economy arising from such exports' he would have discovered if they were 'illusory rather than real'. It later emerged that close to half of the AIBP beef shipments to Iraq, covered on foot of Reynolds' decision, were the product of the United Kingdom. To put it another way, Reynolds had put $60 million of Irish taxpayers money at risk in order to support the export of UK beef from 1987 to 1989.[54] Instead of stimulating the Irish export trade, the Irish taxpayer was underwriting aspects of the British and Northern Irish economies. It was a bewildering decision devoid of basic logic.

Decision to limit cover to AIBP and Hibernia

Goodman complained to Reynolds in November 1987 that rival Irish meat companies were 'causing him difficulties in Iraq by cutting prices'.[55] Reynolds believed that such competition 'was against, in my view, the national interest and the national economic interest to allow foreign consumers the benefits of lower prices'.[56] Subsequent decisions by Reynolds meant that AIBP and Hibernia were the only two companies which benefited from cover for beef exports to Iraq. Applications by non-Goodman controlled beef companies Agra Trading Ltd, Taher Meats Ltd and Halal were refused and an earlier offer to Halal was withdrawn.[57]

The decisions made by Reynolds, the Beef Tribunal found, 'undoubtedly favoured AIBPI and Hibernia Meats . . . and placed other beef exporters at a considerable disadvantage'.[58] This was as far as the Tribunal was prepared to go in its criticisms of the Minister. Instead, the Tribunal accepted that Reynolds made the decisions he did on the basis of the 'conception of the requirements of the national interest and there is no evidence to suggest that his decisions were in any way based on improper motives, either political or personal'.[59]

Unfortunately for Ireland, Reynolds' opaque definition of the national interest, as his rationale for his decision-making process, was one subjectively interpreted by him as the narrow economic interests of the beef industry. In this case, the conception of a national interest was merely what the Minister said the national interest was. As it transpired, the national interest included the Irish exchequer underwriting beef which was not Irish. Reynolds was censured mildly in the report. Hamilton suggested that 'before exposing the state to a potential liability of well in excess of IR£100 million, a more detailed investigation or analysis of the benefits to the economy of such decisions . . . should have been carried out'.[60]

Decision to amend Section 84 of the Finance Act

Section 84 of the Finance Act was a complex tax relief mechanism which originated from a loophole in the Corporation Tax Act, 1976 and then amended by Section 41 of the Finance Act 1984. In essence, it enabled a bank to share its tax saving with a company by lending to that same company at a reduced interest rate. As a consequence of this creative accounting arrangement between companies and banks, companies were the beneficiary of cheap loans and banks were able to avoid their overall tax obligations. The exchequer was destined to lose in this scenario because the tax income it was entitled to was diverted between Goodman International and the banks. The National Economic and Social Council (NESC), a body established with the specific purpose to advise the government on the 'efficient development of the economy', highlighted how Section 84 had 'become extremely expensive to operate, together accounting for IR£170 million of tax revenue forgone in 1985'. From 1987 to 1988, AIBP drew down on IR£106 million from this scheme.[61]

AIBP executives met Reynolds on several occasions and sent the Department of Finance a proposed addition on the Finance Act which would enable the company to take fuller advantage of Section 84 funding. This was agreed and secured with the active assistance of the government agency charged with promoting inward investment, the Irish Development Authority (IDA), in clearing the way with the Revenue Commissioners. The Beef Tribunal report quantified that this amendment to the Act amounted to an estimated IR£30 million in cheap loans given to Goodman International. Thus, 'By the end of the year, Larry Goodman not only had the state subventing his purchase of the beef for Iraq, he also had it guaranteeing payment for it.'[62]

Decision to drop Industrial Development Authority clause
Shortly after Fianna Fáil came to government in 1987, a five-year IDA development plan for Goodman International was announced in great fanfare by the new Taoiseach, Charles Haughey. In return for cheap, exchequer-subsidised loans, at rates of interest in some cases as low as 1 per cent, Goodman promised to stimulate the Irish beef industry by providing more employment. By the end of that year, Goodman International had drawn down IR£81 million but none of the promised development had taken place.[63]

The IDA agreed to the deal on the condition of a performance clause, guaranteeing that money would be paid to the company only after it had created jobs. Goodman met Haughey and sought the removal of this clause and told the Tribunal under oath that he was not 'going along asking for Mr Haughey to remove it' [the clause], but 'if Mr Haughey chose to do something about it, that was great'.[64] Several days after this meeting, Haughey's departmental secretary and close adviser, Pádraig Ó hUiginn, made enquiries to the IDA about the clause. Ó hUiginn believed that Goodman 'had a reasonable case' and advised Haughey accordingly in a note sent into a cabinet meeting. The cabinet amended the clause to the effect that the plan was to be 'interpreted' that the company would use its 'best endeavours' to fulfil job targets.[65]

This cabinet decision was not recorded on the usual pink slip used for cabinet decisions. The decision amounted to direct political interference with the IDA. In his Beef Tribunal report, Hamilton made it clear that the government had no power to force the IDA to drop the performance clause from the agreement. 'There is no doubt whatsoever that the government . . . wrongfully and in excess of its powers . . . directed the Authority [IDA] to remove the performance clause from the grant agreement . . . and that this direction was made either at the instigation of the then Taoiseach or the Secretary to his Department.' Haughey's government, according to the Beef Tribunal report, acted illegally.

The Beef Tribunal: a re-evaluation

Tribunal findings on Reynolds' decisions

'In any other Western democracy, a Prime Minister so resoundingly con-victed of incapacity . . . would have the grace to resign' O'Malley thundered during the Dáil debate on the Tribunal's findings. Reynolds, now Taoiseach, bluntly rejected such assertions. 'My integrity has been vindicated', Reynolds asserted . . . 'I would remind the House that the findings make clear that not a single allegation against me has been sustained, so I have every legitimate entitlement to state that I have been cleared by the report.'[66]

The Beef Tribunal absolutely rejected the allegation that 'blatant' politi-cal favouritism occurred: 'There is no evidence to suggest that either the Taoiseach [Haughey] at the time or the Minister for Industry [Reynolds] at the time was personally close to Mr. Goodman or that Mr. Goodman had any political associations with either of them or that party that they represented.'[67] This allegation, Reynolds told the Dáil on five occasions, was 'clearly, emphat-ically, and unambiguously' wrong.[68] Instead, the Tribunal asserted that the Reynolds' decisions were motivated by a political belief of the national inter-est rather than for any individual personal gain.

The Tribunal unfortunately never defined what it understood the national interest to mean. Any analysis of the five decisions to: (1) reintroduce export insurance to Iraq; (2) to increase the export insurance ceilings; (3) to limit cover to AIBP and Hibernia; (4) to amend Section 84 of the Finance Act; and (5) to drop IDA performance clause, would certainly suggest that Goodman International benefited, more than any other Irish beef company, from these specific decisions made, or strongly influenced by, Reynolds and the Fianna Fáil cabinet. Favouritism, defined as the unfair favouring of one person or group at the expense of another, was undoubtedly a recurring theme. The Tribunal lacked the courage to condemn political favouritism and instead condoned political decisions described as in the national interest.

Beef industry donations to Fianna Fáil

The Tribunal was aware that Fianna Fáil received substantial donations, yet Hamilton decided not to 'refer further to this matter or report thereon as the tribunal is satisfied that such contributions were normal contributions made to political parties and did not in any way affect or relate to the matters being inquired into by the tribunal'.[69] This rather surprising decision had remarkable outcomes. The relationship between the Irish beef industry and Fianna Fáil was not fully disclosed. Reynolds swore four times to the Tribunal on oath that Goodman was 'never ever a guest of mine at a Cáirde Fáil dinner'[70] (the annual Fianna Fáil President's dinner). However, an *Irish Independent* article on 12 December 1987 reported that 'Albert and Kathleen cut quite a dash on the dance floor. And they had Ireland's most important 'Baron' as their guest. Larry Goodman, beef baron extraordinaire even ventured onto the floor for a couple of twirls.'

If political donations were regarded as 'normal' and beyond the scope of Tribunal inquiry, then any implicit conflict of interest between the donor and the recipient was by inference beside the point. In the first two weeks of February 1987, Goodman International donated to Fianna Fáil IR£50,000; Master Meats gave IR£30,000 and Hibernia IR£25,000. This amounted to over 10 per cent of the IR£1 million that Fianna Fáil party headquarters spent on the 1987 national election campaign, held on 17 February.[71]

Oliver Murphy, chief executive of Hibernia, donated a further IR£25,000 to Fianna Fáil in November 1987, shortly after the crucial meeting of 4 September when Reynolds, then Taoiseach and Minister for Industry and Commerce, allocated export credit insurance cover to Murphy's company. Murphy gave the money to the Minister for Finance, Ray MacSharry, who was also the Fianna Fáil joint honorary treasurer. MacSharry's son worked for Murphy. Such donations, it transpired, 'sometimes coincided with key moments in the process of conferring large public benefits on these companies'.[72] Three days before the 1989 election, Murphy donated a further IR£25,000 to Fianna Fáil.[73]

Goodman donated IR£50,000 to Fianna Fáil on the day of the 1989 general election. The former financial controller of the party, Seán Fleming, testified in 2000 to the Moriarty Tribunal that Haughey directed that the donation was recorded as 'anonymous'. Goodman donated a further IR£25,000 to Fianna Fáil two days later. At the Moriarty Tribunal, Goodman described this as a contribution to Brian Lenihan's medical expenses. Yet the cheque was made out to the 'Fianna Fáil (Party Leadership Fund)' which was directly controlled by Haughey, and seems not to have been used for Lenihan's benefit. Murphy also confirmed to the Moriarty Tribunal that he contributed IR£5,000 to the Lenihan fund in 1989.[74] The Tánaiste Brian Lenihan travelled to the Mayo clinic in America that year for a liver transplant, estimated to cost anything from $125,000–$250,000. Faced with the prospect of selling the family home to meet these medical expenses, a group of friends 'made a contribution' because 'they felt that Brian had worked for the country for virtually his whole life, and that he should be able to receive the best treatment'.[75]

The Flood / Mahon Tribunal of Inquiry into Certain Planning Matters and Payments in December 2004, established that Goodman advanced about IR£600,000 to the then-influential Fianna Fáil politician Liam Lawlor and his companies in the late 1980s, of which only IR£350,000 was subsequently repaid.[76] These transactions, which related to the purchase of lands in West Dublin, went through offshore companies. Lawlor had a long association with Goodman. An Oireachtas committee on state sponsored bodies discovered in 1988 that a Goodman company called Food Industries, had an interest in buying the Irish Sugar Company, a semi-state body likely to be privatised. Controversy arose when it transpired that Lawlor, Haughey's appointee as chair of the committee, was also a director of Goodman's Food Industries. Pat O'Malley TD, a PD and member of the committee, objected to this obvious conflict of interest in a parliamentary question to the Minister for Agriculture, Michael O'Kennedy, in November 1988.

Lawlor also had access to detailed financial information about Irish Sugar. His power to defend the public interest was compromised because of his conflict of interest between the private company seeking to acquire the same semi-state company he was obliged as committee chair to protect. Lawlor's position was untenable and he resigned in January 1989. In his testimony to the Beef Tribunal, he disclosed that in the month before he resigned, he was in Baghdad making representations to Iraqi officials on behalf of Goodman International.

Paschal Phelan, founder of Master Meats and personal friend of Reynolds, contributed IR£10,000 to Fianna Fáil and personally donated a further £30,000 in advance of the 1989 election.[77] Reynolds gave a commitment for IR£10 million worth of cover to Master Meats that year, even though the company had no track record in Iraq. In sworn evidence to the Tribunal, Phelan said it was 'entirely a coincidence' that he was present in Reynolds' office the day the government decided to raise the export limits for export insurance cover to Iraq.[78] This valuable cover was transferred to Hibernia. Goodman publicly denied that he was the beneficial owner of Master Meats. He told the 1989 inquiry by the Fair Trade Commission (FTC) that 'I didn't own it. I never owned it and I can put my hand on my heart and say that.'[79] A subsequent High Court action in 2002 established that this was not the case. Goodman accepted that 'for the purpose of the proceedings', as he described it, that he did in fact own and control Master Meats.[80]

However, Professor Paddy Lyons who conducted the inquiry for the FTC subsequently told officials in the Department of Enterprise, Trade and Employment that his inquiry was not a 'Sworn Inquiry' and that Goodman was guaranteed that his evidence was 'given in confidence'.[81] This distinction meant that Goodman had not committed perjury though he had seriously misrepresented a government minister and the FTC. This was a breach of the mergers and monopolies legislation and raised questions whether Goodman had perverted the course of justice by advancing misrepresentations before the Beef Tribunal and thereby benefiting from a Tribunal Cost Order in his favour. Hamilton granted Goodman his legal costs which were taxed by the High Court Taxing Master, James Flynn, appointed by the Fianna Fáil / PD Coalition on 21 October 1992. Flynn awarded Goodman IR£6.7 million in 1996 for costs incurred in the Beef Tribunal. Ms. Justice Mary Laffoy of the High Court later reduced the lawyers' bill by IR£1.2 million and threw out costs awarded to a public relations firm and to caterers.

In all, Fianna Fáil received IR£297,000 from beef processing firms from 1987–91. Fine Gael was also the beneficiary of large donations from the beef industry, totalling some IR£138,550 in that same period. This included IR£63,000 from Goodman, IR£20,000 from Agra Trading, IR£17,500 from Kepak, IR£16,500 from Hibernia Meats, IR£10,000 from Master Meats and IR£11,550 from five other separate beef companies.[82] Although Fine Gael strenuously criticised Fianna Fáil's close relationship with Ireland's beef barons, this did not prevent a party trustee, Sean Murray with close links to the Irish Export Board, make three informal funding approaches to Goodman between August 1994 and July 1995.[83] The timing was both extraordinary and hypocritical. The first solicitation was made just days after the Beef Tribunal report was published in July. The last approach occurred some six months after the new Fine Gael / Labour / Democratic Left Coalition entered office.

The PDs too were not immune from financial contributions from the beef industry. Goodman's IR£20,000 gift made him the party's largest donor in advance of the 1987 election.[84] Murphy's Hibernia Meats gave IR£5,000 in 1987. However Murphy's IR£10,000 donation, sent after the Fianna Fáil / PD coalition was formed in July 1989, was returned the following day.[85] Master Meats donated IR£5,500 in 1989.

Paschal Phelan's Master Meat Packers donated IR£85,500 to Irish political parties between 1987 and 1989. Larry Goodman's Goodman International was by far the biggest benefactor to Irish democracy, donating IR£208,000 in that same period. Oliver Murphy's Hibernia Meats contributed IR£103,000 to Fianna Fáil, Fine Gael and the PDs.[86] Murphy denied anything improper in all this. His barrister, Colm Allen, expressed it this way: 'Any slur or nasty, snide, whingeing, carping suggestion that there was anything involved in these contributions, other than the legitimate support of the legitimate democratic process, is beneath contempt.'[87]

In his evidence to the Tribunal, the general secretary of Fianna Fáil, Pat Farrell, said that these figures only applied to contributions made to party headquarters. He said it would be 'extremely difficult' to ascertain how much money was collected at local level and given to individual TDs. Discrepancies between figures provided by Fianna Fáil and Master Meats during the course of the Tribunal suggested that not all contributions by beef companies are reflected in the various parties' official records.[88]

Financial costs to the state

The complexity of the schemes and an absence of unambiguous information make it difficult to establish the absolute total cost to the exchequer of the Beef Tribunal scandal. Nonetheless, Goodman International did benefit enormously from an abuse of the export credit insurance scheme. In 2009, the Department of Environment confirmed that 'significant defaulting' and 'considerable payments' were made on foot of this protectionist mechanism. In total, the state paid out €67 million, of which €27 million was never recovered. Much of this was due to the Iraqi beef debts, though the Iraqi government has since paid €7.8 million which represents a fraction of the original beef debt, plus interest.[89]

It was disconcerting that these liberties with the public finances were taken at a time when Ireland was undergoing a severe recession. In 1987, Irish GDP per person was 69 per cent of the EU average, unemployment was at 17 per cent and government debt was 112 per cent of GDP. The Fianna Fáil Minister for Finance, Ray MacSharry, earned the nickname Mac-the-Knife for his severe cuts to the public finances. Funding for school capital projects, for instance, fell 50 per cent from IR£40 million in 1987 to around IR£20 million a year from 1988 to 1992. The long-term consequences of halving the commitment to educational infrastructure came home to roost in the 1990s and 2000s. The existing stock of schools is in a state of extensive disrepair and has been unable to meet demographic challenges.[90] The unrecovered €27 million the state was owed from the export credit insurance scheme would have kept the school capital programme intact for one full year.

With regard to the theft of intervention beef within the AIBP factories, the Beef Tribunal report outlined that 'there is no doubt whatsoever but that it was the deliberate practice and policy of the management of AIBP in the state engaged in intervention operations'[91] to give the EU the minimum legal amount of meat from each carcass and to keep the rest. An unpublished report by the European Commission anti-fraud agency, Unite de Coordination de la Lutte Anti-Fraude (UCLAF) found major and sustained abuse of Common Agricultural Policy funds within the Irish beef intervention scheme. It imposed an IR£68 million (€86.3 million) fine on Ireland in 1996 because of the Department of Agriculture's failure to take reasonable steps to recover sums lost to fraudulent claims. This was the largest amount ever demanded from Ireland by the EU.[92] In an out-of-court settlement in 2003, the AIBP group agreed to pay the Department of Agriculture and Food €3.81 million in compensation for intervention beef irregularities.[93] This decision was approved by the Fianna Fáil / PD cabinet on the basis of advice given by counsel and the Attorney General.

Ultimately, the Irish state was at a loss of some €83 million. The state did not bring those responsible for these crimes to justice or get the public's money back.[94] Instead, Des O'Malley noted, 'The taxpayer meekly paid up. The beneficiaries of the fraud paid nothing. They kept their ill-gotten gains. The taxpayer committed no crime. He was simply a convenient and compliant whipping boy.'[95] Goodman remains Europe's largest beef processor and the annual turnover of his companies is estimated at more than a €1 billion.[96]

Failure of accountability

The Tribunal got answers to questions that the Dáil could not. Ray Burke's evidence to the Tribunal demonstrated the cavalier and indifferent manner that the government regarded parliamentary procedure: 'If the other side don't ask the right questions, they don't get the right answers. And it's not for me to lead them as to where they figure they want to go. And if they ask a question, then the question is answered precisely, and that is what would have happened.'[97]

The tone of Burke's response was reflected in evidence to the Tribunal where a senior civil servant congratulated a subordinate for confusing a TD who had asked questions about beef export numbers. For his part, Hamilton claimed in the Beef Tribunal report that 'if the questions that were asked in the Dáil were answered in the way they are answered here, there would be no necessity for this inquiry and an awful lot of money and time would have been saved'. Parliamentary question as a method of accountability was found to be wholly inadequate. The Tribunal exposed the shortcomings of the legislature as a body responsible for the oversight of the executive. The Dáil was regarded as inconvenient, irrelevant and at times wilfully misled. A culture of secrecy, deliberate obstruction, abuse of official discretion and arrogant authority had thoroughly permeated the structures of government and the upper echelons of the civil service.

Civil Service

The Beef Tribunal report did not have any observations on the limited recourse or alternative avenues senior civil servants had when they profoundly objected to decisions and unusual practices carried out by their ministers. Neither was it made clear that where such avenues existed, why civil servants choose not to avail of them. For over a decade, inspectors at the Department of Agriculture investigated meat factories and concluded that abuses within the beef intervention scheme were 'widespread'. Nothing was done. There were no prosecutions, no long-term withdrawal of licences, no consequences.[98] Chapter 25 of the report, titled *Agricultural Recommendations*, was an utterly inadequate response to such failings. It recommended a two week intensive course, training videos, refresher courses and new instruction manuals for Department of Agriculture staff tasked with implementing the intervention scheme.

As it transpired, censure by the Beef Tribunal was not an impediment to career success. The Secretary of the Department of Agriculture, John Malone, reported to the Dáil Public Accounts Committee in 1999 that those civil servants involved in the falsifying or altering of documents on beef intervention had since been promoted or recommended for promotion.[99] Indeed, two key public servants subsequently became high ranking executives for the same meat companies they previously had the responsibility for regulating on behalf of the state. James O'Mahony, Secretary to the Department of Agriculture (1977–88), awarded a medal by Taoiseach Jack Lynch in 1973 for public service during the EEC negotiations, became a non-executive director of a Goodman controlled public company, Food Industries, subsequent to his retirement.

As Secretary to the Department of Industry, Trade, Commerce and Tourism[100] between 1984 and 1991, John Donlon's duties included oversight of the IDA and the Irish Export Board. Donlon became a director of Hibernia Meats in 1992. Ethical guidelines on perceived conflicts of interest and post-employment restrictions for senior civil servants radically changed in the late 1990s to prevent state gamekeepers becoming poachers for private interests.

Pádraig O hUiginn, Ireland's most senior civil servant as Secretary to the Department of the Taoiseach (1982–93) was known as Haughey's 'favourite' public servant. O hUiginn was chair of the National Economic and Social Council, which produced the influential Strategy for National Development 1986–90. This IR£260 million investment strategy would have benefited Goodman Companies IR£170 million under a package of loans from section 84 funding and IR£60 million in assistance from the IDA and the EEC. The ambitious plan never got off the ground. 'Although no government agency made any direct investment in the plan, the Goodman Companies did draw down a considerable portion of Section 84 loan finance.'[101]

O hUiginn became a director of Esat Telecom in 1995, a telephone company then owned by businessman Denis O'Brien. He was said to have 'contacts throughout the system at every level'.[102] O hUiginn was regarded as a valuable board member at Esat, especially when the company complained to the EU in 1996 over interconnection charges charged by Eircom, then Telecom Éireann. The practice of senior civil servants taking up employment with private industry immediately after their retirement in the public sector was not an unusual occurrence. The regular turnover of those charged with maintaining the state's interests to work in companies whose private interests overlapped was nevertheless disconcerting.

Whistleblowers

As in previous incidents throughout the history of the Irish state, those who made the allegations were vilified and accused of being against the state itself. Even those who represented the state were maligned. Des O'Malley reflected: 'I was fiercely attacked by the state, even though I was a minister [Minister for Industry and Commerce] during the tribunal . . . I know now what a whistleblower feels like, with no law or public institution to protect him.'[103] In particular, politicians Pat O'Malley, Pat Rabbitte, Tomas Mac Giolla, Barry Desmond, Dick Spring and John Bruton had their motives impugned: far from seeking to uphold the wider public interest, their critics dismissed them merely as self-interested maverick dissenters' intent on damaging political opponents.

The beef industry accounted for 34 per cent of Ireland's agricultural output – sufficient ammunition for Charles Haughey to accuse Barry Desmond TD, Labour, of national 'sabotage'[104] when the first allegations about Goodman were aired. In similar vein, Goodman was 'disgusted that people of this left-wing calibre and element can do such things to our company, to our country. They are anti-private industry, anti-success, anti-effort, anti-bloody well everything'. Brian Britton, Goodman senior executive, described those who made the allegations as 'fringe TDs looking for cheap publicity' who had been guilty of an 'abuse of public office'.[105] Bertie Ahern also evoked the national interest to criticise the PDs who 'at a time of international economic instability' were 'prepared to halt progress and stability . . . They do not care about the damage this will do to the country, to Ireland's image overseas, or about the negative effect it will have on our currency'.[106] Michael Smith, Minister for Environment, attributed such negativity to naked envy and quoted to that effect from Shakespeare's *Othello* in his Dáil contribution on the Beef Tribunal report: 'O! beware, my Lord, of jealousy; It is the green-ey'd monster which doth mock.'[107] In that same Dáil debate, Michael McDowell TD, PDs, accurately summed up this mindset as one where:

> those who seek and insist on accountability in our democracy are nothing but trouble-makers, begrudgers, character assassins, opponents of enterprise, sabo-teurs of agriculture, economic vandals or anti-employment . . . We are not anti-enterprise or anti-job creation, we just want accountability. We do not moralise, but we seek democratic accountability for the way in which power is exercised in our society.[108]

The key whistleblowers whose actions contributed largely to establishing the Tribunal lived outside the state. As Diarmuid Ferriter acutely observed, 'it often took outsiders to unfold the truth'.[109] Patrick McGuinness, the former senior Goodman accountant and key witness for the Tribunal, was living in Canada and went to considerable pains to ensure that his legal representation were from outside the Irish state. Hamilton noted that 'counsel on behalf of the Goodman group of companies took the unusual course of making submission regarding the credibility of Mr McGuinness' who they described as a 'sub-class of witness'.[110] The only consequences incurred by Goodman were by way of fines imposed not by the Irish government, but the European Commission.

The producer for the World in Action documentary, Susan O'Keeffe, was employed by ITV and living in Britain. In 1995 she was prosecuted for refusing to name her sources to the Beef Tribunal. O'Keefe was subsequently acquitted and was the only person, apart from two low-ranking Goodman employees, brought before the courts as a result of the Tribunal.

The PD Senator, John Dardis, told the Seanad that 'people in the Irish media were intimidated from publishing it [information alleged in the World in Action programme] by writs slapped on them by the Goodman organisa-tion'.[111] In February 1989, some two years prior to the ITV documentary, two RTÉ journalists ran a television story stating that an unnamed Irish company 'has become involved in a meat fraud investigation' in Iraq and that 'the Government's export credit insurance facilities may have been abused' by using it to cover non-Irish meat. Pádraig Mannion, presenter of the *Daily Farm Diary* and Joe Murray, boss of all agricultural programming on TV and radio, were brought before an internal RTÉ disciplinary hearing and found guilty of negligence and incompetence, thereby damaging their professional reputations.

Solicitors for Goodman's AIBP alleged that the report had libelled the com-pany. RTÉ subsequently broadcast an apology to an unnamed company on all news programmes, accepting that the *Daily Farm Diary* story was entirely without foundation. In his book on the history of RTÉ, John Horgan wrote, 'It is difficult to recall any apology issued by any media organisation in relation to any other matter which was more extensive, detailed and specific.'[112] For those involved in journalism, the apology was an implicit message: 'engage in investigative journalism at the likely risk of imprisonment and public censure. A culture of silence radiated at every corner of the state'.[113]

Political costs of the tribunal

The Beef Tribunal report amplified underlying tensions within the Fianna Fáil / PD 1989-92 Coalition and the Fianna Fáil / Labour 1993-94 Coalition and ultimately served to topple both governments. O'Malley stood over the allega-tions he had made in opposition about Reynolds and told the Tribunal that the now Taoiseach had displayed favouritism towards Goodman International and Hibernia Meats when Minister for Industry. O'Malley told the Tribunal that Reynolds' decisions were 'wrong . . . grossly unwise, reckless and foolish'. Reynolds sharply responded that O'Malley's evidence was 'reckless, irresponsible and dishonest'. Reynolds makes the distinction in his memoirs that O'Malley's claim that IR£172 million, owed by the exchequer to Goodman's companies under the export credit insurance scheme, was only a potential liability, not an actual liability.

In truth, the Tribunal only served to air the deeply held personal bitterness between Reynolds and O'Malley, which was simmering beneath the surface since the establishment of the PDs in 1985. As far as Reynolds was concerned 'the PDs were determined to bring down the coalition. They were just waiting for the right excuse. The Beef Tribunal, which was to bedevil me throughout my years as Taoiseach, gave the PDs the opportunity'.[114] Incidentally, this was the only reference Reynolds made to the Beef Tribunal in his 320 page auto-biography. Parties in government operated as hostile opponents rather than coalition partners.[115] It was unprecedented that a serving minister would pub-licly criticise his departmental predecessor, now Taoiseach, in a public forum like a Tribunal. This destabilised an already fragile coalition and precipitated a general election in 1992.

The Fianna Fáil / Labour 1993–94 Coalition was ultimately the Tribunal's second political casualty. The Department of Agriculture released the Beef Tribunal report on the Friday evening of the 1994 August bank holiday weekend to Fianna Fáil advisers. Just before midnight and the newspaper deadline, Sean Duignan, government press secretary, told the *Irish Times* journalist, Jackie Gallagher, that Reynolds had been 'totally vindicated' by the Report.[116] Duignan pointed to Tribunal extracts which found that Reynolds was legally entitled to make the decisions he did and acted in good faith. Coalition partners, the Labour party, had not yet even received the report. Fergus Finlay, chief adviser to the Labour Tánaiste, Dick Spring, was adamant that doors leading to the Taoiseach's private offices were deliberately locked, thus preventing the Labour party gaining access to the Reynolds and the report.[117]

This orchestrated series of events ensured a partisan interpretation of the Beef Tribunal report from the outset. The upshot over the subsequent row between the Labour Tánaiste, Dick Spring, and Reynolds 'was that the media concentrated on the internal government row over the leak rather than on the report itself'.[118] This all served to distract from the intricacies of the allega-tions which were 'swept aside by the hype over the political implications of his [Reynolds] 'putting it up to' O'Malley'. Instead, Duignan noted, the affair came down simply to 'a duel to the death between the most powerful politi-cians in the land'.[119] Moreover, the timing of the Dáil debate, the same day as the announcement of an IRA ceasefire, further diverted attention from the core allegations.

Reynolds' contentious decision to appoint Attorney General Harry Whelehan to the Presidency of the High Court that October further distracted due attention to the report. Whelehan's office had been the subject of severe criticism as a result of delays in the extradition to Northern Ireland of a priest who was suspected of child abuse. The refusal by Reynolds to back down on the appointment ultimately led to Whelehan's resignation and the fall of the government. The Whelehan incident confirmed what had already been implied in the Beef Tribunal report and the Golden Circle scandals. A culture of embedded secrecy rejected principles of openness, accountability and transparency within government in order to avoid scandal.

This perception of unorthodox privilege gained credence following 1994 media reports which outlined how Reynolds' family business, C&D pet foods, had received an IR£1.1 million loan on favourable terms from the Palestinian Masri family, whose members had also received passports in 1992. 'Why, of all the companies in Ireland, did the Masri family choose to invest in C&D Foods, which is owned by the prime minister's family?' asked Jim Kemmy TD, the chair of the Labour party, who called for an investigation.[120] An internal government inquiry into the passports for sale controversy was uneventful. Tánaiste Dick Spring, Labour party, examined the Department of Justice files on the investment and publicly stated that all the legal requirements had been complied with by the Masri family and that the department had acted in 'an ethical, above board and arm's length way'.[121] In return for investment in Irish companies, 163 passports were awarded. By the time the scheme was suspended by the Rainbow Coalition in 1998, IR£95 million had been invested in Irish firms in this way. The scheme was reintroduced by the subsequent Fianna Fáil / PD government. Under its provisions, operated by the Department of Justice, an applicant must make a minimum net investment of IR£1 million and the basis of the investment must be either job creation or job maintenance.

Absence of consequences

The *Irish Times* reported that despite imminent publication of the Beef Tribunal report, Reynolds was 'possibly the most relaxed person at the Galway Races'. Bertie Ahern, Minister for Finance, told the newspaper how pleased he was that the Taoiseach had won after he gave him a betting tip.[122] Reynolds had every reason to be relaxed about the Tribunal findings. His subsequent Dáil speech on the report was regrettably accurate. 'The public are interested in the bottom line, not in the minutiae that appear to be so riveting to a handful of commentators.'[123] Two weeks after the Tribunal findings, the *Irish Times* / MRBI opinion poll found that although many electors were very critical of the action of senior politicians, a minority had a limited knowledge of the contents of the report.

Ultimately, the real casualty of the Tribunal was the Tribunal itself. The original motivation for establishing the inquiry, to investigate the extent of the 'special relationship' between Haughey and Goodman, was sidetracked. To the public mind, Reynolds came to epitomise the Beef Tribunal because of his public and personal spat with O'Malley. Haughey escaped public scrutiny of his private affairs. The opportunity for political accountability was lost. The Tribunal failed to deliver a clear result in the form of punishment, condemnation or significant policy change.

The Tribunal proved to be a counterproductive exercise. Although it exposed incompetent decision-making and the gross mismanagement of public monies, it served only to confirm in the public mind that suspicions of golden circles were not only justified, but beyond legal, political and moral reproach or sanction. The Tribunal did not challenge in any meaningful way a political culture which condoned political favouritism, tolerated conflicts of interest, tax evasion, fraudulent practices, unregulated party funding and the failure of parliamentary mechanisms of accountability. If anything, the report was a public exercise in deciding where the standards of ethical behaviour now lay. The probity of government procedures, the integrity of collective cabinet confidentiality and the veracity of the distinction between public and private interest were not given due consideration by the Tribunal, the political establishment, the media or the public. As the *Business & Finance* magazine sagely noted: 'Larry Goodman has become a household name and people talk about Iraq as if it was the 'in' tourist attraction. All this talk has done little to answer certain questions which remain of considerable concern to those in the trade.'[124] Such concerns included inappropriate political influence, the discretionary allocation by government of scarce export credit, intervention facilities and public money to political allies. Also dismissed were conflict of interest concerns where those same businessmen availing of state facilities were also donating large amounts of money to Fianna Fáil.

Mr. Justice Hamilton's report lacked the courage of its convictions and failed to hold those responsible to account. Pat Rabbitte TD, Democratic Left, was particularly perceptive in his Dáil contribution on the Beef Tribunal report. Hamilton, he believed, had 'made his findings of fact', and refrained 'from allocating blame.' Conclusions were left to hang in the air or avoided altogether.[125] The report was a futile exercise in ambiguity, facilitating such moral uncertainty about political responsibilities that terminology like consequence was absent from any discussion on the Tribunal findings. In effect, the implicit licence to act without impunity was now established explicitly.

Conclusion

In an 1859 lecture entitled 'Self-Made Men' the great Black American leader, Frederick Douglass, asserted that self-made men 'owe little or nothing to birth, relationship, friendly surroundings; to wealth inherited or to early approved means of education; who are what they are, without the aid of any of the favouring conditions by which other men usually rise in the world and achieve great results'.[126] In that respect, Goodman was the Douglass archetype, a man who defied the expectations of his class in a country where the social hierarchy of 'knowing your place' was ever so subtlety defined.

The newly educated and entrepreneurial Irish were aggrieved that the confines of social class prohibited them from achieving their full potential and due recognition that social progress afforded.[127] Since independence, the English and the Protestant ascendancy had now been replaced by the upper middle-class Catholics who dominated the professions, particularly banking and accountancy. Access to, and ascent within, the professions was perceived as bound by discernible privilege. The conventions of class status did not readily embrace new applicants which may account for why so many of the successful Irish business enterprises from the 1960s were populated by self-made men. In popular political parlance, they were known, somewhat dismissively and contemptuously, as the mohair suit brigade. Many of them shared the belief that the very virtue of overcoming the hurdles of perceived class prejudice, united them against the establishment to which they nonetheless yearned to belong.

Charles Haughey and Albert Reynolds would have recognised themselves in Goodman's rising success and shared a mutual sense of deferential admiration towards the beef baron and self-made men like Dermot Desmond and Michael Smurfit. Those that entered politics in the late 1950s and 1960s were characterised by an absence of any pre-political resources in terms of financial security, prestige or power. Although they came from modest social backgrounds and in many cases had minimal professional qualifications (although Haughey had a first class honours degree in commerce at University College Dublin and later qualified as a chartered accountant), emphasis in general was placed on the entrepreneurial ethic as opposed to the merits of formal education and professional certificates. Haughey's insecurity was his greatest flaw according to Geraldine Kennedy, *Irish Times*: 'What he wanted most of all was to be seen to be respectable and he thought he could buy that - and he couldn't, in that Ireland.'[128] These justifications were echoed when sustained scandal hit Haughey in the late 1990s. In an interview with the *Sunday Business Post* in 1998, Patrick Gallagher, son of the property developer and builder Matt Gallagher, revealed a genuine belief that business involvement with Taca was part of a movement which would create a more prosperous Ireland. 'Haughey was financed in order to create the environment which the Anglo-Irish had enjoyed and that we as a people could never aspire to.'[129] Haughey's fabulous lifestyle was initially due to the generosity of Matt Gallagher who was motivated by the sincerely held belief that 'Fianna Fáil was good for builders and builders were good for Fianna Fáil, and there was nothing wrong with that'.[130]

On Gallagher's advice, Haughey purchased his Grangemore home in 1959 for IR£13,000. This was sold to the Gallagher Group, a building firm controlled by Matt Gallagher, a decade later for IR£260,000.

The enormous price differential was due to recently acquired rezoning by Haughey, now Minister for Finance which accounted for the twenty-fold increase in value.[131] This proved controversial because Haughey had availed himself of a device he had personally introduced in the 1968 Finance Act, to avoid paying any tax on his windfall gain. When T. J. Fitzpatrick, Fine Gael TD for Cavan, raised this matter in the context of a 1970 Dáil debate, Haughey's position was robustly defended by P. J. Burke, Ray Burke's father. Burke was adamant that the primacy of private property rights was superseded any such enquiry: 'Is it a mortal sin or is it a sin against the Constitution for a man to sell his private property? . . . Why is he [Fitzpatrick] dealing with a personal thing.'[132]

The Greencore, Telecom and Beef scandals marked a critical juncture in Irish public life. Disturbing questions about the quality of Ireland's public administration, of accountability and of the relationship between business and politics and the issue of political funding were raised in a sustained way. Ultimately, this backdrop of recurring scandal and the circumstances of the coalition's collapse in 1992 created the necessary conditions for unprecedented legislative change on political ethics. For these reasons, the period in office of the Fianna Fáil / PD 1989–92 coalition government represented the most seismic chapter in modern Irish politics.

The Beef Tribunal report failed to excite public attention because Mr. Justice Hamilton wrote it in the context that corruption was narrowly defined as the abuse of public power for direct personal financial gain. Without doubt, decisions taken by Haughey, Reynolds and the 1987–89 Fianna Fáil government benefited the business interests of Larry Goodman and Oliver Murphy. However, because no member of that government was found to have received something as crude and obvious as a monetary bribe, it was gently assumed that no corruption occurred. In a small country such as Ireland, it was evitable that prominent members of the beef industry were on friendly terms with politicians and there was nothing improper or unusual about such relationships. Other justifications sought to evoke the national interest. Although members of the public, media and politics were deeply frustrated that those at the heart of the inquiries were largely immune from consequences, this period did distinguish itself from earlier corruption inquiries.

The political consequences of the inquiry were immense. Two governments collapsed, the reputations of senior political figures were tarnished permanently and the context and tone of political scandal for the 1990s were established. The extensive tax evasion and fraud, shown by the Tribunal to have occurred, impacted on the very ability of the government in the late

1980s to provide basic health, education and social services for the population as a whole. The consequences for those in need of such services were all the worse due to the recession then taking place. The financial impact to the exchequer, because of the political decisions made by the Fianna Fáil government, escaped the sharp attention they deserved.

For the first time, reservations were expressed about the conventional and limited interpretation of impropriety. The integrity of Hamilton's decision to overlook the influence of political donations made by Goodman and Murphy to Fianna Fáil was challenged. This was unprecedented territory for a judiciary naturally immune from political criticism. The concept of mediated corruption and the principle that a gain was not necessarily direct or financial was fermenting within the public consciousness. An unprecedented extension of the definition of corruption was occurring. The gain was now gradually understood to include power, prestige, authority and reputation, such as re-election to government. Successful election campaigns, assisted by a war-chest of political donations from a generous benefactor who also happened to be the recipient of favourable political decisions, could no longer be dismissed as coincidental.

This period ushered in sustained questioning about the mutually beneficial networks of personal friendships that existed across influential sectors of Irish society. Such suspicions had lain dormant since the 1960s and were silently slapped down when journalists such as Joe McAnthony sought to give voice to them. Above all, the scandals provided an insight into how power operated in Ireland. Legal corruption, the undue influence by vested interests over regulation and policy-making, where elites have access to insider information that they use for their private benefit, was now described in Ireland rather politely as a golden circle. Vested interests were entrenched within and facilitated by the political system. Ethical breaches were accepted because they had become normalised.

The belief that what was good for Ireland was good for business prevailed, a sentiment expressed by Reynolds to the Tribunal: 'It has always been said in Ireland, particularly in rural Ireland . . . that the economy was going well if the price of cattle was good. The economy was going badly if the price of cattle was bad.'[133] The Tribunal revealed remarkable degrees of deference by the government and civil service to the private interest of businessmen. For instance, Goodman's jet had 'made a private arrangement' with an Irish air corps officer where space at the state's military aerodrome in Baldonnell, Dublin was rented to the beef baron while facilities were being constructed for him at Dublin airport. The cabinet handbook which outlined the procedures to regulate any relationship between business interests and politicians was ignored.

Apart from challenging the traditional consensus on what the definition of corruption entailed, the Greencore, Telecom and Beef controversies revealed that the phenomenon of state capture was not an abstract concept as far as the relationship in Ireland between politics and business was concerned. The International Monetary Fund (IMF) defines state capture as the influence of private interests on the formulation of public policies, laws and regulations of the state for their own advantage.[134] George Stigler makes the distinction between illicit and legitimate influence in his definition on regulatory capture. Legitimate intervention includes the exercise of political influence such as lobbying. Illicit access occurs through informal, non-transparent and evidently preferential channels. Regulatory capture can occur when parliament votes on legislation which benefits private interests or where illegal contributions to political parties and election campaigns are paid by private interests.[135] The appropriation of public policy for private purposes is not always necessarily illegal. The naïve assumption by developed western economies prevailed that it was only in developing countries that business interests seek to shape decisions taken by the state to gain specific advantages.

The very principles of democracy were undermined during the course of the 1987–89 Fianna Fáil government. 'The boundaries between the interests of a private company and those of the Irish state were, from the summer of 1987 onwards, being blurred.'[136] Goodman enjoyed unrivalled access to members of the cabinet, the civil service and the Irish diplomatic service. The pace at which decisions beneficial to the Goodman companies were made and implemented was astonishing.[137] Within five months of entering government in 1987, Fianna Fáil had reversed previous government policy on economic relations with Iraq and had committed itself to giving Goodman companies IR£30 million under the terms of their development plan. A change had been made in section 52 of the 1987 Finance Act, specifically at his urging, and on the suggestion of Albert Reynolds, which facilitated cheap finance, underwritten by the exchequer to Goodman. The government also abandoned a key element of its employment strategy, gone outside the law, and forced on the IDA a change which it considered very wrong.[138]

Moreover, on 28 August 1990, the Dáil was recalled from its summer break for an emergency session to introduce legislation which would allow the courts to appoint an examiner rather than a liquidator to the Goodman beef companies, which at time had collapsed with debts to the banks of more than €635 million.[139] The potential bankruptcy of a private company was regarded as an urgent national crisis. This allowed the outstanding debts to be rescheduled. The government were fearful that the collapse of Goodman would have had devastating knock on effects for farmers.

The costs of both types of capture, illicit and legitimate, to the exchequer can be significant and are not socially costless and can impact on the 'overall economic performance and the capacity or commitment of the state to provide critical public goods for the development of the market economy'.[140] The Irish exchequer paid €83 million in fines to the European Commission because of fraudulent claims made by Goodman's AIBP group within the Irish beef intervention. The wasteful investment of resources because of monopoly privilege-seeking can impose large costs on an economy. In the Irish case, the professionally organised and systematic abuse of European intervention funds by the beef industry was ultimately paid for by the Irish taxpayer. This ultimately diverted financial resources for public projects such as investment in education, health and other public services. The perception that export intervention quotas were granted to beef interests who financially donated to the party of government also had a corrosive impact on public trust.

The imposition of anti-competitive barriers, for example, can generate highly concentrated gains to selected powerful firms at a significant social cost, such as lost income to the exchequer. When firms 'use their influence to block any policy reforms that might eliminate these advantages, state capture has become not merely a symptom but also a fundamental cause of poor governance'.[141] The inequality of influence generates a self-reinforcing dynamic in which institutions are subverted, thus strengthening the underlying political and economic inequalities and damaging the credibility of institutions.[142]

Thus, a vicious circle is created where the policy and institutional reforms necessary to improve governance are undermined by the collusion between powerful firms and state officials who reap substantial private gains from the continuation of weak governance.[143] There is no political incentive to challenge vested interests when those in authority benefit from the status quo. The incidence of state-capture is lower in countries that have pursued more comprehensive economic reform and political reform, such as access to information, press freedom, citizen participation in decision-making processes, transparent political party financing and civil society monitoring of conflict of interest.[144]

None of which was explicitly evident in the Ireland of the early 1990s.

Notes

1 Des O'Malley appointed Minister for Industry and Commerce; Bobby Molloy appointed Minister for Energy. Mary Harney appointed the state's first ever Minister for Environmental Protection. Stephen O'Byrnes appointed Assistant Government Press Secretary. The PDs had entered into a coalition agreement with Fine Gael during the election campaign but they performed badly.
2 M. Gallagher and R. Sinnott (eds), *How Ireland Voted 1989* (PSAI Press and Centre for the Study of Irish Elections, 1990).
3 M. R. Curran, *Siúicre Éireann c.p.t., Sugar Distributors (Holdings). Limited, Sugar Distributors Limited* (Dublin Stationery Office, 1991).

4 Michael Noonan, Dáil Éireann, *Siúicre Éireann and Related Companies Report: Motion. 417.* (13 March 1992).

5 C. P. Foley and A. G. Barry, *Investigation into the Affairs of Siúicre Éireann C.p.t. and Related Companies / Final Report* (Dublin Stationery Office, 1992), pp. 221–3.

6 J. Maher, 'Subculture of cash and secret deals uncovered', *Irish Times* (27 August 1992).

7 Dick Spring, Dáil Éireann, *Siúicre Éireann.*

8 97/624/EC: Commission Decision of 14 May 1997 relating to a proceeding pursuant to Article 86 of the EC Treaty, IV/34.621, 35.059/F-3 - Irish Sugar plc.

9 *Ibid.*

10 Chestvale Properties Limited (and) Hoddle Investments Limited, *Investigation under Section 14(1), Companies Act, 1990 Final report* (Dublin Stationery Office, 1993), p. 118 (Section 8.2.2).

11 M. Cooper, *Who really runs Ireland? The Story of the Elite Who Led Ireland from Bust to Boom . . . and Back Again* (Dublin: Penguin Ireland, 2009), pp. 138–141, has detailed information on the Glackin Report.

12 Chestvale *Final Report* pp. 78–9 (Section 4.7; 4.7.2).

13 In October 1990, Haughey faced his first no confidence motion during that phase of his political career. Earlier, in 1982–1983, he faced three challenges to his leadership of Fianna Fáil, including a no confidence motion in October 1982, each of which he defeated. The final challenge of that time, in February 1983, was a blunt demand for his resignation. He defeated it by 40 votes to 33.

14 D. Walsh, 'On further mature recollection', *Irish Times* (5 October 1991).

15 F. O'Toole, 'To "know" and not to know facts', *Irish Times* (22 August 2000).

16 Ray Burke and Pat O'Mahony, Dáil Éireann, *Written Answers: Beef and Sheep Exports to Iraq. 388.* (12 April 1989).

17 Irish Food Processors group emerged out of the collapse of Goodman International in 1990.

18 E. Shanahan, 'From scratch to multi-millionaire', *Irish Times* (19 June 1987).

19 F. O'Toole, *Meanwhile Back at the Ranch: The Politics of Irish Beef* (Vintage, 1995), p. 31.

20 Des O'Malley, Dáil Éireann, *Adjournment Debate, Beef Exports to Iraq. 389.* (10 May 1989).

21 Des O'Malley, Dáil Éireann, *Questions, Oral Answers, Beef Exports to Iraq. 392.* (1 November 1989).

22 'Credit meetings recalled', *Irish Times* (30 June 1992); 'June '89 The Wicked Month it all started to go wrong', *Irish Independent* (23 November 1999).

23 That action was concluded in September 2003, when Goodman Holdings withdrew its legal action against the state. Goodman said the cancellation contributed to the firm's collapse into examinership in 1990 when the Iraqi customers defaulted. Today Larry Goodman remains one of Europe's biggest beef processors.

24 Mr. Justice Liam Hamilton, *Report of the Tribunal of Inquiry into the Beef Processing Industry* (Dublin Stationery Office, 1994). pp. 23, 568.

25 Charles J. Haughey, Dáil Éireann, *Request to Move Adjournment of Dáil under Standing Order 30. 408* (14 May 1991).

26 Michael O'Kennedy, Dáil Éireann, *Meat Industry: Motion. 408.* (15 May 1991).

27 Albert Reynolds, Dáil Éireann, *Private Members' Business: Ethics in Government and Public Office Bill, 1991: Second Stage. 407.* (7 May 1991).

28 S. Collins, *Breaking the Mould: How the PDs Changed Irish Politics* (Gill and Macmillan, 2005), p. 125.

29 Hamilton, *Report of the Tribunal of Inquiry into the Beef Processing Industry*, p. 3.

30 E. O'Halpin, "'Ah, they've given us a good bit of stuff . . .' tribunals and Irish political life at the turn of the century', *Irish Political Studies*, 15:1 (2000), p. 185.

31 'Chief Justice who presided over Beef Tribunal and whose inquiry led to the resignation of two judges', *Irish Times* (2 December 2000).

32 J. MacMenamin, 'James Hamilton', in McGuire and Quinn (eds), *Dictionary of Irish Biography: From the Earliest Times to the Year 2002*, www.dib.cambridge. org.

33 Hamilton, *Report of the Tribunal of Inquiry into the Beef Processing Industry*, pp. 334–5.

34 *Ibid.*, p. 330.

35 'Ahern opposed tax amnesty pushed by Reynolds', *Irish Times* (29 September 1999). 21 May 1993 memo.

36 F. Finlay, *Snakes and Ladders* (New Island Books, 1998); R. Quinn, *Straight Left: A Journey in Politics* (Hodder Headline Ireland, 2005).

37 F. O'Toole, 'A culture of total impunity', *Irish Times* (6 June 2004).

38 Hamilton, *Report of the Tribunal of Inquiry into the Beef Processing Industry*, pp. 400–1.

39 *Ibid.*, p. 396–7.

40 *Ibid.*, p. 502.

41 O'Toole, *Meanwhile Back at the Ranch*, pp. 191–2.

42 Charles J. Haughey, Dáil Éireann, *Questions, Oral Answers. Statement by the Minister for Agriculture and Food. 388.* (12 April 1989).

43 O'Toole, *Meanwhile Back at the Ranch*, p. 191.

44 Hamilton, *Report of the Tribunal of Inquiry into the Beef Processing Industry*, pp. 366–406.

45 'Factual position', in *ibid.*, pp. 216–36.

46 *Ibid.*, pp. 76–7.

47 O'Toole, *Meanwhile Back at the Ranch*, p. 139. Beef Tribunal transcript p. 60/58th day of evidence.

48 *Attorney General v The Sole Member of the Tribunal of Inquiry into the Beef Processing Industry [1993] 2* I.R. 250.

49 O'Toole, *Meanwhile Back at the Ranch*, p. 81, 103 - 'Albert Reynolds decision had helped to increase the value of Goodman Iraqi business by $100 million'

50 *Ibid*, p. 147 - Beef Tribunal transcript pp. 19–20/82th day of evidence.

51 Hamilton, *Report of the Tribunal of Inquiry into the Beef Processing Industry*, p. 159.

52 *Ibid*, p. 71.
53 'ICMSA doubtful on FF policy', *Irish Times* (4 March 1987); 'Expansion of meat production urged', *Irish Times* (11 March 1987); 'Beef Industry 'may face crisis'', *Irish Times* (15 June 1987).
54 O'Toole, *Meanwhile Back at the Ranch*, p. 253. The Tribunal noted this figure in dollars rather than pound.
55 Hamilton, *Report of the Tribunal of Inquiry into the Beef Processing Industry*, p. 229.
56 *Ibid.*, p. 229.
57 *Ibid.*, pp. 39–236.
58 *Ibid.*, p. 232. The Tribunal used the ambiguation AIBPI to detonate Allied Irish Beef Processors *International.*
59 *Ibid.*, p. 231.
60 *Ibid.*, pp. 215–16.
61 *Ibid.*, p. 288.
62 O'Toole, *Meanwhile Back at the Ranch*, pp. 128, 133.
63 'Goodman got his pound of flesh through Haughey', *Irish Times* (19 July 1997).
64 O'Toole, *Meanwhile Back at the Ranch*, p.199 181a, 52.
65 *Ibid.*, p. 199 181a 52.
66 Albert Reynolds, Dáil Éireann, *Report of Tribunal of Inquiry into Beef Processing Industry. 445.* (1 September 1994).
67 Hamilton, *Report of the Tribunal of Inquiry into the Beef Processing Industry*, p. 231.
68 *Ibid.*, p. 321.
69 *Ibid.*, p. 12.
70 *Ibid.*, 135c, p. 188.
71 N. Collins and C. O'Raghallaigh 'Political sleaze in the Republic of Ireland', *Parliamentary Affairs*, 48:4 (1994), p. 707.
72 F. O'Toole, 'Failures of Beef Tribunal haunt us yet', *Irish Times* (26 June 2001); O'Toole, *Meanwhile Back at the Ranch*, pp. 69–70, 153.
73 'Party Funding outlined', *Irish Times* (5 June 1992).
74 Mr. Justice Michael Moriarty, *The Moriarty Tribunal Report. Report of the Tribunal of Inquiry into Payments to Politicians and Related Matters. Part 1* (Dublin Stationery Office, 2006), p. 27.
75 A. Lenihan and Angela Phelan, *No Problem: To Mayo and Back* (Blackwater Press, 1990), p. 70–1.
76 L. Reid, 'Goodman 'loaned €600,000' to Lawlor for land', *Irish Independent* (8 December 2004).
77 F. O'Toole and D. de Bréadún, 'Discrepancy in size of donation to Fianna Fáil', *Irish Times* (17 September 1992).
78 *Ibid.*
79 L. Collins, 'Court rerun for Reynolds/O'Malley clash', *Sunday Independent* (8 April 2001).
80 M. Carolan, 'Bitter battle ends as Master Meats case is struck out in High Court', *Irish Times* (14 February 2002).

81 Liam Collins, 'Court rerun for Reynolds/O'Malley clash', *Sunday Independent* (8 April 2001).
82 '£138,550 to Fine Gael', *Irish Times* (16 September 1992).
83 'FG admit seeking Goodman funds', *Irish Independent* (6 March 1996).
84 'List of contributors to the PDs', *Irish Times* (15 December 1997).
85 'Fine Gael looking political gift horse in the mouth', *Irish Independent* (12 February 2001).
86 It gave £75,000 to the minority Fianna Fáil government, between February 1987 and June 1989, in three separate lots of £25,000.
87 F. O'Toole, 'Hidden world of political lobbying', *Irish Times* (6 June 1992).
88 F. O'Toole and D. de Bréadún, 'Discrepancy in size of donation to Fianna Fáil', *Irish Times* (17 September 1992).
89 M. Brennan, 'Payback time as Iraq hands over €6.3m of our beef money', *Irish Independent* (5 January 2009).
90 OECD, '*Education at a Glance 2008* (OECD, 2008); OECD, '*Education at a Glance 2010* (OECD, 2010) www.oecd.org/edu. When compared with other OECD countries, Irish education spending relative to the country's economic wealth and student / teacher ratios are below the OECD average.
91 F. O'Toole, 'Scandal of agriculture officials and their relaxed way with the errant beef barons', *Irish Times* (6 January 1999).
92 P. Smyth, '£75m EU repayment largest ever sought from Ireland', *Irish Times* (31 March 1995).
93 S. MacConnell, 'Goodman firm to pay €3.8m compensation for beef irregularities', *Irish Times* (19 July 2003).
94 F. O'Toole, 'Beef scam quietly condoned', *Irish Times* (22 July 2003).
95 D. O'Malley, 'Lights, cameras, corruption make tribunals effective, put them on TV', *Sunday Independent* (28 January 2007).
96 Cooper, *Who Really Runs Ireland?* p. 391 details his wealth.
97 M. MacCarthaigh, *Accountability in Irish Parliamentary Politics* (Institute of Public Administration, 2005), pp. 202–6.
98 O'Toole, *Meanwhile Back at the Ranch*, pp. 264–5.
99 F. O'Toole, 'Scandal of agriculture officials and their relaxed way with the errant beef barons', *Irish Times* (9 January 1999).
100 This department had a variety of minor name changes in this period.
101 Collins, *Breaking the Mould*, p. 87.
102 'Esat sale would take O hUiginn to front rank of Irish business earners', *Irish Times* (7 January 2000).
103 O'Malley, 'Lights, cameras, corruption make tribunals effective, put them on TV'.
104 Charles J. Haughey, *Order of Business. 388.* (15 March 1989).
105 O'Toole, *Meanwhile Back at the Ranch*, pp. 236, 249.
106 Bertie Ahern, Dáil Éireann, *Supplementary Estimates, 1992: Confidence in Government: Motion 424* (5 November 1992).
107 Michael Smith, Dáil Éireann, *Report of Tribunal of Inquiry.*
108 *Ibid.*, Michael McDowell.

109 D. Ferriter, *The Transformation of Ireland 1900–2000* (Profile Books, 2005), p. 678.

110 Hamilton, *Report of the Tribunal of Inquiry into the Beef Processing Industry*, pp. 491–2.

111 John Dardis, Seanad Éireann, *Tribunal of Inquiry into Beef Processing Industry: Motion. 129.* (29 May 1991).

112 J. Horgan, *Broadcasting and public life: RTÉ news and current affairs, 1926–1997* (Four Courts Press, 2004), p. 204.

113 F. O'Toole, 'A culture of total impunity', *Irish Times* (1 June 2004).

114 A. Reynolds, *Albert Reynolds: My Autobiography* (Transworld Ireland, 2009).

115 Collins, *Breaking the Mould*, p. 138.

116 'Spring rebuts Reynolds's spokesman on report', *Irish Times* (30 July 1994).

117 S. Duignan, *One Spin on the Merry-Go-Round* (Blackwater Press, 1996), p. 114.

118 Collins, *Breaking the Mould*, p. 151.

119 Duignan, *One Spin on the Merry-Go-Round*, pp. 49–50.

120 'Reynolds in passport row', *Sunday Times* (5 June 1994).

121 J. Carroll and Maol Muire Tynan, 'Tough legislation on passports for investors on way – Spring. Statement marks a new low in political cynicism, McDowell says', *Irish Times* (2 June 1994).

122 M. Finlan, 'Horsing around at the Galway races', *Irish Times* (28 July 1994).

123 Albert Reynolds, Dáil Éireann, *Report of Tribunal of Inquiry.*

124 'Toil and trouble in the meat trade', *Business & Finance* (6 July 1989).

125 Pat Rabbitte, *Report of Tribunal of Inquiry.*

126 W. E. Waldo, *The Mind of Frederick Douglass* (University of North Carolina Press, 1984), p. 256.

127 T. Garvin, *Nationalist Revolutionaries in Ireland 1858–1928* (Oxford University Press: 1987).

128 RTÉ Mint Productions, *Haughey* (June 2005).

129 Frank Connolly, *Sunday Business Post*, quoted in Peter Murtagh, 'Power, lies & corruption', *Irish Times* (17 June 2006).

130 'Controversial property dealer', *Irish Times* (18 March 2006).

131 J. Corcoran, 'Farewell to this risen son scorched by the greedy demands of a golden circle', *Sunday Independent* (19 March 2006).

132 P. J. Burke, Dáil Éireann, *Nomination of Member of Government: Motion (Resumed) 246.* (7 May 1970).

133 O'Toole, *Meanwhile Back at the Ranch*, p. 135.

134 T. S. Hellman and D. Kaufmann, 'Confronting the challenge of the state chapter in transition economies', *Finance and Development*, 38: 3 (2001), pp. 31–5, www.imf.org/external/pubs/ft/fandd/2001/09/hellman.htm.

135 G. Stigler, 'The theory of economic regulation', *Bell Journal of Economics and Management Science*, 2:1 (1971), p.2, 3–21.

136 O'Toole, *Meanwhile Back at the Ranch*, p. 115.

137 Hamilton, *Report of the Tribunal of Inquiry into the Beef Processing Industry*, pp. 68–73.

138 O'Toole, *Meanwhile Back at the Ranch*, pp. 136–7, 202–3.

139 C. Keena, 'US attacks taking toll on Phelan outlets', *Irish Times* (14 February 2002).

140 J. S. Hellman G. Jones and D. Kaufmann, *'Seize the State, Seize the Day': State Capture, Corruption, and Influence in Transition* (World Bank, 2000), p. 54.

141 Hellman and Kamfmann, 'Confronting the challenge of state chapter in economies', pp. 31–5.

142 J. S. Hellman and D. Kaufmann, 'The inequality of influence', in J. Kornai and S. Rose-Ackerman (eds), *Building a Trustworthy State in Post-Socialist Transition* (Palgrave Macmillan, 2004).

143 J. S. Hellman and D. Kaufmann, *Confronting the Challenge of State Capture in Transition Economies* (International Monetary Fund, 2001).

144 *Ibid.*

6

The tribunal period: 1990s–2000s

Introduction

A series of state sponsored investigations into political impropriety in the 1990s and 2000s revealed for the first time that unaccountable political decisions were not isolated incidents, as previous episodes seemed to suggest. The various inquiries instead exposed how those at the highest positions of power periodically abused their political discretion to benefit private interests. This chapter demonstrates that an improper relationship existed between the receipt of political donations and discretionary political decisions which at best can be described as being in breach of the most rudimentary conflict of interest considerations.

The entrenched nature of this conduct also suggested that the type of corruption which was exercised could not be dismissed as a minor deviation from existing laws, rules and regulations. Instead, extensive transgressions were tolerated at the policy formulation end of politics. This period of Irish public life witnessed a growing focus on corruption as table 6.1 outlines. There was a concern that grand corruption, rather than petty corruption, was emerging within the political process. In the early 1990s, Ireland's outdated legislative anti-corruption framework was wholly inadequate and relied on voluntary compliance with self-interpreted concepts of ethical behaviour. The threat of the most serious form of corruption, that of systemic corruption, was ominous. In this scenario, the only way to economically engage with the political system was to partake in a corrupt act.

The McCracken, Moriarty and Flood / Mahon Tribunals of Inquiry initiated a prolonged process of public disclosure on the veracity of the political decision-making process. As a consequence, the definition of corruption evolved within the public consciousness to incorporate a much wider acknowledgment of the mediated concept of corruption. The conventional definition of corruption, the abuse of public office for private gain, is reliant on a legal interpretation of the terminology abuse, public and gain. This narrow approach neglects public expectations that the conduct of those in public office should be characterised by a broader moral compass.

Table 6.1 Selected anti-corruption timeline

Year	Development
1989–92	*Fianna Fáil / Progressive Democrat Coalition*
1991–94	The Beef Tribunal
1992	Charles J. Haughey resigns as Taoiseach
1993–94	*Fianna Fáil/Labour coalition government*
1993	Second tax amnesty
1994–97	*Rainbow government – Fine Gael, Labour, Democratic Left coalition*
1995	Ethics in Public Office Act – Public Offices Commission established
1996	Michael Lowry resigns as Minister for Transport, Energy and Communications
1997	Electoral Act
1997–97	The McCracken Tribunal of Inquiry
1997–2002	*Fianna Fáil / Progressive Democrat Coalition*
1997–2011	The Moriarty Tribunal of Inquiry
1997–	The Flood / Mahon Tribunal of Inquiry
1998	The Belfast (Good Friday) Agreement
1998	Dáil Public Accounts Committee DIRT Inquiry
2000	High Court Ansbacher (Cayman) Inspectors reports
2001	Prevention of Corruption (Amendment) Act
2002–07	*Fianna Fáil / Progressive Democrat Coalition*
2002	Publication of Flood / Mahon Tribunal Second Interim report
2004	Commissions of Investigation Act
2006	Publication of the first Moriarty Tribunal report
2007–2011	*Fianna Fáil / Progressive Democrat / Green Coalition*
2008–	Irish economic crisis
2010	IMF/EU bailout deal announced giving Ireland access to €85 billion in funding
2011–	*Fine Gael / Labour Coalition*
2011	Publication of the second Moriarty Tribunal report
2011	Publication of the Nyberg report of the Commission of Investigation into the Banking Sector in Ireland

This was the first time that the distinction between the legal and moral definition of corruption received such extensive public attention. The privatisation of the state's publicly owned resources and an economic boom characterised by a property bubble, created financial incentives of staggering proportions and facilitated fraudulent behaviour. The Tribunal trilogy facilitated the formal recognition that corruption also encompassed the undue influence on the formulation of policy and legislation by vested interests at the expense of the public interest as political actors benefited indirectly and directly as a result of their increased power, prestige, authority and lifestyle.

This chapter will provide empirical evidence which illustrates: (1) how pervasive corruption was within every layer of political action; (2) how those who donated to leading members of the government also benefited from favourable political decisions; (3) how the definition of corruption developed from a narrow interpretation of legal statutes to an emergent awareness of the ethical dimensions of improper political behaviour; and (4) what factors facilitated this transition.

This chapter does not propose to provide exhaustive detail concerning the nuances of the various inquiries. Many of these investigations have received meticulous attention in voluminous tomes.[1] Instead, the wider themes from the McCracken, Moriarty and Flood / Mahon Tribunals of Inquiry will be examined, with particular reference to the relationship between payments to politicians by businessmen and the decision-making process.

The McCracken Tribunal 1997 and Moriarty Tribunal 1997–2011 (volume 1)

The findings of the McCracken Tribunal of Inquiry (Dunnes Payments), March 1997 - August 1997, uncovered significant levels and scope of corruption, thus creating the basis for the Moriarty Tribunal's extended terms of reference that pursued a wider range of activities over a much lengthier period. The McCracken Tribunal established that donations to former Fianna Fáil Taoiseach Charles J. Haughey were lodged in Dublin banks under the name of Ansbacher (Cayman) Ltd. The primary purpose of this secret offshore banking system was to facilitate tax evasion by Irish residents. These deposits became known as the Ansbacher accounts. Although the Tribunal concluded that 'there appears in fact to have been no political impropriety' on the part of Haughey, it denounced his behaviour in the strongest of terms:

> It is quite unacceptable that a member of Dáil Éireann, and in particular a Cabinet Minister and Taoiseach, should be supported in his personal lifestyle by gifts made to him personally. It is particularly unacceptable that such gifts should emanate from prominent businessmen within the state. The possibility that political or financial favours could be sought in return for such gifts, or even be given without being sought, is very high, and if such gifts are permissible they could inevitably lead in some cases to bribery and corruption.[2]

The McCracken Tribunal also examined the relationship between former Fine Gael Minister Michael Lowry and Ben Dunne which it described as: 'an unhealthy business relationship under any circumstances, but was particularly disturbing in view of Mr. Michael Lowry's position as a public representative, and subsequently as Chairman of the Fine Gael parliamentary party and ultimately as a Cabinet Minister'.[3]

The Moriarty Tribunal of Inquiry into Payments to Politicians and Related Matters was established by Dáil Éireann in September 1997 to further investigate payments to Haughey and Lowry. The purpose of this inquisitorial inquiry was to determine the nature of the relationship between the receipt of political donations and any political decisions made when both men held several critical ministerial positions. Mr. Justice Michael Moriarty was appointed as sole member of the Tribunal just a year after his entry to the High Court. The Belfast born judge, whose politics have been described as 'Labour with a small l', published two strikingly forthright reports in 2006 and 2011.

The first report, published in December 2006, uncovered an embedded network of rogue accountants, businessmen, bankers and politicians with Haughey at its centre. The 704 page dossier shed light on how the Mayo-man funded his extravagant lifestyle and revealed Byzantine schemes to avoid tax, all of which was tainted by reservations of political favouritism and grave conflicts of interest.

Charles J. (Charlie) Haughey (1925–2006) was first elected to Dáil Éireann as a TD for Dublin North-East in 1957. He was re-elected at each subsequent election until he stepped down from office in 1992. Haughey held several cabinet posts and succeeded Jack Lynch as leader of Fianna Fáil in 1979 where he went on to serve four terms as Taoiseach.[4] On his death, the state broadcaster, RTÉ, was discerning in its observation: 'Not since the Civil War has an Irish politician been the subject of such adulation and execration as Charlie Haughey.'[5]

The contrived myth around the "Boss," as he was known by close associates, was that of the lovable rouge who endured an improvised childhood and accordingly rebelled by harbouring a life-long anti-establishment streak. This translated as a residual, sneaking regard of Haughey's "cute hoor" temperament. Suspicions about the disproportionality between his relatively modest earnings and 'conspicuously lavish lifestyle' shadowed Haughey's thirty-five year political career. Irish public life however instinctively tolerated this myth.[6]

The Tribunal evidence suggested that Haughey's political survival went hand in hand with his financial survival. In his forensic examination of Haughey's personal finances, Colm Keena presented convincing analysis that when 'in power the money tended to flow in, and when he was out of power the money tended to dry up'.[7] The funds identified as available to Haughey by the Tribunal, the schedule of these payments and his periods as Taoiseach are illustrated in figure 6.1. Haughey's first term as Taoiseach, from December 1979 - June 1981, was complemented by IR£1,184,950 in donations within seventeen months. His second short stint as Taoiseach, between March and December 1982, was rewarded with IR£461,931 in donations. Haughey's opposition period, from December 1982 to March 1987, saw him receive IR£2,065,762 in over four years. Haughey received IR£932,903 during his

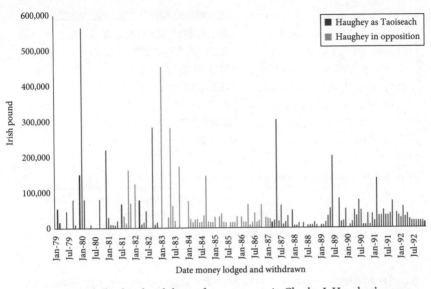

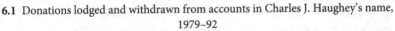

6.1 Donations lodged and withdrawn from accounts in Charles J. Haughey's name, 1979–92

third term as Taoiseach, from March 1987 to June 1989. His final term as Taoiseach, from July 1989 to February 1992, was met with IR£1,389,824 in funds.

Notwithstanding the Tribunal's deliberately 'conservative approach' in identifying payments, it estimated that Haughey received at least IR£9,106,369 in donations between 1979 and 1996 which the Tribunal calculated as €45 million in contemporary terms. At a time when Ireland was facing double digit inflation, rising unemployment, and soaring debt in the 1980s, Haughey was the beneficiary of 171 times his gross salary.[8]

Tracing the origins of much of this money has not been possible because of the complicated and secretive system of transfer of funds between accounts and Haughey's incomplete financial records. In particular, the Tribunal was unable to present a more comprehensive picture for the years 1987–91 'as there were no records of such funds available and there were no bank accounts in Mr. Haughey's name'.[9] Figure 6.2 illustrates just ten sources of the diverse funds available to Haughey from 1979–96.[10]

These difficulties were in part due to the death of Haughey's life-long confidant and accountant, Des Traynor in 1994, before the commencement of the Tribunal process. Traynor joined the board of directors of Gallagher Group in 1961 and later joined the board of Carlisle Trust Ltd, a company set up by property developer John Byrne, another friend of Haughey. The contacts and clients provided by Haughey led Traynor to become one of the most important

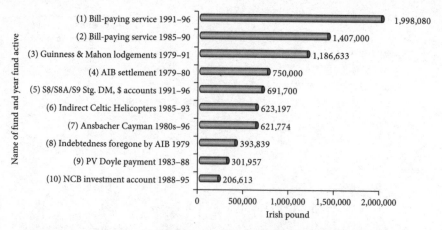

6.2 Top ten funds identified by Moriarty Tribunal available to Charles J. Haughey, 1979–96

financial advisers during the property development boom that took place in Dublin during the 1960s. This in turn brought him into contact with one of Dublin's oldest merchant banks, Guinness & Mahon. Traynor was a director of numerous enterprises including Aer Lingus and New Ireland Holdings.

The Tribunal also examined payments made to Haughey after he ceased to hold office as Taoiseach and his retirement from political life. Although payments to Haughey after 1992 'did not have the potential to influence the discharge of any public office', the Tribunal was nonetheless satisfied that donations were made 'in circumstances giving rise to a reasonable inference that the motive for making the payment(s) was connected with any public office held.'[11] Moreover, in the case of the 'S' series of accounts, for example, the only records available were for the years 1991–96 (see figure 6.2). Yet in his evidence to the Tribunal, Pádraig Collery, a senior bank official with Guinness & Mahon (Ireland) Ltd and a close associate of Traynor, noted that these accounts had been in existence for many years prior to 1992 and in all probability dated back to the mid 1970s.[12] This evidence would suggest the existence of a time delay between the receipt of gifts and donations and the registration of same within Haughey's financial records. For these reasons, donations received and withdrawals made by Haughey after he left political office 1992–96 are included in this analysis.

Dermot Desmond, a key Haughey benefactor, railed against public disquiet about the former Taoiseach's besmirched legacy. In a rare 2004 interview, the financier inquired: 'I keep asking people what did Charlie Haughey do wrong and how was he corrupt?'[13] This section will outline evidence from the Tribunal which challenges the unconvinced tone which underpins Desmond's rhetorical question.

The conventional analysis of Haughey's political decisions has been distracted by his colourful political career where focus is placed on who gave him money and how the brown paper envelopes changed hands. This section will instead examine the timing of payments and (1) how such donations tended to coincide with political decisions which benefited Haughey's financial patrons; (2) benefactors tended to be appointed to influential state bodies; (3) donors tended to be wealthy businessmen or have strong associations with banking and property interests; (4) financial contributions were made by a number of individuals who were formerly members of Taca or Ansbacher account holders.

This will be explored by analysing the indirect or direct benefits (i.e. contracts; intervention in tax matters; favours for families; rezoned land) obtained by prominent Haughey benefactors as listed in figure 6.3 such as Ben Dunne, Dermot Desmond, Mahmoud Fustok and John Byrne. In doing so, it will also demonstrate the challenge faced by the Tribunal of proving any definitive examples of wrong-doing. Despite the passage of time, this is not a definitive list as a comprehensive register of Haughey's funds still remains unidentified. Analysis will also be focused on the relationship between those who donated and were awarded prestigious political appointments and those closely aligned with banking interests.

Ben Dunne

Bernard (Ben) Dunne junior, the then head of the largest privately owned business in the state, donated IR£2,021,292 to Haughey when the latter was Taoiseach from 1987–92. Most of these payments serviced a bill-paying system used by Haughey to fund his extravagant lifestyle. On the eve of his election as Taoiseach in February 1987, Haughey's overdraft with the Guinness & Mahon Bank was over quarter of a million pounds. 'He may also have had a debt at the bank's Cayman Islands subsidiary equal to half a million pounds. He was struggling.'[14] A £282,500 sterling donation by Dunne in May 1987, therefore, was of particular benefit for the Taoiseach.

Haughey arranged a meeting between the Dunnes Stores supermarket tycoon and the chair of the Revenue Commissioners, Seamus Páircéir, within one month of becoming Taoiseach. The timing of Haughey's intervention and the subsequent 'complete about turn in the consistent thinking of Revenue', regarding a capital gains tax issue by the Dunne family Trust, 'cannot be tenably regarded as purely coincidental' the Tribunal argued. Negotiations with Páircéir and the Dunne Family Trust reduced their IR£38.8 million tax bill to IR£16 million, an IR£22.8 million reduction. Revenue argued that this was part and parcel of a normal arbitration process. In any event, the Appeals Commissioner, an independent body which decides on tax disputes between taxpayers and the Revenue, decided that no tax liability was due.

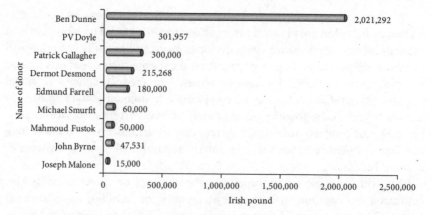

Notes: The Tribunal distinguished between direct and indirect donations. The Tribunal did not compile the total list of donations given by Dunne to Haughey, as was the case with P. V. Doyle in figure 6.2, in order to avoid double-counting as Dunne donated directly to Haughey and to several funds. Figures include Sterling converted to Irish pounds. Further information on Patrick Gallagher in chapter 4.

6.3 Direct and indirect donations identified by the Moriarty Tribunal to Charles J. Haughey from businessmen, 1979–96

Páircéir, who by then had retired and was apparently blind to the perception that a conflict of interest might be apparent, was retained by Dunne to assist in drawing up that appeal before the Appeals Commissioner. Haughey 'acted with a view to intervening improperly in a pending tax case of great magnitude' in return for such payments according to the Tribunal.[15] 'Irrespective of how matters ultimately unfolded, the Tribunal is satisfied that such an option was, at the time, a valuable and substantial benefit conferred on Mr Dunne, directly consequent on Mr Haughey's actions.'[16]

The timing of donations made by Dunne to Haughey and the timing of interventions made by Haughey on Dunne's behalf were quite fortunate for both men. Nonetheless, Dunne was 'aggrieved' at these findings and responded through the words of Shakespeare's *Othello*: 'But he that filches from me my good name / Robs me of that which not enriches him / And makes me poor indeed.'[17] Haughey, incidentally, also shared his benefactor's love of *Othello* and appealed to the Shakespearean tragedy in his 1992 resignation speech as Taoiseach: 'I have done the state some service; they know't / No more of that.' Haughey neglected to quote the rather ominous subsequent lines: 'I pray you, in your letters / When you shall these unlucky deeds relate, / Speak of me as I am; nothing extenuate, / Nor set down aught in malice.'

Dermot Desmond

Dermot Desmond founded National City Bank (NCB) Stockbrokers in 1981 and built it into Ireland's largest independent brokerage. The self-made entrepreneur is credited with helping transform Ireland's economy in the late 1980s with a proposal for Dublin's International Financial Services Centre. *Forbes* magazine calculated his wealth in 2009 at $1.5 billion.[18] Desmond became a tax exile domiciled in Gibraltar in the early 1990s.

Desmond made two payments totalling £125,000 sterling in 1994 and 1996 after Haughey had retired from public life. The Tribunal rejected Desmond's evidence that these were loans and noted that they were made 'in circumstances giving rise to a reasonable inference that the motive for making the payment(s) was connected with any public office held'.[19] The motive for these payments, the Tribunal believed, was connected with Haughey's term in office. The Tribunal rejected Desmond's evidence that he made no direct payments to Haughey before 1994. Although there was no evidence to the contrary, the Tribunal said that it could not 'make a finding to that effect as neither Mr. Haughey's off-shore accounts, nor Mr. Desmond's off-shore accounts were accessible to the Tribunal for the purposes of verifying this matter.'[20]

Desmond's IR£75,546 refurbishment of the Haughey 60-foot steel-hulled family yacht, *Celtic Mist*, in 1990 and 1991 constituted indirect payments to the then Taoiseach according to the Tribunal which noted that they totalled more than Haughey's gross salary at the time. Desmond also invested IR£26,667 and made a IR£55,000 loan to Feltrim, a mining company, in 1990 and 1991 'without agreeing any precise terms as to repayment'. This mining company was owned by Haughey's son Conor. The Tribunal did not believe that the Feltrim episode constituted any indirect payments to Haughey and these are not included in figure 6.3.[21]

Desmond's peers were in awe of his success. In 1991, *Irish Times* financial journalist, Jackie Gallagher, wrote of how Desmond's 'ability to generate business, especially from government quarters, amazed other stockbroking firms'. It negotiated the sale of the Department of Energy's 25 per cent interest in Tara Mines to a Finnish mining company. Gallagher noted that according to other brokers, NCB received three times the normal fee for its effort. NCB won many state contracts in the late 1980s and early 1990s to advise on the potential privatisation of semi-state bodies including Telecom Éireann, Aer Lingus, ESB and Irish Sugar when the latter was floated as Greencore in 1991. NCB was also the government's adviser on the privatisation of the life assurance company, Irish Life, the same year NCB withdrew from the Telecom privatisation study after the Ballsbridge site scandal erupted.

Desmond told Gallagher that suggestions that contracts were received because of his personal relationship with Haughey were begrudgery.

Contracts, he asserted, were awarded on merit because NCB were the only major independent stockbroking and corporate finance house in Ireland.[22] In 2010, the former editor of *Magill* magazine, Vincent Browne, settled a libel action and apologised for a 1998 article which gave 'rise to the inference or innuendo that Dermot Desmond and / or NCB were the beneficiaries of contracts awarded to NCB by the state as a direct result of, or in consideration of, alleged payments made by Dermot Desmond to Charles J Haughey.'[23]

Mahmoud Fustok

The Fustok case illustrates the indirect and Byzantine nature of the implicit and explicit benefits bestowed on Haughey by a benefactor whose relatives and close associates directly gained from the remarkable interventions made by Haughey when he was Taoiseach. Mahmoud Fustok, a Saudi Arabian billionaire bloodstock breeder, diplomat and brother-in-law of the Saudi Crown Prince, became acquainted with Haughey through John O'Connell, a politician with a chameleonic political career. Initially elected as a Labour TD from 1965–81, O'Connell joined the Fianna Fáil parliamentary party the same year that Fustok donated IR£50,000 to Haughey in February 1985 through O'Connell's bank account. O'Connell was later appointed by Haughey to the Seanad in 1987. The Tribunal described Fustok's fax explanation that this was money owed to Haughey for a horse as 'highly unconvincing and improbable.'[24]

Although the payment was made to Haughey when in opposition, fourteen relatives or close associates of Fustok were granted naturalisation between June 1981 and December 1982 when he was Taoiseach with a final naturalisation granted in May 1990 when Haughey was again Taoiseach. The Tribunal determined that Fustok's donation was made in circumstances which influenced the discharge of Haughey's political duties.[25] Haughey's unequivocal involvement in the final naturalisation, that of Faten Moubarak, was particularly obvious and was described by the Tribunal as 'wholly exceptional and disproportionate'. Despite the 'exceptionally explicit level of written and oral departmental (Department of Justice) advice over a lengthy period which had made clear the unanimous view of senior officials' that her application be rejected, Haughey gave a specific direction to the contrary. The senior civil servant, with responsibility for naturalisation, described Haughey's 'sustained and continual series of requests' which accumulated into a direct intervention to grant naturalisation as 'unprecedented'.[26]

Haughey directly intervened in the earlier naturalisation processes by making specific written and verbal requests to his Minister for Justice and ignoring the serious concerns raised by Garda authorities with respect to some of the applications. The Tribunal noted that as Taoiseach, Haughey tended 'to involve himself in the affairs of individual government departments, without any, or any proper reference to the responsible Ministers, and in so doing to deal inappropriately with individual Civil Servants'.[27] Moreover, 'in the teeth of robust departmental advices to the contrary' Haughey's 'consistent and exceptional support' ensured that the coveted Irish passports were granted to these fifteen non-nationals 'in a manner that could on no appraisal be viewed as transparent'.[28]

On his state visit to Ireland in June 1988, Fustok's brother-in-law, the Crown Prince Abdullah of Saudi Arabia, presented Haughey and his wife with a gold and jewel-encrusted dagger and a diamond necklace. The necklace alone was said to have been worth IR£250,000, but Haughey said the value had been exaggerated.[29] Haughey also holidayed at the Crown Prince's French chateau in Chantilly with his mistress, Terry Keane.

John Byrne

John Byrne was a major property developer. Haughey was a long-time associate and was widely believed to have been a "sleeping partner" in Byrne's burgeoning property business.[30] On the day of the 1987 general election, Byrne signed a IR£50,000 cheque made payable to the Guinness & Mahon Bank. The Tribunal concluded that it 'cannot exclude the real possibility that the cheque represented a payment intended for the benefit of Mr. Haughey, but in the absence of evidence that these funds were in fact applied for Mr. Haughey's benefit, the Tribunal equally cannot make a positive finding'.[31] In 1992 / 1993, Byrne invested IR£47,532 into Celtic Helicopters. The Tribunal believes that this payment was 'prompted by the connection to Mr. Haughey'.[32]

Byrne negotiated long-term property leasing agreements with the state in the 1960s, 1970s and 1980s. He received €5.55 million in rents from the state in 2004 alone.[33] For many years Traynor, Haughey's financial organiser and the man who raised the funds for Celtic Helicopters, was on the board of both Carlisle Trust and Dublin City Estates, property companies associated with Byrne. Byrne is a part-owner of the Brandon Hotel in Tralee and in 1988 benefited when urban renewal designation was granted to a site centred on the hotel. Urban renewal designation gave attractive tax incentives to development on designated sites. Byrne also benefited in a similar way in 1990 when Dublin's Liffey Quays designated area was extended to George's Quay. When these two decisions were made - in both 1988 and 1990 - Haughey was Taoiseach while Pádraig Flynn was Minister for the Environment and had the prime responsibility for designating areas for tax incentives.[34] Byrne was identified as an Ansbacher account holder in 2002.

Political appointments

The practice of appointing political supporters to prestigious positions on state boards has been a traditional source of patronage for the government of the day and became particularly evident during the Fianna Fáil and Fine Gael administrations of the 1980s. Appointments are made on the discretion of the relevant minister and are regarded as a reward for allies, friends and those who financially contribute to their political party. Membership of a generously remunerated state board, with additional expenses and perks, ensures influential "networking" opportunities among key political decision-makers and civil servants. Installing friends in top positions throughout the public sector allowed politicians to know what was going on in many different sectors of the economy and was a means of ensuring that the will of the government was implemented.

Joseph Malone, Paul Kavanagh and P. V. Doyle were three close associates of Haughey who were appointed to influential state bodies. Joseph (Joe) Malone was not a notable donor to Haughey but was closely associated with Fianna Fáil fundraising in the 1960s through to the 1980s. He was a prominent subscriber to Taca in the 1960s and helped establish the "Friends of Fianna Fáil" political fundraising organisation in the United States in the 1980s.[35] Malone served as Haughey's special adviser in the March 1982 election and was the chair of the Fianna Fáil fund-raising committee in the early 1980s. He invested IR£15,000, in the name of his son Joe, into the Celtic Helicopters account in March 1985. Malone's financial association with this commercial rival of Aer Lingus was at odds with his role as a director of the airline state body. Malone was an Ansbacher account holder and consequently paid a €108,759 settlement to the Revenue in 2004.

Malone's close association with Haughey and Fianna Fáil coincided with his political appointment to influential state bodies. The nature of his unorthodox appointment to the prestigious position of North American general manager to Bord Fáilte in 1966, caused uproar in the Dáil. There were apparently no other candidates for the unadvertised post which Michael Mullen TD, Labour, described as 'disgraceful'.[36] The Fianna Fáil Minister for Transport and Power, Erskine Childers, belittled Mullen's concerns by explaining that there were always 'exceptional occasions in regard to appointments at absolutely top level' and that such posts were often not advertised 'because one may want someone so eminent and so well known that the mere fact of that person applying through a public advertisement might cause difficulties for himself and for others. Everybody who has experience of the business world knows what I mean'.[37] Malone was appointed director general of Bord Fáilte under a Fine Gael / Labour government in 1976. He was reappointed to the Bord Fáilte board in November 1982 and as an Aer Lingus director in the early 1980s and 1990s under Fianna Fáil governments.

Paul Kavanagh was appointed by Haughey as Fianna Fáil's chief fundraiser in 1982. Like Malone, he was also appointed to a number of state boards, including Telecom Éireann, CTT, Aer Lingus, the IDA and An Post. In 1989, for a brief period, he was a Senator.

Paschal Vincent (PV) Doyle was one of Ireland's most successful hoteliers and building contractors and made payments amounting to IR£301,957 to Haughey from 1983–88. Doyle was appointed to the Bord Fáilte board in 1970 and remained in-situ until his death in 1988. The Tribunal was judicious in its view that 'the only possible inference is that they (the payments) were connected with Mr. Haughey's Public Office and as such must have had the potential to influence the discharge of such offices'.[38] Doyle and his son David were both named in the Ansbacher report as account holders.

Banking interests

The Moriarty Tribunal exposed an extraordinary degree of deference by regulatory authorities towards the Irish banking system and, similarly, absolute reverence by banking authorities towards politicians. This dual attitude of intense trust and submissiveness towards banking and political authority was not checked for over three decades. An overlap between prominent Haughey donors and associates and those keenly allied with banking interests appeared to exist in the cases of Guinness & Mahon Bank (G&M), Allied Irish Bank (AIB) and National Irish Bank (NIB).

Guinness & Mahon (G&M)

For instance, inspectors from the Central Bank examined the G&M loan book in 1976 and 1978 and expressed concern that 'Guinness & Mahon was facilitating a tax avoidance scheme . . . [which] was tantamount to facilitating tax evasion'.[39] Since 1972, when the Cayman Islands left the sterling area, it had been unlawful to send money to offshore trusts there without declaring it for exchange controls.

The system worked like this: money, probably undeclared, was lodged in the Ansbacher deposits. No tax was paid on the interest that accrued. A loan was taken out, secretly backed or secured by the deposits. The person or business who took out the loan then claimed tax relief on the interest which accrued on the loan. It was a double tax fraud. Not only had G&M set up a structure that allowed some of the foremost business figures in the state, including the most powerful politician in the state, Charles Haughey, to avoid the exchange control regulations of the 1970s and 1980s, it also allowed some of them to salt away what were probably undeclared fortunes offshore.

Despite the misgivings of the Central Bank, it decided to trust a commitment made by Traynor, the then de facto chief executive of G&M, that G&M would wind down loan business to Irish residents that was backed by offshore deposits. The 1978 Central Bank inspection found that one of its own

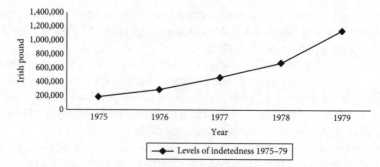

6.4 Charles J. Haughey's indebtedness to Allied Irish Bank, 1975–79

directors, Ken O'Reilly-Hyland, had a loan of IR£416,000 secured by a deposit of IR£230,000 in Cayman.

The Tribunal noted that the 'ultimate responsibility for the supervisory and other roles of the Central Bank rests with the Board, which comprises a Governor and nine Non-Executive Directors. The sole shareholder and therefore the owner of the Bank is the Minister for Finance.' O'Reilly-Hyland, a Central Bank board appointee from 1973 to 1983, was a well-known member of Taca and the chair of Fianna Fáil's general election fund-raising committee in the 1970s and 1980s. Governments are responsible for the level of regulation, and there was clearly a massive regulatory failure. This systematic evasion went on for over two decades, unhindered by the Central Bank, the Revenue Commissioners, company law regulators or prosecuting authorities.

Allied Irish Bank (AIB)
Haughey's indebtedness to AIB, as figure 6.4 illustrates, spiralled from IR£188,844 to IR£1,143,839 within a four year period.[40] The Tribunal noted that the bank 'exhibited a marked deference in its attitude' towards Haughey, despite the six-fold increase in his personal debt.[41] This was exemplified in a 1976 AIB memorandum which outlined Haughey's response to the AIB Banking Department Lending Committee which sought to adopt a 'very hard line' on the then opposition TD's debt: 'Haughey became quite vicious and told Mr. Denvir [bank official] that "He would not give up his cheque books as he had to live," and "That we were dealing with an adult and no banker would talk to him, Mr. Haughey, in this manner." Furthermore he stated that if any drastic action were taken by the bank he could be a "very troublesome" adversary.'[42]

On his election as Taoiseach in December 1979, Haughey's personal overdraft was seventy-seven times his IR£14,717 gross annual salary. In terms of contemporary worth, in 2010, seventy-seven times the Taoiseach's annual salary amounted to €6,618,054. Traynor met with senior AIB bank officials, including Niall Crowley, that same month and negotiated a IR£393,000 write-down of Haughey's debt. The Tribunal described this 'somewhat unorthodox' bank discount, which amounted to a third of Haughey's overall arrears, as conferring 'a substantial benefit on Mr. Haughey in circumstances referable to his political office' and as 'an indirect payment'.[43]

Conor Crowley, member of the Fianna Fáil fundraising committee in the early 1980s, was a brother of Niall Crowley, chair of AIB from 1977 to 1989. When Peter Murtagh noted this sibling relationship in a 1983 *Irish Times* article, the newspaper issued an apology for 'the inadvertent context of the reference' and stated that it had 'no intention to imply that Niall Crowley was in any way connected with Fianna Fáil fundraising, nor the bank of which he is chairman'.[44]

Other prominent Haughey benefactors with banking interests included Michael Smurfit who donated IR£60,000, by a transfer of funds to an off-shore account, to Fianna Fáil at the 1989 election. Haughey ultimately applied this for his personal benefit. Smurfit was a director of AIB from 1978–83. He testified to the Moriarty Tribunal that he was not aware that Haughey was an AIB account holder and had no knowledge of the then Taoiseach's indebtedness.[45] Smurfit was appointed as the chair of semi-state body, Telecom (see chapter five) and was appointed as Ireland's honorary consul to Monaco where he resides as a tax exile.

National Irish Bank (NIB)

Haughey misappropriated state funds and money intended for Fianna Fáil for personal use. These abuses of public office for personal gain above all garnered in the public mind Haughey's personal venality. The Party Leader's Allowance was paid by the Exchequer to the leaders of the Irish political parties for the purposes of meeting expenses incurred in connection with the party's parliamentary activities. Although drawings were made to meet legitimate expenses of the Fianna Fáil party 'the Tribunal is nonetheless left with the clear impression that Mr. Haughey treated the account, and the funds held to the credit of the account, as being available to him. . .for his personal use'. In all, IR£598,208 was drawn from the party leader's account, held at AIB, between 1984 and 1991.[46] An absence of records makes it difficult to quantify how much of this Haughey used for personal or party purposes. It is however public knowledge that Haughey withdrew money from the state-funded allowance in 1992 to pay his personal expenses with Le Coq Hardi restaurant in Dublin, the Parisian shirt-making firm Charvet and other private bills.

Haughey did use the allowance to pay IR£26,000 of John Ellis's personal debts in 1989. If NIB were successful in its bankruptcy proceedings against the Sligo-Leitrim Fianna Fáil TD, his automatic disbarment from Dáil Éireann would have left Haughey with a potential by-election loss at a politically crucial time. This was a naked instance of abusing public funds to preserve personal power. Reminiscent of AIB's deferential treatment of Haughey, NIB subsequently wrote off IR£243,000 of Ellis debts and settled for IR£20,000.

The Irish public were especially galled at the revelation that Haughey had stolen IR£130,000 in donations to Fianna Fáil in 1989 intended for the US medical treatment of his friend, the then popular Tánaiste, Brian Lenihan, who he described to the Tribunal as 'closer to me than one of my own brothers'.[47] Edmund Farrell, managing director of the Irish Permanent Building Society 1975–93, made payments amounting to IR£180,000 to Haughey. IR£140,000 of this was from funds provided by Irish Permanent Building Society. Farrell intended that IR£20,000 was for the Lenihan fund but this was misappropriated by Haughey. The Tribunal was satisfied 'beyond doubt' that 'a sizeable proportion of the excess funds collected [for Lenihan] were misappropriated by Mr Haughey for personal use'.[48] Haughey also 'deliberately and skilfully' diverted IR£85,000 in donations intended for the party's 1989 general election campaign for his own discretionary use. The journalist Vincent Browne has estimated that sums in excess of IR£1 million intended for Fianna Fáil, both in donations and funds from the leader's account, were diverted to Haughey's personal accounts.[49]

Fianna Fáil has never sought to repatriate any of this stolen money from the Haughey estate. Immediately after the publication of the Moriarty Tribunal report, Lenihan's sister, Mary O'Rourke, said that matters relating to Haughey and the Lenihan family were now a 'closed book'.[50] The response by Bertie Ahern TD, leader of Fianna Fáil and Taoiseach from 1997 to 2008 was more intricate. At the party's Ard Fheis (annual conference) in 1997, Ahern unequivocally disavowed his former mentor with the words 'There would be no place in our party today for that kind of past behaviour.' In his graveside oration for Haughey in 2006, six months before the Moriarty Tribunal was published, Ahern described "The Boss" as 'a legend and a man. A political leader of peerless acumen and commanding talent. He was a patriot to his fingertips. I have no doubt but that the ultimate judgement of history will be positive'.

Ahern, Ray MacSharry and Haughey were the three signatories on the Leader's Allowance Account and in his report, Mr. Justice Moriarty outlines several instances where discrepancies between those that donated to the party and the party's records should have been obvious.[51] Moriarty's explanation for why these discrepancies were not pursued also serves to explain why the party deliberately chose to remain firmly silent on Haughey's embezzlement of Fianna Fáil's funds: 'The only reasonable explanations for all of these omissions are that: either those concerned were deeply embarrassed by what had occurred and chose to adopt a diplomatic approach to the issue, or that there was a tacit understanding between them that the matter had arisen in a former era and that its details were best left undisturbed'[52]

Conclusion

When asked if it was appropriate that politicians should accept such large donations from the business community for his personal benefit, Haughey said that it depended on 'the meaning of the word beholden . . . There are many public-spirited people who subscribe to political parties and to individual politicians and who have no anticipation of anything other than the political success of the individual'. Haughey made the distinction between donations seeking influence and those alleviating 'the financial difficulties of a particular politician' where 'a group of friends would come together and out of purely altruistic motives assist a particular politician in a particular spot of difficulty'.[53]

Nonetheless, Haughey's wealthy benefactors tended to benefit from influential political appointments to state bodies such as Aer Lingus and Bord Fáilte, boards with heavily subsided foreign travel. For many within the Haughey golden circle, serving the public interest was rewarded by personal gain. As outlined, donations tended to coincide with political decisions which benefited Haughey's financial patrons. Colm Keena, *Irish Times* journalist, made the observation that those named in the Ansbacher report 'included a number of people who were at the heart of the Haughey / Taca / Fianna Fáil fund-raising scene from the 1960s to the 1980s. There was common ground between Taca and Ansbacher, and between Ansbacher and the people who gave money to Haughey. Given the size of the economy at the time it would be surprising if it was otherwise'.[54]

The Tribunal was unequivocal in its findings. The 'inescapable conclusions must be drawn that he [Charles Haughey] received a wide range of substantial payments and that certain of the acts or decisions on his part while Taoiseach, were referable to some of those payments'.[55] The tone of the language used by the inquiry was clear-cut. Although the timing of these donations did not always coincide with when Haughey was Taoiseach or in politics, the Tribunal determined that the 'invariably secretive nature of payments from senior members of the business community, their very incidence and scale . . . can only be said to have devalued the quality of a modern democracy'.[56] Haughey was a corrupting influence on the public life of the Irish state. His use of public power for personal gain was so entrenched that it took a family feud within the Dunne family and the JMSE building company plus three Tribunals to expose what most of those around him already knew.

The McCracken Tribunal 1997 and Moriarty Tribunal 1997–2011
(volume 2)

Mr. Justice Michael Moriarty published his second and penultimate Tribunal report a month after the February 2011 general election. A link to the two volume 2,395 page report, was issued on the Tribunal's website without any media notice or public forewarning. The inconspicuous manner in which the high-profile inquiry into political corruption was published was probably a deliberate strategy by a judge accustomed to the threat of legal injunctions which had beset the fourteen-year investigation.

Of the eight public inquiries established since the foundation of the state to probe political corruption, the Moriarty Tribunal was the most significant. Yet, unlike the Great Southern Railway, Ward, Locke, McCracken, Beef and Mahon / Flood Tribunals, governments did not fall, nor did prominent political personalities prematurely resign as a consequence of tribunal's scrutiny. Moriarty was however more far-reaching than its predecessors because it sought to comprehensively redefine the traditional interpretation of legal corruption and introduce a wider understanding of fraudulent behaviour by instead focusing on the power of influence in political action.

The primary purpose of the second Moriarty report was to examine the financial relationship between Michael Lowry, and businessmen Ben Dunne and Denis O'Brien, in order to determine if the Fine Gael minister had used his public office to confer a benefit to the supermarket tycoon and the Telecoms entrepreneur. Lowry was the recipient of large direct or facilitated financial contributions (i.e. loan support; payment in kind; beneficial business arrangements) from the two benefactors as listed in figure 6.5. Dunne and O'Brien also contributed to Fine Gael. According to the second Moriarty

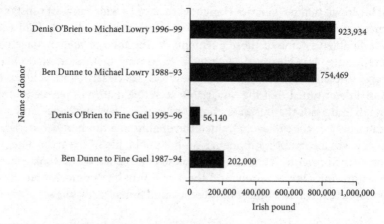

6.5 Direct and indirect donations identified by the Moriarty Tribunal to Michael Lowry and Fine Gael

report, Dunne and O'Brien were the potential beneficiary or direct beneficiary of two decisions which Lowry sought to influence (a rent arbitration and
a mobile phone licence evaluation process) during his period as Minister for
Transport, Energy and Communications. Lowry became chair of the trustees
of the Fine Gael parliamentary party in 1993 with responsibility for fund-
raising. Appointed as minister in 1994, in what was known as the Rainbow
Coalition, Lowry resigned from the Fine Gael, Labour/Democratic Left coalition government in November 1996 when it emerged that he had failed to
disclose substantial payments from Dunne. The North-Tipperary TD also
neglected to make a full disclosure of his tax affairs, as he was obliged to do on
his appointment as minister.

The investigation into Lowry and O'Brien almost did not happen.
Proceedings instituted by Haughey against the Tribunal held up the anticipated conclusion of its work in 2000. Unfortunately for Lowry, journalist
Matt Cooper published a series of articles in the *Sunday Tribune* in February
and March 2001 regarding a $50,000 donation to Fine Gael. This initiated a
new line of inquiry for the Tribunal to a STG£420,000 Investec / Woodchester
loan involving both Lowry and O'Brien.

Ben Dunne

Ben Dunne donated IR£202,000 to the Fine Gael party and party representatives between 1987 and 1994. This included three separate contributions to
the Opposition party of IR£30,000, IR£50,000 and IR£100,000 in 1989, 1991
and 1993 respectively.[57]

Lowry was pivotal in eliminating Fine Gael's substantial debts in the early
1990s and in assisting individual party candidates to raise funds from Dunne.
It was Lowry, for instance, who arranged and was present at the meeting in
Dunne's home in May 1991 when the director of Ireland's largest supermarket chain gave John Bruton, the newly elected leader of Fine Gael, a IR£50,000
cheque for the party. The timing of this contribution was providential for Fine
Gael given the prospect of an imminent election due to deepening fault lines
emerging within the Fianna Fáil / PD Coalition government. Five Fianna Fáil
cabinet ministers had said they did not believe that Haughey would lead the
party into the next election. Haughey's leadership crisis revolved around his
denials that he had held a meeting with the Greencore chair about the privatisation of Irish Sugar (see chapter 5).

Dunne also donated IR£22,000 to individual politicians. Michael Noonan,
Minister for Justice 1982–86, was the beneficiary of IR£3,900, via Lowry,
towards his 1992 general election expenses. Noonan's Limerick East constituency received contributions totalling IR£3,000 from Dunne in 1993 and 1994.
Lowry rang rising political star, Ivan Yates, during the 1992 campaign to tell
him there was IR£5,000 cash from Dunne for his election expenses waiting

to be collected by him at a Dublin hotel. Yates told the McCracken Tribunal that this donation amounted to half the total costs of his campaign and was by far the biggest donation he had ever received.[58] Dunne also donated sums ranging from IR£1,000 to IR£5,000 to prominent Fine Gael office holders, Jim Mitchell, Seán Barrett, Fintan Coogan and John Bruton. McCracken classified these payments as 'ordinary political donations' and that there was 'no ulterior motive for making of any of these payments.'[59]

Vincent Browne disagreed with McCracken's conclusion that the motivation behind Dunne's generous contributions was 'to ensure a stable opposition to the government.'[60] McCracken acknowledged that Fine Gael was 'facing serious financial difficulties' in 1991. Yet, as Browne noted, the party were 'bankrupt in late 1994. Within a year it was flush with cash'.[61] The journalist has repeatedly made the case for a more thorough examination of Fine Gael's finances from the early to mid-1990s.

The aggregate of payments made to Lowry by Dunne in the five-year period from 1988–93, approximated to IR£754,469.[62] These were very often indirectly given by Dunne to Lowry via the latter's company, Streamline Enterprises, which was responsible for the supply and maintenance of refrigeration equipment in all the Dunnes Stores outlets within the state. This unorthodox business agreement between Dunne and Streamline, McCracken noted, was 'never reduced to writing, and in financial terms, were vague in the extreme'. Payments were also disguised as bonuses to Lowry and his staff and were frequently disbursed through offshore accounts in the Isle of Man and Jersey. The Dunne Group also contributed, as a payment in kind, to the refurbishment of Lowry's Tipperary home in Holy Cross which cost IR£395,000. Although Lowry has always maintained that all of these payments were for work done by Streamline, the money was lodged to personal accounts and it was not declared for tax purposes.

McCracken described the financial relationship between Dunnes Stores, Lowry and Streamline Enterprises as 'an unhealthy business relationship under any circumstances' which was aggravated by the fact that 'a Government Minister and Chairman of a Parliamentary Party can be seen to be consistently benefiting from the black economy from shortly after the time he was first elected to Dáil Éireann.' McCracken also determined that by his tax evasion Lowry had 'made himself vulnerable to all kinds of pressures from Dunnes Stores, had they chosen to apply those pressures'. Despite these missives, McCracken found that 'there was no political impropriety' on the part of Lowry.[63]

Moriarty went much further than McCracken and explicitly linked the receipt of large contributions from businessmen with the bestowal of implicit influence and inappropriate decision-making by those in public office. This formal acknowledgement of the impropriety of such behaviour left little room for any ambiguity which had characterised earlier inquires, such as the Beef Tribunal. The investigation into Lowry's intervention within an arbitration being conducted to fix the revised rent payable in respect of Marlborough House in 1995, underlined the significance which Moriarty now placed on influence.

The parties to the arbitration were Dunne who had recently acquired the landlord's interest in the property, Telecom Éireann and Lowry, who as the Minister for Communications, was the ultimate shareholder. In what amounted to a grave conflict of interest, Lowry sought, but fortunately was foiled in his attempt, to confer on Dunne a benefit amounting to approximately IR£2.38 million in the short term. He endeavoured to do so by seeking to influence Mark FitzGerald, the business partner of the arbitrator. FitzGerald, a trustee of Fine Gael with a long-standing family history of association with the party, gave evidence that after he rebuffed the Minister, Lowry responded: 'What are "we" going to do, as Ben Dunne has contributed £170,000 to Fine Gael?' There was no equivocation on the part of Moriarty who was clear cut in his conclusion that Lowry's request of FitzGerald 'was inextricably linked to Mr. Ben Dunne's status as a financial supporter and benefactor of Fine Gael.'[64]

If this unwarranted rent increase had been secured, it would have resulted in a capital value of Dunne's property of IR£12.75 million, a virtual doubling of his investment of IR£5.4 million made just months earlier. Moreover, Lowry's actions would not only have improperly enriched Dunne but 'burdened public funds within his Ministerial remit.' This 'particularly flagrant dereliction of duty', Moriarty said, 'was profoundly corrupt to a degree that was nothing short of breathtaking'. The strength of the judge's estimation of Lowry's conduct can be gauged from the fact that this was the only occasion throughout the 2,395 page, two-volume report, that the word corrupt was evoked to describe a political action.

Denis O'Brien

O'Brien was in his mid-thirties when he had attained the reputation as a businessman of international repute. The Corkyman and son of a veterinary supplier founded Esat Telecommunications Limited in 1991 for the purpose of providing competitive telecommunications services both in Ireland and worldwide. The ambitious UCD history and politics graduate was already successful with 98 FM, the Dublin commercial radio station. His triumphant bid for the state's second mobile phone licence in 1996 dramatically propelled his business career and financial resources. In 2001 he established and became chair of the privately-owned Digicel Group, one of the fastest growing cellular companies in the world. *Forbes* listed him as Ireland's second richest billionaire in 2011 and he was ranked at 254 internationally.[65]

O'Brien has engaged in spectacular acts of philanthropy, most notably in post-earthquake Haiti. Appointed to the Bank of Ireland board in 2000, he was then promoted as deputy to the Bank governor in 2005, one of the most prestigious positions in Irish business. In many ways he is a synonymous public figure and is a powerful individual in the business, sporting, philan-thropy and media communities in Ireland. O'Brien's commanding wealth is just one source of his power. His immense media interests include national radio stations, Newstalk, Today FM and 98FM and two local radio stations and he is the largest shareholder in Independent News and Media (INM).

O'Brien donated IR£923,934 in 'clandestine circumstances' and loan sup-port to Lowry between July 1996 and December 1999. These came in three separate instalments, the first less than seven weeks after the mobile phone licence was granted, and include IR£147,000, STG£300,000 and a 'benefit equivalent to a payment' in the form of support for a loan of STG£420,000.[66] The £147,000 payment was returned by Lowry when the McCracken Tribunal was established in February 1997.

O'Brien contributed substantially less to Fine Gael, just IR£56,140. This figure includes the controversial IR£33,000 Esat/Telenor donation (see p. 65). The timing of these donations, within an eighteen-month period between March 1995 and June 1996, was part of 'a strategy of promoting himself and his companies with members of Fine Gael.' The Tribunal also believed that O'Brien's attendance at fourteen Fine Gael fundraising events during this time formed part of his preparations for the second mobile licence bid, as they occurred 'during the currency of the GSM competition and subsequent licensing negotiations'.[67] The Former Minister of communications and serving Fine Gael TD, Jim Mitchell and prominent party member, Dan Egan, were appointed as political consultants for the purposes of advising on financial contributions and effecting meetings with senior Fine Gael ministers.

The Tribunal investigated if Lowry intervened or influenced the outcome of an evaluation process which decided the destination of Ireland's valuable second mobile phone license, the single largest procurement award in the history of the state. As Minister for Transport, Energy and Communications, Lowry's Department had responsibility for the competitive process which had six bidders. O'Brien was chair of, and a significant beneficiary in Esat Digifone, the eventual winner of the licence in 1996. Esat was later sold in 2000 to British Telecom for IR£2.3 billion. O'Brien was reported to have netted IR£289 million from the sale and his decision to become a tax exile in Portugal is estimated to have saved him IR£55 million in capital gains tax.[68]

The timing of O'Brien's donations to Lowry and Fine Gael, and the inter-ventions by Lowry, appear to coincide with critical stages in the evaluation process. (1) The government decision to authorise the holding of a process in March 1995 coincided with two small donations of IR£2,000 and IR£1,000 by O'Brien to Fine Gael. (2) Moriarty was unable to disguise his scepticism regarding Lowry and O'Brien's account of their 15 September 1995 chance encounter where both men:

> happened to attend the All-Ireland Football Final at Croke Park. They happened to be seated in the same area; they happened to encounter each other during the half time interval; and they happened to arrange to meet later . . . [they] repaired across the road together to Hartigans licensed premises, where they remained alone for some half hour and talked of nothing other than the match, and Mr. O'Brien's fixed-line business.[69]

Relying solely on circumstantial evidence, Moriarty determined that O'Brien 'must have shared with Mr. Lowry the single matter that was preoccupying his thoughts, namely, his strategy of strengthening the Department's perception of his side of the finances of Esat Digifone'. (3) Two weeks later, at the beginning of October, Lowry conceived the notion of 'bankability' as a solution to the financial frailties of Esat's bid. Although Esat were the top-ranked applicant at this time, they did not meet the precondition of financial capability. Bankability however allowed for the prospect that banks would regard the mobile phone project as an attractive investment and seek to invest after the licence was issued. The introduction of bankability into the evaluation criteria by Lowry, some eight months after the process commenced, was crucial to the success of Esat's bid and circumvented stated government policy.

(4) In mid-October, Esat donated IR£4,000 in what the Tribunal described as 'a deliberately discreet if not anonymous sponsor, of a Fine Gael Golf Classic' which was distinguished by 'its proximity in time to the conclusion of the evaluation process.' (5) Lowry applied a guillotine to the work of the Project Group the following week. The Project Group, comprised of civil servants and external Danish consultants, had responsibility for evaluating the competitive process and were not convinced that Esat should be nominated as the winner of the process. Confused about the weightings applied and how the result had emerged, they sought more time to revisit and review the evaluation. Lowry prevented them from doing so.[70] (6) A $50,000 (IR£33,000) donation by Esat, via Telenor - the Norwegian shareholder in Esat - was made to Fine Gael immediately after it emerged that that Esat had won the competition. The Fine Gael party leader, John Bruton, later rejected the donation. (7) O'Brien donated IR£147,000 to Lowry in July 1996, a month after the licence was granted.

Despite a voluminous report saturated with convoluted detail, the essence of it is straightforward. Lowry was the recipient of direct or facilitated financial contributions, as was his political party, by a businessman who benefited from a decision made by his department. Aside from the money-trail, a cocktail of irregularities within the evaluation process was complemented by the 'insidious and pervasive influence' of a minister. The wordy report can be reduced to this paragraph by the judge:

> Lowry displayed an appreciable interest in the substantive process, had irregular interactions with interested parties at its most sensitive stages, sought and received substantive information on emerging trends, made his preferences as between the leading candidates known, conveyed his views on how the financial weakness of Esat Digifone should be countered, ultimately brought a guillotine down on the work of the Project Group, proceeded to bypass consideration by his Cabinet colleagues, and thereby not only influenced, but delivered, the result that he announced on 25th October, 1995, that Esat Digifone had won the evaluation process, which ultimately led to the licensing of Esat Digifone on 16th May, 1996.[71]

Conclusion

The Moriarty Tribunal slayed the myth that unethical political exploits were the exclusive preserve of Fianna Fáil. Membership of this particular political party was not a necessary prerequisite for unorthodox behaviour. The Tribunal report instead attested that it was due to a proximity to power. Moriarty determined that both Haughey and Lowry, in their 'cynical and venal abuse of office . . . displayed qualities similar in nature'. Although both men were in separate governments of entirely different political composition, they showed 'favour to wealthy or prominent individuals, and in recompense obtain payments or other benefits, in each instance bringing improper influence to bear on public servants for the end as sought'.[72]

No previous Tribunal had to endure such sustained criticism of its work which Moriarty referred to as 'splenetic outpourings of abuse'.[73] O'Brien depicted the work of the Tribunal as 'totally biased', and that its activities constituted 'a new low in Irish judicial history'.[74] O'Brien, who personally made over a quarter of a billion Irish pounds arising from the sale of an asset granted by the state and immediately afterwards became a tax exile, became an unlikely knight in shining armour for the Irish taxpayer. He focused trenchantly on the implications of the Tribunal findings regarding the possibility of substantial compensation from rival bidders who failed to win the lucrative mobile phone licence and the legal costs of the Tribunal. 'We've had to take the fight to the tribunal otherwise the Government will be faced with a massive claim for damages', he told the *Sunday Times*.[75] He also established a website, www.moriartytribunal.com, to present his own views on the Tribunal evidence, which was described by the director general of the Law Society, Ken Murphy, as a 'sustained polemic against the Moriarty Tribunal and certain named individuals associated with it'.[76]

Lowry alleged that 'Moriarty's credibility was shattered because of his selective approach to evidence during the private and public enquiry.'[77] In essence, both O'Brien and Lowry implied that a judge regarded as the epitome of judicial sobriety and propriety had gone rogue and become obsessed with destroying Ireland's international reputation.[78] The intensity, of what amounted to a direct attack on the very integrity of the judiciary, was such that the Minister for Justice, Alan Shatter, felt it necessary to publicly defend the 'independent and impartial role of the judiciary'.[79]

For instance, a key point of contention between the Moriarty Tribunal and O'Brien and Lowry, was the judge's interpretation of the evidence by the experienced Professor Michael Andersen, the lead consultant in the Project Group. Andersen, a Danish expert who was involved in over 120 such licence processes in almost fifty jurisdictions worldwide prior to the Irish competition, testified that the bid by Esat was one of the best he had ever seen.[80] Both Andersen and the two key civil servants who steered the evaluation said that they witnessed no indication of any political interference on the part of Lowry. Nonetheless, Moriarty concluded that the civil servants' concern for administrative efficiency of the project meant that they 'unwittingly lost sight of its adjudicative character'. Moriarty also dismissed Andersen's deposition, instead asserting that:

> The retention of expert consultants provided no guarantee of an objective process, free of political influence . . . That the consultants presided over and endorsed an evaluation process, that deviated so markedly from their recommended methodology, was at odds with any reasonable expectation that the rigour of the process would be underwritten by their input.[81]

The conclusions by Moriarty have been vehemently contested on the grounds that that he inferred transactions, exchanges and conversations between Lowry and O'Brien on the basis of circumstantial evidence.[82] *The People (A.G.) v William Sullivan* however determined that circumstantial evidence may be corroborative evidence where a collection of circumstantial evidence has a cumulative effect and tends to implicate the accused.[83] Or, as Moriarty put it:

> Put more bluntly, surveying the odd backdrop of happenstance, silence and implausibility comprised by much of the evidence, and the manner and time in which it came to be recounted, it is inevitable that a stage is reached when the Tribunal must ask "does all this have the ring of truth?", and conclude that much emphatically does not.[84]

Furthermore, at the heart of Lowry and O'Brien's objections was this assertion by Lowry that the High Court judge, with over four decades of legal experience, had 'outrageously abused the Tribunal's ability to form opinions which are not substantiated by evidence or fact'.[85] In essence this amounted to a tension between two diverse interpretations in how corruption is defined.

An understanding between the distinction of corruption and influence is important in order to appreciate the very different analysis of the Tribunal report by Lowry and O'Brien on the one hand, and that which was adhered to by Moriarty.

A traditional definition of corruption necessitates that a finding of corrupt behaviour is one where a direct exchange of public goods or state resources has occurred in return for private financial gain. The corruption is therefore direct and explicit. The world has not worked like that for some time. By its very nature corruption is secretive, complex and is generally not of the obliging kind that provides an arsenal of smoking guns. Influence, however, is indirect and implicit. It is an informal misuse of power which occurs where personal relationships, lobbying, political favours and political donations unduly influence the decision-making process even if no laws are broken.

Chapter 8 details how the role of influence within the definition of corruption is internationally recognised. Article 18 of the United Nations Convention Against Corruption, for example, is dedicated to 'Trading in Influence'. The 1999 Council of Europe Criminal Law Convention on Corruption has defined influence as 'background corruption'. The Tribunal terms of reference reflected these international conventions.

> Term of Reference (e) embraces substantial payments made directly or indirectly to Mr. Michael Lowry in circumstances giving rise to a reasonable inference that the motive for making the payment was connected with any public office held by him or had the potential to influence the discharge of such office.[86]

Moriarty stopped short of making a definitive finding of corruption regarding the decision by Lowry to award the lucrative licence to Esat in 1996. Indeed, despite the 2,395 pages of the corruption report, the word 'corrupt' was directly used on just one occasion à propos of Lowry's 'profoundly corrupt' relationship with Dunne. Moriarty instead, and very deliberately, used the word influence. In doing so, this challenged public opinion to reassess its own acquiescence to the adage of the harp as a metaphor for the use of influence - in order to get anything.

The Flood / Mahon Tribunal 1997–

The consequences of a decade of political instability marked by constant campaigning and opportunities for personal financial gain arising from political decisions, began to emerge publicly from the early 1990s. A Green Party councillor, Tervor Sargent TD, caused uproar in Dublin County Council chamber in February 1993 when he held up a £100 cheque from an unnamed property development manager acting on behalf of a landowner seeking a rezoning decision and asked if other councillors had received such cheques from developers in order to influence their decisions. The property development manager later told the *Irish Times* that he regularly made personal representations to politicians and that the cheque did not 'constitute an improper advance or to exercise undue influence, but sufficient to stimulate the readings of the enclosed brochure'.[87]

The *Irish Independent* published claims by Joan Burton, Minister of State for Labour, in 1993 that 'a loose coalition of FG and FF councillors has pushed through a series of rezonings . . . Observers of this process have been shocked at the sight of developers, their agents and lobbyists, including some with notorious political connections, crowding the council's antechamber and gallery, ticking off lists of councillors as they arrive and vote for decisions that multiply at a stroke the value of lands they own or control'.[88] Forty-one Fianna Fáil and Fine Gael Dublin councillors claimed the article was defamatory, sought an apology and sued for compensation.

On foot of the Sargent and Burton incidents, the Minister for the Environment, Michael Smith, openly stated that zoning in the Dublin County Council area was a 'debased currency.' In response to what he described as 'a frightening degree of irresponsibility' in the planning process, Smith reorganised the seventy-eight member Dublin County Council into three separate bodies – Fingal, South Dublin and Dun Laoghaire / Rathdown – as a means of ensuring that councillors were held more directly accountable for their decisions.[89] Smith also ordered a Garda Investigation where all seventy-eight members of the council were interviewed and a file was sent to the DPP. No-one was prosecuted. Frustrated by perceived wrongdoing within the planning process, environmental campaigners, Michael Smith and Colm MacEochaidh, placed an anonymous advertisement in the *Irish Times* in 1995: '£10,000 Reward Fund. Information leading to the conviction of (*sic*) indictment of a person or persons for offences relating to Land Re\zoning in the Republic of Ireland'. Six specific allegations were subsequently forwarded to the Gardaí.

This created the momentum for the establishment of the Flood / Mahon Tribunal into Certain Planning Matters and Payments, established on 4 November 1997. It focused on corruption within the local government planning process over a thirty-year period and cast a light on the relationship between the networks of developers, politicians at national and local level, local authority officials and lobbyists in the rezoning of those lands.[90] It highlighted how allegations of bribery involved relatively small sums of cash, on average IR£1,300.[91]

A 1997 public advertisement by the Tribunal seeking information in relation to corruption returned 184 submissions and complaints. These did not fall into any particular geographic pattern or location, but from all parts of the country, urban and rural, suggesting that irregularities within the planning process were wide-ranging.[92] This lengthy time-span and the diverse range of actors across the political spectrum under investigation were reflected in the dense detail of the Tribunal's four interim reports, published between 1998 and 2004.[93] The range of topics investigated were widened to include radio broadcasting and offshore trusts and corporations. Indeed, when Mahon indicated on 29 October 2008 that the Tribunal had effectively ended its public sittings, the Tribunal had sat for a total of 916 days, generated 60,000 pages of evidence and some 76,000 pages of correspondence with 400 witnesses.

A large portion of the 2002 second interim Flood Tribunal report, which sold in excess of 25,000 copies to members of the public, some of whom had queued overnight to buy the €1 publication, was dedicated to political decisions made by Ray Burke. Chapter 4 has already outlined several matters of concern in relation to Burke's period as a local government councillor (1967–78; 1985–87) and TD for Dublin North (1973–97). Burke's nine terms in ministerial office spanned the key portfolios of Industry, Commerce and Energy, Environment, Energy, Communications, Justice and Foreign Affairs. This section will explore the beneficial relationships that existed between Burke and Century Radio, Joseph Murphy Structural Engineering and developers Tom Brennan and Joseph McGowan, thus demonstrating the ubiquitous nature of corruption and the protracted abuse of political discretion.

Ray Burke

Joseph Murphy Structural Engineering (JMSE)

Burke's enduring association with JMSE reveals the degree to which planning legislation was manipulated for private ends. The planning appeals board, An Bord Pleanála, was established in 1976 and allowed third parties the right to appeal planning decisions made by local authorities. Planning law requires those who wish to develop agricultural land for residential or commercial use, to seek a 'rezoning' decision from the County Council, based on a vote by a majority of council councillors. The rezoning of land from agricultural to residential or commercial use had the potential for large profit margins. This served as an incentive for corrupt developers to bribe councillors or officials to secure the rezoning land. This system of incentives was further exacerbated by a system of weak regulation, oversight and enforcement of existing planning law.

James Gogarty worked for property developers JMSE and turned star whistleblower for the Tribunal. He gave evidence that in the week before the June 1989 general election, Burke, then the outgoing Minister for Industry and Commerce, received substantial cash at his Briargate home in Swords from JMSE representatives.

The purpose of his payment was to ensure that Burke used his political influence 'on councillors so as to achieve the rezoning and planning changes required to alter the status of approximately 700 acres of land' associated with JMSE. The Tribunal found that Burke 'was undeniably paid at least £30,000 of JMSE's money'. The inquiry described this as 'an extraordinarily large donation for any individual or company to make to a politician' and were satisfied that this was a 'corrupt payment and all present at the meeting were aware that it was such' in return for altering Murphy's North Dublin land from agricultural to development land'.[94] Michael Bailey, Joseph Murphy and James Gogarty were present at this meeting and the payment was made with the prior knowledge of Murphy executives, Joseph Murphy Snr., Frank Reynolds, and Roger Copsey.

Brennan & McGowan

Joe McAnthony's public exposé about Burke's personal finances in 1974 (see chapter 4), was followed by a short-lived and unsuccessful Garda investigation into Burke. The Tribunal investigation unearthed a 1974 letter from a Bank of Ireland branch assistant manager which was 'written for the sole purpose of satisfying the Gardaí as to how he (Burke) had paid for his house' suggesting that the then Garda investigation was less than thorough and painstaking.[95] The inquiry determined that Burke's family home 'amounted to a corrupt payment' from developers Tom Brennan and Joseph McGowan in 1973.[96] Burke later sold his Swords home for IR£3 million in the 1990s.

Burke was in receipt of £150,000 sterling in corrupt payments from Brennan and McGowan between 1982 and 1985 which were deposited in offshore bank accounts. The Tribunal was 'satisfied on the balance of probabilities, that he [Burke] acted in their [Brennan and McGowan] interests in the performance of his public duties'. Although the Tribunal were 'unable to discover what specific action' Burke had completed in return for this money, it is not beyond the bounds of probability that he assisted in the rezoning of land from agricultural to development purposes, making the land extremely valuable for the property developers.[97]

Century Radio

The proclivity of political and business actors to exploit opportunities for corruption was facilitated by a non-rules-based system where discretionary decisions were the order of the day. In January 1989, Century Radio was awarded the first national independent radio licence. As the Minister for Communications, Burke was responsible for matters relating to the granting of broadcasting licences and in March 1989 issued a Ministerial Directive, under Section 16 of the Radio and Television Act 1988, which obliged the state broadcaster, RTÉ, to provide equipment and transmission facilities to Century, then in financial difficulty, which were considerably less than what was sought by RTÉ. This Directive was 'contrary to the advices of his

Department and was unsupported by any independent evaluation'. Had Century remained in business and fulfilled its contract, this would have amounted to almost IR£2½ million savings for the private company. The Tribunal was satisfied that the Directive 'was heavily weighted in Century's favour'.[98]

Burke received a IR£35,000 donation in May that same year from Oliver Barry who was centrally involved in Century Communications Limited. The Tribunal described this as a 'bribe' and that it was sanctioned by fellow Century promoters, James Stafford and John Mulhern. The Tribunal also judged that Burke had solicited this bribe and treated this 'money as his own, to do with as he pleased'.[99] Incidentally, Stafford was a close associate of Haughey and acted as best-man at Mulhern's wedding to Haughey's daughter. Mulhern featured in the Moriarty report and the report of the inspectors into the secretive Ansbacher operation, run by Traynor.

Burke rejected the Tribunal's findings. His reputation was irrevocably damaged and he became the first former minister to be jailed on foot of investigations by a Tribunal. After pleading guilty to two counts of lodging false tax returns, Burke was sentenced to six months imprisonment at Arbour Hill prison in 2005. Judge Desmond Hogan justified this penalty because at the time of the offences, Burke was a member of the Oireachtas and due to his special position as a legislator; he committed a gross breach of trust. The Criminal Assets Bureau (CAB) identified €300,000–€400,000 in undeclared income from 1973 to the early 1990s. Burke subsequently made a €600,000 settlement with CAB.

George Redmond

The Flood / Mahon Tribunal investigation into George Redmond was a defining moment for the public inquiry. It revealed that corruption was not the unique preserve of senior elected public representatives. It existed not only in every layer of political action but also among public officials. Redmond worked for Dublin Local Authorities since 1941, was promoted to the Planning Department of Dublin Corporation in 1965 and retired as Assistant City and County Manager for Dublin in 1989. He was the most important planning official in Dublin for over a quarter of a century. The Tribunal investigated the context of his dealings with JMSE employee, James Gogarty, and the JMSE property developers Joseph Murphy Snr., Joseph Murphy Jnr. and Michael Bailey.

In its 2004 third interim report, Redmond was found by the Tribunal to have solicited a 10 per cent payment from Joseph Murphy Jnr in 1988 in return for fixing service charges and levies relating to lands owned by two Murphy companies at Forrest Road, Swords at 1983 levels instead of the more expensive 1988 charges. This corrupt payment amounted to IR£12,246 and was a 'substantial financial benefit' for Murphy with IR£1.45 million in savings. Bailey also made three cash payments to Redmond amounting to IR£16,000–IR£20,000 in the eighteen months before July 1989. The Tribunal was satisfied that those were corrupt payments made in 'circumstances which could give rise to a reasonable inference that they were made to influence him [Redmond] in the performance of his duties as assistant city and county manager for Dublin.'[100]

For twenty-eight years since the 1960s, Redmond had 'been in receipt of regular and substantial payments from builders and developers in the Dublin area . . . the equivalent of receiving one substantial house per annum free'.[101] Although Redmond's legitimate annual after-tax earnings were IR£19,380 when he retired, the Tribunal estimated that by 1996 he had IR£1,051,360 million in assets and accumulated capital (excluding his Castleknock private residence) which could not 'be explained as being the proceeds of savings from Mr Redmond's salary or the interest earned on savings'.[102]

Redmond was arrested in 1999 at Dublin airport when he arrived from the Isle of Man carrying a bag of Irish and sterling notes and four stockbroker cheques with a total value of approximately IR£300,000. He subsequently served eight months of a one-year sentence for corruption. This was the first high-profile conviction of a senior public figure on corruption charges arising from the planning Tribunal. This conviction was quashed by the Court of Criminal Appeal in 2004 following new evidence. In two separate corruption cases, Redmond was found not guilty in one while the jury failed to reach a verdict on the other. Speaking outside the court Redmond unapologetically defended his actions, insisting that the planning assistance he gave was within the law. 'I think I did a lot more good than harm. I helped people and put a lot of them on the straight road.'

Redmond, the Tribunal resolved, had persistently 'hindered and obstructed' its work with false denials and claims and as a consequence was offered only minimal relief on an estimated €1 million legal bill. His lawyers claimed he was "effectively destitute" after paying the Revenue Commissioners IR£782,000 in tax, interest and penalties. Redmond's tenure before the Tribunal, the Garda, CAB and the Revenue Commissioners ended in 2008 when the state announced that they would not press any further criminal charges of corruption against the eighty-three-year old.

Conclusion

At the time of writing in 2010, the Tribunal has yet to issue its final report. The range of matters under active inquiry, sixty-one at the time of the 2002 interim report, suggests that corruption within the planning system was an entrenched component of the political process. Indeed such was the extensive reach of its inquiry, that an investigation was initiated into alleged payments to a sitting Taoiseach. Bertie Ahern announced his resignation as Taoiseach on 2 April 2008 as a consequence of conflicting evidence before the Tribunal with his former secretary Gráinne Carruth. As of that date, he had yet to explain contradictory statements and evidence he gave under oath to the Tribunal. Ahern has rejected claims that he received IR£80,000 to block a tax break for a rival shopping centre development.[103]

The pervasive nature of corrupt behaviour within diverse layers of political action became acutely obvious on 19 April 2000. The Pauline conversion of Frank Dunlop, former government press secretary and political lobbyist, on "Spy Wednesday" laid bare the corrupt nature of dealings between well known landowners, property developers and councillors. Dunlop admitted that in 1992 and 1997, he paid bribes to Dublin city and county councillors in return for their votes on more than twenty property development and zoning transactions. He was charged with bribing eight different councillors, and pleaded guilty to five of the sixteen charges against him. Dunlop was sentenced to two years' incarceration, with six months suspended because of his cooperation with the authorities.

Despite the far-reaching list of corruption allegations under investigation, this list is not an exhaustive inventory of dubious political peccadilloes. It represents just a sample of the fraudulent political culture prevalent in Ireland from the 1960s to 1990s. A series of issues will never be examined. For instance, Mrs. Justice Susan Denham's 2007 Supreme Court judgment held that the Tribunal had not complied with its amended 2004 terms of reference and, consequently, had no jurisdiction to hold a public hearing in relation to the Fitzwilton Group's €30,000 political contribution to Fianna Fáil, made in June 1989. Other issues outside of the Tribunal's jurisdiction for public hearings include the alleged connections between Liam Lawlor and the planned development of a racecourse project at Phoenix Park and the tax designation issues, connected to the Urban Renewal Act during the 1990s when Bertie Ahern was Finance Minister.[104]

Yet, given the level of corruption in urban planning decisions as exposed by the Tribunal, it is surprising that the status quo remains insofar as the gains from the rezoning decisions of public officials have been pocketed in their entirety by private-sector developers. There is a marked reluctance in Irish public life to systematically examine the decision-making processes which have instigated poor urban and regional planning and which, in turn, have created a lack of adequate infrastructure such as school places in newly developed commuter areas.[105]

The routine failure to review draft county development plans in a timely manner contributed to an over-burdened local government administrative system which neglected to take into account rapidly changing population trends. The Sargent and Burton incidents, for example, occurred in a context where the Dublin County Council development plan had not altered in ten years, an extraordinary precedent for a country's capital city. The principal planning officer of the Council, Al Smith, described this policy drift as 'horrendous'. As a consequence, councillors had to run the gauntlet of representations from developers and opponents of development. The Democratic Left councillor, Eamon Gilmore TD, told the Council that the sheer scale of population expansion made it difficult to distinguish between proposals for rezoning on valid social and economic grounds and those which were purely speculative.[106]

The Tribunal process: a balance sheet

The Tribunal process has been influenced by an intrinsic tension between the moral expectations foisted upon it by the public, and legal parameters it is obliged to work within. The friction between these two distinct objectives has consequently prejudiced the very character of the outcomes by the various Tribunals.

The Tribunal process has six primary purposes or functions. (1) A Tribunal seeks to establish the facts, especially in circumstances where the facts are disputed, or the course and causation of events is not clear. (2) By learning from what happened, it helps to prevent recurrence by synthesising or distilling lessons, which can be used to change practice. This includes identifying shortcomings in law or regulations. (3) Tribunals provide catharsis or therapeutic exposure in providing an opportunity for reconciliation and resolution, by bringing protagonists face to face with each other's perspectives and problems. (4) It provides reassurance, by rebuilding public confidence after a major failure. (5) It establishes accountability – holding people and organisations to account, and sometimes indirectly contributing to assigning mechanisms for retribution. The sixth function is for political considerations – serving a wider political agenda for government either in demonstrating that "something is being done" or in providing leverage for change.[107]

Nonetheless, these six functions elicit confusion among the public. The expectations by the public and the realities of the Tribunal legislative framework are two very different phenomena. The purpose of inquiry is to investigate facts and make recommendations, not to punish individuals through criminal sanction, establish liability or assign blame.[108] It does not apportion consequences. This desire to establish liability is particularly strong where the matter under investigation is high-profile or controversial. A Tribunal is an inquisitorial process rather than an adversarial judicial procedure. The task of the judicial system is to administer justice which is inconsistent with the very

Tribunal process because Tribunals are not courts of law. The Tribunal will never accomplish what the public perceive it should do - assign legal responsibility for specific actions – because it is limited to what it can do - assign moral responsibility for specific actions. The Tribunal process consequently is condemned to operate within a context where it is confined to the prospect of being a square peg in a round hole.

The Tribunals have had tangible and intangible outcomes. Direct effects have included the investigation into allegations of corruption; the issuance of public recommendations to reform legislation and the scrapping of a law or policy that creates an environment conducive or even contributing to corruption. Instances of high-profile censure, impeachment, or forced resignation of corrupt politicians and public officials has included former Taoiseach Charles Haughey, former minister Ray Burke, former official George Redmond and public affairs consultant Frank Dunlop. This has not been the case with Michael Lowry, whose voting record has risen exponentially as a consequence of two Tribunal inquiries, and as a result is conceivably the most expensive Irish public representative ever elected. The Tribunal process has provided the intangible outcome of providing crucial insights into how power operated in Ireland. The inquiries have acted as a deterrent to future negative activities because the social costs of committing corruption have increased.

As an upshot of the elaborate nature of corruption, relevant legislation is often non-existent, broad or vague and convictions are rare. The conventional methods of punishment, such as jail, are hence more challenging to secure. Adverse media reaction to the Beef, Flood / Mahon and Moriarty Tribunals placed pressure on the inquiries to not only conclude their work quickly and cost effectively but to satisfy a public appetite hungry for explanation.

The Law Reform Commission has actually felt it necessary to counsel against punishing an individual 'under the guise of an inquiry, by "naming and shaming" the culprit' which may account for the 'intense application by the courts of the rules of constitutional justice to inquiries'.[109] A series of Supreme Court judgments agreed that the exceptional inquisitorial powers of Tribunals may unnecessarily expose the private lives of citizens and thereby run 'the risk of having baseless allegations made against them' which could cause 'injury to their reputations, and may interfere with the applicant's constitutional right to privacy'.[110] However, the *Redmond v Flood* 1999 Supreme Court decision determined that 'the right to privacy is, however, not an absolute right. The exigencies of the common good may outweigh the constitutional right to privacy . . . particularly when such inquiries are necessary to preserve the purity and integrity of public life'.[111] Accordingly, the courts have reached the unexceptionable conclusion that a public inquiry is not, in principle, unconstitutional. The constitutional right of citizens to privacy can be outweighed by the primacy of the public interest.

The refusal of legal costs to witnesses who were uncooperative or who wilfully obstructed the Tribunal was a familiar instrument of proportionate punishment used by the chair of the Tribunal. The Flood / Mahon Tribunal, for instance, refused 15 per cent of those seeking legal costs, representing 67 per cent of the original cost estimate.[112] Costs were awarded or partially awarded to witnesses who, though involved in corruption, had chosen to cooperate with the Tribunal. In the absence of whistleblower legislation, this was interpreted as a 'whistleblower's charter'.[113] Seventeen individuals were not awarded their costs. They included: Ray Burke, former Fianna Fáil minister, €10 million; Tom Brennan and Joseph McGowan, builders, €2.6 million; Oliver Barry, Century Radio promoter, €611,000; James Stafford, Century Radio promoter, €310,515 and John Finnegan, auctioneer, €125,000.

Nonetheless, a Supreme Court decision in 2010 ruled that the Flood / Mahon Tribunal has no authority to determine that any person has hindered or obstructed its work, because this is a criminal offence and not therefore legitimate ground upon which to deny costs. Property developers Joseph Murphy Jnr and Frank Reynolds will now be paid their substantial costs from the public purse and there is a possibility that others who had their costs withheld might seek now to have their decisions overturned in the light of this judgment. The principle of judicial discretion with regard to the awarding of costs was undermined by enormous financial implications; worse, the decision amounted to a severe blow to the credibility of the inquiry.

The Law Reform Commission has described the Tribunal process as the 'Rolls-Royce' of public inquiries because of the unusual and amorphous character of its investigations.[114] A Comptroller and Auditor General 2008 report into tribunals concluded that their lengthy nature was due to the wide terms of reference, adversarial procedures, extended cross-examination, procedural shortcomings, legal challenges and the obstruction or non-cooperation of witnesses.[115]

The constraints of the archaic legal parameters of the Tribunal of Inquiry process are evidenced by the thirty-nine time-consuming legal challenges which have been filed against it. This includes twenty-nine against Flood / Mahon, four against Moriarty and six against Morris, at an approximate cost of €4 million thus far.[116] Instances of protracted procedural delays involved over four days of reading the statement of Joseph Murphy senior into the Flood / Mahon Tribunal record. Repeated pleas from Mr. Justice Flood for additional judges and greater resources fell on deaf ears for many years.

The open-ended terms of reference for the Flood / Mahon Tribunal were particularly corrosive to any timely conclusion of its investigations. Although initially limited to investigating possible acts of corruption committed on or after 20 June 1985, the then Flood Tribunal's request to extend its terms of reference before this date were granted in 1998. The merits of a meandering inquiry would always be unpredictable from the outset. The secretive and sophisticated nature of corruption inevitably means that such investigations were not straightforward but oblique. Moreover, it was difficult to specify what was going to be discovered until it was first investigated. Much depends on the integrity of public records, the existence of paper trails and expert scrutiny of financial and corporate documents. The absence of systematic records at the Department of Public Enterprise, with regard to the evaluation process of the mobile phone licence award, meant that the Moriarty Tribunal had to engage in a protracted analysis of 119 files which amounted to some 30,000 pages of documentation. It also involves confronting cultural norms and making subjective comparisons between a person's personal wealth, their lifestyle and their actual income.

Herein lies the tension between due process, robust inquiry and the ambit of an inquiry which seeks to address concerns of length, complexity, cost and timely outcomes. Attempts to narrow the terms of reference have political implications and are bound with the perception that matters are deliberately not being investigated to save political face. The 1921 Tribunal Act prescribes that the establishment of such a process is necessary where there is a 'definite matter described in the resolution as of urgent public importance'. In its report on the reform of the Tribunal process, the Law Reform Commission felt it necessary to revert to the Oxford English Dictionary in order to clarify the word 'definite'. This was a polite way of suggesting that Tribunals should only occur where there there the terms of reference are as 'clearly stated and precise as possible'.[117]

The overemphasis on the role of the judiciary, to whom the task of renewing the political class and purifying the whole system was delegated, may have had a boomerang effect. Since the Beef Tribunal report in 1994, the public perception has held that impunity reigns because of the ineffective attempts at prosecution. This is ultimately detrimental to the very concept of justice. In other jurisdictions, such as the Italian *mani pulite* corruption inquiries for instance, the appointment of judges to chair political inquiries has had the undesirable effect of tarnishing the reputation of judicial integrity and independence with accusations that the judiciary have unnecessarily intruded into the political realm.[118] Media attention in Italy has shifted from the allegations of corruption to disputes about the alleged bias of judges. The Italian public no longer pay any attention to their corruption inquiries and focus is directed on the method of inquiry rather than the underlying allegations themselves.[119] This is also the case in Ireland where the outdated legislative infrastructure has facilitated disconnection from the very serious substantive issues at the heart of the Tribunal. In his second Tribunal report, Judge Moriarty wistfully observed that the Tribunals of the 1940s were an 'almost Arcadian picture of a serene, orderly and cooperative process, that is greatly at odds with contemporary experience'.[120] This disparity is largely due to the wholly changed jurisprudence landscape which now emphasises the rights and fair procedures that must be accorded to affected persons.

Public opinion too has grown more hostile towards the escalating cost of the inquiries. The Flood / Mahon Tribunal 'has created 14 Tribunal millionaires' with one barrister earning a reported €5.3 million because of his work at the Tribunal.[121] The forthright language used by Mr. Justice Adrian Hardiman, in his 2010 Supreme Court decision against the Flood / Mahon Tribunal, has underlined questions about the veracity of that inquiry. So too has the acknowledgment by the chair of the Moriarty Tribunal that he made an error in relation to the Attorney General's view on a matter affecting the legality of the licence issued to O'Brien's Esat Digifone in 1996. Mr. Justice Michael Moriarty felt it necessary to issue an unprecedented statement in April 2010 to 'assert the integrity of the Tribunal' following sustained media criticism.[122]

A saturation effect has occurred where the constant drip-feed of scandal has dulled a coherent and sustained sense of public outrage about matters which are under investigation for over a decade. 'Like medicines that become the less effective the more you take them, so it is with inquiries, legal notifications and indictments: the more they follow one after the other, the less people pay any attention to them, and the less they give rise to public judgments that count or have any lasting impact.'[123]

A recurring theme within the three Tribunals was the failure of the Revenue Commissioners to systematically collect taxes and the absence of political will to enforce compliance. The case study analyses of the Flood / Mahon and Moriarty Tribunals have underscored examples of how those at the highest level of politics, and their associates, personally benefited from flawed laws and procedures, an absence of checks and balances and inadequate enforcement in relation to tax matters. Those tasked with formulating tax policy processed a patent conflict of interest. The Tribunals exposed the extent to which tax evasion was facilitated by the banks, accountants and other professionals. In particular, they disclosed the irregular banking practices and financial transactions, insider trading, offshore operations and the inadequate checks and balances system which characterised Ireland's financial management structure. Although these episodes were not directly corrupt, they served to illustrate just how omnipresent and organised the culture of non-compliance was within every layer of society in Ireland during the 1970s, 1980s and 1990s. The ultimate consequences of this were long-term institutional credibility issues, unaccountable power and grossly diminished tax revenue which prevented much needed exchequer investment into public infrastructure.

Indeed a policy of tax amnesty was regarded as a method of achieving tax

Table 6.2 A balance sheet: estimated cost of tribunals and direct yields to
exchequer because of tribunals (€ million)

Investigation / initiative	Estimated cost (including third party costs)	Yield (tax, interest and penalties)
McCracken Tribunal 1997–97	6.5	–
Ansbacher 2002–10 (arising from McCracken)	–	107.3
Moriarty Tribunal 1997–2011	200	8.44
Flood / Mahon Tribunal 1997–	300	32.6
DIRT / bogus non-resident accounts 1998–2010 (arising from Moriarty)	–	872.4
Total	506.5	1,020.74

Source: Author's analyses from C. Keena, 'Pressure grows as €200m tribunal faces
more scrutiny', *Irish Times* (27 May 2010); C. Keena, 'Mahon Tribunal ends 11 years
of hearings', *Irish Times* (30 October 2008); July 2010 data from correspondence
with Revenue Commissioners including spreadsheet entitled: 'Yield from various
Revenue Special Investigations / Initiatives at 31.3.2010'.

compliance. The controversial 1988 and 1993 tax amnesties, introduced by
two different governments - Fianna Fáil and Fianna Fáil / Labour-collected
IR£500 million and IR£260 million respectively (without interest or penalties demanded) and long-fingered any meaningful confrontation of deeper
issues.[124] An MRBI poll for the *Irish Times* after the 1993 amnesty, which
comprised 37,500 separate payments to the exchequer, found that the highest incidence of disapproval on the amnesty was evident in Dublin and
urban areas. The highest approval ratings were in farming homes and among
Fianna Fáil supporters.[125] High personal tax rates during the 1980s and early
1990s (the top rate was 58 per cent until 1987) were suggested as causes of
tax evasion.[126] The McCracken and Moriarty Tribunals spawned a series of
special investigations by Revenue which were of significant net worth to the
exchequer, as table 6.2 demonstrates.

The McCracken Tribunal unearthed the existence of offshore accounts
designed to avoid tax, known as the Ansbacher deposits. Company inspectors appointed to investigate the affairs of Ansbacher (Cayman) Ltd, published their report in July 2002. The Moriarty Tribunal revealed that offshore
accounts were used to evade tax and launder payments to politicians. The
subsequent Dáil Public Accounts Committee investigation into tax evasion
(DIRT Inquiry) published its report in 1999 and revealed that financial institutions opened 300,000 bogus non-resident accounts as a means of evading
Deposit Interest Retention Tax (DIRT). Revenue and the Department of

Finance were aware that Irish banks offered their well-heeled customers this tax avoidance measure as a means of attracting business but never confronted those involved. The 1986 Finance Act which empowered Revenue to inspect non-residence declarations held by financial institutions was not invoked.

A consequence of the DIRT / Bogus Non-Resident (BNR) Accounts investigation was the 'offshore assets' investigation which in turn initiated two supplementary investigations relating to – 'Single Premium Insurance Policies' and 'offshore trusts'. When the Revenue's special investigations into tax evasion, as a direct and indirect consequence of Tribunal investigations, are taken into account, the exchequer netted €2,473,890,000 billion.[127] Justifiable public concerns about the expense of the Tribunals must also consider that the financial yield to the exchequer as a direct consequence of the inquiries is twice their estimated cost. When indirect revenue is considered, the yield to the exchequer is over four times their outlay.

Irish public life will never again have to resort to establishing a Tribunal of Inquiry. Members of the judiciary are as pleased about this prospect as the public, with many judges privately describing the process as 'fundamentally deeply flawed'. The shortcomings of the Tribunal process – the inability to breach the divide between its perceived moral expectations and its legal obligations – have been somewhat addressed by new legislation. The Commissions of Investigation Act 2004 provides an alternative method of inquiry. This private investigation process is designed to encourage cooperation and has a lower likelihood of a need for legal representation which will allow for timelier and cost effective outcomes. The far-reaching Proceeds of Crime (Amendment) Act 2005 has effectively broadened the statutory definition of corruption because it eliminates the previous legislative obligation which required that a specific instance of corruption must be linked to a specific payment and a specific favour. Under this Act, a lower burden of proof is necessary for CAB to confiscate the assets of corrupt individuals and seize a gift suspected of being a bribe. These departures are welcome, but represent a closing of the stable door after the horses have bolted.[128]

Conclusion

Irish public life has witnessed a permanent process of institutional self-scrutiny since 1990. In the twenty year period between 1990 and 2010, thirty-two public inquiries have been initiated to examine matters of ethical concern within politics, business, church, police, finance, public service, professions and health. Ten non-statutory inquiries, nine Companies Act inquiries, eight Tribunals of Inquiry and five parliamentary inquiries have publicly questioned the character of authority. Self-regulated institutional authority has been comprehensively challenged and a sea change in attitudes towards the integrity of power has occurred. This marks an overdue and positive development in Irish public life. Traditional values of blind deference, misguided loyalty and the fear of asking questions have undergone an electrifying process of transformation. This has had the effect of fostering public accountability.

Did the overriding focus on armed conflict in Northern Ireland from 1968 to 1998 prevent due attention to domestic matters such as political corruption? Did this dynamic enable the transition of the public awareness of corruption from that of a narrow legal construct to one of a broader moral realisation? The nature of how a state develops can account for the incidence of political corruption within a society.[129] For instance, the collapse of the Berlin Wall and the end of the Cold War coincided with a re-evaluation of the absolutes and certainties that had heretofore characterised political action. The shadow of the thirty year Northern Ireland conflict had various direct and indirect implications for public life. The 'national question' tended to expediently intervene to deter due attention on questions relating to political ethics and the relationship between political, social and economic institutions.

A new surge of IRA activity from the late 1960s threatened the political stability of the Republic. The dismissal by the Taoiseach, Jack Lynch, of two cabinet ministers, Charles J. Haughey and Neil Blaney, and the consequent investigation into the alleged use of government money to import arms for the IRA threatened to inflame Civil War and induced an internal split within Fianna Fáil which lasted for twenty-five years. Chapter 4 has outlined how the Northern Ireland conflict distracted attention from the serious allegations of corruption concerning Ray Burke and builders Brennan and McGowan. These allegations only received due consideration in the Flood / Mahon Tribunal, subsequent to the end of the Northern conflict.

The peace process, which began in earnest with the signing of the Anglo Irish Agreement in 1985, was regarded as one of the main priorities for the public through this period. An IMS *Irish Independent* 1991 opinion poll found that three times as many people believed the peace process was more significant than the political abuse of power. The poll was taken at a time when a dramatic series of corruption incidents occurred which accumulated in the establishment of the Beef Tribunal. When serious incidents of alleged impropriety arose, overwhelming reasons of state tended to divert resolute attention from corruption issues. The overwhelming sense of national interest, defined by Reynolds during the Beef Tribunal, was uncontested by a public more preoccupied by Goodman's assurance of employment in his meat factories for example. It was only when the conflict entered into the phase of protracted negotiations for peace that allegations of corruption received mainstream attention.

It was not until the intensification of the peace process from the early 1990s, exemplified by the 1993 Downing Street Declaration issued by the Irish and British Prime Ministers, that political, public, media and legislative attention began to meaningfully focus on corruption. The 1998 Good Friday Agreement, signed by both the British and Irish governments, was endorsed by most of the Northern Ireland political parties and by the voters from the North and South. The conclusion of armed conflict and the parallel introduction of qualified political stability in the North engendered a re-prioritisation of issues in the South. This coincided with a period where civil society became more vibrant, the media were now more vigilant and the electorate adopted a more demanding and questioning outlook, though this concern did not necessarily translate itself with regard to the outcome of the 2007 general election. Moreover, the international media and international community, timely convened to prioritise matters relating to corruption in political life.

Eithne FitzGerald attributed the delay in introducing ethics legislation to the national economic and political crises that permeated the 1970s and 1980s. 'Legislation is often a response to the times that people are in. If you look at what was going on in the 70s such as the oil crisis, and in the 80s the priority was things like the economy and Northern Ireland . . . Times are tough and let's batten down the hatches mentality.'[130] A spate of media investigations in the 1990s exposed unprecedented questions regarding wrongdoing at the highest leverages of power. For instance, the privatisation of Irish Sugar Company (1991), Frank McDonald and Mark Brennock *Irish Times* rezoning articles (1993), Passports for sale (1994), Colm MacEochaidh *Irish Times* advertisements for information on land rezoning (1995), Ben Dunne / Michael Lowry donation (1996), Pick-me-ups (1998),[131] DIRT investigation (1998) were revealed following media exposés. The economic boom of the 1990s and the moves toward peace in Northern Ireland may however have muted the impact of the scandals and Tribunals that dominated much of the 1990s.

The consensus of party policy positions over Northern Ireland, and the convergence of party positioning on key issues generally, now meant that political parties had to discover new issues to distinguish themselves to their core supporters. In this vacuum, ethical concerns now held more attraction than previously.[132] In particular, the approach undertaken by the Flood / Mahon Tribunal in its investigations into Ray Burke marked a watershed for Irish political life because for the first time a distinction between the legal and moral definition of corruption received wide-ranging attention. The forthright language of the Tribunal report left no ambiguity as to its conclusions. In the absence of *explicit* evidence, but in the knowledge of *implicit* evidence, it made findings based on the principle of 'the reasonable inference to be drawn from the facts proved'.

This was exemplified in Burke's unprecedented personal statement to the Dáil in September 1997, in response to media allegations that he was the recipient of large payments from property developers. The then Minister for Foreign Affairs said:

> As all Members of this House will be aware, the last 25 years have seen a funda-mental change in the operation of politics ... Soliciting or accepting such con-tributions was not outlawed or discouraged through legislation or the Standing Orders or rules of this House ... I am being judged under the rules of 1997 ... although the contribution was received in 1989 when there were no rules in place ... [it] has been the tradition of this House in relation to confidentiality regard-ing contributions and I do not intend to comment further on the matter.[133]

Burke resigned as Minister one month later. He defended the solicitation and acceptance of contributions on the basis that they were entirely permitted within the legal parameters of the time. This justification neglected to point out that the existing legislation was inadequate which allowed the defence to emerge that because there was no law, then no law was broken. The nature of politics had changed but the legislation governing politics had not. Burke had failed to acknowledge that his responsibilities to public office included duties to public trust, which involved moral expectations as well as legal obligations. His failure to separate his public and private lives made it difficult to distin-guish what a conflict of interest was. In his evidence to the Tribunal, Burke was emphatic: 'My life was seamless. I was a politician from the time I got up in the morning until I went to bed at night.'[134] Indeed, when Burke resigned from politics, his bank manager recorded his 'political fund' which contained IR£118,000, as a personal asset.[135]

Burke's defence shares many similarities with the justifications evoked by Alan Cranston, a Californian Democrat reprimanded by the 1991–92 US Senate Select Committee on Ethics. Cranston defended the receipt of large donations on the basis that it was part and parcel of the normal competitive process whereby politicians are encouraged by the political system to solicit support and bestow favours in order to win elections. This was the very nature of the system.[136] Like Burke, Cranston believed that because everybody knew what was occurring, it was therefore acceptable.

The Cranston case established a moral precedent within the Committee on Standards of Official Conduct of the US Congress which has similar appli-cability to Ireland: 'Because Senators occupy a position of public trust, every Senator always must endeavour to avoid the appearance that the Senator, the Senate, or the governmental process may be influenced by campaign con-tributions or other benefits provided by those with significant legislative or governmental interests.'[137] In a similar vein, the Burke case signalled a trans-formation not only of Irish political culture but the legal position regarding the acceptance of undisclosed, large financial donations. The sharp separation between the public and private lives of politicians was no longer held sacred and the distinction between legal and moral definitions of corruption became more prominent.

The case of Bertie Ahern is illustrative of how the conclusion of the Northern Ireland conflict created the context for public life to focus attention on ethical matters rather than internal political instability. Ahern, one of Europe's longest-serving leaders and Ireland's second longest serving Taoiseach, was regarded by many as the most popular and successful Taoiseach of the modern era and was closely involved in the negotiations that finally brought peace to Northern Ireland. As a consequence of cross-examination by counsel for the Flood / Mahon Tribunal, it became clear that there were serious contradictions given in evidence about Ahern's personal finances. His former secretary, Gráinne Carruth, had sworn that she had never handled sterling for Ahern. However, the Tribunal had found £15,000 in sterling lodgements. Her loyalty was tested when she was warned that it was a criminal offence to lie. Carruth then broke down on the witness stand and acknowledged that 'on the balance of probability' she had made the lodgements. In his autobiography Ahern said that this was 'a turning point for me'.

Ahern announced his surprise resignation as Taoiseach a week later on 3 April 2008, so that 'the work of my ministerial colleagues is not distracted from by incessant publicity about the Tribunal.' Ahern was adamant that 'I have done no wrong and wronged no-one.' He later claimed that the sterling transaction was as a consequence of accumulated sterling savings and from the proceeds of horse racing bets which came from 'a few good wins over the years, including one or two successful bets in 1996'.

The morning after his announcement Ahern addressed the Institute for British-Irish Studies Conference, in what was the only official commemoration of the tenth anniversary of the Good Friday Agreement in the Republic of Ireland. Ahern movingly told the audience: 'Thousands of people died, thousands more were injured. Thousands of families were left broken and grieving – without fathers or mothers, sons or daughters, brothers or sisters. This happened in our country. In our lifetimes. Whatever the circumstances, whatever the motivation, whatever the hurt felt before hurt was caused, none of that violence was justified.' This historic celebration of peace was overshadowed by Ahern's inability to disguise his anger at the Flood / Mahon Tribunal. In the press conference immediately afterwards he criticised the Tribunal's legal team in the strongest terms, describing their 'harangued' cross-examination of Carruth as 'appalling' and 'lowlife stuff'.[138]

The chronology of Ahern's final month in office was populated by momentous public occasions which duly focused attention on his critical contribution to the peace process. His address to the joint Houses of the United States Congress was met with international acclaim when he declared that 'Ireland is at peace'. His official opening of the interpretative centre at the Battle of the Boyne site, so long a symbol of division, with the Northern Ireland First Minister Rev Ian Paisley was groundbreaking. The public endorsement of his legacy to the establishment of peace on the island of Ireland is justified. This series of public engagements complemented a narrative which emphasised the primacy of Ireland's national interest, the security of the state, which superseded all other concerns.

This narrative was particularly evident in his autobiography where references to his unorthodox personal financial affairs that ultimately led to his disgrace are noticeable by their absence. This selective portrayal of history is standard practice as a means of offsetting any negative connotations. Instances of moral indiscretions are consciously relegated to the footnotes. This was the approach employed by *Sunday Independent* columnist, Eoghan Harris, in his robust defence of Ahern who was then under siege by questions regarding his personal finances from the Tribunal. On *The Late Late Show* on RTÉ in the last weekend of campaigning for the 2007 general election, Harris emphasised Ahern's credentials on peace while those that had the audacity to raise concerns about Ahern's ethical qualifications belonged to the 'Puritan priesthood... of Platonic perfection'. Beyond its wildest expectations, Fianna Fáil earned a greater percentage of votes than its phenomenal 2002 results. Harris, appointed to the Seanad by an appreciative Taoiseach, observed that 'the Irish people have little time for moral innocents - or moral prigs'.[139] He was perceptively accurate.

The traditional 'national question' of Northern Ireland cyclically intervened to divert due attention from underlying questions relating to political ethics. It may now have been replaced by the overwhelming "national question" of economic sovereignty and the constraints wrought from Ireland's financial bailout by the European Commission, European Central Bank and International Monetary Fund troika. One, which Professor Morgan Kelly has predicted, will induce 'a prolonged and chaotic national bankruptcy'.[140]

Notes

1 In particular Cullen, *With a Little Help from My Friends*; Keena, *The Ansbacher Conspiracy*; N. Collins and M. O'Shea, *Understanding Corruption in Irish Politics* (Cork University Press, 2000).

2 Mr.' Justice Brian McCracken, *Report of the Tribunal of Inquiry (Dunnes Payments)* (Dublin Stationery Office, 1997) pp. 19–20, 73.

3 *Ibid.*, p. 69.

4 Minister for Justice 1961–64, minister for agriculture 1964–66, minister for finance 1966–70, minister for health 1977–79 and minister for social welfare 1977–79. Taoiseach 1979–81, March 1982 – December 1982, 1987–89 and 1989–92

5 RTÉ News, 'Obituaries, Charles J. Haughey (1925–2006)', www.rte.ie/news/ ob_cjhaughey.html.

6 Mr. Justice Michael Moriarty, *The Moriarty Tribunal Report. Report of the Tribunal of Inquiry into Payments to Politicians and Related Matters. Part 1,* (Dublin Stationery Office, 2011) p. 23.

7 C. Keena, *Haughey's Millions: Charlie's Money Trail* (Gill and Macmillan, 2001), p. 44.

8 *Ibid.,* 2006: pp. 544–5.

9 Moriarty, *The Moriarty Tribunal Report: Part 1,* p. 169.

10 With reference to figure 6.2, (1/2) The bill-paying service was money lodged to a variety of domestic and offshore accounts administered initially by Des Traynor and latterly by Jack Stakelum. This was used to pay Haughey's household and personal expenses; (3) Guinness & Mahon (Ireland) Limited were a licenced Irish bank which formed a small offshore investment company in the Cayman Islands in 1969; (4) the AIB settlement was made to the bank in 1979–80. Developer Patrick Gallagher paid £300,000 and the source of the remaining £450,000 is unknown; (5) the "S" accounts were confidential offshore accounts which were intended as payments to Haughey or represented the proceeds of investments for Haughey's benefit. (6) Celtic Helicopters, a company closely associated with his son Ciaran, was 'a vehicle for the transmission of other funds' for Haughey's own benefit; (7) Ansbacher (Cayman) Ltd was an offshore bank founded by Traynor which facilitated tax evasion; (8) department forgiven by AIB shortly after Haughey became Taoiseach in 1979; (9) donation by PV Doyle, hotelier and building contractor; (10) A series of accounts opened by Traynor in National City Bank (NCB) Stockbrokers for Haughey's benefit characterised by an 'unusual routing' of funds. Desmond was the contact point in NCB.

11 Moriarty, *The Moriarty Tribunal Report: Part 1,* p. 573.

12 *Ibid.,* p. 187.

13 'Inside the mind of Dermot Desmond', *Irish Independent* (23 October 2004).

14 Keena, *Haughey's Millions,* p. 121.

15 Moriarty, *The Moriarty Tribunal Report: Part 1,* p. 545.

16 *Ibid.,* p. 601.

17 J. Corcoran, 'He that filches from me my good name makes me poor indeed', *Sunday Independent* (24 December, 2006).

18 'The world's billionaires', *Forbes Magazine* (3 November 2009).

19 Moriarty, *The Moriarty Tribunal Report: Part 1,* p. 573.

20 *Ibid.,* p. 573.

21 *Ibid.,* pp. 249–253, 262–3.

22 J. Gallagher, 'A man who would be a merchant banker', *Irish Times* (20 July 1991).

23 'Desmond action over "Magill" article settled', *Irish Times* (11 February 2010).

24 Moriarty, *The Moriarty Tribunal Report: Part 1,* p. 422.

25 *Ibid.,* pp. ix, 423.

26 *Ibid.,* p. 605.

27 *Ibid.,* 2006: p. 546.

28 *Ibid.*, p. 604.
29 T. Harding, 'Is this a dagger I see before me?', *Sunday Business Post* (8 October 2000).
30 F. McDonald and K. Sheridan, *The Builders* (Penguin, 2009), p. 28.
31 Moriarty, *The Moriarty Tribunal Report: Part 1*, p. 564.
32 *Ibid.*, p. 584.
33 A. Beesley, 'OPW leases on property cost €100m', *Irish Times* (27 February 2004).
34 M. Brennock, 'Investors who benefited from Haughey decisions', *Irish Times* (13 February 1999).
35 'Moneybags', *Irish Business* (1 February 1989).
36 Michael Mullen, Dáil Éireann, *Committee on Finance Vote 41 – Transport and Power. 230.* (9 November 1967).
37 Erskine Childers, Dáil Éireann, *Committee on Finance Vote 41 – Transport and Power (Resumed). 231.* (16 November 1967).
38 Moriarty, *The Moriarty Tribunal Report: Part 1*, p. 103.
39 *Ibid.*, p. 612.
40 *Ibid.*, p. 30.
41 *Ibid.*, p. 550.
42 Moriarty Tribunal, *Transcripts,* (16 February 1999) www.moriarty-tribunal.ie., p. 68.
43 *Ibid.*, pp. 29, 551.
44 'Mr. Niall Crowley', *Irish Times* (28 January 1983).
45 F. McHugh, and J. Burns, 'Smurfit paid £50,000 to Haughey', *Sunday Times* (25 June 2000).
46 Moriarty, *The Moriarty Tribunal Report: Part 1*, pp. 631–3.
47 Moriarty Tribunal, *Transcripts,* (23 May 2001), www.moriarty-tribunal.ie.
48 Moriarty, *The Moriarty Tribunal Report: Part 1*, p. 164.
49 V. Browne, 'No hard questions asked of Charles Haughey, then or now', *Village Magazine* (14 December 2006).
50 RTÉ News at One, (19 December 2006).
51 Moriarty, *The Moriarty Tribunal Report: Part 1*, pp. 159–63.
52 *Ibid.*, pp. 162–3.
53 'Friends would assist a politician in difficulty', *Irish Times* (20 December 2006).
54 Keena, *The Ansbacher Conspiracy*, p. 50.
55 Moriarty, *The Moriarty Tribunal Report: Part 1*, p. 543.
56 *Ibid.*, p. 544.
57 McCracken, *Report of the Tribunal of Inquiry*, pp. 19–20.
58 M. Brennock, 'FG leaders' active role in fund raising revealed', *Irish Times* (29 April 1997).
59 McCracken, *Report of the Tribunal of Inquiry*, pp. 19–20, 68.
60 *Ibid.*, p. 70.
61 *Ibid.*, p. 20; V. Browne, 'No hard questions put to FG', *Irish Times* (9 July, 2003).
62 Mr. Justice Michael Moriarty, *The Moriarty Tribunal Report. Report of the Tribunal of Inquiry into Payments to Politicians and Related Matters. Part 2,*

Volume 2 (Dublin Stationery Office, 2011) p. 1057; McCracken, *Report of the Tribunal of Inquiry*. This figure includes STG£220,000 in payments converted into Irish pounds.

63 McCracken, *Report of the Tribunal of Inquiry*, pp. 69–70.

64 Moriarty, *The Moriarty Tribunal Report: Part 2, Volume 1*, p. 420.

65 Forbes Rich List 2011, www.therichest.org/nation/richest-irish-2011.

66 Moriarty, *The Moriarty Tribunal Report: Part 2, Volume 2*, p. 1058.

67 *Ibid.*, p. 1064.

68 Jamie Smyth, 'Angry O'Brien hits back at his critics', *Irish Times* (24 October 2003).

69 Moriarty, *The Moriarty Tribunal Report: Part 2, Volume 2*, p. 406.

70 *Ibid.*, p. 1053.

71 *Ibid.*, p. 1050.

72 *Ibid.*, p. 1059

73 *Ibid.*, p. 16.

74 *Ibid.*, p. 16.

75 Mark Tighe, 'O'Brien licence award "illegal"', *Sunday Times* (26 July 2009).

76 Colm Keena, 'Law Society refused O'Brien advert', *Irish Times* (31 October 2009).

77 Statement by Michael Lowry (23 March 2011), www.michaellowry.ie/moriarty-tribunal.

78 F. O'Toole, 'To impunity and beyond: brazenness of tribunal's shamed is well founded', *Irish Times* (26 March 2011).

79 Statement by the Minister for Justice, Equality and Defence, www.merrionstreet.ie (25 March 2011).

80 Website created by Denis O'Brien, www.moriarty.com; Colm Keena, 'Judge rejected O'Brien evidence on how Desmond came on board' *Irish Times* (26 March 2011).

81 Moriarty, *The Moriarty Tribunal Report: Part 2, Volume 2*. p. 1049.

82 Pat Leahy, 'A truly murky tale', *Sunday Business Post* (27 March 2011).

83 *People (AG) v William O'Sullivan* [1930] I.R. 552.

84 Moriarty, *The Moriarty Tribunal Report: Part 2, Volume 1*, p. 18.

85 Statement by Michael Lowry (30 March 2011), www.michaellowry.ie/moriarty-tribunal.

86 Moriarty, *The Moriarty Tribunal Report: Part 2, Volume 2*, p. 65.

87 Padraig Yeates, 'Developer confirms he sent cheque to Greens', *Irish Times* (23 January 1993).

88 'Rezone Bribes Bid No Surprise', *Irish Independent* (22 February 1993).

89 F. McDonald, 'Dublin county rezonings: calls for the Minister to intervene', *Irish Times* (11 December 1993).

90 Mr. Justice Feargus Flood chaired the Tribunal until his retirement in 2003. Then chaired by Mr. Justice Alan Mahon and assisted by Ms. Justice Mary Flaherty and Mr. Justice Gerald Keys.

91 Flood, *Second Interim Report*.

92 *Ibid.*, pp. 150–1.

93 February 1998, September 2002, January 2004 and June 2004 respectively.

94 Flood, *Second Interim Report*, pp. 74, 115, 140, 148.

95 *Ibid.*, p. 13.

96 *Ibid.*, p. 34.

97 *Ibid.*, pp. 138–9.

98 *Ibid.*, p. 45.

99 *Ibid.*, pp. 48, 53.

100 *Ibid.*, p. 19.

101 *Ibid.*, p. 8.

102 *Ibid.*, p. 8.

103 M. Clifford, and Shane Coleman, *Bertie Ahern and the Drumcondra Mafia* (Hodder Headline, 2009).

104 J. Burke, 'Mahon Tribunal has been laid low by a self-inflicted blow', *Sunday Business Post* (8 July 2007).

105 F. Barry, 'Institutional capacity and the Celtic Tiger', *8th International Network for Economic Research annual conference* (University College Cork, September 2006), p. 3.

106 Padraig Yeates, 'Councillor criticises claims of bribery at rezoning meeting', *Irish Times* (27 February 1993).

107 Law Reform Commission of Ireland (LRC), *Public inquiries including Tribunals of Inquiry: Report 73* (Law Reform Commission, 2005), p. 20.

108 R. Brady, *Reflections on Tribunals of Inquiry* 3 (Bar Review, 1997), p. 121; LRC 2005, p. 15; *Boyhan v Beef Tribunal [1993]* 1 I.R. 210, 222.

109 Law Reform Commission of Ireland, *Consultation paper on public inquiries including Tribunals of Inquiry: Report 22* (Law Reform Commission, 2003), p. 10.

110 Quoted in *Redmond v Flood [1993]* 3 I.R. 79, 87–88. Also see *Haughey v Moriarty [1999]* 3 I.R. 1, 57–59.

111 *Redmond v Flood [1993]* 3 I.R. 79, 87.

112 Some 3.5 per cent of parties were only awarded partial costs, As of December 2007: Comptroller and Auditor General, *Special Report Tribunals of Inquiry* (Government of Ireland, December 2008).

113 E. Byrne, 'Ireland: Global Corruption Report', in J. Kotalik and D. Rodriquez (eds), *Transparency International Global Corruption Report 2006* (Pluto Press, 2007).

114 LRC 2003, pp. 2, 13.

115 Comptroller and Auditor General, *Special Report Tribunals of Inquiry*.

116 Byrne, 'Ireland: Global Corruption Report', pp. 173–4.

117 LRC 2005, p. 35.

118 A. Vannucci, 'The controversial legacy of "Mani Pulite": a critical analysis of Italian corruption and anti-corruption policies', *Bulletin of Italian Politics*, 1:2 (2009), pp. 233–64.

119 *Ibid.*, pp. 241–2.

120 Moriarty, *The Moriarty Tribunal Report: Part 2, Volume 1*, p. 20.

121 P. Cullen, 'Top-earning barrister earns more than €5m', *Irish Times* (13 October 2008).

122 Statement of Mr Justice Michael Moriarty, (23 April 2010), www.moriarty-Tribunal.ie.

123 A. Pizzorno, *Il potere dei giudici*, (Laterza, 1998), p. 114.

124 *Irish Times* (3 May 2001).

125 Bertie Ahern, Dáil Éireann, *Written Answers, Tax Amnesty Deadline. 445.* (18 October 1994). J. Jones and A. O'Donoghue, *In Your Opinion: Political and Social Trends in Ireland through the Eyes of the Electorate* (Town House, 2001), p. 144.

126 S. Dorgan, 'How Ireland Became the Celtic Tiger', *The Heritage Foundation*, (23 June 2006), www.heritage.org/research/worldwidefreedom/bg1945.cfm. Committee of Public Accounts, Sub-Committee on Certain Revenue Matters, *Examination of the Report of the Comptroller and Auditor General of Investigation into the Administration of Deposit Interest Retention Tax and Related Matters during 1 January 1986 and 1 December 1998* (Dublin Stationery Office, 1999), p. 98.

127 Correspondence with Revenue Commissioners, 'Spreadsheet: Yield from various Revenue Special Investigations/Initiatives at 31.3.2010', (July 2010).

128 Byrne, 'Ireland: global corruption report'.

129 J. LaPalombara, 'The structural aspects of corruption', in Trang (ed.), *Corruption and Democracy*; J. Williamson and C. Shen, 'Corruption, state strength, and democracy: a cross-national structural analysis', *Annual Meeting of the American Sociological Association* (Philadelphia, August 2005).

130 Eithne FitzGerald, interview, (February 2006).

131 Fine Gael made illegal under-the-counter cash payments to staff thus avoiding payment of PAYE and PRSI contributions. The party subsequently made a IR£111,000 tax settlement with the Revenue Commissioners in 1999.

132 McGraw, 'Managing change: party competition in the new Ireland'.

133 Ray Burke, Dáil Éireann, *Personal Statement. 480.* (10 September 1997).

134 Cullen, *With a Little Help from My Friends*, p. 103.

135 *Ibid.*, pp. 122–3.

136 Thompson, 'Mediated corruption: the case of the Keating five', pp. 369–70.

137 Senate Select Committee on Ethics, 102–223, 102d Cong., 1st Sess. 11–12, 'Investigation of Senator Alan Cranston, S. Rep.' (1991), www.ethics.house.gov.

138 M. Lord, 'Boyscout Bertie begins his next adventure', *Irish Times* (4 April 2008).

139 E. Harris, 'The Greens can't be moral innocents', *Sunday Independent* (17 June 2007).

140 Morgan Kelly, 'Ireland's future depends on breaking free from bailout', *Irish Times* (7 May 2011).

7

Political funding and the legislative response: 1980s–2010

Introduction

Democracy is not free and money is necessary for political parties to perform their basic democratic functions. These include selecting, recruiting, and training candidates for public office; mobilising voters; participating in elections; forming government or serving as the Opposition; designing and implementing policy alternatives and providing the main link between citizens and government.

Yet, unorthodox inflow of private sources of capital to a political party compromises the very premise of democracy. Corrupt political financing is defined as political contributions that contravene existing laws on political donations; the unauthorised use of state resources for partisan political purposes; the acceptance of money in return for an unauthorised favour or the promise of a favour in the event of election to an office and the use for campaign or party objectives of money that a political officeholder has received from a corrupt transaction.[1]

It creates collusive power blocs, which capture the political market and undermine the democratic principles of civic equality and equitable electoral competition. Moreover, the decision-making capacity of political parties is eroded by a procured conflict of interest. At the heart of the three corruption Tribunals outlined in chapter 6 were serious concerns about how the practice of political action was funded. Irish academia however, has paid inadequate attention to illicit political finance and how such influence has been used to subdue or defeat democratic processes for private gain. The study of flows of money within political life has not received the same scrutiny as, say, voting statistics or electoral systems. Although the exact effects of the financing of elections are difficult to quantify because there so many factors that can shape candidate and party appeal (e.g. incumbency, a candidate's unquantifiable appeal to voters, etc.), money undoubtedly plays a vital role in democratic politics.[2] Benoit and Marsh's detailed study of the 1999 local government election and the 2002 general election, for example, found that 'spending is positively and significantly related to electoral success.'[3]

Fianna Fáil's financial reliance on the beef industry in the 1980s was replaced by property and construction interests in the 1990s and 2000s. This chapter explores if this dependence impacted on policy decisions and if this reliance exacerbated the depth of Ireland's economic collapse from 2008–10. The upshot of the financial crash was the subsequent intervention by the International Monetary Fund and the European Central Bank in November 2010 and the loss of Irish economic sovereignty.

Political funding: 1980s

The professionalisation and competitiveness of politics, which began in the 1960s, was amplified in the 1980s as presidential style election campaigns based on personality politics took hold.[4] The consequence of three highly charged elections, during an eighteen month period between 1981 and 1982, was an abiding legacy of financial vulnerability for political parties and individual politicians. Fianna Fáil's spend was estimated at IR£2,750,000 while Fine Gael spent in the region of IR£1,250,000, significant sums of money in a then depressed economy.[5] The parties were estimated to have spent a similar amount at the 1987 election.[6] The 1989 election, the fifth in eight years, proved to be the most expensive yet. The ballpark figure for Fianna Fáil's spend was IR£2.5-IR£3 million, Fine Gael IR£1.5 million, the PDs IR£400,000 and Labour IR£50,000.[7]

In all, the five elections from 1981–89 cost Fianna Fáil and Fine Gael approximately IR£7,500,000 and IR£3,960,000 respectively. Figure 7.1 illustrates the escalating expenditure on political campaigns by Fianna Fáil and Fine Gael. At that time state funding for parties did not exist and all financing was self-raised. This conservative figure does not include the price of four contentious referendum campaigns, a local election and six by-elections. At the close of the 1992 election campaign, Fianna Fáil were more than IR£3.5 million in debt while Fine Gael owed more than IR£1 million. Fianna Fáil were said to have scheduled to clear its debt by the end of the 1994. 'Such a financial transformation is an astounding achievement, noted the *Irish Times*.[8]

Then and now, political parties were notorious for their sensitivity regarding the source of party funding. In an RTÉ *Morning Ireland* radio interview, after the 1989 election, journalist Cathal MacCoille's query about the source of Fianna Fáil's funds was met with an angry response by the party. He subsequently made a written apology to Seamus Brennan, Minister for Transport and Tourism, for the manner in which he conducted the interview. 'I made it clear I was asking a question, not making an accusation' he told the *Irish Times*.[9] MacCoille's question was made within a context where any such inquiry into political donations was greeted with outright contempt.

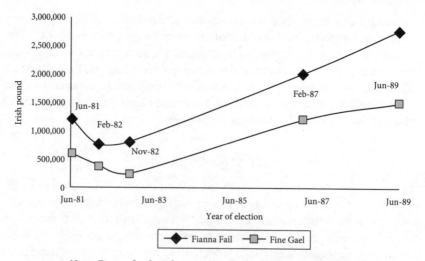

7.1 Estimated campaign spend by Fianna Fáil and Fine Gael, 1981–89

Note: Figures for the Labour party and other parties were sporadic.

The Moriarty Tribunal revealed why the issue of political donations was so sensitive. Haughey, Ray Burke, Minister for Justice and Communications, and Pádraig Flynn, Minister for the Environment, 'had all used the 1989 election campaign to raise enormous amounts of cash for their own personal use from a variety of wealthy Fianna Fáil supporters'.[10] Burke received three separate IR£30,000 donations from Rennicks (subsidiary of the Fitzwilton Group), James Gogarty and Century Radio boss Oliver Barry. Flynn accepted a IR£50,000 blank cheque from property developer Tom Gilmartin.[11]

The idea that the relationship between business subscriptions and politics depends on the proximity to power was not a revelation born from Tribunal investigations in the late 1990s. Writing in 1989, journalist James Downey noted, 'there is good reason to suspect that FF in particular do improper favours for businessmen in return for contributions to party funds. It is discouraging to think that a good proportion of the electorate would appear to see little wrong with this.'[12]

The cloak of secrecy and an absence of figures outlining the personal indebtedness of individual politicians, necessitates reliance on anecdotal references. The experiences of Emmet Stagg TD, Labour, as a politician in the 1980s was mirrored across the political spectrum: 'I was in constant debt arising from the costs of being a TD. That's the period that the Tribunals are investigating now. It left politicians and public representatives very vulnerable to awards of unauthorised money, if you like, to put it that way. And that did occur. And it was very tempting because you were broke.'[13] When Martin Cullen, PDs, lost his Waterford seat in 1989, 'he was said to be in such financial difficulty that he would be forced to sell his car to pay his mortgage'.[14] So severe were the financial difficulties within the PDs at the time that prominent PD TD, Mary Harney, contended that if the party had not entered into coalition with Fianna Fáil in 1989: 'I don't think the party would still be around. We wouldn't have been able to sustain the organisation or financially sustain the show if we hadn't been in government.'[15]

Political funding: 1990s-2000s

A growing public unease about 'accountability in relation to standards applicable to the holding of public office' motivated Brendan Howlin TD, Labour, to introduce a private members Ethics in Government and Public Office Bill in February 1991.[16] Albert Reynolds, Minister for Finance, rejected the Bill on the grounds that the code of conduct within the Government Procedure Instructions, media scrutiny and 'most importantly, the people of Ireland, who have the sovereign right to decide through the ballot box' were sufficient deterrants to dishonourable transgressions. Reynolds accused the Wexford TD of exaggerating the problem of gift-giving to politicians, noting donations merely reflected 'the personal bond that may exist between donor and recipient'. Indeed, Reynolds went so far as to suggest that any introduction of provisions governing members' private financial interests 'would run the risk of being in breach of the spirit – if not the letter – of the Constitution'.[17] The Bill was lost at the second stage by two votes when voted down by the Fianna Fáil / PD government. The Beef Tribunal was established two weeks later in February 1991.

The implementation of Howlin's Ethics Bill was a precondition for the Labour party in its 1992 programme for government negotiations with Fianna Fáil. The ensuing Ethics in Public Office Act, 1995 was the first substantive legislation on political corruption since the Prevention of Corruption Act, 1916. In the intervening seventy-nine years, Ireland's anti-corruption framework had derived from eight British statutes implemented between 1854 and 1916. The Ethics Act ended this rather naive assumption about the sanguine ability of politicians to self-regulate their own conduct. Eithne FitzGerald, Minister of State at the Department of Finance, with responsibility for introducing the ethics legislation, attributed this delay in legislative reform to the civil service embargo. Laney Bacon, who had retired from the Attorney General's office, drafted the Act in his eighties.[18] Tony Killeen TD, Fianna Fáil, became the first Chair of the Committee on Members' Interests of Dáil Éireann under the Act. He attributes this delay to Ireland's insularity, a 'reluctance to copy what was happening in the UK' and 'I suppose the very practical consideration, politicians are working sixteen or seventeen hours a day just to keep afloat and they really haven't the time to be thinking about this kind of stuff.'[19]

This era of political reform was wrought by fortuity rather than design, which had counterproductive implications for Ireland's accountability framework over the next fifteen years. A crisis-led approach to legislation was devoid of a systematic early consideration of the long-term benefits, enforcement and compliance issues of new regulatory proposals. This contributed to a dense, and at times contradictory, legislative framework which necessitated several attempts to reform the reforms. Mr. Justice Brian McCracken, chair of the 1997 McCracken Tribunal, described this as 'a knee jerk reaction . . . They are now just throwing things in without thinking about them and if they had, if somebody had sat down for two or three months and bring out one decent act covering everything'.[20]

In total, some twenty-five pieces of legislation focusing directly or circuitously on corruption were initiated in the ten year period 1995–2005. The hotchpotch nature of the legislation is such that a bribery offence alone is punishable with four different sentences under the Prevention of Corruption (Amendment) Act, 2001 and the Criminal Justice (Fraud and Theft Offences) Act, 2001. The 1997 Electoral Act for instance had been amended six times before 2006. The prevention, detection, investigation and prosecution of corruption is divided between Tribunals of Inquiry, Commissions of Inquiry, High Court Inspectors, the Financial Regulator, the Standards in Public Office Commission (SIPO), Local Authorities, the Dáil and Seanad Committees on Members Interests, the Garda Bureau of Fraud Investigation, CAB, and the Office of the Director of Corporate Enforcement. Those charged with implementing the anti-corruption legislative framework find it cumbersome because of the quantity of amendments made to ethics legislation in recent years.[21]

This piecemeal approach was also reflected within the legislation governing the financing of Irish political parties. The Council of Europe Body, the group of states against corruption (GRECO), concluded in its 2009 evaluation report that Ireland's 'regulatory framework on political financing is very fragmented . . . [and] far from ideal'.[22] The regulatory framework on political finances is indicative of the political approach to public ethics. The legislation often expresses objectives without considering in sufficient detail how to implement these worthy intentions. The letter rather than the spirit of the law is honoured. Legal statutes hold fast to the 'three Ps' principle - print the legislation, post it up for all to see and pray that it works. In the haste to legislate, personal ethical responsibilities were forsaken for legislation which has allowed for the legalistic political defence to emerge that: 'I have broken no law; therefore I have done no wrong'. In this scenario the law will always play

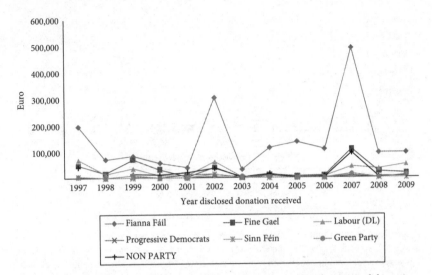

Notes: The Electoral Acts distinguish between donations made to political parties and those given to political individuals such as TDs, Senators and MEPs. Fianna Fáil representatives were by far the largest beneficiaries of disclosed political donations, receiving 62 per cent, €1,630,072 million, between 1997 and 2007. Individuals from all the other parties combined, including Fine Gael, Labour, Greens, Sinn Féin, PDs, Socialist and non-party, received one-third of all disclosed donations.

7.2 Donations disclosed by political individuals, 1997–2009

catch up. The public perception has arisen that public officials seek to merely fulfil legislative obligations rather than moral expectations.

Figure 7.2 illustrates the total donations per year disclosed by Irish political individuals since the establishment of the political disclosure regime introduced under the Electoral Act 1997. This Act necessitated that annual statements of donations and elections expenditure must be submitted to SIPO. Since the Electoral (Amendment) Act 2001, money donated to individual candidates in Dáil, Seanad, Presidency and European elections (exceeding €635) must now be disclosed and must not exceed €2,539 (for elected representatives and candidates) in any given year by the same donor.

Donations significantly increase in election years. Fianna Fáil representatives attracted almost twice as much as all the other parties combined during the 2002 and 2007 general elections. The quantity of Fianna Fáil donations, 931, makes it difficult to break down the sources of this money. The fact that Fianna Fáil candidates are the beneficiaries of more disclosed donations than candidates from other parties is not surprising because proportionate to other parties, Fianna Fáil has traditionally run more candidates. Of the 466 candidates that ran in the 2002 election, 22 per cent were from Fianna Fáil. Nonetheless, during that election year, Fianna Fáil received two-thirds of all

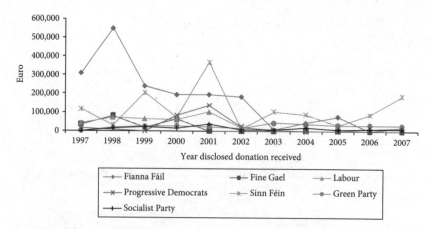

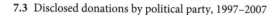

Notes: Total Figures rounded to the nearest euro. 1998-2000 figures converted from punt to euro. Australian and US dollars also converted to euro. Converted on the first of January of the year of disclosure using currency converter: www.wolsink.com/currencyconv.php. Total figures exclude monies (1) returned to donors and (2) returned because monies exceeded disclosure limit. Labour figures include small number of Democratic Left (DL) donations. DL merged with Labour in 1999. Large numbers of donations received during 1998 were given on foot of the Belfast Peace Agreement.

7.3 Disclosed donations by political party, 1997–2007

the funding disclosed which means that candidates from that party obtained seven times more donations than a non-Fianna Fáil candidate.

Although donation limits to political parties (€6,349, see below) are pitched at a higher threshold, political individuals attract significantly more financial contributions. Disclosed donations to political individuals in 2007 amounted to €855,995. Excluding subscriptions from the salaries of elected representatives to their parties, disclosed donations to political parties in 2007 amounted to just €43,693. It is evidently more attractive to donate to political representatives than political parties. As loyalty to political parties has declined, the "franchise" nature of political parties has increased. Candidates from the same party increasingly present themselves to the electorate as individual choices. As candidates, not parties, become the focus of financing, the opportunity structures for illicit influence may increase.

Figure 7.3 illustrates the total donations per year disclosed by Irish political parties to SIPO since 1997. Before the introduction of the Electoral (Amendment) Act 2001, there was no cap on the value of donations to be disclosed. Figure 7.3 illustrates a deliberate pattern by all political parties to disclose less since the introduction of this Act. Since 2001, donations to political parties (exceeding €5,079) must now be disclosed and must not exceed €6,349 in any given year by the same donor. The acceptance of foreign donations was prohibited.

Donations peaked in 1999 and 2001 as parties were positioning their finances in advance of the European Parliament, Local Government and general elections. Apart from the monthly or annual subscriptions from the salaries of Labour, the Greens, Sinn Féin and the Socialist Party elected representatives, donations disclosed by all political parties amounted to €753,523 in 2001, the year before the 2002 election. In the year before the 2007 election, which was anticipated to be one of the most expensive yet undertaken, just €17,000 in donations, excluding subscriptions, was disclosed.[23] This extraordinary decline in disclosure is attributable to a deliberate policy by the political parties of soliciting donations below the disclosure thresholds. This is due to the relatively small difference in the maximum donation that can be accepted by a political party (€6,349) and the amount that must be disclosed (€5,078).

For instance, the PDs issued a letter to 400 potential donors in advance of the 2007 election and suggested a contribution of €5,000 which was 'below the declarable limit' and 'will not be the subject of any disclosure, either voluntary or statutory'.[24] Fine Gael has returned a nil disclosure to the standards commission from 2001–10. Incredibly, Fianna Fáil, Fine Gael and Labour disclosed a zero return in disclosed donations for 2009, the year that all three parties ran substantial local, European, by-election campaigns and a Lisbon Treaty referendum.

GRECO concluded that 'a significant shortcoming' of the donations disclosure system was 'the lack of provisions to account for the total annual finances of political parties'.[25] The absence of full sets of income and expenditure, debts and assets has in effect made the existing legislation meaningless. For instance, of the €10.1 million spent by parties and candidates in the 2007 general elections, only €1.3 million was disclosed with no information available as to the origin of the remaining €8.8 million.[26] This is a minimal figure; the legislation requires that election expenditure is only expected to be accountable for the period between the dissolution of the Dáil to polling day, usually three to five weeks. Electioneering prior to this period is not accounted for. Election campaigning for the 2007 election began in earnest in 2004 – not only with the Mullingar Accord between the Opposition parties Fine Gael and Labour (a pre-election statement of intent between both parties) – but also the regular campaigning and billboards from that time forward.

As figure 7.4 illustrates, 35 per cent (€635,970), of Fianna Fáil's disclosed donations were sourced from property and construction interests from 1997–2007 (see notes to figure 7.4 for full explanation). Fianna Fáil received substantial donations in 1998 for the specific purpose of campaigning on the 1998 Good Friday Agreement (GFA) referendum. When these donations are excluded, disclosed donations from property and construction interests amount to 39 per cent (€545,818) overall. Treasury Holdings, which also

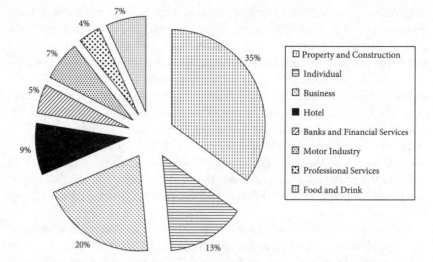

Notes: This period 1997–2007 coincides with the height of the Celtic Tiger and the three elections of 1997, 2002 and 2007 when Fianna Fáil were the dominant coalition partner in the 1997–2002 and the 2002–07 Fianna Fáil / PD governments. This is an incomplete picture of how Fianna Fáil were funded because there is no statutory obligation to disclose donations below the legal threshold. Figure 7.4 does however indicate trends in the sources of political donations. Fianna Fáil was the largest beneficiary of disclosed donations, among all the political parties receiving €1,819,210. Eighty per cent of which was raised between 1997 and 2001, before donation limits of €6,349 and legal disclosure above €5,078 were introduced.

7.4 Disclosed donations to Fianna Fáil by sector 1997–2007

donated under Castlemarket Holdings and Spencer Dock Developments, proved the most generous. In all, the property company associated with John Ronan, donated €98,408 to Fianna Fáil and its representatives and €69,302 to the PDs.[27]

Business interests were the next largest donors, contributing 20 per cent (€367,109) of Fianna Fáil's disclosed donations. Individuals donated 13 per cent (€245,801) of all disclosed funds. The hotel industry, banks and financial services, motor industry, food and drinks interests and professional services, such as solicitors and auctioneers, donated a third of all disclosed donations. These included solicitor, auctioneer and chartered accountant firms Ernst & Young, Fintan Gunne, KPMG, William Fry Solicitors and CB Richard Ellis Gunne and hoteliers such as Doyle Hotels, O'Callaghan Hotels and Fitzpatrick Hotels, New York.

The banks and insurance companies were also charitable to Fianna Fáil, donating 5 per cent (€90,190) of all disclosed donations. These included American General Investment Management Group - $10,000, American International Group (AIG) $10,000, AIB $10,000 and Anglo Irish Bank

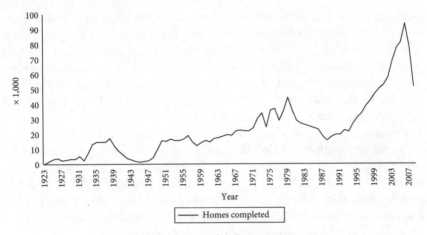

7.5 Homes completed, 1923–2008

IR£9,600. Irish Life donated IR£35,000 for the purposes of the GFA referendum. Loretta Brennan Glucksman, wife of the late Lew Glucksman, former chair of the global investment group Lehman Brothers, gave $10,000. Thomas J. Moran, president and chief executive of life insurance group, Mutual of America, donated $20,000. Moran was appointed Bank of Ireland director in 2001–07. The Irish-American sits as non-executive director of Aer Lingus.

Fianna Fáil's financial reliance on the beef industry in the 1980s was replaced by property and construction interests in the 1990s and 2000s. From Paltiel's perspective, 'the flow of funds into any party system reflects the economic and social structure of its society . . . The search for funds may induce politicians to listen more to those who give to their campaigns than to those who vote for them, or for their party'.[28] In order to retain the support of the electorate, the government intervened in the housing market to initiate marginal changes to stamp duty, tax rates and grants which assisted first-time home purchasers. The state lowered capital gains tax, allowed developers to forego their affordable and social housing obligations and promoted a laissez faire planning system. The Irish policymaking system failed to counteract the property-market bubble, because of the susceptibility of government to interest-group pressures. This is reflected by Fianna Fáil's dependence on funding from these quarters and from an expectant electorate demanding concessions within the housing market. This had devastating consequences for Irish economic sovereignty.

The robust tradition of housing sentiment in Ireland, combined with competitive market conditions and cheap money, created an inelastic supply of housing from 1997 to 2007 as figure 7.5 illustrates. The extent of the property boom was such that almost a third of Ireland's housing stock was built during this boom period. Ireland had the highest per capita building rate in Europe in 2005 and one of the highest home ownership rates in the EU with 77 per cent of households living in tenure.[29] By 2007, Ireland, along with Spain, was producing more than twice as many units per head of population than elsewhere in Europe.[30] More than a fifth of the Irish workforce were employed in building houses in a property market which accounted for 17 per cent of total tax revenue in 2006, up from 5 per cent in 1998.[31]

Key political decisions were insulated from critical debate because they were executed within a closed and cartelised system which facilitated regulatory capture.[32] The absence of clear lines of demarcation between expert advice and political decision-making allowed both sides to evade responsibility, even though the doctrine – whereby accountability is vested solely in the Minister – is notionally designed to avoid this possibility. Forensic probing only occurred when a complete systems failure transpired.[33]

This systems failure occurred in September 2008. A near-paralysis of the international markets for short-term liquidity occurred after Lehman Brothers, the fourth-largest U.S. investment bank, filed for bankruptcy on 15 September. A report commissioned by the government in the causes of Ireland's economic crisis found that although the collapse of Lehman Brothers was a 'trigger' for the economic collapse, it was not the 'decisive' factor.[34] Irish residential property prices had already been falling for more than 18 months. An analysis by the National Asset Management Agency (NAMA) and through the Prudential Capital Assessment Review (PCAR) process has since revealed that the loan portfolio of Anglo Irish Bank was at this point 'well on the road towards insolvency'.[35]

In September 2008, the government offered a comprehensive State Guarantee for the liabilities of the six Irish-owned banks. The blanket bank guarantee, as it became known, amounted to €440 billion of Irish bank liabilities which was later increased to €485 billion to cover foreign-owned banks with significant operations in Ireland. Brian Lenihan, the Minister for Finance, regarded the viability of Anglo Irish Bank as 'of systemic importance to Ireland', and in January 2009 the bank was nationalised.

By the end of 2010, a capital bailout of €46 billion had been injected into the Irish banks, of which, almost €30 billion had been put into Anglo. This was the equivalent to nearly a fifth of Ireland's national output.[36] Anglo was the most exposed Irish bank to the property crash and virtually all of it's €72 billion loan book was to builders and property developers. Between September 2008 and December 2010, Anglo reported a loss of €30.4 billion, setting a new record in Irish corporate history. This compares with Ireland's total tax take during 2010 of €31.75 billion.[37]

Kevin Cardiff, the secretary general of the Department of Finance, told the Dáil Public Accounts Committee in July 2010 that Anglo had been 'extremely disingenuous' in its communication to government about the strength of its loan book and its capital-raising powers right up until its nationalisation.[38] This underestimation by the government of Anglo's liabilities undermined the government's banking policy. The decision to introduce the blanket banking guarantee thus over-exposed the state. According to market traders, this decision damaged the government's credit rating and led ultimately to the €85 billion international bailout by the European Union and International Monetary Fund in November 2010.[39]

The 2010 preliminary investigation by the Governor of the Central Bank (Honohan report) into the causes of Ireland's dramatic economic collapse found that the 'significant factors contributing to the unsustainable structure of spending in the Irish economy', were due to the 'Government's procyclical fiscal policy stance, budgetary measures aimed at boosting the construction sector, and a relaxed approach to the growing reliance on construction-related and other insecure sources of tax revenue.'[40] Ireland was awash with tax reliefs, incentives schemes and income tax exemptions for developers and investors which inflated the price of land and overheated the market. These included tax allowances on 'multistorey car parks, student accommodation, buildings used for third-level educational purposes, hotels and holiday camps, holiday cottages, rural and urban renewal, park-and-ride facilities, living over the shop, nursing homes, private hospitals and convalescent facilities, sports injury clinics and childcare facilities'.[41] Lenihan also commissioned the Regling and Watson *Preliminary Report on The Sources of Ireland's Banking Crisis*. This report noted these tax reliefs 'directed to the property sector, often in particular regions of the country . . . contributed to a more general misallocation of resources as some of the tax concessions seem to have been granted on an ad-hoc basis in a not fully transparent way'.[42]

This includes the 2000–07 Special Incentive Tax Rate for developers which sought to free up land for development by taxing proceeds from the sale of land at 20 per cent instead of the higher rate of up to 42 per cent. The cost to the exchequer because of this tax incentive is estimated in the region of €800 million.[43] In 2010, the excess supply of houses was estimated at 345,116, or 17 per cent of all housing and more than 620 half-empty or unfinished 'ghost estates'.[44]

Moreover, the Finance Act 1994 and Chapter 1, Part 9, of the Taxes Consolidation Act (TCA) 1997 provided for accelerated capital allowances for hotels. Although this special provision for hotels was terminated in Budget 2003, the Finance Act 2003 included transitional arrangements that allowed for the continued availability of a 100 per cent write off over seven years provided certain conditions were met. This arrangement was further extended in the Finance Acts 2004 and 2005. The Finance Act 2006 effectively extended the transitional period by introducing a phase-out period. A report by economist Peter Bacon for the Irish Hotels Federation asserted that 'the tax allowance scheme allowed hotels to access both equity and debt finance easier than would be the case otherwise . . . the total value of tax allowance related to hotels that have not been open 7 years at end 2009 would be just over €1.5 billion'.[45] Bacon believes that there is an oversupply of between 12,300 to 15,300 hotel rooms nationally. Paul Ryan, principal officer at the Department of Finance, has stated that €329 million in capital reliefs were provided from 2004–07 for new hotel developments. The total hotel bedroom capacity of the sector grew by almost 50 per cent from 1999–2008 with 26,802 new hotel bedrooms bringing the total to 60,000.[46]

In 2002, Part V of the Planning and Development Act, 2000 was amended to allow developers to negotiate their way out of providing 20 per cent social and affordable housing in any development through a land swap, payment to the council or building equivalent social and affordable housing elsewhere. In 2004, the chair of the Revenue Commissioners told the Comptroller and Auditor General (C&AG) that not paying tax was seen as a way of gaining competitive advantage in the construction industry. In his 2005 report, the C&AG found that compliance with the Relevant Contracts Tax scheme, introduced to counter tax evasion by subcontractors in construction, was just 57 per cent.

Thirty-five per cent of Fianna Fáil's €1,819,210 disclosed donations were sourced from those who directly benefited from these tax incentives. In the case of Fianna Fáil's 1997–2007 coalition partners, the Progressive Democrats, 34 per cent of their €262,241 disclosed donations came from the property sector. In his Dáil contribution in 1996, Bertie Ahern, the then leader of the Fianna Fáil opposition, observed that 'There is nothing wrong with seeking a greater contribution from those who have rather than from those who have not . . . Ministers and politicians also need to look very carefully at any aspect of their activities that could undermine public confidence in our democratic system.'[47] Yet the main source of Fianna Fáil's disclosed donations for the 1997, 2002 and 2007 elections, when Ahern was Taoiseach, came from property and construction interests.

The Opposition political parties did not disclose any donations from property interests. Fine Gael did disclose €197,914 in donations between 1997 and 2000 from a variety of businesses and individuals but did not disclose donations above the legal threshold from 2001–10. Almost two-thirds of the Labour party's €392,255 in disclosed donations came from the trade union movement.

Conclusion

It will never be known how much Fianna Fáil, the Progressive Democrats or any other political party received in donations below the disclosure limit.

'A list of rich political donors once read like a Who's Who of Irish property developers. Indeed, Fianna Fáil's in house magazine, *The Nation*, was at one point so stuffed with ads from friendly builders that it was a Who's Who of property tycoons.'[48] Many of those property developers who were prominent Fianna Fáil donors, such as Seán Dunne, Ray Grehan, Seán Mulryan, Paddy Kelly, Johnny Ronan, Gerry Gannon, Séamus Ross and the Cosgrave Brothers, are now major clients of the National Asset Management Agency (NAMA). So too is Bernard McNamara, a former local councillor for the party. This agency was established in 2009 to clean up the Irish banking system by taking €81 billion in property-linked loans off their balance sheets with a projected 50 per cent discount on the vast majority of these loans.[49]

In 2010, the Fianna Fáil / Green government declined to extend the terms of reference of the Nyberg Commission of Investigation into the Banking Sector into political decisions made when it was in office. The inquiry, reported in March 2011, did not examine any undue influence by vested interests over regulation and policymaking nor explored those elites who had access to insider information and if they used it for their private benefit. The extent to which political decisions were initiated following lobbying from special interests were not investigated nor were the extraordinary proliferation of tax-incentive schemes during the property boom. It instead examined the behaviour of the banks but not the political decisions which contributed to the economic conditions in which they operated.

The US Financial Crisis Inquiry Commission (FCIC), which published its report in January 2011 into the causes of the American financial and economic crisis, did not have any such reservations about making the relationship between financial contributions and weak regulation. The FCIC found that the 'dramatic failures of corporate governance and risk management at many systemically important financial institutions were a key cause of this crisis.' It noted that 'the financial sector expended $2.7 billion in reported federal lobbying expenses; individuals and political action committees in the sector made more than $1 billion in campaign contributions' which deprived America 'of the necessary strength and independence of the oversight necessary to safeguard financial stability'.[50] The Federal National Mortgage Association, Fannie Mae, for example, 'used their political power for decades to ward off effective regulation and oversight – spending $164m on lobbying from 1999–2008'.[51]

A 2010 report by the National Institute for Regional and Spatial Analysis (Nirsa) at Maynooth called for an independent inquiry to investigate decisions within the planning system and alleged close links between politicians and property speculators.[52] The perception of unorthodox links between politicians, bankers and property developers ultimately led to a series of events which resulted in the resignation of Brian Cowen as leader of Fianna Fáil, though he remained as Taoiseach, and the early dissolution of the Dáil with a 25 February 2011 election.

It emerged for the first time in January 2011 that the Taoiseach played a seven-hour golf round with Seán FitzPatrick, chairman of Anglo Irish Bank, on 28 July 2008, two months before the introduction of the blanket banking guarantee.[53] Cowen and FitzPatrick then had a private dinner at Druids Glen and were joined by Gary McGann, a director of Anglo and Alan Gray, a director of the Central Bank. Anglo was on the verge of collapse with shares valued at €5.30 that day, compared to a €14.40 high the previous October. The Taoiseach has insisted that there was nothing improper with this contact and has strenuously denied that he discussed any of matters relating to Anglo during the golf game or the dinner. The 2010 Honohan report into the causes of Ireland's deepest economic crisis since the foundation of the state, made the finding that 'deference and diffidence on the part of the CBFSAI (Central Bank & Financial Services Authority of Ireland) led to insufficient decisive action or even clear and pointed warnings'.[54]

Ironically, the Moriarty Tribunal, established in 1997 to investigate payments to politicians, was given the remit to make specific recommendations regarding 'the dependence of party politics on financial contributions from undisclosed source'. The terms of reference also requested proposals concerning 'the role and performance of the Central Bank as regulator of the banks and of the financial services sector'. The Tribunal issued its first report in 2006 and its penultimate report in March 2011.

Notes

1 M. Pinto-Duschinsky, 'Political party funding', in R. Stapenhurst, N. Johnson, R. Pelizzo (eds), *The role of parliament in curbing corruption* (World Bank, c. 2006), pp. 190–1.

2 K. Benoit and Michael Marsh, 'The campaign value of incumbency: a new solution to the puzzle of less effective incumbent spending', *American Journal of Political Science*, 52:4 (2008), pp. 874–90.

3 K. Benoit and M. Marsh, 'For a few Euros more: campaign spending effects in the Irish local elections of 1999', *Party Politics*, 9:5 (2003), p. 1; K. Benoit and M. Marsh, 'Incumbent and challenger campaign spending effects in proportional electoral systems: the Irish elections of 2002', *Political Research Quarterly*, 63:1 (2010) pp. 159–73.

4 P. Mair and M. Marsh, 'Political parties in electoral markets in postwar Ireland', in, P. Mair, W. Muller and F. Plasser (eds.), *Political Parties and Electoral Change: Party Responses to Electoral Markets*, (Sage, 2004).

5 F. McDonald, 'Fianna Fáil tightlipped on election funding', *Irish Times* (8 February 1982); P. Murtagh, 'Big money backers switch to Fine Gael', *Irish Times* (11 November 1982); D. Coglan, 'FF's debts may be as high as £600,000', *Irish*

Times (27 January 1983); G. Kennedy, 'Haughey's use of power for financial advantage is exposed', *Irish Times* (30 January 1999).

6   S. Kenny and F. Keane, *Irish Politics Now* (RTÉ, 1987), p. 50.

7   D. Coglan, 'No answer to the £2m political question', *Irish Times* (30 May 1989).

8   'Political Funding', *Irish Times* (25 October 1994).

9   'Journalist apologises to Minister', *Irish Times* (9 October 1989).

10   Collins, *Breaking the Mould*, p. 89.

11   Although Gilmartin said that the donation was meant for Fianna Fáil, the money ended up in foreign bank accounts in the names of Flynn and his wife, Dorothy. Collins, *Breaking the Mould*, p. 92.

12   J. Downey, *All Things New: The 1989 General Election and Its Consequences* (Aisling, 1989), p. 31.

13   RTÉ Six One News, 'Allowances and expenses, interview with Emmet Stagg', (14 September 2009).

14   Collins, *Breaking the Mould*, p. 111.

15   *Ibid.*, p. 109.

16   Brendan Howlin, Dáil Éireann, *Private Members' Business: Ethics in Government and Public Office Bill, 1991: Second Stage. 407.* (7 May 1991).

17   Albert Reynolds, Dáil Éireann, *Private Members' Business. Ethics in Government and Public Office Bill, 1991: Second Stage. 407.* (7 May 1991).

18   Eithne FitzGerald, interview.

19   Tony Killeen, interview, (February 2001).

20   Mr. Justice Brian McCracken, interview, (February 2001).

21   Standards in Public Office Commission, interview (July 2006).

22   GRECO, *Third Evaluation Round Evaluation Report on Ireland Transparency of Party Funding (Theme II)* (Strasbourg, Council of Europe, September 2009), www. coe.int, p. 21.

23   E. Byrne, 'Parties pay lip-service to rules on donations', *Irish Times* (27 June 2007).

24   M. Hennessy, 'PDs defend fundraising letters', *Irish Times* (12 February 2007).

25   GRECO, *Third Evaluation Round*, p. 22.

26   E. Byrne, 'Worrying fall in disclosure of funding by parties', *Irish Times* (22 May 2009).

27   Also in the name of two of its directors and the wife of a director.

28   K. Z. Paltiel, 'Campaign finance: contrasting practices and reforms', in D. Butler, H. R. Penniman and A. Ranney (eds), *Democracy at the Polls* (AEI, 1981), p. 138; also see K. H. Nassmacher (ed.), *Foundations for Democracy – Approaches to Comparative Political Finance: Essays in Honour of Herbert E. Alexander* (Nomos Verlag, 2001).

29   Royal Institute of Chartered Surveyors, *European Housing Review 2005/2006* (2007): www.rics.org.

30   DepartmentoftheEnvironment,HeritageandLocalGovernment,*HousingStatistics (2009)*,   www.environ.ie/en/Publications/StatisticsandRegularPublications /HousingStatis.

31 Davy Research, *Irish Property: Government Finances Exposed to a Correction* (2006), www.davydirect.ie/other/pubarticles/irishpropertyoct2006.pdf.
32 F. Barry, *Politics and Economic Policymaking in Ireland* (Trinity College Dublin, working paper, October 2009) pp. 1–15.
33 F. Barry, 'Public policymaking and the marketplace for ideas', *Transforming Public Services* (Trinity College Dublin, 15 September 2009).
34 P. Honohan, *The Irish Banking Crisis Regulatory and Financial Stability Policy 2003–2008: A Report to the Minister for Finance by the Governor of the Central Bank* (Government Publications Office, 2010), p. 16, 32.
35 *Ibid.*, p. 7.
36 Julia Kollewe, Henry McDonald, 'Anglo Irish Bank bailout could total €34bn', *The Guardian* (30 September 2010).
37 Colm Keena, 'Loss of €17.6bn a corporate record', *Irish Times* (9 February 2011).
38 Eoin Burke-Kennedy and Steven Carroll, 'Anglo "disingenuous" in claims to government', *Irish Times* (22 July 2010).
39 John Murray Brown, 'Cowen under pressure over Anglo Irish funding', *Financial Times* (11 January 2011).
40 Honohan, *The Irish Banking Crisis*, p. 6.
41 *Ibid.*, p. 31.
42 Klaus Regling and Max Watson, *A Preliminary Report on the Sources of Ireland's Banking Crisis* (Government Publications Office, 2010), p. 27.
43 Pat Leahy, 'No hiding place', *Sunday Business Post* (13 June 2010).
44 B. Williams, B. Hughes and B. Redmond, *Managing an Unstable Housing Market* (Urban Institute Ireland: University College Dublin, working paper 10/02, 2010).
45 P. Bacon, *Over-Capacity in the Irish Hotel Industry and Required Elements of a Recovery Programme* (Irish Hotel Industry, November 2009), p. 39, 41.
46 C. Kelpie, 'Tax breaks impaired viable hotels – Shortall', *Irish Times* (12 March 2010).
47 Bertie Ahern, Dáil Éireann, *Private Members' Business. Inquiry into Alleged Payments by Dunnes Stores Ltd.: Motion. 472.* (10 December 1996).
48 N. Webb and E. Williams, 'For politics' sake, may the giving hand never falter', *Irish Independent* (1 April 2010).
49 S. Carswell, 'Eight months a long time as reality bites for Nama', *Irish Times* (9 July 2010).
50 Financial Crisis Inquiry Commission, *The Financial Crisis Inquiry Report: Final Report of the National Commission on the Causes of the Financial and Economic Crisis in the United States*, (2011), p. xviii: www.fcic.gov/report.
51 *Ibid.*, p. xxvi.
52 R. Kitchin, J. Gleeson, K. Keaveney and C. O'Callaghan, *A Haunted Landscape: Housing and Ghost Estates in Post-Celtic Tiger Ireland* (National Institute for Regional and Spatial Analysis, working paper 59, July 2010).
53 Tom Lyons and Brian Carey, *The FitzPatrick Tapes: The Rise and Fall of One Man, One Bank and One Country* (Penguin Ireland, 2011).
54 Honohan, *The Irish Banking Crisis*, p. 12.

8

Political corruption in Ireland: 1922–2010

Introduction

This book reveals a hidden Irish history between the inauguration of political independence in 1922 and the loss of economic sovereignty in 2010. It has presented the context within which political culture responded to corruption since the foundation of the state. The integrity of political activity was analysed to assess what the critical junctures were that caused behaviour to change. It found that the type of corruption altered as a transformation of Ireland's political, economic and social structures occurred. The decline of standards is best represented with the contrast between the 1924 episode where the Minister for Finance charged ministers for their £4.9:6 in subsistence during the Civil War, as described in chapter 2, and the systematic exploitation of the taxpayer since the 1970s as outlined in chapters 5 and 6. This chapter will present the main features of corruption in the twentieth century and that of Ireland in the new century. It will also examine three variables – Irish party system, Irish political culture and Irish media – which facilitated discretionary political decision-making.

Political corruption in the twentieth century

Ireland's political culture, like that of Southern Europe, was influenced by the manner in which the state developed. The Act of Union, 1801 alienated native decision-making to a Dublin Castle administration. Ireland was now governed in a more centralised way than England, Scotland and Wales. Relegated from an independent Irish legislature to that of colony status, special coercive legislation was enforced for all but five years of the Union's first fifty years. Nationalist sentiment against the Union fermented much later and sought to attribute responsibility for Irish economic backwardness to malevolent Westminster rule. During the first Dáil of 1919, Sinn Féin went as far as accusing the Union of facilitating four artificial famines and twenty-seven partial famines.[1] The perception of a debased political elite complicit in the economic and political ruin of their country lingered in the collective Irish memory for generations.

A significant casualty of the Union was that of trust. The hostility to British rule warranted dependence by Dublin Castle on short-term material induce-ments to secure political support in the eighteenth century, such as clien-telism and patronage. These methods by the political establishment to defend and maintain the Union was ultimately counter-productive. The long-term implication of promoting a tainted loyalty to a contested administration was a robust allegiance to the townland, village, town and city. The weak legitimacy of the formal political system ensured weak affinity with the state and a dis-tinct distrust and lack of commitment to the rule of law. Those who cooper-ated with the British authorities were regarded as traitors or informants and treated accordingly by their peers. In his poem, *The Act of Union*, the Nobel prize winning Irish poet Seamus Heaney highlighted these enduring lega-cies of the Union as 'the big pain / That leaves you raw, like opened ground, again'.[2]

A sense of loyalty to the state was undermined because, for the most part, it was politically and administratively identified with another state, one which was hostilely regarded by many as repressive and adversarial. In these circumstances, if fidelity was demanded, it had to be paid for rather than bequeathed benevolently. This mindset may account for the large number of election petitions contesting elections, because of allegations of corruption, which had become common practice in Ireland.[3] The system of justice too was emasculated because the courts system existed not to do justice and enforce the rule of law, but to sustain the imposition of colonialism, which reinforced a sense of unaccountability by the state. Ultimately, this 'style of governance was characterised by government being "done" to the people, rather, than a people being governed by consent'.[4] More than two centuries after the Act of Union was introduced, the term 'establishment' remains a pejorative term in Irish political folklore.

The profound patriotism of those that founded the state in the 1920s sub-consciously elevated an instinctive deference to authority. The institutions of the state assumed a tone of sacredness which in due course earned an authority that rested on the assumption that it is was above reproach, without question and beyond criticism. The maintenance of the rule of law became an end in itself. Political culture placed a premium on continuity, consensus and permanence which over time translated into innate conservatism. This shaped the context of political action and the character of the public mindset for the first ninety years of Irish independence.

Like Ireland, Southern Europe is typified by strong clannish parties which prevailed over any sense of state.[5] The *comatarhis* of Greece, *mafiosi* of Italy and *caciques* of Spain act as political brokers to negotiate access to state struc-tures in a system distinguished by a centre-periphery relationship. Entry into politics was largely without any pre-political resources in terms of financial security, prestige or power. Political careers were often distinguished by obscure social origins and little professional qualifications.[6] Strong nuclear family ties were rooted historically in autocratic and patrimonial institutions, exemplified by the traditional structure of land ownership which emphasised hierarchy and hence inequality.

In this context, the practice of machine politics becomes entrenched within political action. This non-ideological organisation is interested less in political principle than in securing and holding office for its leaders and distributing wealth to those who work for it. Informal means of influence, such as patronage, clientelism and brokerage, were used by those outside the formal system because of social class, religious belief and other cleavages.[7] The preference of conducting political activity endowed Irish politics with certain characteristics such as committed loyalty to the political party / leader / candidate, traditional distrust of the rule of law, hierarchical structures reinforced by a strong party whip, central political identification of the family, dependence upon short-term material inducements to secure political support and reciprocal obligation between politicians and voters.

Ireland also shares similar traits to how Southern European democracies intervened in their economies.[8] This interventionism has taken four broad forms. An all-embracing regulation of economic activity, an extensive state role in the ownership of industries and utilities, the development of a welfare state which, whilst not extensive by Northern European standards, is well equipped to provide selectively generous benefits to particular political constituencies and finally, a large public administration which like state industries, has served to absorb excess labour as much as the provision of public service.[9]

These four instruments of intervention have been employed by political parties for their own partisan interests. The over-regulation of economic life has provided rent seeking opportunities for parties to grant favours to business interests through particularistic deregulation and privatisation. A significant public sector and large welfare state offer the means to mobilise votes and support in exchange for targeted material benefits, as well as providing a state-funded salary for key party workers. For instance, of the €649.2 billion in government expenditure spent during Ireland's boom from 1995 to 2009, public sector salaries and pensions were the largest source of spending at €178.9 billion.[10]

The state is widely perceived as a resource to be exploited. In this scenario, irregular banking practices, insider trading and offshore operations and the poor regulation of financial and economic imprudence warranted pervasive tax evasion which was considered normal practice. The government had in its gift, for example, the allocation of contracts, regulations, tariffs, quotas, subsidies, tax deductions, foreign exchange allocation, planning permission and other economic control mechanisms such as monopoly arrangements. The distribution of state resources may also include the rights to offshore oil and gas exploration and radiomagnetic spectrum, used for broadcasting and for telephony.

Opportunities: rent-seeking behaviour

The World Bank has argued that incentives and bad systems, rather than bad ethics, induce people to act corruptly.[11] The motivation to act corruptly is rationalised because of a high degree of state ownership and service provision, excessive business regulation and taxes and the arbitrary application of regulations and trade restrictions which contribute to an uncompetitive private sector.[12] Rent-seeking behaviour, where individuals seek to obtain special privileges from government by petitioning for tax concessions or regulatory policies that benefit the lobbyist at the expense of the taxpayer, becomes more evident. Dysfunctional access to the market creates an artificial gap between demand and supply and provides discretionary opportunities for public officials to seek rents in decision-making processes.

This was certainly the case in the early half of the twentieth century. The Great Southern Railways, Ward and Locke Tribunals of the 1940s were, in some measure, due to the narrow restrictions placed on domestic industry by the Control of Manufacturing Acts 1932–34. The Irish economy was then a highly regulated environment where varying degrees of political discretion were exercised in the issuing of public resources such as licences, shares, leases and export quotas. The type of conduct exposed at these tribunals included conflict of interest, kickbacks, improper disclosure of confidential information, use of position to ascertain favourable access to key decision-makers and the circumvention of normal bureaucratic procedures.

Irish society after independence was characterised by a generation which had inherited their social and economic status by virtue of incumbency. The 1960s, a period when the state officially rejected protectionism and embraced the outside world, was accompanied by ambitious self-made men such as Patrick Gallagher, Larry Goodman, Dermot Desmond, Albert Reynolds, and Charles Haughey. Just as the 1830s were signified by the 'fierce collision between the people and the gentry',[13] the 1960s were defined by the struggle between old and emerging political and economic elites. This narrative also applies to the Ireland of the 1990s and 2000s. The nouveau riche developers, bankers and legal practitioners, such as Sean Dunne, Seán FitzPatrick and Michael Lynn, came from humble origins to rise to the height of their respective professions, only to dramatically subside in the recession that followed.[14]

The economic confidence of the property developers, beef barons and financiers now became more evident. These new economic actors demanded access to markets which were traditionally closed and limited to incumbent influence which had historical and formal ties to the state and therein substantial advantages in terms of marketplace share and secure property and contractual rights. In order to compete against such influence, this hard-nosed generation from the 1960s sought to cultivate network capital and thereby challenge these assumed rights to economic power through unorthodox means. From this perspective, because entry to the market was intrinsically unequal, alternative and innovative action, such as a policy of state capture, was regarded by some as a justified strategy.

This process was accentuated in the late 1980s and early 1990s. As Ireland sought to reduce and reorient the state's role in the economy, the opportunity for substantial rent, facilitated rent-seeking behaviour because of the potential for excessive profits.[15] Many key parts of the economy, such as civil aviation and telecommunications, were wholly or partially opened by the government from the 1980s to private sector competition. This deregulation of the market and retreat of the state - as well as the proliferation of EU funds through complicated and poorly monitored channels – coincided with a spate of corruption inquiries. The Hamilton, Flood / Mahon and Moriarty Tribunals, for instance, focused on the government's role in allocating quotas of import non-EU beef, radio broadcasting licences and second-generation mobile phone licences. 'Entrepreneurial' actors took advantage of an archaic bureaucratic and political system which was incapable of meeting the demands of those who traditionally felt excluded from the allocation of the state's discretionary resources. The formal political system was unable to cope with the scale of rapid social mobilisation, urbanisation and politicisation and the consequent demands that this initiated.

The golden circle scandals involving Greencore and Telecom Éireann, for example, demonstrated how well placed individuals exploited the uncertainty associated with the transition to the market and how the ethical framework was inadequate to account for the privatisation process. In a comparative analysis with other European states, Chari and McMahon have noted that the Irish experience of privatisation is denoted by the closed and 'rather elitist' nature of the negotiation process where 'disproportionate influence by capital actors' is exercised.[16] The privatisation process in Ireland attracted controversy when government decisions to award public resources through licence have lacked transparency. Such licences have generally had a zero or nominal value placed on them 'known to be well below the likely market value . . . [which] are then allocated through a so-called beauty contest process'.[17]

Colm McCarthy has observed that the state never used auction or tender processes for the allocation of assets, other than physical property, despite its revenue potential and the value added perception of transparency. McCarthy asks whether structural features of the Irish decision-making process were particularly susceptible to corruption because of 'the desire of politicians, and possibly bureaucrats, to retain the levers of patronage and to enable the pursuit of essentially political objectives through surrogate and opaque processes'.[18] That bureaucracy may favour a deliberate policy of interventionism because it increases its power is perhaps a daunting prospect. The capacity of civil servants to be effective protectors of the public interest in negotiations with private sector has not been met with universal enthusiasm.[19]

Opportunities: property and the growth of the state

Although the 1940s are not comparable in terms of the scale of corruption with the latter half of the twentieth century, both periods were distinguished by a marked acceleration in corruption. One explanation proposed is that both episodes were discerned by different degrees of government involvement in the market. Victor Tanzi suggests that 'the growth of corruption is closely linked with the growth of some of the activities of the government in the economy'.[20]

The late 1950s onwards, for example, witnessed a major expansion in the scale, scope and size of state activity. The demographic and economic character of the state dramatically changed within a relatively short period of time. A new breed of professional and career orientated politicians exercised greater political intervention within the economy within the context of an escalating hybridisation of the state and market. The growth of public spending as a share of gross national product (GNP) almost doubled between 1960 and 1985.[21] The Irish economic model underwent a transformation from a mostly rural and agriculturally based market to a largely urbanised, technology and service industry-based economy. The Whitaker reforms of the late 1950s officially abandoned the ideological policies of economic nationalism and protectionism and embraced a new economic departure. Ireland's urban population rose from 40 per cent in 1960 to over 60 per cent in 2000. The upshot of economic success was a greater demand for housing and public services.

The demand for housing in the 1960s was defined by an economic boom which initiated the urbanisation of Ireland and in turn created unprecedented pressure within the housing market. This was also the case in the 1990s, a period characterised by extraordinary immigration rather than just migration. From 1993 to 2002, Ireland experienced sustained economic growth where GDP growth per annum was more than double than that of its European neighbours and its wealth levels, in terms of average income, rose to among the highest of any developed nation.[22] This reversed a trend of emigration towards one of immigration and saw the population increase by 16.8 per cent between 1996 and 2006.

As discussed in chapter 4, the City and County Management (Amendment) Act 1955 institutionalised opportunity structures for potential clientelism through the notorious section four motion of the Act. The cost of creating large tracts of building land reserves, through favourable planning decisions at local government level, was far lower than its market price. The limited availability of building land and favourable planning decisions at local government level placed enormous discretionary powers in the hands of officials and politicians. The political will to address the discrepancies of the 1963 Planning Act was absent. The Attorney General's clear advice in 1974 on the need for conflict of interest legislation was ignored while other legislation on ethics was repealed. Local councillors now had the extraordinary power to override management decisions on land rezoning and planning permission decisions.

This did not change significantly in the second housing boom of the 1990s. Local councillors still held the power to formulate and adopt development plans and make zoning decisions without any obligation to take recommendations of experts into account. In a 2007 RTÉ 1 television *Prime Time Investigates* programme, for instance, Councillor Hughie McElvaney, Fine Gael, from Clones, Co Monaghan outlined his planning logic: 'We are not experts in planning. If there's not a hill on it . . . if it's suitable for sewage, then it's suitable for planning'.[23] Although eighty-eight separate local planning authorities adjudicated over planning applications, they did so within a local authority system overseen by local councillors. Section 140 of the Local Government Act 2001 (formerly section four of the City and County Management (Amendment) Act, 1955) allowed councillors to override specific planning decisions.[24] Indeed, John O'Connor, An Bord Pleanála chairman, described local councillors as responding to the 'special pleadings of landowners and other vested interests' on the occasion of his 2007 annual report.[25]

The nature of the Irish state was shaped by its political culture and a specific economic context which facilitated intermittent but notable instances of corruption. The strong sense of republican public spiritedness in post-independent Ireland, exemplified by the introduction of meritocracy in the civil service and local government, was rigorously contested from the late 1950s.

Political corruption: Ireland in the new century

As Ireland passed from one set of standards to another, indiscretions which were previously accepted and tolerated began to be scandalised. A range of social forces undermined the role of traditional hierarchical power structures. The transition from a predominantly rural to a predominantly urban society was accompanied by greater degrees of geographical mobility, increased educational attainment and higher levels of social capital which provided alternative means of accessing the state. As Ireland's white-collar and middle-class strata multiplied, quality of life issues such as health, education, transport, and infrastructure became the most prominent items on the political agenda as evidenced by the greater prioritisation of such issues within the manifestos of the political parties.[26]

A redefinition of political ethics was facilitated by heightened political competition and growing international socialisation on the positive implications of governance. The moral costs of disreputable transgressions increased as the probability of being discovered by a more inquisitive media was more likely. The severity of reputational punishment was greater as public attitudes towards illegality changed. The political will to strengthen anti-corruption legislation was in larger supply and the culture of secrecy and misplaced loyalty was challenged. Previous recourse to reasons of state was less evident. Weak institutions, poor governance and inadequate legislative controls were tempered by an independent judiciary and the competitive nature of the political system. A shift from traditional self-regulation to a legislative impetus occurred with the introduction of anti-corruption legislation, ethics codes, internal reporting, whistleblowing, audit requirements, and investigative bodies.

Corruption, however, did not cease to exist as the nature of the state transformed but instead embraced new clothes. This difficulty of reconciling old and new definitions of corruption is best understood by examining Irish legislators' relationship with the 1999 Council of Europe Criminal Law Convention on Corruption. In their 2009 evaluation of Ireland's compliance with this Convention, the Council of Europe noted that Ireland had failed to introduce a specific criminal statute prohibiting 'trading in influence'. Ireland was also rapped on the knuckles for the absence of consistency and clarity in the terminology it used. This suggests that Irish legislators found modern terminologies of corruption, such as trading in influence, difficult to grasp.[27] The intricacy of existing Irish legislation is a reflection of both a century of incremental legislative change and an uncertainty among legislators about the broader definition of corruption.

The trading in influence provision seeks to establish transparency and impartiality into the political and administrative decision-making system by buttressing trust and fairness into the process, thereby preventing what it describes as, an 'atmosphere of corruption'. The 1999 Convention also seeks to criminalise a corrupt trilateral relationship where a person gives an undue advantage to another person ('the influence peddler') who claims, by virtue of his professional position or social status, to be able to exert an improper influence over the decision-making of officials and political representatives.

The influence peddler is the one who receives the undue advantage, not the public official, but who misuses his real or alleged influence on other persons. This distinction is significant, in that it is immaterial whether the influence peddler actually exerted influence or not as is whether the influence leads to the intended result.[28] Irish legislation has been criticised by GRECO for not accounting for 'corrupt behaviour of those persons who are close to power and who try to obtain advantages from their situation by influencing the decision-maker'.[29] As chapter 7 demonstrated, over a third of the disclosed donations to Fianna Fáil, the main party of government from 1997 to 2007, originated from construction and property related donors. This dependence may have impacted on policy decisions which exacerbated the depth of Ireland's economic collapse from 2008–10 because policy makers failed to counteract the property-market bubble.

Described as 'background corruption' by the 1999 Convention and as 'legal corruption' by the Transparency International 2009 Country Study of Ireland, the phenomenon of undue influence is one that legislators, politicians and wider Irish society find it taxing to wholly appreciate.[30] Legal corruption may be defined as undue, but not illegal, influence by vested interests over regulation and policy-making where elites have access to insider information which they utilise for their private benefit. This informal misuse of power occurs where personal relationships, patronage, lobbying, political favours and political donations unduly influence the decision-making process even if no laws are broken. It is in this context that distinctions between moral and legal corruption, as outlined in chapter 1, become more evident.

In her study on the allocation of capital expenditure in Ireland from 2001–07 by government department, Jane Suiter finds that individual ministers 'deliver significant additional resources to their own personal bailiwicks'.[31] For instance, the constituencies of the Minister for Arts and Sports and the Minister for Finance were statistically predisposed to receive more in capital grants to sports clubs than elsewhere. The Minister for Sport's constituency receives a mean of €2.2 million compared with €1.5 million elsewhere; sports clubs in the Minister for Arts and Sports and Minister for Finance constituencies are more likely to be successful in their applications at 12 per cent and 15 per cent respectively, than clubs in other districts; individual clubs in the Minister for Arts and Sports and Minister for Finance constituencies receive larger grants at over €70,000 compared with €53,000 elsewhere.[32]

Suiter also finds a similar pattern when examining capital grants to primary schools within the constituencies of the Minister for Education and Minister for Finance. 'The Minister for Finance's constituency receives an average €7.4 million a year in grants to primary schools compared with €3.7 million elsewhere and €4.1 million for the Minister for Education's constituency;

Individual schools in the Minister for Finance's constituency also receive more money. Primary schools in the Minister for Finance's constituency can expect 20 per cent additional funding at over €145,922 compared with €120,636 elsewhere'.[33]

In relation to the constituencies of the Minister for the Environment and the Minister for Community Rural and Gaeltacht Affairs, these constituencies 'receive more money in non-national roads funding with a mean €15.9 million allocated to the Minister for the Environment compared with €3.6 million elsewhere'.[34]

Other policy areas most vulnerable include the public contracting system of procurement, appointments to public bodies and undue effect in the budgetary cycle and the planning process. The pervasiveness of undue influence by private interests undermined the reliability of policy design and decision-making processes in relation to taxation, licensing, procurement, and quota, grant and budget allocations. Clientelism becomes politically professionalised and more competitive as rival patrons compete to control public resources in order to distribute individual benefits. In this new form of clientelism, the political party systematically infiltrates the machinery of the state in order to allocate state jobs, pensions, subsidies, and collective benefits such as roads, housing, education buildings and sports facilities, all in exchange for electoral backing. Legal corruption, or undue influence, is enabled by a decision-making process which is not subject to direct measures of accountability.

Difficult decision-making was delegated to extra-parliamentary state institutions such as the courts, state agencies, social partnership, the European Union and the increased use of referendums. Controversial decisions are sidestepped, thus avoiding unnecessary confrontation. The reversion to Tribunals of Inquiry has allowed parties to relegate the potentially damaging effects of official corruption to mechanisms that provided a degree of cover for themselves. This Irish experience of 'agencification' has been particularly pronounced from a comparative perspective.[35] Since the mid-1980s, a sharp upward trend in creating these new bodies has occurred.[36] Many regulatory agencies have been removed from direct public accountability. Bodies such as the Arts Council, Irish Prison Service, Courts Service, National Roads Authority, Health Service Executive and the Office of Public Works are no longer subject to oversight by members of the Dáil through parliamentary questions (PQs). Moreover, holding the executive to account has been undermined by the increased use by parliamentarians using PQs as a means of meeting constituency demands.

'There seems to have been just a preference, every time there was a problem: set up a new outfit'.[37] This emphasis away from due process and instead towards efficiency and output can increase the possibility of discretion. The

2008 OECD report commented that the result is a confusion of lines of accountability, with poor coordination and duplication of function.[38] As John Stuart Mill noted in 1861, 'responsibility is null and void when nobody knows who is accountable'.[39]

This is further compounded by the unclear and mixed criteria for appointing board members of state bodies. Boards tend to be political appointees: rather than having the benefit of independent outsider expertise and are often the product of cronyism and patronage.[40] Bertie Ahern, when Minister for Finance received IR£16,500 and £33,000 sterling in 'dig-outs' payments from 1993–94.[41] When asked during an extended 2006 interview with Bryan Dobson on RTÉ TV's *Six One News*, about making appointments to state boards for alleged favours, the then Taoiseach defended himself by saying: 'I might have appointed somebody but I appointed them because they were friends, not because of anything they had given me'.[42]

A tradition of self-regulation was complemented by a reluctance to legislate for political conduct and a crisis-led approach to tackling corruption.[43] Ireland's accountability framework is characterised by an absence of clearly defined rules, regulations, policies and legislation governing conflict of interest, political party and campaign finance and political lobbying. For instance, the Freedom of Information 1997 Act sought to open up government. However, the Act has been weakened by the introduction of fees for access to non-personal information and charges of €150 for appeals. The fees which are amongst the highest in the world, have led to a dramatic fall in the number of requests for information from both the media and the public.[44] The Public Service Management Act 1997, in line with public service reform priorities, gave Secretaries General of departments more responsibility and therefore greater accountability for what goes on in their departments. Yet the 2005 Travers report on nursing home charges, for example, still found 'persistent and systemic corporate failure within the Department of Health and Children'.[45]

Concerns about undue influence have also been raised within the Comptroller and Auditor General's (C&AG) annual reports. The C&AG, which reports to the Dáil Public Accounts Committee (PAC) has problems doing value-for-money reports in a timely way; there is often quite some time lag because of its ex-post role. The C&AG and PAC have repeatedly asserted that ongoing parliamentary scrutiny of major expenditure projects is almost non-existent and have raised serious questions about the ability of parliament to examine public procurement practices. The annual procurement market for the island of Ireland is estimated at €19 billion.[46] The September 2007 C&AG special report into the National Education Welfare Board found that only one of 122 individual IT purchases were the subject of a tender process. Lapses within internal audit controls 'were exploited by a member of staff, apparently in collaboration with a supplier' and have ultimately cost the taxpayer over €700,000.[47] The 2008 C&AG special report criticised the underlying 'failures relating to the procurement process, governance and financial management' within FÁS (Irish national training and employment authority), the Abbey Theatre, the National Library of Ireland, the Irish Blood Transfusion Service, Science Foundation Ireland and Beaumont Hospital.[48] Since it came into operation in 2009, the process of valuing individual assets and the transfer of property loans into NAMA, the biggest property portfolio in the world, is not subject to the Freedom of Information Act because of commercially sensitive reasons.[49]

Three corruption variables?

Irish party system

A local, rather than national, identification of politics may account for a recurring predisposition by the Irish electorate to reward self-serving political activity. Irish voters do not as a rule punish individual candidates – or their parties – for corruption. Journalist Pat Leahy made the observation of the Irish electorate in 2007 as one where 'The public do care about standards in public office. It's just that they often make a different – one is tempted to say more nuanced, but relaxed is probably a better word – judgement on its importance relative to other political issues'.[50]

This approach was evident with regard to a number of renowned politicians who became identifiable in the public mind with value laden agendas. Public statements by Niall Andrews, Fianna Fáil, that he would confront alleged conflict of interests within local government planning decisions were not rewarded when he lost his Dublin County Council seat in 1974. Pat O'Malley lost his PD Dáil seat at the 1989 election, notwithstanding his prominent parliamentary contributions which contributed to the establishment of the Beef Tribunal. This propensity to rebuke rather than recompense ethical action was particularly manifest during the Dáil debates which preceded the establishment of the Beef Tribunal. The observation by Ben Briscoe TD, Fianna Fáil: 'I have been in this House 26 years and I have seen many Members come and go. Sometimes I think the 'holier than thou" Members last the shortest time in the House'[51] was corroborated by the findings of an *Irish Times* MRBI opinion poll some months later. Sixty per cent of the electorate held the view that Fianna Fáil was responsible for a drop in standards in Irish politics and that Haughey should now resign as Taoiseach, though 70 per cent did not want a general election.[52] The Irish public wanted accountability but did not want the ultimate consequences of responsibility – a change in government.

In retrospect, Eithne FitzGerald Labour, TD noted that her high-profile role as the Minister who pioneered the introduction of ethics legislation was electorally counter-productive: 'To say that someone was of high moral ground was a way of putting them down'.[53] Her vote collapsed and she failed to be re-elected in 1997. A similar fate bedevilled Jim Mitchell, Fine Gael. Although he held his Dublin seat for twenty years between 1977 and 1997, he was not elected at the 2002 election, despite his highly acclaimed chairmanship of the Dáil Public Accounts Committee investigation into tax evasion.

Politicians subject to scrutiny have tended to record exceptional electoral results. When questions of impropriety first arose in the case of Charles Haughey, Ray Burke and Michael Lowry, the electorate's response was to accord them their largest first preference vote to date. Lowry resigned as Minister for Transport, Energy and Communications in 1996 and was then expelled from Fine Gael following media revelations of an unorthodox financial relationship with businessman Ben Dunne. The response of the North Tipperary electorate in the subsequent June 1997 election was to grant Lowry his highest return ever, recording over a third more votes than his previous election.

The McCracken Tribunal report, published in August 1997, found that apart from knowingly assisting Dunne to evade tax, Lowry was the beneficiary of IR£395,000 in renovations to his Holycross home by the supermarket tycoon. Mr. Justice Brian McCracken reproached Lowry's indiscretions with the words: 'a person in the position of a government minister and member of cabinet was able to ignore, and indeed cynically evade, both the taxation and exchange control laws of the state with impunity'.[54] Despite this strong missive, Lowry's electoral success continued to grow. Lowry also recorded exceptional poll-topping results at the 1999 local elections and the 2002 and 2007 general elections.

Perceived as an anti-establishment protagonist within his own constituency, Lowry is the quintessential prodigal son who returned to the Tipperary periphery from the Dublin centred corruption inquiries. Ireland's PR-STV (proportional representation-single transferable vote) electoral system richly rewards responsive constituency service. It reduces the likelihood of exposure and censure for wrongdoing because voters use it to ensure a focus on intra-party rather than inter-party competition. Political candidates not only compete with those from opposition parties but contenders from their own party. This personalises and localises politics and places emphasis on cultivating not only party loyalty but also candidate loyalty, the basis of clientelistic politics. In the case of Lowry, this loyalty was motivated in response to the resoundingly negative public media saturation aimed at Tipperary's local personality which in turn warranted analogous compensation by local voters.

Irish politicians and parties are insulated from the adverse effects of corruption. Fianna Fáil's ability to continually form governments in an era when two of its longer serving party leaders, Charles Haughey and Bertie Ahern, came under intense pressure because of corruption charges strengthens this claim. Haughey's resignation, while certainly precipitated in part by growing opposition to him stemming from the allegations of corruption, came only after he had survived an internal vote of no-confidence within Fianna Fáil. It was not corruption charges that led immediately to his resignation from within Fianna Fáil, but rather the discovery that Haughey had been aware of illegal phone-tapping in the early 1980s that had forced his then Minister for Justice Seán Doherty to resign.

Fianna Fáil 'suffered little or no electoral backlash for the highly publicised misdeeds of their party leaders'.[55] The 2002 election, for example, was preceded by distinctive instances of erroneous political behaviour. Revelations from the Moriarty and Flood / Mahon Tribunals had effectively destroyed the political reputations of dominant Fianna Fáil personalities, Charles Haughey, Pádraig Flynn, Ray Burke and Denis Foley. Other Fianna Fáil notables also became the centre of scrutiny. Lawlor, devoid of the Fianna Fáil whip, had the ignominy of being imprisoned on three occasions (January 2001, January 2002 and February 2002, for a total of six weeks) for contempt of court arising from his persistent non-cooperation with the Flood / Mahon Tribunal. Beverley Cooper-Flynn was expelled from Fianna Fáil in 2001 when she lost a libel action against RTÉ. The jury in the case found that RTÉ had proven that she advised and encouraged four people to evade tax in her previous work with National Irish Bank. Frank Dunlop, former press secretary for Fianna Fáil, confessed to bribery in 2000.

Massive tax fraud and criminal activity on the interface between politics and big business was uncovered in the Dáil Public Accounts Committee investigation into tax evasion (DIRT Inquiry) which published its report in 1999. Aside from these ethical scandals, two potentially explosive inquiries into financial and political malfeasances were awaiting imminent publication. The Ansbacher (Cayman) Inspectors delayed publishing its thirteen volumes of evidence until two months after the 2002 election. The Flood / Mahon Tribunal decided against hearing any new evidence in the months before the May election and waited until September 2002 to publish its report. Never before was malpractice within politics exposed to such media and public enquiry.

The logic of Irish public opinion prescribed that Fianna Fáil deserved high political office but only if the PDs exercised the role of ethical watchdog. Opinion polls have shown that this is not an isolated phenomena as Fianna Fáil voters have indicated a preference for coalition rather than a single party government since the 1990s.[56] The infamous Michael McDowell lamp post campaign stunt, during the last week of the May 2002 election campaign, ostensibly provided an acceptable measure of public indignation for the Irish electorate. The 'Single Party Government: No Thanks. Vote Progressive Democrats' poster highlighted the PDs role as protecting the integrity of the

Fianna Fáil led government despite a decade of corruption charges. Public anger subsided as the economy boomed.

As it happened, Fianna Fáil was just deprived of an overall majority in the election and for the first time since 1969, a government was re-elected to office. The eternally popular Bertie Ahern led Fianna Fáil to its third straight general election victory in 2007 despite lingering allegations about the Taoiseach's personal finances. A 2006 MRBI poll revealed that 64 per cent of respondents believed that the Taoiseach was wrong to have accepted IR£50,000 in extramural payments from his friends while he was Minister for Finance in 1993. Another 66 per cent felt that Ahern was wrong to accept £8,000 sterling from his friends in Manchester, United Kingdom, while he was Minister for Finance in 1994. Nevertheless, only one year later an RTÉ exit poll after the 2007 election found that 75 per cent of voters felt that these questions did not affect their vote.[57] Ahern remained Taoiseach for an additional year before resigning and only did so when concern emerged among party elites that his finances would adversely affect Fianna Fáil's efforts in the 2009 local and European elections.[58] Chapter 7 has also outlined the circumstances of the resignation of Taoiseach Brian Cowen as leader of Fianna Fáil in 2011. It was historically low opinion ratings for the party and a pending election which provoked an internal leadership heave and not the underlying controversy of Cowen's previously undisclosed contacts with the chair of Anglo Irish Bank in the months leading up to the 2008 blanket bank-guarantee.

The 2002 and 2007 electoral feats occurred despite the shadow of political scandal overhanging Fianna Fáil in advance of those elections. A punch-drunk electorate choose to consistently ignore the ethical shortcomings of their political masters who adopted a Teflon ability to deflect undue public attention. Why has this been the case? Sean McGraw makes the case that Fianna Fáil's electoral success throughout the period of increased perception of corruption (1992–2007), garnering 40 per cent of the vote, 'supports the conclusion that Fianna Fáil loyalists may indirectly enjoy the benefit of influence-peddling or other questionable practices, as a result of engaging in precisely these practices'. This he believes is because Fianna Fáil successfully portrayed 'itself as the best broker of individual needs of Irish citizens when dealing with the increasingly intricate government apparatus'.[59] A view supported by Anderson and Tverdova:

> Those elected in the incumbent government are less likely to seek out information about corruption and less likely to interpret such information negatively. Moreover, we posit that, when corruption occurs, it is more likely to benefit supporters of the government than supporters of the opposition. As a result, corruption should produce less of a negative impact on political support among those who elected the incumbent government (the majority) than among those who supported the opposition (the minority).[60]

The electorate have frequently made the deliberate choice of voting for those with impugned probity records. The character of Ireland's consociative democracy was also responsible for stymieing legislative response to ethical breaches. Cross-party consensus between political parties on the government and opposition benches, over a sustained period of time, warranted that political culture was not meaningfully challenged. Despite the public objections to perceived conflict of interests and concerns about political ethics, the Fine Gael / Labour coalitions of 1973–77 and 1981–87 did not introduce reform. Instead, it was 'outsiders', not political opponents who challenged the unspoken accord between institutions of power.

The Irish party system has been characterised by stability and hegemony and has witnessed extended periods when the same political party experienced longevity in power.[61] Fianna Fáil has been one of the most successful parties in Western Europe, holding two sixteen-year periods of uninterrupted government, from 1932 to 1948 and 1957 to 1973. The decision by Fianna Fáil to enter into coalition government in 1989 warranted the perception of permanent Fianna Fáil government. With the brief exception of an unanticipated Rainbow government from 1994–97, Fianna Fáil has been in power for twenty-one years from 1987–2011. When permanence in power becomes so prevalent, an assumption of eventual reciprocity can become deep-rooted while the distinction between government and state can become distorted in the eyes of those in power. This was the case with the Christian Democrats in Italy and the Liberal Democrats in Japan, where both parties retained national hegemony for more than a generation before corruption scandals led to their downfall.[62]

The protective activities of parties only become destabilised when the fortunes of political parties decline. On the two occasions where the Irish party system experienced high degrees of electoral volatility, atypical concentration on political ethics occurred. Elevated levels of unpredictability occurred during the multi-party periods of the 1940s and the late 1980s and 1990s.[63] These two periods coincide with an intensity of formal corruption investigations. The 1940s were distinguished by three Tribunals, legislative reform and two convictions for bribery. The late 1980s and 1990s were marked by four Tribunals, considerable legislative reform, substantial tax settlements by prominent politicians and three convictions directly and indirectly related to Tribunal investigations.

Hence, low degrees of electoral volatility have corresponded with the absence of official inquiry by the state into corruption. New entrants to politics prompt a review of old practices. This was the case with the emergence of the PDs as a political force in the late 1980s and their demand for the establishment of the 1991 Beef Tribunal. The Spring Tide in 1992 more than doubled the number of Labour TDs to 33 and facilitated a meaningful campaign on ethical reform. This suggests that when the Irish political system has been at its most competitive, the opportunity for corruption allegations to emerge has been greater. This does not mean that meaningful political responses necessarily occur. Research on political activity within American states, for instance, has shown that those states with a high degree of political competition record low instances of corruption.[64] This suggests that political incumbency and the absence of electoral competition increase the risk of behaviour favourable to corruption.

The effect of electoral volatility is reflected within the content of political manifestos. Sean McGraw's analysis of political programmes reveals that the issue of corruption received negligible attention, if it was referenced at all. In the seventeen elections between 1948 and 2002, Fianna Fáil mentioned corruption on four occasions, Fine Gael six times, and Labour five times.[65] Clann na Poblachta referenced corruption in ten per cent of their election materials. Chapter 3 has outlined the context of Clann's emergence during the tribunals of the late 1940s. The 2011 election campaign was distinguished by all political parties identifying political reform as a key election issue. The economic collapse which resulted in the IMF / ECB / EU intervention was perceived by Labour to be a consequence of 'abuses of corporate and political power that have risked our country's sovereignty'.[66]

Irish political culture and religion

The long-term implications of the prodigious influence of the Catholic Church on the nature of Ireland's political development are threefold. They include the consequences of the authoritarian nature of the political culture, articulated through the acceptance of hierarchy and espousal of conservatism, the expression of public trust though the prism of familial values and finally the blanket emphasis on loyalty which embraced deference as a core virtue.

The absence of a focused campaign against the church's institutional power and influence within Ireland's everyday civic and political life was perhaps because the church in nineteenth-century Ireland was identified as anti-establishment and was not a major landowner nor linked to the old regime unlike its European neighbours. Ireland thus did not experience the same tradition of anti-clericalism as mainland Europe. Resistance to British colonial rule was associated with the campaign to grant greater religious rights to the Catholic majority. In the Nationalist movement, loyalty to the concept of the Irish and Gaelic nation became identified with faithfulness to the Catholic religion. Indeed the strength of the relationship between Irish political and religious freedom was such that contemporary Irish Protestants believe that they are not perceived as being 'really Irish' by their Catholic compatriots.[67]

This view gained prominence in late nineteenth-century Ireland. The

Dominican priest, Thomas N. Burke, articulated this in his famous 1872 sermon, 'Catholicity as revealed in the character of the Irish people', where he merged the Irish character, nationality and religion. 'Every nation and every race on the face of the earth has its own peculiar characteristics, its sympathies and antipathies, its notions of things, its line of conduct, and so on; and all these things go to make up what is called the national character of a people'.[68] For Burke and his contemporaries in the Irish Catholic Church, Irishness was defined as membership of the Catholic faith which accepted a Catholic mindset. The corollary of this nationally circumscribed Catholicism was a political culture which embraced authoritarian authority, hierarchical values and deferent conservatism.

In the wake of the 'Devotional Revolution' in the late nineteenth century and the creation of a quasi-confessional state in the 1920s and 1930s, the Catholic Church permeated every aspect of Irish society in the twentieth century.[69] Despite W. T. Cosgrave's attempts to politically consolidate Protestants within the Senate after Irish independence, the national definition of Irishness came to implicitly become equated with membership of the national religion, that of Catholicism. The secular tone of the 1922 Free State Constitution was abandoned in the 1937 Constitution. The presence of God, as articulated in Catholic theology, was enshrined in the preamble of Bunreacht na hÉireann.

In Ireland, all meaningful networks of association and relationships of reciprocity - the essential elements of social capital – found their source and substance in the Catholic Church.[70] Individual sexual, religious and private morality was firmly regulated by the church hierarchy. Deep suspicion and hostility was directed to the outsider, defined as someone not a member of family nor the village, which contributed to a self-interested culture. Not only were outsiders regarded with deep suspicion, but so too were any ideas that challenged the consensus. This was a society that prided itself in thwarting intellectualism, perceived as the liberal fancy of Protestants and wealthy educated Catholics, the very antithesis of Burke's definition of Irishness.

The Process of Aggiornamento, Second Vatican Council, initiated by Pope John XXIII from 1962–65, failed to produce the same measure of intellectual ferment in Ireland that was prompted in other Catholic countries. The national mind grew paranoid that any lapse in moral fundamentalism would cause horrific social disintegration and destroy the roots of family life and any semblance of moral decency. Archbishop John Charles McQuaid's 1967 Lenten Regulations for the Dublin Diocese included the missive: 'Parents have the serious duty to be vigilant and to supervise the use by their children, especially their adolescent children, of the modern means of communication: books, magazines, press, radio, television, stage and cinema'.[71] Cold suspicion of critical reflection and foreign influence distinguished traditional Irish Catholicism with narrow-minded, anti-intellectual and morally rigorist qualities which permeated into wider society.[72] Church and state dedicated substantial resources to keeping out new ideas. Irish writers and artists emigrated not just of economic necessity but due to an unresponsive and apathetic intellectual environment.

In the space of one generation, the attitudes of a relatively homogeneous Catholic nation, characterised by a broad consensus congregating around conservative social attitudes, have undergone sweltering change. This is evident in the liberalisation in attitudes toward religious and moral issues, notably abortion, divorce and homosexuality. Regular mass attendance collapsed from an astonishingly high 91 per cent in 1974 to 55 per cent in 2005, and even smaller percentages are reported in the working-class areas of Dublin and the other main cities.[73] A liberal emphasis on individual moral responsibility, on equality rather than hierarchy, on participation rather than submission to authority has occurred. In this increasingly secular Ireland, 'a reformation of the Catholic Church or a Protestantisation of Catholic belief and practice' has been taking place where Catholics are increasingly guided by conscience rather than by church teaching.[74] The space previously occupied by the Church in shaping the public agenda has been replaced by the media. A series of scandals erupted in the 1990s and placed the church in a permanent crisis of authority. The horrific revelation of decades of clerical child sexual and physical abuse, as revealed in the Murphy and Ryan Reports, has accentuated a fundamental shift in the relationship between the Irish people and the Catholic Church.

The 2009 Commission to Inquire into Child Abuse, chaired by Justice Seán Ryan, revealed an uncomfortable history of how institutional power was practically defined since the foundation of the state. The absolute authority of the Catholic Church rested on the assumption that it is was above reproach, without question and beyond criticism. This hierarchical power was characterised by absolute obedience, unwavering loyalty and naïve deference, based on a premise of respectability, and buttressed by a 'culture of confidentiality' as described in the Ryan report. The moral depravity of religious authority was a proxy for the corruption of political power which permeated every structure of the state. The Ryan report found that the Department of Education 'had considerable powers, but it lacked the initiative and authority to do anything more than maintain the status quo'. The intense trust and 'deferential and submissive attitude' by the department toward the religious orders endorsed a culture that vilified complainants. The department's attitude to the repeated complaints by victim Tim O'Rourke 'was not about how to investigate his complaint, but about what to do about a troublemaker who had complained'.

In a damning finding, the 2010 Dublin Archdiocese Commission of Investigation into allegations and suspicions of clerical child sexual abuse, chaired by Justice Yvonne Murphy, concluded that the church was preoccupied by 'the maintenance of secrecy, the avoidance of scandal, the protection of the reputation of the Church and the preservation of assets . . . All other considerations, including the welfare of children and justice for victims, were subordinated to these priorities'.

The Ryan and Murphy reports represented a critical juncture in Irish public life because they exposed the outcome of corrupted power. The institutional decline of the Catholic Church and a growing secularism within the Irish population coincided with a judicious discussion on political ethics. The belated process of anti-clericalism, the leftovers of an imperfect revolutionary sentiment expressed at independence, has emasculated the ethical monopoly of puritanical morality. Christian teaching has been emancipated from Irish Catholicism.

Apart from the influence of the Irish version of Catholicism on Irish political culture, researchers have pointed to a positive correlation between hierarchical forms of religion, such as Catholicism and Eastern Orthodox and corruption.[75] Catholicism, organised as a ruling body of clergy structured into orders or ranks where each is strictly subordinated to the one above it, places emphasis on the inability of man to escape sin and the consequent need for the church to be forgiving and protecting. The clergy, as mediators between mankind and God, facilitate confession and therefore the possibility to be absolved of guilt.[76]

The egalitarian organisation typical of Protestantism believes that each individual has the autonomy to have a direct relationship with God. Protestants cannot buy absolution nor rely on the institutional forgiveness of the church but are instead personally responsible for the avoidance of sin. The Protestant, Weberian 'spirit of capitalism', advances the concept of individual responsibility and personal access to divine revelation. The Protestant ethos is less understanding when lapses from grace occur. The institutionalisation of virtue and the compulsion to cast out the wicked is underlined more explicitly. The implication therefore is that Protestants are less inclined to commit a sin because they do not have the same faculty of achieving pardon as Catholics do. Thomas N. Burke profoundly disagreed with the Protestant concept of salvation through personal accountability and instead emphasised the ritual of mediated redemption:

> The Protestant man has no other judge than society. He is afraid of his life as to what his fellow men think of him, and of the judgement they will pass upon him . . . [confession] teaches a man that the opinion of the world is not to be valued, that he need not care what men think of him if he knows that he is right before God.[77]

The distinction between Catholic and Protestant societies is also discernible when it comes to expressions of public trust. Trust or social capital, defined as the propensity of people in a society to cooperate to produce socially efficient outcomes, determines the performance of a society's institutions. The more civic a society, the greater the degree of trust by citizens in their political institutions. Social capital helps prevent the emergence of corruption because norms of reciprocity are well developed which prevent opportunities to engage in corruption. The extension of trust to strangers, rather than that confined to the family, facilitates collective action which is essential for the provision of public goods and consequently enhanced governance.[78] 'Trusting societies have less corruption. People who have faith in others are more likely to endorse strong standards of moral and legal behaviour'.[79]

The separation between church and state tends to be further pronounced in Protestant societies which instead promote an autonomous civil society. Robert Putnam regards Protestant churches as particularly important for American civic society and characterises a healthy civic community by its strong sense of civic engagement, political equality, solidarity and social capital.[80] The motivation to secure scarce economic resources through unorthodox means may not be as manifest because 'the dominant forces in a political system usually have no reason to resort to corruption to make their influence felt, for the state is institutionalised to serve their purposes'.[81] Of course, dominant groups may also avail of informal means of influence to consolidate their position.

Irish media

A final factor that impacts on the extent of corruption is media scrutiny. Without information there is no accountability. The role of the media is critical in promoting good governance. It not only raises public awareness about corruption, its causes, consequences and possible remedies, but also investigates and reports incidences of impropriety.[82] Brunetti and Weder find evidence of a significant negative relationship between press freedom and corruption in a large cross-section of countries.[83] The direction of causation runs from higher press freedom to lower corruption. The assumption therefore is that the effectiveness of the media, in turn, depends on access to information and freedom of expression, as well as a strong tradition of independent journalism.

If a country's media acts as a mirror that reflects the integrity of the government, how competent were the Irish media in exposing scandalous wrongdoing and holding those in positions of power accountable?[84] Figure 8.1 compares the level of debate on corruption in the Houses of the Oireachtas, (the Dáil and Seanad) and the incidence of corruption stories within the *Irish Times*, Ireland's longest surviving broadsheet newspaper which has a reputation as the paper of record. Overall, a similar pattern was replicated within

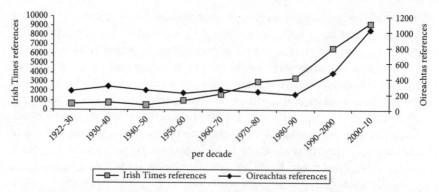

Note: Corrupt,* denotes the different deviations of corruption – corrupt, corrupted, corruption, corrupting, corruptive and so forth – and is a cursory and crude attempt at representing the quantity of national political debate. Moreover, Oireachtas debate may only contain a passing reference to corruption while others are decidedly more intense. Corrupt may be used in an entirely different context to that of political corruption. A parliamentary or newspaper archival search which limits itself to corruption does not capture other euphemisms and colloquialisms which may have wider public currency. Analysis of newspaper literature in America, Germany, England, France, Japan and Spain found that the generic word "corruption" was used half as much again as bribery and its associated terminology in all the western language dailies.

8.1 Reference to corrupt* in Oireachtas records, 1922–2010 and *Irish Times* newspaper articles, 1922–2010

both the Oireachtas and *Irish Times* records - decades of relative inertia punctuated by a spike in scandal. The deviation, however, notably occurred earlier in relation to the *Irish Times* and was much more pronounced.

Of course, public discourse is not confined to the parliament or newspapers but takes place in other forums such as radio, television, books, political meetings, on bar stools and in taxis-cabs. Nevertheless, it is not possible to measure the topicality of a subject matter in a conversation over a period of time. An indicator of the newsworthiness of a subject, and consequently its pervasiveness within the 'national conversation' of a country, can be approximated by examining the occurrence of corruption stories within a newspaper. The premise of examining the *Irish Times* archives is that an analogous analysis of other newspaper collections would echo a pattern of comparability with the data. Comparing debate within the Oireachtas and the degree of coverage a newspaper affords to a certain topic is not evaluating like with like. Parliamentary debate is restricted to the parliamentary calendar which enjoys long holidays and thus leaves less opportunity for regular discussion unlike newspapers which are published daily. However, unlike newspapers, the Oireachtas is protected from libellous proceedings by parliamentary privilege which allows public representatives to speak more freely in the knowledge that they will not incur the wrath of legal action. When corruption is cited in the Oireachtas, it is primarily in relation to Ireland which is distinct from newspapers which report more extensively on world affairs. For instance, from 2000–10, over a third of the *Irish Times* newspaper stories referred to international citations on corruption.[85]

Despite these qualifications, figure 8.1 provides a rudimentary overview of the volume of public discourse on corruption. These figures demonstrate a remarkable consistency in the incidence of corruption references within the Oireachtas and the *Irish Times*, despite the coarseness of the data. In the absence of other measurements, figure 8.1 offers the possibility to sketch the development of public dialogue on this issue. It also clearly demonstrates that the newspaper began to direct its attention on corruption significantly earlier than the Oireachtas.

Within Oireachtas debate, corruption was cited an average of 242 times per decade between the 1920s and the 1980s. There is one anomaly in this timeframe. Oireachtas discussion on corruption recorded the lowest references from 1980 to 1990, with just 199 citations. This is especially curious given that the findings of the Hamilton, McCracken, Flood / Mahon and Moriarty Tribunals exposed grave instances of political favouritism, conflict of interest and corruption within Irish public life.

In the decade of Haughey's ascent to power, the Oireachtas record suggests that public debate on corruption was least. Yet, during the 1980s it was a Fine Gael Taoiseach, Garret 'the Good' FitzGerald who dominated political life.[86] On the occasion of Haughey's nomination as Taoiseach in 1979, FitzGerald controversially remarked about his opponent's 'flawed pedigree'. FitzGerald went on to say that Haughey's 'motives can be judged ultimately only by God but we cannot ignore the fact that he differs from his predecessors in that these motives have been and are widely impugned . . .'.[87] However, in his six years as Taoiseach, FitzGerald failed to introduce any legislative measure which sought to address the lapses that he supposed Haughey was guilty of.

FitzGerald's speech was controversial at the time not because of *what* he was alleging but the very fact that he *was* making an allegation about the personal character of an individual politician. Brian Lenihan, Fianna Fáil Tánaiste and Presidential candidate, subsequently wrote that FitzGerald had 'plumbed to a new depth in Irish political rhetoric'.[88] FitzGerald failed to substantiate his charge and skirted around the issue by vaguely stating he could not be more specific 'for reasons that all in this House understand'. His comments had the reverse effect of evoking sympathy for Haughey because public opinion adjudicated that they were inappropriate for the occasion, particularly given that Haughey's seventy-nine-year-old mother was in the Dáil gallery to see her son formally elected Taoiseach. In retrospect, FitzGerald expressed regret at his remarks: 'When I made my speech, that was extremely unpopular including my own party, people would say, "what did you do that for, you can't say things like that about people." A very negative reaction and I am afraid that it discouraged myself and other people in pursuing matters subsequently'.[89] Honesty as a political trait was not regarded as a positive attribute by the body public. Enemies of Jack Lynch in Fianna Fáil began using the nickname of 'Honest Jack' as a derisory term. FitzGerald remarked that ' . . . people would sort of damage us by saying that we were good, does argue for a very curious mentality in the electorate, if people think that's a way of damaging you there is something wrong with society'.[90]

Discussion on corruption within the Oireachtas increased from 1990. This can be attributed to a rising number of scandals which surfaced in the early 1990s as outlined in chapter 5. A heightened awareness of the implications of political indiscretions, a higher reputational cost and a correspondent implementation of ethical legislation also occurred at this time. Indeed, 2000–10 witnessed more than a threefold increase on the entire period of 1922–90, with some 1,032 debates. This significant spike suggests an abrupt topicality and politicisation of the subject.

The first years of the Free State 1922–30 recorded 651 corruption stories. Impropriety was referenced least in the *Irish Times* from 1940 to 1950, with just 523 stories, despite an intense phase of tribunals, court cases and the emergence of a political party which campaigned on anti-corruption as part of its policy platform. This perhaps imitates the newspaper's reluctance to be perceived as anti-government in time of war with a deliberate wide berth of controversial political issues complemented by vigorous anti-censorship legislation. A focus on political ethics by the newspaper became more evident from the 1960s when citations rose exponentially. A change in editor in 1963 encouraged a sharper journalistic edge which was rewarded by a dramatic increase in circulation. In an analogous pattern to references within the Oireachtas records, newspaper stories in the 1980s were relatively static.

Although this new editor, Douglas Gageby, was regarded as having a soft spot for Haughey, stories on corruption featured strongly in the newspaper by-lines of the 1970s. Fintan O'Toole, assistant editor of the *Irish Times* (2006-) described the *Irish Times* under Gageby and his successor Conor Brady (1986–2002), as 'for most of that period the paper was, in broad terms, editorially supportive of Fianna Fáil'.[91] Environment editor, Frank McDonald, asserts that Gageby 'basically didn't want stuff that was "damaging" to Haughey to appear in the paper – other than the usual political stuff' and 'buried' a heavily researched piece McDonald wrote on Haughey's wealth in December 1979.[92]

Developments in Northern Ireland meant the introduction of regressive measures which restricted media freedom. The 1976 Broadcasting Act, introduced by the Labour Minister for Posts and Telegraphs, Conor Cruise O'Brien, prevented the publication of news items which 'might reasonably be regarded as likely to promote, or incite to crime or as tending to under-mine the authority of the state'. This legislation, combined with existing libel statutes, advanced justifications for censorship. Irish libel law posed a barrier to investigative journalism and deterred the reporting of allegations in main-stream media. Throughout the 1970s blank pages in the body of the *Hibernia* magazine contained the simple statement:

> Our printer, the *Irish Times* Limited, has advised the editor of *Hibernia* that it is not prepared to print the material that was proposed by *Hibernia* to appear on these pages, as its legal advisers are of the opinion that such material is defama-tory or is capable of being construed as defamatory of certain persons named.[93]

Figure 8.1 depicts a divergence after 1990 by both the Oireachtas and *Irish Times* in their treatment of corruption which suggests a telling shift in public attitudes. A number of journalists pre-empted the matters under Tribunal inquiry into beef irregularities, Haughey's finances, planning corruption and Burke's donations by some twenty or thirty years. They were proven right in their observations, but a culture of secrecy, deliberate obstruction, abuse of official discretion and conceited authority dismissed their concerns. Questions of accountability and transparency were disregarded as the typical Irish begrudgery of political opponents. For instance, information alleging systematic irregularities in the beef industry first received media attention in the 1970s, some twenty years before the Beef Tribunal. Julian de Kassel had a front page *Irish Press* story in 1975 with the headline 'EEC to investigate Irish beef stocks: £10m irregularities?' The agriculture correspondent for the *Irish Independent,* Aengus Fanning, wrote articles that same year out-lining concerns by the Department of Agriculture about abuses within the beef intervention scheme.[94] Joe Meade, the C&AG, highlighted instances of beef export irregularities in his 1987 annual report. People did know, or at least suspected that wrongdoing was occurring, but chose to ignore their suspicion.

Sunday Independent journalist, Joe McAnthony, published a 1973 article alleging financial unorthodoxy within the National Sweepstakes scheme, an Irish hospitals lottery granted a government licence in the 1930s. McAnthony contended that 'Irish hospitals are receiving less than 10 per cent of the value of tickets marketed' while large sums of money were diverted to the McGrath family which operated the lottery. It subsequently transpired many years later that McAnthony's story was entirely accurate.[95] The McGrath's had impeccable political connections. The Director of the Irish Hospitals Trust was Joseph McGrath, a close associate of the revered Irish Nationalist Michael Collins. McGrath served as Minister for Labour and as Minister for Industry and Commerce from 1922 to 1924. His brother Patrick, manag-ing director of the Trust, was appointed to the Seanad by Taoiseach Liam

Cosgrave in 1973. Incensed, the McGrath's withdrew their lucrative advertising from the newspaper for two months.[96] This incident ultimately destabilised a potential takeover by the McGrath family of the Murphy and Chance controlled Independent newspapers. Opportunistically, businessman Tony O'Reilly purchased 20 per cent of controlling shares that year and incrementally increased his holdings until 1980 when he was appointed chair of the Independent Group.

McAnthony wrote extensively in 1974 on a conflict of interest exercised by Ray Burke TD, Fianna Fáil, who voted on planning decisions within local government while at the same time contracted as an auctioneer or consultant for those seeking the rezoning. McAnthony recalled that after his coverage of the Ray Burke story in 1974, 'My life was pretty much over as a journalist . . . everything I worked on in RTÉ was closed down . . . I couldn't work in the *Independent* anymore, nobody else would hire me . . . I had four children so we had to go . . . here I was essentially expelled from Ireland'.[97]

Some twenty years later, in March 1996, Frank Connelly published an article in the *Sunday Business Post* which alleged that a 'senior Fianna Fáil politician' had received IR£30,000 in corrupt payments in relation to the planning process. Matt Cooper, *Sunday Tribune*, named Ray Burke as the recipient of this alleged political contribution from Michael Bailey in July 1997. Almost seventeen months after the first media reports, the Minister for Foreign Affairs claimed in the Dáil that he had been the 'victim of a campaign of calumny and abuse' and threatened legal action if any of these allegations were repeated.[98] The Taoiseach, Bertie Ahern, described the media attention afforded to Burke as the 'persistent hounding of an honourable man'.[99] Charlie McCreevy, Minister for Finance, and Jim McDaid, Minister for Tourism, Sport and Recreation, suggested that a media conspiracy or 'politarazzi' was responsible for Burke's subsequent resignation.[100] The Flood / Mahon Tribunal concluded that Burke's Dáil statement 'was a deliberate attempt . . . to forestall any further investigation into his affairs'.[101] The Tribunal also found that the basis for many of the media allegations of corrupt payments were in fact accurate. These four instances of investigative journalism exposed the depths of just how lack lustre the response by those in political, police and revenue authority was to act on well-founded assertions of ethical misdemeanours.

In 1983, the journalist Des Crowley was issued with libel proceedings following an article into Haughey's Allied Irish Bank (AIB) debt. Joe Joyce and Peter Murtagh's book, *The Boss: Charles J. Haughey in Government*, published transcripts of recorded conversations between ministers discussing rumours of Haughey's financial difficulties and the Baldoyle rezoning in 1983. That too was overlooked. So too was Frank McDonald's 1985 book, *The Destruction of Dublin*, which accurately described Traynor as Haughey's 'bagman' but was later changed to 'close personal friend and financial adviser'. The book was effectively suppressed when the country's leading book distributor refused to handle it for fear of a libel action.[102]

Dedicated journalism on the corrupt relationship between developers and local councillors was published in a series of articles in September and October 1982 by Frank Kilfeather and Frank McDonald and again in February and July 1993 by McDonald and Mark Brennock, but were largely ignored. A front page story by *Irish Independent* reporters Brian Dowling and Tom Brady in 1989 revealed that an unnamed Dáil deputy had demanded £100,000 from a developer to ensure that planning permission was granted for a major suburban commercial complex in Dublin.[103] In a separate article, the newspaper also stated that North Dublin builder Peter Loughran, of Carmen builders, made a full statement to Gardaí alleging corruption in the planning process and had named Dublin Assistant City and County Manager George Redmond.

Ireland's prescriptive libel laws, combined with inadequate resources for investigative journalism are often cited as reasons for why the media did not expose more cases of political indiscretion. Journalists have been required to prove the truth of their allegations, while apologies can be used as an admission of liability in a defamation case. More often, the very threat of a libel action by the subjects of investigation and media scrutiny has deterred the reporting of allegations. The couched message was that those who engaged in investigative journalism did so at the likely risk of public censure with implicit consequences for employment prospects. The Irish Constitution also poses additional barriers. Article 40.3.2 provides for the statutory and unqualified protection of an individual's 'good name'. Punitive damages can be considerable, for example, the Supreme Court awarded €750,000 in 2007 against the *Irish Daily Mirror* to Irish businessman Denis O'Brien over false claims made by the paper in 1998.[104] In 2007, the High Court ruled that two journalists from the *Irish Times* had to answer questions on the source of leaked Flood / Mahon Tribunal evidence on payments to the former Taoiseach, Bertie Ahern. However, a 2009 Supreme Court ruling established the legal recognition of the right of journalists to protect their sources. Nonetheless, this came at a cost with the newspaper ordered to pay legal costs, estimated at more than €600,000, because of the 'exceptional circumstances' in the case – namely the journalists' destruction of documents related to the source – which justified departure from the normal rule that costs go to the winning side in litigation.

Apart from libel and constitutional difficulties, was the type of journalist inquiry in Ireland responsible for failing to mobilise public opinion to address the fundamental causes of corruption that persistently repeated themselves from the 1960s through to the 1990s? As Mary Holland observed in her *Irish Times* column:

Irish journalists had been accustomed to treating politicians with discretion, rather priding themselves on not reporting on either the financial affairs or the private lives of individual TDs or ministers . . . I've certainly been guilty of softening reports, or not writing at all about politicians of whom I could have been extremely critical, either because I knew they had a domestic problem or dreaded the phone calls from angry friends attacking me for 'picking' on this or that individual.[105]

Haughey, in particular, embraced the explosion of media influence in Irish politics. He enthusiastically facilitated the new young breed of photographers and journalists, thus steadily cultivating his cult of personality which in turn possibly distracted from underlying reservations regarding his personal wealth. The well known social columnist, Mary Kenny, would write of her lunch with Haughey in 1972: 'The nice thing about Charlie is that he doesn't show off; I mean, he shows off by driving posh cars and buying yearlings at the bloodstock sales, but that's a very acceptable and civilised indulgence; he doesn't show off pompously . . . meantime, he just quietly orders the Krug '62. And there's a lot to be said for a man who quietly orders Krug '62'.[106]

The media tend to focus on sensational and personal accounts because it is easier to sell the game of politics than it is to convey the content of public issues. The substance is not as attractive to sell as is the sensational, the negative, and the scandalous.[107] Larry J. Sabato attributes this to the 'feeding frenzy' where the media 'prefers to employ titillation rather than scrutiny; as a result, its political coverage produces trivialization rather than enlightenment'.[108] Press emphasis is shifted to those who made the allegations and not the allegations themselves. Media coverage of the Locke Tribunal, as outlined in chapter 3 for example, was awash with attention on Oliver J. Flanagan. So too was the Beef Tribunal, which was saturated with narratives about the personal history between Albert Reynolds and Des O'Malley. This personality scenario was repeated when ethical controversy later engulfed Charlie Haughey and Bertie Ahern.

Despite the threat of libel and the cost of investigative journalism, newspapers did in actual fact report on corruption in a sustained way. State authorities failed to act on allegations because the party system and political culture failed to demand it. Widespread complicity by all sections of Irish society facilitated a quiet tolerance of not asking questions. Public opinion did not check disreputable behaviour. As the nineteenth-century Irish Nationalist, J. G. Swift McNeill, sagely advised a Trinity College Dublin student society: 'In some instances public opinion rapidly ripens, in others a great length of time elapses between the discovery of the need of reform by precocious genius, and its adoption by the public vote'.[109] The incessant media focus on corruption, and on the work of the tribunals since the 1990s, may have actually rendered corruption as commonplace and almost a source of boredom, causing even some of the most interested citizens to tune out at the mere mention of the work of the Tribunals. 'Irish voters are often numbed by what they hear and choose not to let this information affect their voter preferences'.[110]

Conclusion

The durability of Irish corruption has been due to the combined influence of several variables: the absence of alternating government made negligible by a homogenic political culture, which reinforced the possibility and expectation of reciprocal control; the escalating costs of politics and the weakness of regulations governing the public financing of parties and the absence of legal or social sanctions against corrupt politicians and business actors. Moreover, the de-facto arbitrariness of many decision-making processes, where excessive formal regulation coexisted with the provenance of political discretion; the extent of state intervention and the over-regulation of economic and social activities intertwined with a lack of competition in the markets. The structure of social values and political culture orientated both to strong religious and nationalistic attachments and the lack of a 'sense of the state'.

Social sanctions and stigma against entrepreneurs and other private agents involved in corruption have been non-existent. The crisis of political funding exacerbated these difficulties. An anti-corruption legislative framework was largely absent in Ireland until the mid 1990s, some seventy years after the foundation of the state. Inadequate avenues of transparency and oversight further contributed to a perception of unaccountable conduct.[111] The inadequate funding of politicians and political parties led to demands for alternative sources of funding. The increased costs of campaign expenditure, the bureaucratisation of party organisations and a change in the nature of political competition coalesced with a decline of traditional means of party finance such as membership dues, voluntary donations and local fund-raising events.

One of the most striking features of Irish corruption, as revealed by Tribunal inquiries in the 1990s, is that illegal activities were often closely interrelated because of elaborate networks of corrupt exchange. In other words, corruption operated within a *system* rather than the mere aggregation of isolated illegal acts. It had become a market, which, as in the case of every functioning market, has developed internal rules governed by the laws of supply and demand.[112]

There was a limited appreciation of the corrosive effects of clientelism and patronage. Political will failed to tackle corruption and a self-interested definition of national interest and impunity from consequences for impropriety characterised Irish political culture. The role of clientelism and patronage was understood from within a narrow interpretation of the terms involved, as discussed in chapter 1. The focus upon personalised descriptions of corruption incidents and their subsequent politicisation at the expense of a broader and deeper analysis of why such corruption occurred subdued demands for anti-corruption reform.

Ultimately, the exercise of corruption is intrinsically undemocratic because it seeks to bestow unfair and unjust advantage to the few which is contrary to the belief in liberty, equality and fraternity.[113] It undermines and delegitimises the principle of democratic action. The relationship between power and citizenship is dependent on a voluntary contract of trust. In the September 2009 Eurobarometer poll, Ireland had virtually the lowest level of public trust in government across the twenty-seven European countries surveyed, with only Hungary, Latvia, Lithuania and Greece returning lower degrees of trust.[114] This is not normal for Ireland. In June 2008, confidence in the government was at 46 per cent. This dramatically dropped by 36 percentage points to 10 per cent only a year later.[115]

Evidence suggests that trust is greater when there is a general belief that 'we're all in it together', and that no group is being disproportionately advantaged or disadvantaged by discretionary state actions or selective receipt of state benefits.[116] High trust in public services also increases compliance rates in revenue payment and reduces the incidence of welfare fraud, reducing the cost of monitoring.[117] In the absence of trust, political action characterised by short-termism seeks to garner the support of the electorate. The courage to adhere to high standards of probity is eroded when the definition of public interest is distorted by those that seek to promote the interests of vested individuals. This perception of corruption within political leadership ultimately reduces loyalty towards a sense of state by its citizens.

Irish authoritarianism was curiously juxtaposed with a flexible attitude toward laws and rules. Partly as a result of hostility to British rule, a popular ambivalence towards authority developed in Ireland. Personalism, where people are valued for who they are and whom they know – not solely for what technical qualifications they possess – was regarded as the 'workable alternative' and 'built in check' to the harsh realities of austere authoritarianism.[118] The political psychology of the Irish citizen was one that blindly trusted authoritarian decision-making and wholeheartedly embraced strong and centralised political leadership. This was deferentially expressed through the subtle distinctions of class, the structures of institutional authority, the organisational character of the Catholic Church and the closed taciturn nature of economic power.

The philosophy of authority was moulded by a fear of offending the powerful where a culture of ingrained learned powerlessness became normalised. This subservient way of thinking became a shroud of impunity for those in positions of power. The self-perpetuating abuse of power became systematic when internalised over a long period of time. This is a learned behaviour, dutifully passed down by successive generations without challenge. The cycle of abuse infects every facet of public and private morality. Thus, this complacent outlook passively condones breaches of trust in all aspects of our lives. The reporting of suspicions of corruption to the authorities was disincentivised through a legacy of negative association with informing. Political culture implicitly punished whistleblowing which contributed to a 'culture of silence' in both public and private sector bodies. Those who sought to speak out were labelled as traitorous informers which created a fear of breaking the conspiracy of silence when obvious wrongs were committed.

Individual indifference embraced the luxury of believing in what Irish people were told by those in power. The responsibility to constructively challenge such orthodoxies was ignored. The corruption of power by those in positions of authority perpetuated a loss of trust in the integrity and capability in Irish public life. Institutions devoid of accountability and naked of responsibility pretended to live in a Republic, deep-rooted conservatism sought to preserve the status quo and an island mentality reinforced by intellectual isolation is determined to maintain a social order which rejects the uncomfortable truths about ourselves.

Since the foundation of the state, Ireland has born witness to an incremental legal revolution which emphasised individual rights instead of moral responsibilities. The chronology of incidents as outlined, and more ominously, Ireland's spectacular economic collapse from 2008 to 2010, has incentivised the demand for a balance between legal and ethical obligations. The contention that 'corruption scandals can then be a sign of a country's growing political maturity. They show that citizens are beginning to recognize the difference between the public and the private spheres and to complain when the border is crossed'[119] may have embryonic merit in the Irish case.

This book has presented a narrative of the context in which the inauguration of political independence in 1922 was realised. The memory of the Act of Union, which sacrificed legislative independence for self-interest, served to motivate politicians from across the political divide to build a political framework on ethical foundations. Ireland's loss of economic sovereignty in 2010, due to a perception of political failure and the unorthodox influence of vested interests, may yet motivate Irish public life to engage in state-building and reimagine Irish society with an emphasis on the moral duties of citizenship.

Notes

1 National Library, Dublin, IR94109 p90, Sinn Féin, The Case of Ireland: 'Sinn Féin Series No. 12'. 1919.

2 S. Heaney, 'Act of Union', *Opened Ground: Poems 1966–1996* (Faber and Faber 1998).

3 Byrne, *Nineteenth and Twentieth Century Political Corruption in Ireland.*
4 Pope, 'Ethics, Accountability and Transparency', p. 41.
5 R. Theobald, *Corruption, Development, and Underdevelopment.*
6 D. della Porta and A. Vannucci, 'Corruption as a normative system', *International Conference on Corruption Control in Political Life and the Quality of Democracy: A Comparative Perspective Europe – Latin America.* (CIES – ISCTE, May 2005).
7 Scott, 'Corruption, machine politics, and political change', pp. 1146–9.
8 G. Sapelli, *Southern Europe since 1945: Tradition and Modernity in Portugal, Spain, Italy, Greece and Turkey* (Longman, 1995).
9 R. A. W. Rhodes, *Understanding Governance: Policy Networks, Governance, Reflexivity and Accountability* (Open University Press, 1997).
10 'How we spent the boom', *Irish Times* (29 October 2010).
11 Stapenhurst *et al.*, *The Role of Parliament in Curbing Corruption*, p. 16.
12 M. Johnston, 'Political corruption: historical conflict and the rise of standards', in L. Diamond and M. F. Plattner (eds), *The Global Resurgence of Democracy* (Johns Hopkins University Press, 1993), p. 198.
13 National Library, London. House of Parliament, 1837a, p. 102.
14 Dearbhail McDonald, *Bust* (Penguin, 2010).
15 J. N. Bhagwati, 'Directly unproductive, profit-seeking activities', *Journal of Political Economy*, 90:5 (October 1982), pp. 988–1002; A. O. Krueger, 'The political economy of the rent seeking society', *American Economic Review*, 64:3 (June 1974), pp. 291–303; S. Rose-Ackerman, *Corruption: A Study in Political Economy* (Academic Press, 1978); Mauro, 'Corruption and growth'.
16 R. S. Chari and H. McMahon, 'Reconsidering the patterns of organised interests in Irish policy making', *Irish Political Studies,* 18:1 (June 2003), pp. 27–50.
17 C. McCarthy, 'Corruption in public office in Ireland: policy design as a countermeasure', *Economic and Social Research Institute, Quarterly Economic Commentary* (2003), p. 13.
18 *Ibid.*, p. 14.
19 W. Kingston, *Interrogating Irish policies* (Dublin University Press, 2007).
20 Tanzi, *Policies, Institutions and the Dark Side of Economics*, p. 133.
21 Central Statistics Office, Dublin, 34 per cent in 1960 to 65 per cent in 1985, www.cso.ie.
22 Kitchin *et al.*, *A Haunted Landscape*, p. 9.
23 RTÉ One, 'The pressure zone', *Prime Time Investigates* (26 November 2007); also see: M. Clifford, 'Zealotry battles corruption as Leitrim planning row turns septic', *Sunday Tribune* (17 November 2002).
24 A total of 29 County Councils, 5 County Borough Corporations, 5 Borough Corporations and 49 Town Councils.
25 'Planning laws and best practice', *Irish Times* (7 November 2008).
26 McGraw, 'Managing change: party competition in the new Ireland', p. 260.
27 Council of Europe, *Criminal Law Convention on Corruption, Explanatory Report, Article 12* (2009), www.conventions.coe.int/Treaty/en/Reports/Html/173.htm.
28 *Ibid.*,
29 GRECO, *Third Evaluation Round*, p. 16.

30 E. Byrne and J. Devitt, *National Integrity Systems, Transparency International Country Study Report on Ireland* (Transparency International Ireland, 2009), p. 16.
31 J. Suiter, 'Chieftains delivering: political determinants of capital spending in Ireland 2001–07' (PhD dissertation, Trinity College Dublin, 2007).
32 *Ibid.*, p. 269.
33 *Ibid.*, p. 270.
34 *Ibid.*, p. 270.
35 C. Pollitt, C. Talbot, J. Caulfield and A. Smullen, *Agencies: How Governments Do Things through Semi-Autonomous Organizations* (Basingstoke, Palgrave Macmillan, 2004).
36 Hardiman and Whelan, *Politics and Democratic Values*; M. MacCarthaigh, *Parliamentary Scrutiny of the Administration* (Geary Institute: University College Dublin, working paper, November 2009).
37 C. McCarthy, *Prime Time* RTÉ 1 television quoted in E. Byrne, 'McCarthy shows up so many divisions among us', *Irish Times* (21 July 2009).
38 OECD Public Management Reviews, *Ireland: Towards an Integrated Public Service* (OECD, 2008), pp. 295–8.
39 J. S. Mill, 'Considerations on representative government', in J. S. Mill, *Utilitarianism, Liberty and Representative Government* (Dent, Everyman's Library, 1964).
40 P. Clancy and G. Murphy. *Outsourcing Government: Public Bodies and Accountability* (Tasc at New Ireland, 2006).
41 Cooper, *Who Really Runs Ireland?* pp. 59–65, detailed information benefits Ahern's friends received. Also see M. Clifford and Shane Coleman, *Bertie Ahern and the Drumcondra Mafia* (Hodder Headline, 2009).
42 RTÉ Six One News, (26 September 2006).
43 Byrne, *Nineteenth and Twentieth Century Political Corruption in Ireland*.
44 Byrne and Devitt, *National Integrity Systems*, p. 16.
45 J. Travers, *Interim Report on Certain Issues of Management and Administration in the Department of Health and Children associated with the Practice of Charges for Persons in Long Stay Health Care in Health Board Institutions and Related Matters* (Dublin Stationery Office, Oireachtas Joint Committee on Health and Children, 2005), para 6.2.
46 E. Byrne, 'New crisis looms in shadowy corridors of Ireland Inc'., *Irish Times* (3 October 2008).
47 E. Byrne, 'Public pays high price for financial mismanagement', *Irish Times* (2 December 2008).
48 *Ibid.*
49 E. Byrne, 'Nama must be accountable to the taxpayer', *Irish Times* (4 August 2009).
50 P. Leahy, *Showtime: The Inside Story of Fianna Fáil in Power* (Penguin, 2009), p. 73.
51 Ben Briscoe, Dáil Éireann, *Private Members' Business: Ethics in Government and Public Office Bill, 1991: Second Stage (Resumed). 408.* (14 May 1991).

52 J. Jones, '*Irish Times* MRBI opinion poll', *Irish Times* (11 December 1991).

53 Eithne FitzGerald, interview, (February 2006).

54 Mr. Justice Brian McCracken, *Report of the Tribunal of Inquiry (Dunnes Payments)* (Dublin Stationery Office, 1997) pp. 68–9.

55 McGraw, 'Managing change: party competition in the new Ireland', p. 211.

56 M. Marsh, 'Voting for government coalitions in Ireland under Single Transferable Vote', *Electoral Studies*, 29:3 (2010).

57 See RTÉ Exit Poll, (25 May 2007), www.rte.ie/news/2007/0525/ RTEExitPoll2007details.ppt.

58 Thanks particularly to McGraw, 'Managing change: party competition in the new Ireland', p. 241.

59 *Ibid.*, p. 214.

60 C. J. Anderson and Y. V. Tverdova, 'Corruption, political allegiances, and attitudes toward government in contemporary democracies', *American Journal of Political Science*, 47:1 (January 2003), pp. 91–109.

61 M. N. Pedersen, 'The dynamics of European party systems: changing patterns of electoral volatility', *European Journal of Political Research*, 7:1 (1979), pp. 1–26; and R. Sinnott, *Irish Voters Decide: Voting Behaviour in Elections and Referendums Since 1918* (Manchester University Press, 1995), p. 109.

62 P. Heywood, 'Political corruption: problems and perspectives', *Political Studies*, 45:3 (1997), pp. 417–35.

63 M. Gallagher, 'Stability and turmoil: analysis and results', in M. Gallagher, M. Marsh and P. Mitchell (eds), *How Ireland Voted 2002* (Palgrave Macmillan, 2003), p. 104; Sinnott, *Irish Voters Decide,* p. 112.

64 J. E. Alt and D. Dreyer Lassen, 'The political economy of institutions and corruption in American States', *Mancur Olson Lecture Series* (University of Maryland, April 2002), p. 13.

65 McGraw, 'Managing change: party competition in the new Ireland', p. 296.

66 Labour party, *One Ireland, Jobs, Reform, Fairness* (Labour party manifesto, 2011), p. 42.

67 H. K. Crawford, *Outside the Glow: Protestants and Irishness in Independent Ireland* (University College Dublin Press, 2010).

68 T. N. Burke, 'Catholicity as revealed in the character of the Irish people delivered in St. Gabriel's Church, New York 4 June 1872' *Lectures and Sermons* (Haverty, 1873), p. 9.

69 E. Larkin, *The Historical Dimensions of Irish Catholicism* (Catholic University of America Press and Four Courts Press, 1984).

70 See R. Putnam, *Making Democracy Work: Civic Traditions in Modern Italy* (Princeton University Press, 1993).

71 *Irish Times* (6 February 1967).

72 V. Twomey, *The End of Irish Catholicism?* (Veritas, 2003).

73 With thanks to McGraw, 'Managing change: party competition in the new Ireland', for compiling this data. Communications Office, Irish Bishop's Conference.

74 T. Inglis, *Moral Monopoly: The Rise and Fall of the Catholic Church in Modern Ireland*, 2nd edn (University College Dublin Press, 1998), p. 204.

75 della Porta and Mény, *Democracy and Corruption in Europe*; D. Treisman, 'The causes of corruption: a cross-national study', *Journal of Public Economics*, 76:3 (2000); M. Paldam, 'Corruption and religion: adding to the economic model' (unpublished manuscript, Aarhus University, Denmark, 1999).

76 *Catechism of the Catholic Church* (Liguori Publications, 1994). Para. 980.

77 Burke, 'Catholicity as revealed in the character of the Irish people' pp. 34–5.

78 J. Coleman, *Foundations of Social Theory* (Harvard University Press, 1990); F. Fukuyama, *Trust: The Social Virtues and The Creation of Prosperity* (Free Press, 1995); S. Knack and P. Keefer, 'Does social capital have an economic payoff? A cross-country investigation', *Quarterly Journal of Economics*, 112:4 (November 1997); Putnam, *Making Democracy Work*.

79 E. M. Uslaner, 'Trust and corruption'.

80 R. Putnam, *Bowling Alone: The Collapse and Revival of American Community* (Simon and Schuster, 2000); Putnam, *Making Democracy Work*, p. 333.

81 Scott, 'Handling Historical Comparison Cross-Nationally', in Heidenheimer *et al.*(eds), *Political Corruption*, p. 139.

82 R. Stapenhurst, *The Media's Role in Curbing Corruption* (World Bank Institute, working paper, 2000).

83 A. Brunetti and B. Weder, 'A free press is bad news for corruption', *Journal of Public Economics*, 87:7–8 (2003).

84 E. Byrne, A. K. Arnold and F. Nagano, *Building Public Support for Anti-Corruption Efforts Why Anti-Corruption Agencies Need to Communicate and How* (UNDOC, 2010).

85 Figure 8.1 includes international references to corruption because the *Irish Times* archives began distinguishing its categories of articles from only 1996. From 2000 to 2010, 2,689 of the 9,253 articles on corruption were categorised as 'world' stories.

86 Served as Taoiseach July 1981 to February 1982; December 1982 to March 1987.

87 Garret FitzGerald, Dáil Éireann, *Nomination of Taoiseach. 317.* (11 December 1979).

88 Lenihan, *For the Record*, p. 221.

89 Garret FitzGerald, interview, (February 2001).

90 *Ibid.*,

91 F. O'Toole, 'A reflection on the times', *Irish Times* (25 October 2008).

92 M. O'Brien, *The Irish Times: A History* (Four Courts Press, 2008), p. 223. Correspondence to author from journalist Frank McDonald.

93 *Hibernia* (24 September 1976).

94 E. Swift, 'The making of a scandal and how the beef barons tried to bury it', *Hibernia* (11 July 1975).

95 RTÉ, *Hidden History: Irish Sweepstakes* (1 December 2003).

96 S. Dodd, 'Irish Sweepstake scandal remains a lesson to us all', *Irish Independent* (7 December 2003).

97 McAnthony, interview.

98 'Mr. Burke Responds', *Irish Times* (8 August 1997); Ray Burke, Dáil Éireann, *Personal Statement. 480.* (10 September 1997).

 99 Bertie Ahern, Dáil Éireann, *Resignation of Member: Statements. 481.* (7 October 1997).
100 'Fearful FF moves to shoot the messenger', *Irish Times* (10 October 1997).
101 Flood, *Second Interim Report*, p. 105.
102 F. O'Toole, 'Threat of legal action used to silence journalists', *Irish Times* (20 October 2003).
103 *Irish Independent* (31 July 1989).
104 *Irish Times* (25 November 2006).
105 M. Holland, 'Attacks on media must not deter them from doing job', *Irish Times* (9 October 1997).
106 M. Kenny, 'Mary Kenny's London dairy', *Hibernia* (6 October 1972).
107 Byrne *et al.*, *Building Public Support for Anti-Corruption Efforts.*
108 Larry J. Sabato, *Feeding Frenzy: How Attack Journalism Has Transformed American Politics* (Lanahan, 1991), p. 6.
109 National Library, Dublin, P 1398, J. G Swift MacNeil, Trinity Law Student's Debating Society: Individuality in its effects on public opinion. An address delivered on the 17th of October, 1875, p. 17.
110 McGraw, 'Managing change: party competition in the new Ireland', p. 209.
111 For example, the Moriarty Tribunal Report refers a total of 28 times to 'payments shrouded in secrecy' and other forms of secrecy. Moriarty, *The Moriarty Tribunal Report: Part 1.*
112 D. della Porta and A. Vannucci, 'The "perverse effects" of political corruption', *Political Studies* 45 (1997); S. Belligni, *Il volt simoniaco del potere* (Giappichelli, 1998).
113 A. Moreno, 'Corruption and democracy: a cultural assessment', *Comparative Sociology* 1 (2002), pp. 495–507.
114 N. Hardiman, *The Impact of the Crisis on the Irish Political System* (University College Dublin, working paper, November 2009).
115 'Irish Times/MRBI poll', *Irish Times* (3 September 2009).
116 S. Kumlin, and Bo Rothstein, 'Making and breaking social capital: the impact of welfare-state institutions', *Comparative Political Studies*, 38:4 (2005), pp. 339–65; Bo Rothstein, 'Creating political legitimacy: electoral democracy versus quality of government', *American Behavioural Scientist*, 53:3 (2009); Bo Rothstein and Jan Teorell, 'What is quality of government? A theory of impartial government institutions', *Governance*, 21:2 (2008), pp. 165–90.
117 M. Levi, 'A state of trust', in Valerie Braithwaite and M. Levi (eds), *Trust and Governance*, (Russell Sage Foundation, 1998), pp. 77–101.
118 D. Schmitt, *The Irony of Irish Democracy: The Impact of Political Culture on Administrative and Democratic Political Development in Ireland* (DC Heath, 1973), pp. 54, 62–4, 159.
119 S. Rose-Ackerman, *Corruption and Government* (Cambridge University Press, 1999), p. 225.

Bibliography

Alt, J. E. and D. Dreyer Lassen, 'The political economy of institutions and corruption in American States', Mancur Olson Lecture Series (University of Maryland, April 2002).

Anderson, C. J. and Y. V. Tverdova, 'Corruption, political allegiances, and attitudes toward government in contemporary democracies', *American Journal of Political Science*, 47:1 (January 2003).

Andvig, J. C. Odd-Helge Fjeldstad, I. Amundsen, K. Tone Sissener and Tina Soreide, *Corruption A Review of Contemporary Research* (Christian Michelsen Institute, NUPI Report NO 268 NOK 175, 2002).

Arndt, C. and C. Oman, *Uses and Abuses of Governance Indicators* (OECD Development Centre Studies, 2006).

Bacon, P., *Over-Capacity in the Irish Hotel Industry and Required Elements of a Recovery Programme* (Irish Hotel Industry, November 2009).

Bardon, J. and D. Keogh, 'Ireland, 1921–84', in J. R. Hill (ed.), *A New History of Ireland VII: Ireland 1921–1984* (Oxford University Press, 2003).

Barry, F., 'Institutional capacity and the Celtic Tiger', *8th International Network for Economic Research annual conference* (University College Cork, September 2006).

Barry, F., 'Public policymaking and the marketplace for ideas', *Transforming Public Services* (Trinity College Dublin, 15 September 2009).

Barry, F., *Politics and Economic Policymaking in Ireland* (Trinity College Dublin, working paper, October 2009).

Bax, Mart, *Harpstrings and Confessions: Machine-Style Politics in the Irish Republic* (Van Gorcum, 1976).

Bayley, D. H., 'The effects of corruption in a developing nation', *Western Political Quarterly*, 19:4 (1966).

Belligni, S., *Il volto simoniaco del potere* (Giappichelli, 1998).

Benoit, K. and M. Marsh, 'For a few Euros more: campaign spending effects in the Irish local elections of 1999', *Party Politics*, 9:5 (2003).

Benoit K. and M. Marsh, 'The campaign value of incumbency: A new solution to the puzzle of less effective incumbent spending', *American Journal of Political Science*, 52:4 (2008).

Benoit K. and M. Marsh, 'Incumbent and challenger campaign spending effects in proportional electoral systems: the Irish elections of 2002', *Political Research Quarterly*, 63:1 (2010).

Berg-Schlosser, D. and J. Mitchell (eds), *Conditions of Democracy in Europe 1919–1939* (Macmillan/St Martin's, 2000).

Bew, P., *Ireland: The Politics of Enmity, 1789–2006* (Oxford University Press, 2007).

Bhagwati, J. N., 'Directly unproductive, profit-seeking activities', *Journal of Political Economy*, 90:5 (October 1982).

Bielenberg, A., *Locke's Distillery: A History* (Lilliput, 1993).

Boland, K., *The Rise and Decline of Fianna Fáil* (Mercier Press, 1982).

Bolton, G. C., *The Passing of the Irish Act of Union: A Study in Parliamentary Politics* (Oxford University Press, 1966).

Brady, R., *Reflections on Tribunals of Inquiry* 3 (Bar Review, 1997).

Brunetti, A. and B. Weder, 'A free press is bad news for corruption', *Journal of Public Economics*, 87:7–8 (2003).

Burgmann, M., 'Constructing legislative codes of conduct lecture in the Department of the Senate', *Occasional Lecture Series at Parliament House Australia* (23 July 1999).

Burke, T. N., 'Catholicity as revealed in the character of the Irish people delivered in St Gabriel's Church, New York, 4 June 1872', *Lectures and Sermons* (Haverty, 1873).

Byrne, E., 'Ethics in Public Office Act 1995: public, political & legislative responses' (degree dissertation, University of Limerick, 2001).

Byrne, E., 'Ireland: Global Corruption Report', in J. Kotalik and D. Rodriquez (eds), *Transparency International Global Corruption Report 2006* (Pluto Press, 2007).

Byrne, E., 'Nineteenth and Twentieth Century Political Corruption in Ireland' (PhD dissertation, University of Limerick, 2007).

Byrne E. and J. Devitt, *National Integrity Systems, Transparency International Country Study Report on Ireland* (Transparency International Ireland, 2009).

Byrne, E., A. K. Arnold and F. Nagano, *Building Public Support for Anti-Corruption Efforts Why Anti-Corruption Agencies Need to Communicate and How* (World Bank, UNDOCK, 2010).

Catechism of the Catholic Church (Liguori Publications, 1994).

Chari R. S. and H. McMahon, 'Reconsidering the patterns of organised interests in Irish policy making', *Irish Political Studies*, 18:1 (June 2003).

Chestvale Properties Limited (and) Huddle Investments Limited, *Investigation under Section 14(1), Companies Act, 1990: Final Report* (Dublin Stationery Office, 1993).

Chubb, B., 'Going about persecuting civil servants: the role of the Irish parliamentary representative', *Political Studies*, 11:3 (1963).

Clancy, P. and G. Murphy, *Outsourcing Government: Public Bodies and Accountability* (Task at New Ireland, 2006).

Clifford, M. and Shane Coleman, *Bertie Ahern and the Drumcondra Mafia* (Hodder Headline, 2009).

Cohen, A. K., 'The study of social disorganization and deviant behaviour', in R. K. Merton, L. B. Broom and L. S. Cottrell, Jr. (eds), *Sociology Today* (Basic Books, 1959).

Coleman, J., *Foundations of Social Theory* (Harvard University Press, 1990).

Collins, N. and C. O'Raghallaigh, 'Political sleaze in the Republic of Ireland', *Parliamentary Affairs*, 48:4 (1994).

Collins, N. and M. O'Shea, *Understanding Corruption in Irish Politics* (Cork University Press, 2000).

Collins, S., *Breaking the Mould: How the PDs Changed Irish Politics* (Gill and Macmillan, 2005).

Committee of Public Accounts, Sub-Committee on Certain Revenue Matters, *Examination of the Report of the Comptroller and Auditor General of Investigation into the Administration of Deposit Interest Retention Tax and Related Matters during 1 January 1986 and 1 December 1998* (Dublin Stationery Office, 1999).

Comptroller and Auditor General, *Special Report Tribunals of Inquiry* (Dublin Government of Ireland, December 2008).

Coogan, T. P., *De Valera: Long Fellow, Long Shadow* (Hutchinson, 1993).

Cooper, M., *Who Really Runs Ireland? The Story of the Elite Who Led Ireland from Bust to Boom . . . and Back Again* (Penguin Ireland, 2009).

Crawford, H. K., *Outside the Glow: Protestants and Irishness in Independent Ireland* (University College Dublin Press, 2010).

Creighton, L., *The Life and Letters of Mandell Creighton* (Longmans, 1904).

Cullen, P., *With a Little Help from My Friends: Planning Corruption in Ireland* (Gill and Macmillan, 2002).

Curran, M. R., *Siúicre Éireann c.p.t., Sugar Distributors (Holdings).Limited, Sugar Distributors Limited* (Dublin Stationery Office, 1991).

de Vere White, T., *Kevin O'Higgins* (Methuen, 1948).

della Porta D. and Y. Mény (eds), *Democracy and Corruption in Europe: Social Change in Western Europe* (Pinter, 1997).

della Porta, D. and A. Vannucci, 'The "perverse effects" of political corruption', *Political Studies*, 45 (1997).

della Porta, D. and A. Vannucci, 'Corruption as a normative system', *International Conference on Corruption Control in Political Life and the Quality of Democracy: A Comparative Perspective Europe – Latin America* (CIES – ISCTE, May 2005).

Devlin Report, *Report of Public Services Organisation Review Group 1966–1969* (Dublin Stationery Office, 1969).

Dixit, A., 'On the modes of economic governance', *Econometrica, Econometric Society*, 1: 2 (2001).

Dobel, P. J., 'The Corruption of a State', *American Political Science Review*, 72:3 (September 1978).

Dorgan, S., 'How Ireland Became the Celtic Tiger', *The Heritage Foundation* (23 June 2006), www.heritage.org/research/worldwidefreedom/bg1945.cfm.

Downey, J., *All Things New: The 1989 General Election and Its Consequences* (Aisling, 1989).

Downey, J., *Lenihan: His Life and Loyalties* (New Island Books, 1998).

Duignan, S., *One Spin on the Merry-Go-Round* (Blackwater Press, 1996).

Dunlop, F., *Yes, Taoiseach* (Penguin, 2004).

Dunphy, R., *The Making of Fianna Fáil Power in Ireland* (Clarendon Press, 1995).

Durkheim, E., *De la division du travail social: étude sur l'organisation des societies supérieures,* trans. G. Simpson (Macmillan, 1933).

Eisenhardt, K. M., 'Building theories from case study research', *Academy of Management Review,* 14:4 (1989).

Eisenstadt, S. N. and L. Roniger, *Patrons, Clients and Friends: Interpersonal Relations and the Structure of Trust in Society* (Cambridge University Press, 1984).

Fanning, R., *The Irish Department of Finance 1922-58* (Institute of Public Administration, 1978).

Fanning, R., *Independent Ireland* (Educational Company of Ireland, 1998).

Farrell, B., *Seán Lemass* (Gill and Macmillan, 1991).

Ferriter, D., *The Transformation of Ireland 1900-2000* (Profile Books, 2005).

Finlay, F., *Snakes and Ladders* (New Island Books, 1998).

FitzGerald, Desmond, *Memoirs of Desmond FitzGerald, 1913-1916* (Liberties Press, 2006).

Flood, Mr. Justice Feargus M., *Tribunal of Inquiry into Certain Planning Matters and Payments: Second Interim Report* (Dublin Stationery Office, 2002).

Foley C.P. and A.G. Barry, *Investigation into the affairs of Siúicre Éireann C.p.t. and Related Companies: Final Report* (Dublin Stationery Office, 1992).

Friedrich, C.J., 'Political pathology', *Political Quarterly,* 37 (January-March 1966).

Fukuyama, F., *Trust: The Social Virtues and The Creation of Prosperity* (Free Press, 1995).

Gallagher, M., 'Stability and turmoil: analysis and results', in M. Gallagher, M. Marsh and P. Mitchell (eds), *How Ireland Voted 2002* (Palgrave Macmillan, 2003).

Gallagher, M. and R. Sinnott (eds), *How Ireland Voted 1989* (PSAI Press and Centre for the Study of Irish Elections, 1990).

Gallagher, M. and Lee Komito, 'The constituency role of Dáil deputies', in J. Coakley and M. Gallagher (eds), *Politics in the Republic of Ireland,* 5th ed (Routledge, 2009).

Gambetta, D., *The Sicilian Mafia: The Business of Private Protection* (Harvard University Press, 1993).

Gardiner, J. A., 'Defining corruption', *Corruption and Reform,* 7. (1993).

Garvin, T., *Nationalist Revolutionaries in Ireland 1858-1928* (Oxford University Press, 1987).

Girvin, B., 'The republicanisation of Irish society: 1932-1948', in J. R. Hill (ed.), *A New History of Ireland VII: Ireland 1921-1984* (Oxford University Press, 2003).

Glackin, John A., *Chest vale Properties Limited (and) Huddle Investment Limited, Investigation under Section 14(1) Companies Act, 1990* (Dublin Stationery Office, 1993).

GRECO, *Third Evaluation Round Evaluation Report on Ireland Transparency of Party Funding (Theme II)* (Strasbourg: Council of Europe, September 2009), www.coe.int.

Hamilton, Mr. Justice Liam, *Report of the Tribunal of Inquiry into the Beef Processing Industry* (Dublin Stationery Office, 1994).

Hardiman, N., *The Impact of the Crisis on the Irish Political System* (Geary Institute: University College Dublin, working paper, November 2009).

Hardiman, N. and C. T. Whelan (eds), *Politics and Democratic Values* (Gill and Macmillan, 1994).

Harkness, D., 'Patrick McGilligan: man of commonwealth', *Journal of Imperial and Commonwealth History*, 5 (1979).

Harling, H., 'Rethinking "old corruption"', *Past and Present*, 141:1 (May 1995).

Hartley, L. P., *The Go-Between* (Hamish Hamilton, 1953).

Heaney, S., 'Act of Union', *Opened Ground: Pomes 1966–1996* (Faber and Faber, 1998).

Heidenheimer, A. J., M. Johnston and V. LeVine (eds), *Political Corruption: A Handbook* (Transaction 1989).

Hellman, J. S. and D. Kaufmann, *Confronting the Challenge of State Capture in Transition Economies* (International Monetary Fund, 2001).

Hellman, J. S. and D. Kaufmann, 'The inequality of influence', in J. Kornai and S. Rose-Ackerman (eds), *Building a Trustworthy State in Post-Socialist Transition* (Palgrave Macmillan, 2004).

Hellman, J. S., G. Jones and D. Kaufmann, *"Seize the State, Seize the Day" State Capture, Corruption, and Influence in Transition* (World Bank, 2000).

Henchy, Mr. Justice Seamus, *Report of the Tribunal Appointed by the Taoiseach on 4 July 1975 (Allegations against Minister for Local Government)*. (Purl 4745, July 1975).

Heywood, P., 'Political corruption: problems and perspectives', *Political Studies*, 45:3 (1997).

Hill, P. B. E., *The Japanese Mafia Yakuza, Law, and the State* (Oxford University Press, 2003).

Honohan, P., *The Irish Banking Crisis Regulatory and Financial Stability Policy 2003–2008: A Report to the Minister for Finance by the Governor of the Central Bank* (Government Publications Office, 2010).

Hope K. R. and B. C. Chikulo (eds), *Corruption and Development in Africa: Lessons from Country Case Studies* (Palgrave, 1999).

Hopkinson, M., 'Civil War and aftermath, 1922–4', in J. R. Hill (ed.), *A New History of Ireland VII: Ireland 1921–1984* (Oxford University Press, 2003).

Horgan, J., *Seán Lemass: The Enigmatic Patriot* (Gill and Macmillan, 1997).

Horgan, J., *Irish Media: A Critical History since 1922* (Routledge, 2001).

Horgan, J., *Broadcasting and Public Life: RTÉ News and Current Affairs, 1926–1997* (Four Courts Press, 2004).

Huntington, S. P., *Political Order in Changing Societies* (Yale University Press, 1968).

Hutchcroft, P. D., 'The politics of privilege: rents and corruption in Asia', in A. J. Heidenheimer and M. Johnston (eds), *Political Corruption: A Handbook* (Transaction: 2002).

Indridason, I. H., 'Coalitions and clientelism: explaining cross-national variation in patterns of coalition formation' (Department of Political Science, University of Iceland, 26 July 2006), www.notendur.hi.is/ihi/CoalitionsClientelism.pdf.

Ingles, T., *Moral Monopoly: The Rise and Fall of the Catholic Church in Modern Ireland*, 2nd edn (University College Dublin Press, 1998).

Jennings, R., *Land Transactions and Prices in the Dublin Area 1974–1978* (An Foras Forbartha, 1980).

Johnston, M., 'Political Corruption: Historical Conflict and the Rise of Standards', in

L. Diamond and M. F. Platter (eds), *The Global Resurgence of Democracy* (Johns Hopkins University Press, 1993).

Johnson, M., 'The search for definition: the vitality of politics and the issue of corruption', *International Social Science Journal*, 48: 149 (1996).

Jones, J. and A. O'Donoghue, *In Your Opinion: Political and Social Trends in Ireland through the Eyes of the Electorate* (Town House, 2001).

Karvonen, L., *Fragmentation and Consensus: Political Organisation and the Interwar Crisis in Europe* (Boulder, 1993).

Kaufmann, D., 'Economic corruption: some facts', *Eighth International Anti-corruption Conference in Lima* (1997), www.8iac.org/papers/kaufmann.html.

Kaufmann, D. and Apart Kraay, *Growth Without Governance* (World Bank: Policy research working paper 2928, November 2002).

Keena, C., *Haughey's Millions: Charlie's Money Trail* (Gill and Macmillan, 2001).

Keena, C., *The Ansbacher Conspiracy* (Gill and Macmillan, 2003).

Kenny, Mr. Justice John, Report (of the) Committee on the Price of Building Land to the Minister for Local Government (Kenny Report). (Dublin Stationery Office, 1973).

Kenny, S. and F. Keane, *Irish Politics Now* (RTÉ, 1987).

Keogh, D., *Twentieth-Century Ireland: Nation and State* (Gill and Macmillan, 1994).

Kingston, W., *Interrogating Irish policies* (Dublin University Press, 2007).

Kinsella, T., *Nightwalker and Other Poems* (Dolmen Press, 1968).

Kissane, B., *Explaining Irish Democracy* (University College Dublin Press, 2002).

Kitchell C. K., *The Literary and Scientific Repository and Critical Review* (Wiley and Halsted, 1821).

Kitchin, R., J. Gleeson, K. Keaveney and C. O'Callaghan, *A Haunted Landscape: Housing and Ghost Estates in Post-Celtic Tiger Ireland* (National Institute for Regional and Spatial Analysis, working paper 59, July 2010).

Kitschelt H. and S. I. Wilkinson (eds), *Patrons Clients, and Policies: Patterns of Democratic Accountability and Political Competition* (Cambridge University Press, 2007).

Knack S. and P. Keefer, 'Does social capital have an economic payoff? A cross-country investigation', *Quarterly Journal of Economics*, 112:4 (November 1997).

Komito, L., 'Development plan rezoning: the political pressures', in J. Blackwell and F. Convery (eds), *Promise and Performance: Irish Environmental Policies Analysed* (Dublin: Resource and Environmental Policy Centre, University College Dublin, 1983), www.ucd.ie/lkomito.

Komito, L., 'Irish clientelism: a reappraisal', *Economic and Social Review*, 15:3 (1984).

Krueger, A. O., 'The political economy of the rent seeking society', *American Economic Review*, 64:3 (June 1974).

Kumlin, S. and Bo Rothstein, 'Making and breaking social capital: the impact of welfare-state institutions', *Comparative Political Studies*, 38:4 (2005).

Labour Party, *One Ireland: Jobs, Reform, Fairness* (Labour Party manifesto, 2011).

Lambsdorff, J. G., 'Consequences and causes of corruption: what do we know from a cross-section of countries' (2005). Internet Center for Corruption Research, www.icgg.org/corruption.research_contributions.html.

LaPalombara, J., 'The structural aspects of corruption', in V. D. Trang (ed.), *Corruption and Democracy: Political Institutions, Processes and Corruption in Transition States in East-Central Europe and in the Former Soviet Union* (Institute for Constitutional and Legislative Policy, Open Society Institute, 1994).

Larkin, E., *The Historical Dimensions of Irish Catholicism* (Catholic University of America Press and Four Courts Press, 1984).

Law Reform Commission of Ireland, *Consultation Paper On Public Inquiries Including Tribunals of Inquiry: Report 22* (Law Reform Commission, 2003).

Law Reform Commission of Ireland, *Public Inquiries Including Tribunals of Inquiry: Report 73* (Law Reform Commission, 2005).

Leahy, P., *Showtime: The Inside story of Fianna Fáil in Power* (Penguin, 2009).

Lee, J. J., *Ireland 1912–1985, Politics and Society* (Cambridge University Press, 1989).

Leff, N. H., 'Economic development through bureaucratic corruption', *American Behavioural Scientist*, 7:3 (November 1964).

Lenihan, A. and Angela Phelan, *No Problem: To Mayo and Back* (Blackwater Press, 1990).

Lenihan, B., *For the Record* (Blackwater Press, 1991).

Levi, M., 'A state of trust', in Valerie Braithwaite and M. Levi (eds), *Trust and Governance* (Russell Sage Foundation, 1998).

Lewis, C. W. and Stuart Gilman, *The Ethics Challenge in Public Service: A Problem-Solving Guide*, 2nd edn (Jossey-Bass, 2005).

Lowenstein, D. H., 'Legal efforts to define political bribery', in A. J. Heidenheimer, M. Johnston and V. LeVine (eds), *Political Corruption: A Handbook* (Transaction 1989).

Lyons Tom and Brian Carey, *The Fitzpatrick Tapes: The Rise and Fall of One Man, One Bank and One Country* (Penguin Ireland, 2011).

MacBride Seán and Caitriona Lawlor, *That Day's Struggle: A Memoir 1904–1951* (Curragh Press, 2005).

MacCarthaigh, M., *Accountability in Irish Parliamentary Politics* (Institute of Public Administration, 2005).

MacCarthaigh, M., *Parliamentary Scrutiny of the Administration* (Geary Institute: University College Dublin, working paper, November 2009).

Machiavelli, N., *The discourses*, trans. L. J. Walker (Yale University Press, 1950).

Magill C. W., (ed.), *From Dublin to Stormont Castle: The Memoirs of Andrew Philip Magill, 1913–1925* (Cork University Press, 2003).

Mair P. and M. Marsh, 'Political parties in electoral markets in post-war Ireland', in P. Mair, W. Muller and F. Passer (eds), *Political Parties and Electoral Change: Party Responses to Electoral Markets* (Sage, 2004).

Maltby, A. and B. McKenna, *Irish Official Publications, A Guide to Republic of Ireland Papers, with a Breviate of Reports 1922–1972* (Pergamon Press, 1981).

Manning, M., *James Dillon: A Biography* (Wolfhound Press, 1999).

Mansergh, N., *The Irish Free State: Its Government and Politics* (Allen and Unwin, 1934).

Martin, W. E., *The Mind of Frederick Douglass* (University of North Carolina Press, 1984).

Marsh, M., 'Voting for government coalitions in Ireland under Single Transferable Vote', *Electoral studies*, 29:3 (2010).

Mauro, P., 'Corruption and growth', *Quarterly Journal of Economics*, 110:3 (August 1995).

Mays, M., *Nation States: The Cultures of Irish Nationalism* (Lexington Books, March 2007).

McBride, L., *The Greening of Dublin Castle: The Transformation of Bureaucratic and Judicial Personnel in Ireland, 1892–1922* (University of America Press, 1991).

McCarthy, C., 'Corruption in public office in Ireland: policy design as a countermeasure', Economic and Social Research Institute, *Quarterly Economic Commentary* (2003).

McCracken, Mr. Justice Brian, *Report of the Tribunal of Inquiry (Dunnes Payments)* (Dublin Stationery Office, 1997).

McCullagh, David, *A Makeshift Majority: First Inter-party Government 1948–51* (Institute Public Administration, 1998).

McCullagh, David, *The Reluctant Taoiseach: A Biography of John A. Costello* (Gill and Macmillan, 2010).

McDonald, Dearhail, *Bust* (Penguin, 2010).

McDonald, F., *Destruction of Dublin* (Gill and Macmillan, 1985).

McDonald, F., *The Construction of Dublin* (Gandon Editions, 2000).

McDonald, F. and K. Sheridan, *The Builders* (Penguin, 2009).

McDowell, R. B., *The Irish Administration, 1808–1914* (London, 1964).

McGraw, Sean, 'Managing change: party competition in the new Ireland' (PhD dissertation, Department of Government: Harvard University, 2009).

McGuire, J. and J. Quinn (eds), *Dictionary of Irish Biography: From the Earliest Times to the Year 2002*, 4 (Royal Irish Academy, Cambridge University Press, 2009).

McKittrick, D., S. Kelters, B. Feeney and C. Thornton, *Lost Lives: The Stories of the Men, Women and Children Who Died as a Result of the Northern Ireland Troubles* (Mainstream, 1999).

Meany, Stephen Joseph, Speeches from the Dock (Project Gutenberg eBook, Part I, June 1867), www.gutenberg.org.

Meleady, D., *Redmond the Parnellite* (Cork University Press, 2008).

Mill, J. S., 'Considerations on representative government', in J. S. Mill, *Utilitarianism, Liberty and Representative Government* (Dent, Everyman's Library, 1964).

Moody, T. W., R. B. McDowell and C. J. Woods, 'A review of the conduct of administration during the seventh session of Parliament, by an independent Irish Whig, ie Tone, 6 April 1790', *The Writings of Theobald Wolfe Tone 1763–98: Volume I: Tone's Career in Ireland to 17 June 1795* (Oxford University Press, 1998).

Moreno, A., 'Corruption and democracy: a cultural assessment', *Comparative Sociology*, 1 (2002).

Moriarty, Mr. Justice Michael, *The Moriarty Tribunal Report. Report of the Tribunal of Inquiry into Payments to Politicians and Related Matters. Parts 1 and 2* (Dublin Stationery Office, 2006, 2011).

Moroff, H. and Verena Blechinger, 'Corruption terms in the world press: how languages differ', in A. J. Heidenheimer, M. Johnston and V. LeVine (eds), *Political Corruption: A Handbook* (Transaction, 1989).

Mulcahy, Roistered, *A family Memoir* (Aurelia Press, 1999).

Nassmacher, K. H. (ed.), *Foundations for Democracy – Approaches to Comparative Political Finance: Essays in Honour of Herbert E. Alexander* (Nomos Verlag, 2001).

National Industrial Economics Council, *Report of Physical Planning. Report No. 26* (Dublin Stationery Office, 1969).

Noonan, J. T., *Bribes* (Macmillan 1984).

Nye, J. S., 'Corruption and political development: a cost-benefit analysis', *American Political Science Review*, 61:2 (June, 1967).

O Broin, L., *The Chief Secretary: Augustine Birrell in Ireland* (Chatto & Windus, 1969).

O Broin, L., *No Man's Man: A Biographical Memoir of Joseph Brennan* (Institute of Public Administration, 1982).

O'Brien, J., *The Arms Trial* (Gill and Macmillan, 2000).

O'Brien, M., *De Valera, Fianna Fáil and the Irish Press* (Irish Academic Press, 2001).

O'Brien, M., *The Irish Times: A History* (Four Courts Press, 2008).

O'Flaherty, L., *The Informer* (Jonathan Cape, 1925).

O'Halpin, E., 'The Dáil Committee of Public Accounts, 1961–1980', *Administration*, 32:4 (1985).

O'Halpin, E., '"Ah, they've given us a good bit of stuff . . ." tribunals and Irish political life at the turn of the century', *Irish Political Studies*, 15:1 (2000).

O'Halpin, E., 'Politics and the State 1923–32', in J. R. Hill (ed.), *A New History of Ireland VII: Ireland 1921–1984* (Oxford University Press, 2003).

O'Leary, C., *Irish Elections 1918–1977: Parties, Voters and Proportional Representation* (Gill and Macmillan, 1979).

O'Neill T. P. and F. A. Pakenham, Earl of Longford, *Éamon de Valera* (Arrow Books, 1974).

O'Toole, F., *Meanwhile Back at the Ranch: The Politics of Irish Beef* (Vintage, 1995).

OECD, *Education at a Glance 2008* (OECD, 2008), www.oecd.org/edu.

OECD, *Education at a Glance 2010* (OECD, 2010), www.oecd.org/edu.

OECD, Public Management Reviews, *Ireland: Towards an Integrated Public Service* (OECD, 2008).

Officer, L. H., 'Five ways to compute the relative value of a UK pound amount, 1830–2006', www.measuringworth.com, 2010.

Oireachtas Select Committee on Building Land, *Report of the Joint Committee on Building Land* (Dublin: Stationery Office, 5 June 1985).

Paldam, M., 'Corruption and Religion. Adding to the Economic Model' (unpublished manuscript, Aarhus University, Denmark, 1999).

Paltiel, K. Z., 'Campaign finance: Contrasting practices and reforms', in D. Butler, H. R. Penniman and A. Ranney (eds), *Democracy at the Polls* (American Enterprise Institute, 1981).

Pedersen, M. N., 'The dynamics of European party systems: changing patterns of electoral volatility', *European Journal of Political Research*, 7:1 (1979).

Philip, M., 'Defining political corruption', *Political Studies*, 45: 3 (1997).

Piattoni, S. (ed.), *Clientelism, Interests, and Democratic Representation* (Cambridge University Press, 2001).

Pinto-Duschinsky, M., 'Political Party Funding', in R. Stapenhurst, N. Johnson, R. Pelizzo (eds), *The Role of Parliament in Curbing Corruption* (World Bank, c2006).

Pizzorno, A., *Il potere dei giudici* (Laterza, 1998).

Plato, *The Republic*, trans. H. D. P. Lee (Penguin, 1987).

Pollitt, C., C. Talbot, J. Caulfield and A. Smullen, *Agencies: How Governments Do Things Through Semi-Autonomous Organizations* (Palgrave Macmillan, 2004).

Pope, J., 'Ethics, Accountability and Transparency', in L. Adamolekun, Guy de Lusignan, A. Atomate (eds), *Civil Service Reform in Francophone Africa* (World Bank, 1996).

Putnam, R., *Making Democracy Work: Civic Traditions in Modern Italy* (Princeton University Press, 1993).

Putnam, R., *Bowling Alone: The Collapse and Revival of American Community* (Simon and Schuster, 2000).

Quinn, R., *Straight Left: A Journey in Politics* (Hodder Headline Ireland, 2005).

Regan, J. M., *The Irish Counter-Revolution 1921–1936 Treatyite Politics and Settlement in Independent Ireland* (Gill and Macmillan, 1999).

Regling, Klaus and Max Watson, *A Preliminary Report on The Sources of Ireland's Banking Crisis* (Government Publications Office, 2010).

Report of the Committees of Dáil Éireann 1950–53, *Report of the Committee on Procedure and Privileges on the Assault Committed by a Member on another Member in the Oireachtas Restaurant on 31 January 1952* (February 1952).

Report of the Tribunal of Inquiry into Dealings in Great Southern Railway Stocks between the 1st Day of January and the 18th Day of November 1943 (Dublin Stationery Office, 1944).

Reynolds, A., *Albert Reynolds: My Autobiography* (Transworld Ireland, 2009).

Rhodes, R. A. W., *Understanding Governance: Policy Networks, Governance, Reflexivity and Accountability* (Open University Press, 1997).

Rose-Ackerman, S., *Corruption: A Study in Political Economy* (Academic Press, 1978).

Rose-Ackerman, S., 'Democracy and 'grand' corruption', *International Social Science Journal*, 158:3 (1996).

Rose-Ackerman, S., *Corruption and Government* (Cambridge University Press, 1999).

Rothstein, Bo., 'Creating political legitimacy: electoral democracy versus quality of government', *American Behavioural Scientist*, 53:3 (2009).

Rothstein, Bo and Jan Teorell, 'What is quality of government? a theory of impartial government institutions', *Governance*, 21:2 (2008).

Ryle Dwyer, T., *Haughey's Forty Years of Controversy* (Mercier Press, 2005).

Sabato, Larry J., *Feeding Frenzy: How Attack Journalism Has Transformed American Politics* (Lanahan, 1991).

Sacks, P., *Donegal Mafia: An Irish Political Machine* (Yale University Press 1976).

Sapelli, G., *Southern Europe since 1945, Tradition and modernity in Portugal, Spain, Italy, Greece and Turkey* (Longman, 1995).

Schmitt, D., *The Irony of Irish Democracy: The Impact of Political Culture on Administrative and Democratic Political Development in Ireland* (DC Heath, 1973).

Scott, J. C., 'Corruption, machine politics, and political change', *American Political Science Review*, 63:4 (December 1969).

Scott, J. C., 'Handling historical comparison cross-nationally', in A. J. Heidenheimer, M. Johnston and V. LeVine (eds), *Political Corruption: A Handbook* (Transaction 1989).

Senate Select Committee on Ethics, 102–223, 102d Cong., 1st Sess. 11–12, 'Investigation of Senator Alan Cranston, S. Rep.' (1991) www.ethics.house.gov.

Shah, A., 'Tailoring the fight against corruption to country circumstances', in A. Shah (ed.), *Performance Accountability and Combating Corruption* (World Bank, 2007).

Shang-Jin Wei, *Why Is Corruption So Much More Taxing Than Tax?* (NBER working paper 6255, 1997).

Sinnott, R., *Irish Voters Decide: Voting Behaviour in Elections and Referendums Since 1918* (Manchester University Press, 1995).

Stapenhurst, R., *The Media's Role in Curbing Corruption* (World Bank Institute: working paper, 2000).

Stevenson, R. L., 'Truth of intercourse', *Cornhill Magazine* (May 1879).

Steves F. and A. Rousso, *Anti-Corruption Programmes in Post-Communist Transition Countries and Changes in the Business Environment, 1999–2002* (European Bank for Reconstruction and Development, working paper 85, 2003).

Stigler, G., 'The theory of economic regulation', *Bell Journal of Economics and Management Science*, 2:1 (1971).

Suiter, J., 'Chieftains delivering: political determinants of capital spending in Ireland 2001–07' (PhD dissertation, Trinity College Dublin, 2007).

Sullivan, T. D., *Recollections of Troubled Times in Irish Politics* (Sealy, Bryers & Walker, M.H. Giull & Son, 1905).

Swift MacNeil, J. G., *What I have Seen and Heard* (Little Brown, 1925).

Tanzi, V., *Policies, Institutions and the Dark Side of Economics* (Edward Elgar, 2000).

Temby, Commissioner Ian, 'Report on Investigation into the Metherall Resignation and Appointment' (Sydney: ICAC, June 1992), quoted in: M. Philp, 'Defining political corruption', *Political Studies*, 45:3 (1997).

Theobald, R., *Corruption, Development, and Underdevelopment* (Macmillan, 1990).

Thompson, D. F., 'Mediated corruption: the case of the Keating five', *American Political Science Review*, 87:2 (1993).

Tobin, F., *The Best of Decades: Ireland in the 1960s* (Gill and Macmillan, 1984).

Townshend, C., *The British Campaign in Ireland 1919–1921* (Oxford, 1975).

Travers, J. *Interim Report on Certain Issues of Management and Administration in the Department of Health and Children associated with the Practice of Charges for Persons in Long Stay Health Care in Health Board Institutions and Related Matters* (Dublin Stationery Office, Oireachtas Joint Committee on Health and Children, 2005).

Treisman, D., 'The causes of corruption: a cross-national study', *Journal of Public Economics*, 76:3 (2000).

Twomey, V., *The End of Irish Catholicism?* (Veritas, 2003).

Uslaner, E. M., 'Trust and corruption', in J. G. Lambsdorff, M. Taube and M. Schramm (eds), *The New Institutional Economics of Corruption* (Routledge, 2005).

Vannucci, A., 'The controversial legacy of 'Mani Pulite': a critical analysis of Italian corruption and anti-corruption policies', *Bulletin of Italian Politics*, 1:2 (2009).

Waldo, W. E., *The Mind of Frederick Douglass* (University of North Carolina Press, 1984.

Walsh, J., *Patrick Hillery: The Authorised Biography* (New Island Books, 2008).

Waterbury, J., 'Endemic and planned corruption in a monarchical regime', *World Politics*, 25:4 (July 1973).

Whitaker, T. K., *Interests* (Institute of Public Administration, 1983).

Williams, B., B. Hughes and B. Redmond, *Managing an Unstable Housing Market* (Urban Institute Ireland: University College Dublin, working paper 10/02, 2010).

Williamson, J., and C. Shen, 'Corruption, state strength, and democracy: a cross-national structural analysis', *Annual Meeting of the American Sociological Association* (Philadelphia, August 2005).

Yin, R. K., *Case Study Research, Design and Method*, 3rd end (Newbury Park: Sage Publications, 2002).

Dáil debates

Ahern, Bertie, Dáil Éireann, *Supplementary Estimates, 1992: Confidence in Government: Motion. 424.* (5 November 1992).

Ahern, Bertie, Dáil Éireann, *Written Answers, Tax Amnesty Deadline. 445.* (18 October 1994).

Ahern, Bertie, Dáil Éireann, *Private Members' Business. Inquiry into Alleged Payments by Dunnes Stores Ltd.: Motion. 472.* (10 December 1996).

Ahern, Bertie, Dáil Éireann, *Resignation of Member: Statements. 481.* (7 October 1997).

Aiken, Frank, Dáil Éireann, *Orders of the Day: Local Government Bill, 1931. 39.* (17 June 1931).

Boland, Kevin and Gerry L'Estrange, Dáil Éireann, *Planning Appeals Bill, 1967: Second Stage (Resumed). 233.* (13 March 1968).

Boland, Kevin, Dáil Éireann, *Committee on Finance. Vote 26: Local Government (Resumed). 245.* (11 March 1970).

Briscoe, Ben, Dáil Éireann, *Private Members' Business: Ethics in Government and Public Office Bill, 1991: Second Stage (Resumed). 408.* (14 May 1991).

Browne, Noel, Dáil Éireann, *Private Members' Business: Office of Taoiseach, Motion. 171.* (12 December 1958).

Burke, P. J., Dáil Éireann, *Nomination of Member of Government: Motion (Resumed). 246.* (7 May 1970).

Burke, Ray, Dáil Éireann, *Local Government (Planning and Development) Bill, 1983: Motion. 344.* (30 June 1983).

Burke, Ray and Pat O'Mahony, Dáil Éireann, *Written Answers: Beef and Sheep Exports to Iraq. 388.* (12 April 1989).

Burke, Ray, Dáil Éireann, *Personal Statement. 480.* (10 September 1997).

Ceann Comhairle, Dáil Éireann, *Report of Committee on Procedure and Privileges, Deputy Reprimanded. 129.* (5 March 1952).

Childers, Erskine, Dáil Éireann, *Committee on Finance Vote 41: Transport and Power (Resumed). 231.* (16 November 1967).

Cole, John and Seán Lemass, Dáil Éireann, *Questions: Reorganisation of Great Southern Railways Company. 91.* (17 November 1943).

Coogan, Eamonn and Patrick McGilligan, Dáil Éireann, *Report of (Ward) Tribunal: Adjournment Debate. 102.* (11 July 1946).

Cosgrave, Liam, Dáil Éireann, *Financial Resolutions. Statement by Taoiseach and Motion re Tribunal of Inquiry. 283.* (3 July 1975).

Costello, John A., Dáil Éireann, *Private Deputies' Business: Dáil Restaurant Incident. 129.* (31 January 1952).

Dáil Committee on Procedure and Privileges, *Draft Report from the Parliamentary Secretary to the Taoiseach.* (4 December 1975).

Dardis, John, Seanad Éireann, *Tribunal of Inquiry into Beef Processing Industry: Motion. 129.* (29 May 1991).

de Valera, Éamon, Dáil Éireann, *Proposed Sale of Distillery: Motion for Tribunal 108.* (5 November 1947).

de Valera, Éamon, Dáil Éireann, *Questions, Oral Answers: Parliamentary Secretaries and Business. 109.* (11 December 1947).

de Valera, Major Vivion, *Dáil Éireann, Private Deputies' Business: Motion for a Select Committee – Question of Members' Conduct. 101.* (15 May 1946).

de Valera, Éamon and Oliver J. Flanagan, Dáil Éireann, *Financial Resolutions Report (Resumed) – Proposed Sale of Distillery: Motion for Select Committee (Resumed). 108.* (30 October 1947).

de Valera, Éamon, Alfie Byrne, Eamonn Coogan and General Richard Mulcahy Dáil Éireann, *Powers and Privileges of the Oireachtas: Motion. 104.* (11 March 1947).

de Valera, Éamon, Luke Joseph Duffy, Thomas Foran, Michael Hayes and William Quirke, Seanad Éireann, *Allegations Against Parliamentary Secretary: Motion for Tribunal. 31.* (5 June 1946).

Dillon, James, Dáil Éireann, *Motion for Tribunal. 101.* (10 June 1946).

Dillon, James and Seán Lemass, Dáil Éireann, *Sheepskin (Control of Export) Bill, 1934: Committee Stage. 51.* (22 March 1934).

Dillon, James and Oliver J. Flanagan, Dáil Éireann, *Motion for Select Committee. Proposed Sale of Distillery. 108.* (29 October 1947).

Figgis, Darrell and Professor William McGinnis, Dáil Éireann, *The Prevention of Corrupt Practices at Elections. 1.* (20 October 1922).

FitzGerald, Garret, Dáil Éireann, *Nomination of Taoiseach. 317.* (11 December 1979).

Flanagan, Oliver J., Dáil Éireann, *Private Deputies' Business. Motion for a Select Committee: Question of Members' Conduct. 101.* (15 May 1946).

Flanagan, Oliver J., Dáil Éireann, *Order of Business Social Welfare Bill. 532.* (31 January 1952).

Haughey, Charles J., *Order of Business. 388.* (15 March 1989).

Haughey, Charles J., Dáil Éireann, *Questions, Oral Answers. Statement by the Minister for Agriculture and Food. 388.* (12 April 1989).

Haughey, Charles J., Dáil Éireann, *Request to Move Adjournment of Dáil under Standing Order 30. 408.* (14 May 1991).

Howlin, Brendan and Albert Reynolds, Dáil Éireann, *Private Members' Business. Ethics in Government and Public Office Bill, 1991: Second Stage. 407.* (7 May 1991).

Lemass, Seán and Patrick McGilligan, Dáil Éireann, *Committee on Finance Vote 57: Industry and Commerce (Resumed). 57.* (19 June 1935).

Lemass, Seán, Dáil Éireann, *Wicklow Mining Lease: Appointment of Select Committee. 57.* (25 June 1935).

Lemass, Seán, Dáil Éireann, *Transport (No. 2) Bill, 1944: Committee (Resumed). 94.* (28 September 1944).

Lynch, Jack and Michael Moran, Dáil Éireann, *Deputies' Allegations: Censure Motion. 228.* (25 February 1976).

MacCarvill, Dr. Patrick, 'Letter addressed to Government dated 22 May 1946', *Seanad Éireann* (5 June 1946).

MacEntee, Seán, Dáil Éireann, *Public Business: Finance Bill, 1935: Second Stage (Resumed). 57.* (18 June 1935).

McDowell, Michael and Michael Smith, Dáil Éireann, *Report of Tribunal of Inquiry into Beef Processing Industry: Motion (Resumed). 445.* (2 September 1994).

McGilligan, Patrick, Dáil Éireann, *Twenty-Seventh Report of the Committee of Selection: Mines and Minerals Bill, 1931: Committee. 40.* (19 November 1931).

McGilligan, Patrick, Dáil Éireann, *Finance Bill, 1935: Second Stage (Resumed). 57.* (14 June 1935).

McGilligan, Patrick, Dáil Éireann, *Transport Bill, 1944: Second Stage (Resumed). 93.* (9 May 1944).

McGilligan, Patrick, Dáil Debates, *Committee on Finance: Vote 5, Office of the Minister for Finance. 116.* (21 June 1947).

Molloy, Robert, Dáil Éireann, *Questions. Oral Answers: Road Safety. 276.* (12 December 1974).

Molloy, Robert, Dáil Éireann, *Personal Explanation by Minister. 283.* (2 July 1975).

Molloy, Robert, Dáil Éireann, *Local Government (Planning and Development) Bill, 1973: Committee Stage (Resumed). 282.* (25 June 1975).

Mulcahy, General Richard Dáil Éireann, *Questions. Oral Answers. Wicklow Mining Lease. 57.* (25 June 1935).

Mulcahy, General Richard and William Davin, Dáil Éireann, *Transport (No. 2) Bill. Committee (Resumed: Amendment No. 18). 94.* (21 September 1944).

Mullen, Michael, Dáil Éireann, *Committee on Finance Vote 41: Transport and Power. 230.* (9 November 1967).

Noonan, Michael and Dick Spring, Dáil Éireann, *Siúicre Éireann and Related Companies Report: Motion. 417.* (13 March 1992).

O'Higgins, Kevin, Dáil Éireann, *Precedence for Ministerial Business. 1.* (27 September 1922).

O'Kennedy, Michael, Dáil Éireann, *Meat Industry: Motion. 408.* (15 May 1991).

O'Malley, Des, Dáil Éireann, *Adjournment Debate, Beef Exports to Iraq. 389.* (10 May 1989).

O'Malley, Des, Dáil Éireann, *Questions, Oral Answers, Beef Exports to Iraq. 392.* (1 November 1989).

Reynolds, Albert and Pat Rabbitte, Dáil Éireann, *Report of Tribunal of Inquiry into Beef Processing Industry. 445* (1 September 1994).

Seanad Éireann, *Private Business: Appropriation Bill, 1969 (Certified Money Bill): Second Stage. 67.* (2 December 1969).

Spring, Dick, Dáil Éireann, *Local Government (Planning and Development) Bill, 1983: Second Stage. 344.* (28 June 1983).

Tully, James, Dáil Éireann, *Local Government (Roads and Motorways) Bill, 1973 Second Stage. 270. 1974). 270.* (7 February 1974).

Newspapers and Periodicals

Newspapers

Financial Times
Freeman's Journal
The Guardian
Irish Independent
Irish Press
Irish Times
The Nation
Sunday Business Post
Sunday Independent
Sunday Times
Sunday Tribune
The United Irishman

Periodicals

Business and Finance
The Economist
Forbes Magazine
Hibernia
Magill Magazine
Nusight
Village Magazine

Archives

Archbishop John Charles McQuaid Archives, Dublin: Bishops House. Finance 1111 A. Book 4. 1939–46.

National Archives, Dublin, AGO/2002/15/166, Justice: Complaint by Sweetman and O'Higgins addressed to Bar Counsel, 'Bar Counsel letter', 30 December 1947.

National Archives, Dublin, AGO/2002/15/166, Justice: Quirke letter to MacEntee, 25 February 1952.

National Archives, Dublin, S 13866/A, Taoiseach: Allegations against Dr., F. Ward.

National Archives, Dublin, S 13866/B, Taoiseach: Memorandum to Taoiseach, 19 January 1948.

National Archives, Dublin, S 14153/B, Taoiseach: Locke's Distillery Kilbeggan, Purchase by Aliens 1947.

National Archives, Dublin, S 15153/C, Taoiseach. 1947.

National Archives, Dublin, 2000/6/104, Taoiseach: Local Appointments Commission, 30 November 1966.

National Archives, Dublin, 2001/6/12, Taoiseach: Ministers, Parliamentary Secretaries and Ministers of State, 3 December 1968.

National Archives, Dublin, 99/1/521, Taoiseach: Planning Appeals, 1968.

National Archives, Dublin, 2000/6/650, Taoiseach: Planning Appeals General (Planning Appeals Board), 21 July 1969.

National Archives, Dublin, 2003/16/393, Taoiseach: Planning Appeals General: Planning Appeals Board, 2 September 1971, 18 October; 29 November and 11 December 1972.

National Archives, Dublin, 2005/3/43, President: Price of Building Land Kenny Report, 31 January 1974.

National Archives, Dublin, 2005/7/488, Taoiseach: County councils: corruption; conflict of interest, June 1974.

National Archives, Dublin, 2005/7/520, Taoiseach: Members of Oireachtas and Members of Local Authority. Financial and other interests, June 1974.

National Archives, Dublin, 2005/7/223, Taoiseach: Local Government (Planning and Development) Act, 1976, 18 October 1974.

National Archives, Dublin, S 10553C, Taoiseach: Cabinet Minutes, 2005–06.

National Archives, Dublin, 2008/79/724 408/137/2 Pt IX, Foreign Affairs: ECE - Housing Sub Committee - Housing, Building and Planning. 1971–75.

National Library, Dublin, P 189A(6), London. House of Parliament, 1837a. An abridgment of the Evidence given before the Select Committee, Appointed in 1835, to consider the most effectual means of preventing Bribery, Corruption and Intimidation, in the Election of Members to Serve in Parliament. Printed for 'The Reform Association'.

National Library, Dublin, P 1032, London. House of Commons, 1837b. Breviate of the Evidence before the Select Committee of the House of Commons, in 1835, on Bribery, Corruption and Intimidation in the Election of Members to Serve in Parliament. London: J. Ridgway, 1839.

National Library, Dublin, P 1398, J. G. Swift MacNeil, Trinity Law Student's Debating Society: Individuality in its effects on public opinion. An address delivered on the 17th of October, 1875.

National Library, Dublin, LOP 414; LOP 417, East Clare election literature: 'Placehunter v Patriot', 1917.

National Library, Dublin, IR94109 p90, Sinn Féin, The Case of Ireland: 'Sinn Féin Series No. 12'. 1919.

National Library, Dublin, 2A 2571, William Norton, Civil Service Reference Book, 1929.

National Library, Dublin, OPIE PP / 36/4, Interim and Final Report Select Committee on the Demise of Certain State Mining Rights, Dáil Éireann Reports of Committees 1932–35. May 1936.

University College Dublin Archives, Dublin, P4/66, P4/617, P4/529, P4/737 7, P4/742 Hugh Kennedy Papers 1920–29.

University College Dublin Archives, Dublin, P7a/95; P7b/23, 24, 25. Richard Mulcahy Papers, 1927.

Law judgements

Attorney General v The Sole Member of the Tribunal of Inquiry into the Beef Processing Industry [1993] 2 I.R. 250.

Blake v Attorney General [1982] I.R. 117.

Boyhan v Beef Tribunal [1993] 1 I.R. 210, 222.

Haughey v Moriarty [1999] 3 I.R. 1, 57–59.

Redmond v Flood [1999] 3 I.R. 79, 87–88.

97/624/EC: Commission Decision of 14 May 1997 relating to a proceeding pursuant to Article 86 of the EC Treaty. IV/34.621, 35.059/F-3 - Irish Sugar plc

Interviews and correspondence

Liam Cosgrave, interview (March 2008).

Declan Costello, interview (February 2006).

Eithne FitzGerald, interview (February 2006).

Garret FitzGerald, interview (February 2001).

Stuart Gilman, head of the Global Programme against Corruption and the Anti-Corruption Unit of the United Nations Office on Drugs and Crime, interview (October 2007).

Tony Killeen, interview (February 2001).

Joe McAnthony, interview by Bob Quinn. (Clare 2005). DVD of interview courtesy of Joe McAnthony.

Mr. Justice Brian McCracken, interview (February 2001).

Standards in Public Office Commission, interview (July 2006).

Correspondence with Revenue Commissioners, 'Spreadsheet: yield from various Revenue Special Investigations/Initiatives at 31.3.2010' (July 2010).

Websites

Central Statistics Office, Dublin: www.cso.ie.

Council of Europe, *Criminal Law Convention on Corruption, Explanatory Report, Article 12* (2009): www.conventions.coe.int/Treaty/en/Reports/Html/173.htm.

Dáil Committee of Public Accounts, *Northern Ireland Relief Expenditure Final Report* (13 July 1972): www.193.178.2.84/test/R/1972/en.toc.com.REPORT_13071972_0.html.

Davy Research, *Irish Property: Government Finances Exposed to a Correction* (2006): www.davydirect.ie/other/pubarticles/irishpropertyoct2006.pdf.

Department of the Environment, Heritage and Local Government, *Housing Statistics (2009)*:   www.environ.ie/en/Publications/StatisticsandRegularPublications/Hous ingStatis.

Enhanced British Parliamentary Papers on Ireland: www.eppi.ac.uk.

EuroBaramoter Polls, *Public Opinion Analysis Sector of the European Commission*: www.ec.europa.eu/public_opinion/index_en.htm.

Financial Crisis Inquiry Commission,*The Financial Crisis Inquiry Report: Final Report of the National Commission on the Causes of the Financial and Economic Crisis in the United States* (2011): www.fcic.gov/report.

Moriarty Tribunal, *Transcripts (*16 February 1999, 22 May 2001, 23 May 2001): www. moriarty-tribunal.ie.

Royal Institute of Chartered Surveyors, *European Housing Review 2005/2006* (2007): www.rics.org.

Statement of Mr Justice Michael Moriarty (23 April 2010): www.moriarty-Tribunal.ie.

Stewart Macalister, R. A. (ed.), and M. Murphy, *Lebor Gabála Érenn: The Book of the Taking of Ireland, Part 6* (2008): www.ucc.ie/celt/LGQS.pdf.

United Nations Office on Drugs and Crime, *Fact Sheet 2, Convention Against Corruption: Q&A (2003)*: www.un.org/webcast/merida/pdfs/03-89373_factsheet2. pdf.

Television

RTÉ Exit Poll (25 May 2007), www.rte.ie/news/2007/0525/RTEExitPoll2007details. ppt.

RTÉ Mint Productions, *Haughey (*June 2005).

RTÉ News, 'Obituaries, Charles J. Haughey (1925–2006)', www.rte.ie/news/ob_ cjhaughey.html.

RTÉ News at One (19 December 2006).

RTÉ One, *The Big Story (*16 August 2009).

RTÉ One, 'Family Fortune: De Valera's Irish Press', *Hidden History* (November 2004)

RTÉ One, 'Irish Sweepstakes', *Hidden History* (1 December 2003).

RTÉ One, 'The Pressure Zone', *Prime Time Investigates* (26 November 2007).

RTÉ Six One News (26 September 2006).

RTÉ Six One News, 'Allowances and expenses, interview with Emmet Stagg' (14 September 2009).

Index